Russian Fairy Tales

A CHOICE COLLECTION

OF

MUSCOVITE FOLKLORE

BY

W. R. S. Ralston, M.A.

Edited and Annotated by Frank Prem

WILD ARANCINI CLASSICS

2024

Publication Details

Russian Fairy Tales - A Choice Collection of Muscovite Folklore was first published in 1887 by Hurst and Co, New York.

This edition first published in Australia in 2024 by Wild Arancini Classics an Imprint of Wild Arancini Press.

ISBN: 978-1-923166-07-3 (pbk)

Author

W. R. S. Ralston, 1828–1889

Text Source

Project Gutenberg, August 22, 2007, https://www.gutenberg.org/ebooks/22373

Book Design

Frank Prem

Editor

Frank Prem

Annotations

Frank Prem

ACKNOWLEDGEMENTS

Wild Arancini Classics is proud to have produced a new edition of W. R. S. Ralston's extraordinary collection of myths and folk tales from old Russia – *Russian Fairy Tales - A Choice Collection of Muscovite Folklore.*

Starting from the raw text of the book, sourced from Project Gutenberg, the book has been lovingly reconstituted, edited and annotated.

I commend the book to you and hope you will enjoy reading *Russian Fairy Tales - A Choice Collection of Muscovite Folklore* as much as I have enjoyed bringing it to life.

Special acknowledgements are due to the following organisations and people, without which I could not have created this work:

- Project Gutenberg for the source text.
- Goodreads for information about the Author.
- Internet Archive for a PDF copy of the 1887 original publication.

Frank Prem–Wild Arancini Classics

ABOUT THE AUTHOR

William Ralston Shedden-Ralston (1828–1889) was a noted British scholar of Russia and translator and Russian.

He was the only son of W. P. Ralston Shedden, who made his fortune as a merchant in Calcutta and set up home in Palmira Square, Brighton, when he returned to England. William spent most of his early years there. Together with three or four other boys he studied under the Rev. John Hogg of Brixham, Devonshire, until he went to Trinity College, Cambridge in 1846, where he graduated with a BA in 1850.

During this period William's father entered into a lengthy but unsuccessful litigation over his claim to the Ralston estates in Ayrshire. The cost dissipated his fortune. The family pressed the claim for many years. Shedden's only sister took up the pleadings, and at one stage conducted the case before a committee of the House of Lords for more than thirty days. William had been called to the bar before the litigation began but the change in the family's fortunes forced him to seek immediate remunerative employment. He also adopted the additional surname of Shedden.

In 1853 he went to work as a junior assistant in the printed-book department of the British Museum, where his zeal and ability won the respect of his superiors. The work began with the requisite two years copying titles for the printed books catalogue, and thereafter he rose slowly through the ranks. When he saw a need for someone who could catalogue Russian books, he began studying Russian, and even learned pages of the dictionary by heart.

He also studied Russian literature. He translated 93 of Ivan Andreevich Krylov's two hundred fables, and this work, published in 1868 as Krilof and his Fables, ran to numerous editions. The following year he brought out a translation of Ivan Turgenev's Nest of Gentlefolk as Liza; in 1872, his

439-page Songs of the Russian People as Illustrative of Slavonic Mythology and Russian Social Life, and in 1873 a bloodthirsty collection of Russian Folk Tales. He made two or three journeys to Russia, formed numerous literary acquaintances there, and had a lasting friendship with Turgenev. He also became a corresponding member of the Imperial Academy of Sciences of St. Petersburg. He visited Serbia twice, and made numerous visits to Germany, Belgium, and Switzerland.

In 1874 he published Early Russian History, the substance of four lectures delivered at the Taylor Institution in Oxford. His visits to Russia were mainly to collect material for another, more comprehensive account. Having contracted for its publication with Messrs. Cassell & Co, at the last moment he allowed them to cancel the agreement and publish instead Donald Mackenzie Wallace's book Russia.

He also possessed a gift for narrating stories orally. He devised a novel form of public entertainment, telling stories to large audiences in lecture-halls, making several successful appearances at St. George's and St James's Halls. He gave story-tellings to the young princes and princesses at Marlborough House, and to other social gatherings; and also, in aid of charities, to audiences in east London and the provinces.

His health failing, he resigned from the British Museum in 1875 and sought to devote himself to literary work but he was susceptible to acute depression and became increasingly withdrawn. Nevertheless he wrote for the Athenæum magazine and the Saturday Review, as well as the Nineteenth Century and other magazines.

(Source: Goodreads)

INTRODUCTION TO THE 2024 EDITION

As a poet/author I have long been inspired by the mythologies and folklore of ancient cultures and early human civilisations, and have been an avid reader of Joseph Campbell's work in particular, returning often to that well for inspiration and reminder of the archetypal stories that humankind has always told and been fascinated by.

This collection of *Russian Fairy Tales - A Choice Collection of Muscovite Folklore*, which dates back to 1887 has created a sense of awe in myself as a reader from my growing awareness that it is a source document that may well have been consulted by Campbell and the other heroes of my mythical and folkloric learning. The sense of walking in the footsteps of giants.

Here, among the gathered stories and anecdotes of rural and peasant Russia I have been introduced to the vagaries of humanity - fickleness and greed as well as kindness and generosity. Unexpected rewards and the punishments that so often accompany such moral tales.

This collection introduces us to early acccounts of witches and warlocks, the Baba Yagas, Vampires and Zombies.

In my initial reading of the book I had considered removal of much of the explanation and discussion and cross referencing that is contained within it to create an abridged edition, concentrating simply on the telling of the stories. I have since decided, however, that the explanatory notes are critical as they provide a context for these fairy tales in the broader realm of all fairy and folk tales, to that date, at least. In that sense, the book remains as much an authorative text as a collection of stories.

I commend *Russian Fairy Tales - A Choice Collection of Muscovite Folklore* as a collection of folk tales that are of interest in their own right, but which also serve as a reference for scholars and a source of inspiration for authors.

Note: A number of the footnote references refer to 'governments'*, for example 'the Government of Astrakhan'. Pre-World War 1 Europe was divided into many individual principalities and independant states. These references appear to be pointing a geographical location within old Europe as origins for particular stories.*

Frank Prem
Wild Arancini Classics

DEDICATION TO THE FIRST (1887) EDITION

To the memory of Alexander Afanasief I dedicate this book.
To him so deeply indebted.

PREFACE TO THE FIRST (1887) EDITION

The stories contained in the following pages are taken from the collections published by Afanasief, Khudyakof, Erlenvein and Chudinsky. The South-Russian collections of Kulish and Rudchenko I have been able to use but little, there being no complete dictionary available of the dialect or rather the language, in which they are written. Of these works that of Afanasief is by far the most important, extending to nearly 3,000 pages and containing 332 distinct stories—of many of which several variants are given, sometimes as many as five. Khudyakof's collection contains 122 skazkas—as the Russian folktales are called—Erlenvein's 41 and Chudinsky's 31. Afanasief has also published a separate volume, containing 33 "legends," and he has inserted a great number of stories of various kinds in his "Poetic views of the Old Slavonians about Nature," a work to which I have had constant recourse.

From the stories contained in what may be called the "chapbook literature" of Russia, I have made but few extracts. It may, however, be as well to say a few words about them. There is a Russian word *lub*, diminutive *lubok*, meaning the soft bark of the lime tree, which at one time was used instead of paper. The popular tales which were current in former days were at first printed on sheets or strips of this substance, whence the term *lubochnuiya* came to be given to all such productions of the cheap press, even after paper had taken the place of bark.[1]

---

1 So our word "book," the German Buch, is derived from the Buche or beech tree, of which the old Runic staves were formed. Cf. *liber* and βίβλος.

The stories which have thus been preserved have no small interest of their own but they cannot be considered as fair illustrations of Russian folklore, for their compilers in many cases took them from any sources to which they had access, whether eastern or western, merely adapting what they borrowed to Russian forms of thought and speech. Through some such process, for instance, seem to have passed the very popular Russian stories of Eruslan Lazarevich and of Bova Korolevich. They have often been quoted as "creations of the Slavonic mind," but there seems to be no reason for doubting that they are merely Russian adaptations, the first of the adventures of the Persian Rustem, the second of those of the Italian Buovo di Antona, our Sir Bevis of Hampton. The editors of these "chapbook skazkas" belonged to the pre-scientific period and had a purely commercial object in view. Their stories were intended simply to sell.

A German version of seventeen of these "chapbook tales," to which was prefixed an introduction by Jacob Grimm, was published some forty years ago,[2] and has been translated into English.[3] Somewhat later, also, appeared a German version of twelve more of these tales.[4]

Of late years several articles have appeared in some of the German periodicals,[5] giving accounts or translations of some of the Russian Popular Tales. But no thorough investigation of them appeared in print, out of Russia, until the publication last year of the erudite work on "Zoological Mythology" by Professor Angelo de Gubernatis. In it he has given a summary of the greater part of the stories contained in the collections of Afanasief and Erlenvein and so fully has he described the part played in them by the members of the animal world

2 "Russische Volksmärchen in den Urschriften gesammelt und ins Deutsche übersetzt von A. Dietrich." Leipzig, 1831.

3 "Russian Popular Tales," Chapman and Hall, London, 1857.

4 "Die ältesten Volksmärchen der Russen. Von J. N. Vogl." Wien, 1841.

5 Such as the "Orient und Occident," "Ausland," &c.

that I have omitted, in the present volume, the chapter I had prepared on the Russian "Beast-Epos."

Another chapter which I have, at least for a time, suppressed, is that in which I had attempted to say something about the origin and the meaning of the Russian folktales. The subject is so extensive that it requires for its proper treatment more space than a single chapter could grant; and therefore, though not without reluctance, I have left the stories I have quoted to speak for themselves, except in those instances in which I have given the chief parallels to be found in the two collections of foreign folktales best known to the English reader, together with a few others which happened to fall within the range of my own reading. Professor de Gubernatis has discussed at length and with much learning, the esoteric meaning of the skazkas and their bearing upon the questions to which the "solar theory" of myth-explanation has given rise. To his volumes and to those of Mr. Cox, I refer all who are interested in those fascinating enquiries. My chief aim has been to familiarize English readers with the Russian folktale; the historical and mythological problems involved in it can be discussed at a later period. Before long, in all probability, a copious flood of light will be poured upon the connexion of the Popular Tales of Russia with those of other lands by one of those scholars who are best qualified to deal with the subject.[6]

Besides the stories about animals, I have left unnoticed two other groups of skazkas—those which relate to historical events and those in which figure the heroes of the Russian "epic poems" or "metrical romances." My next volume will be devoted to the Builinas, as those poems are called and in it the skazkas which are connected with them will find their

---

6 Professor Reinhold Köhler, who is said to be preparing a work on the Skazkas, in co-operation with Professor Jülg, the well-known editor and translator of the "Siddhi Kür" and "Ardshi Bordschi Khan."

fitting place. In it, also, I hope to find space for the discussion of many questions which in the present volume I have been forced to leave unnoticed.

The fifty-one stories which I have translated at length I have rendered as literally as possible. In the very rare instances in which I have found it necessary to insert any words by way of explanation, I have (except in the case of such additions as "he said" or the like) enclosed them between brackets. In giving summaries, also, I have kept closely to the text and always translated literally the passages marked as quotations. In the imitation of a finished work of art, elabouration and polish are meet and due but in a transcript from nature what is most required is fidelity. An "untouched" photograph is in certain cases infinitely preferable to one which has been carefully "worked upon." And it is, as it were, a photograph of the Russian storyteller that I have tried to produce and not an ideal portrait.

* * * * *

The following are the principal Russian books to which reference has been made:—

- AFANASIEF (A.N.). Narodnuiya Russkiya Skazki[7] [Russian Popular Tales]. 8 pts. Moscow, 1863-60-63. Narodnuiya Russkiya Legendui[8] [Russian Popular Legends]. Moscow, 1859. Poeticheskiya Vozzryeniya Slavyan na Prirodu [Poetic Views of the Slavonians about Nature].[9] 3 vols. Moscow, 1865-69.
- KHUDYAKOF (I.A.). Velikorusskiya Skazki [Great-Russian Tales]. Moscow, 1860.
- CHUDINSKY (E.A.). Russkiya Narodnuiya Skazki, etc. [Russian Popular Tales, etc.]. Moscow, 1864.

---

7 In my copy, pt. 1 and 2 are of the 3d and pt. 3 and 4 are of the 2d edition. By such a note as "Afanasief, i. No. 2," I mean to refer to the second story of the first part of this work.
8 This book is now out of print and copies fetch a very high price. I refer to it in my notes as "Afanasief, *Legendui*."
9 This work is always referred to in my notes as "Afanasief, P.V.S."

- ERLENVEIN (A.A.). Narodnuiya Skazki, etc. [Popular Tales, collected by village schoolmasters in the Government of Tula]. Moscow, 1863.
- RUDCHENKO (I.). Narodnuiya Yuzhnorusskiya Skazki [South-Russian Popular Tales].[10] Kief, 1869.

* * * * *

Most of the other works referred to are too well-known to require a full setting out of their title. But it is necessary to explain that references to Grimm are as a general rule to the "Kinder- und Hausmärchen," 9th ed. Berlin, 1870. Those to Asbjörnsen and Moe are to the "Norske Folke-Eventyr," 3d ed. Christiania, 1866; those to Asbjörnsen only are to the "New Series" of those tales, Christiania, 1871; those to Dasent are to the "Popular Tales from the Norse," 2d ed., 1859. The name "Karajich" refers to the "Srpske Narodne Pripovijetke," published at Vienna in 1853 by Vuk Stefanovich Karajich and translated by his daughter under the title of "Volksmärchen der Serben," Berlin, 1854. By "Schott" is meant the "Walachische Mährchen," Stuttgart und Tubingen, 1845, by "Schleicher" the "Litauische Märchen," Weimar, 1857, by "Hahn" the "Griechische und albanesische Märchen," Leipzig, 1864, by "Haltrich" the "Deutsche Volksmärchen aus dem Sachsenlande in Siebenbürgen," Berlin, 1856 and by "Campbell" the "Popular Tales of the West Highlands," 4 vols., Edinburgh, 1860-62.

A few of the ghost stories contained in the following pages appeared in the "Cornhill Magazine" for August 1872 and an account of some of the "legends" was given in the "Fortnightly Review" for April 1, 1868.

---

10 There is one other recent collection of skazkas—that published last year at Geneva under the title of "Russkiya Zavyetnuiya Skazki." But upon its contents I have not found it necessary to draw.

CONTENTS

Russian Fairy Tales

PART I
INTRODUCTORY

The Folk-tale in general, and the Skazka in particular—Relation of Russian Popular Tales to Russian Eife—Stories about Courtship, Death, Burial and Wailings for the Dead—Warnings against Drink, Jokes about Women, Tales of Simpletons— A rhymed Skazka and a Legend *1*

PART II
MYTHOLOGICAL

On the " Mythical Skazkas "—Male embodiments of Evil : 1. The Snake as the Stealer of Daylight; 2. Norkathe Beast, Lord of the Lower World ; 3. Koshchei the Deathless, The Stealer of Fair Princesses—his connexion with Punchkin and " the Giant who had no?Ieart in his Body "—Excursus on Bluebeard's Chamber ; 4. The Water King or Subaqueous Demon—Female Embodiments of Evil : 1. The Baba Yaga or Hag, and 2. The Witch, feminine counterparts of the Snake *71*

PART III
MYTHOLOGICAL

One-eyed Likho, a story of the Polyphemus Cycle—Woe, the Poor Man's Companion—Friday, Wednesday, and Sunday personified as Female Spirits—The Leshy or Wood-Demon—Legends about Rivers—Frost as a Wooer of Maidens—The Whirlwind personified as a species of Snake or Demon—Morfei and Oh, two supernatural beings *193*

PART IV
MAGIC AND WITCHCRAFT

The Waters of Life and Death, and of Strength and Weakness — Aid given to Children by Dead Parents—Magic Horses, Fish, &c.—Stories about Brides won by a Leap, &c.—Stories about Wizards and Witches—The Headless Piincess—Midnight Watchings over Corpses—The Fire Bird, its connexion with the Golden Bird and the Phoenix *249*

PART V
GHOST STORIES

Slavonic Ideas about the Dead—On Heaven and Hell—On the Jack and the Beanstalk Story—Harmless Ghosts—The Rip van Winkle Story—the attachment #f Ghosts to their Shrouds and Coffin-Lids—Murderous Ghosts—Stories about Vampires—on the name Vampire, and the belief in Vampirism....... 313

PART VI
LEGENDS

1. *Saints, &*

Legends connected with the Dog, the Izba, the Creation of Man, the Rye, the Snake, Ox, Sole, &c.; with Birds, the Peewit, Sparrow, Swallow, &c.—Legends about SS. Nicholas, Andrew, George, Kasian, &c.............................. 351

2. *Demons, &*

Part played by Demons in the Skazkas—On " Hasty Words," and Parental Curses; their power to subject persons to demoniacal possession—The dulness of Demons; Stories about Tricks played upon them—Their Gratitude to those who treat them with Kindness and their General Behavior—Various Legends about Devils—Moral Tale of the Gossip's Bedstead. 382

STORIES

THE FIEND.

The way to deal with an evil one . . . 11

THE DEAD MOTHER.

A power to sustain . . . 20

THE DEAD WITCH.

A hot water cure for demons . . . 22

THE TREASURE.

The consequences of greed . . . 25

THE CROSS-SURETY.

The power of a promise . . . 30

THE AWFUL DRUNKARD.

Dealing with devils . . . 36

THE BAD WIFE.

The tricking of a wife and a demon . . . 43

THE GOLOVIKHA.

A comeuppance for greedy ambition . . . 47

THE THREE COPECKS.

A morality tale of reward in return for humility . . . 49

THE MISER.

There is never enough loose change to return a copeck . . . 53

THE FOOL AND THE BIRCH-TREE.

An ox, a treasure, a murder and a goat . . . 57

THE MIZGIR.

A spider's cunning and a little snuff . . . 63

THE SMITH AND THE DEMON.

And if they haven't dies, they are ling still . . . 65

IVAN POPYALOF.

Ivan deals with many-headed snakes . . . 76

THE NORKA.

Ivan achieves three weddings . . . 83

MARYA MOREVNA.

Even chopped in pieces, Ivan pursues his love . . . 96

KOSHCHEI THE DEATHLESS.

With the help of friends, even death may be conquered . . . 113

THE WATER SNAKE.

Selfishness destroys the life and love of another . . . 128

THE WATER KING AND VASILISSA THE WISE.

Husbandly forgetfulness can be cured, it seems . . . 133

THE BABA YAGA.

To defeat a Baba Yaga, tend her familiars . . . 152

VASILISSA THE FAIR.

Vasilia, her dolly and the Baba Yaga . . . 163

THE WITCH.
The perils of fishing when a witch is close by . . . 177
THE WITCH AND THE SUN'S SISTER.
Treating strangers with kindness brings reward . . . 185
ONE-EYED LIKHO.
if you go in search of evil . . . 194
WOE.
Perhaps, even Woe can be outsmarted . . . 201
FRIDAY.
Do not upset Mother Friday . . . 216
WEDNESDAY.
Beat your pails together and make a sign of the cross . . . 218
THE LÉSHY.
A priest's daughter. a wood-demon and a hunter . . . 223
VAZUZA AND VOLGA.
The competitive nature of rivers . . . 226
SOZH AND DNIEPER.
To determine which river will be the strongest . . . 228
THE METAMORPHOSIS OF THE DNIEPER, THE VOLGA, AND THE DVINA.
To become a river . . . 230
FROST.
It pays to properly respect the elements . . . 234
THE BLIND MAN AND THE CRIPPLE.
The legless and the blind are heroes . . . 259
PRINCESS HELENA THE FAIR.
With the assistance of a magical horse . . . 276
EMILIAN THE FOOL.
By the Pike's command . . . 283
THE WITCH GIRL.
The cossack and the witch . . . 289
THE HEADLESS PRINCESS.
A removable head leads to a stake through the heart . . . 292
THE SOLDIER'S MIDNIGHT WATCH.
God knows who breaks in whom . . . 295
THE WARLOCK.
The way to the Warlock's fortune . . . 310
THE FOX-PHYSICIAN.
Do not place your faith in a Fox-Physician . . . 315
THE FIDDLER IN HELL.
A bridge to be rekeased from hell . . . 322
THE RIDE ON THE GRAVESTONE.
The consequence of too-jovial feasting . . . 327
THE TWO FRIENDS.
Promises that endure beyond the grave have consequences . . . 328

THE SHROUD.
The obligations of the shroud . . . 331
THE COFFIN-LID.
The corpse cpntrolled by means of a coffin lid . . . 334
THE TWO CORPSES.
The hunger of corpses . . . 337
THE DOG AND THE CORPSE.
Do not abandon those who try to help you . . . 339
THE SOLDIER AND THE VAMPIRE.
The way to deal with a dead Warlock . . . 341
ELIJAH THE PROPHET AND NICHOLAS.
The saints competing amongst themselves . . . 365
THE PRIEST WITH THE GREEDY EYES.
So greedy he ate the loaves . . . 376
THE HASTY WORD.
Taking a bride from the devil . . . 391
"The Gossip's Bedstead."
It is all on fire and runs on wheels . . . 403

RUSSIAN FAIRY TALES

PART I

Introductory

The Folk-tale in general, and the Skazka in particular—Relation of Russian Popular Tales to Russian Eife—Stories about Courtship, Death, Burial and Wailings for the Dead—Warnings against Drink, Jokes about Women, Tales of Simpletons— A rhymed Skazka and a Legend

THERE ARE BUT FEW among those inhabitants of Fairyland of whom "Popular Tales" tell, who are better known to the outer world than Cinderella—the despised and flouted younger sister, who long sits unnoticed beside the hearth, then furtively visits the glittering halls of the great and gay and at last is transferred from her obscure nook to the place of honour justly due to her tardily acknowledged merits. Somewhat like the fortunes of Cinderella have been those of the popular tale itself. Long did it dwell beside the hearths of the common people, utterly ignored by their superiors in social rank. Then came a period during which the cultured world recognised its existence but accorded to it no higher rank than that allotted to "nursery stories" and "old wives' tales"—except, indeed, on those rare occasions when the charity of a condescending scholar had invested it with such a garb as was supposed to enable it to make a respectable appearance in polite society.

At length there arrived the season of its final change, when, transferred from the dusk of the peasant's hut into the full light of the outer day and freed from the unbecoming garments by which it had been disfigured, it was recognised as the scion of a family so truly royal that some of its members deduce their origin from the olden gods themselves.

In our days the folktale, instead of being left to the careless guardianship of youth and ignorance, is sedulously tended and held in high honour by the ripest of scholars. Their views with regard to its origin may differ widely. But whether it be considered in one of its phases as a distorted "nature-myth," or in another as a demoralised apologue or parable—whether it be regarded at one time as a relic of primeval wisdom or at another as a blurred transcript of a page of mediæval history—its critics agree in declaring it to be no mere creation of the popular fancy, no chance expression of the uncultured thought of the rude tiller of this or that soil. Rather is it believed of most folktales that they, in their original forms, were framed centuries upon centuries ago; while of some of them it is supposed that they may be traced back through successive ages to those myths in which, during a prehistoric period, the oldest of philosophers expressed their ideas relative to the material or the spiritual world.

But it is not every popular tale which can boast of so noble a lineage and one of the great difficulties which besets the mythologist who attempts to discover the original meaning of folktales in general is to decide which of them are really antique and worthy, therefore, of being submitted to critical analysis. Nor is it less difficult, when dealing with the stories of any one country in particular, to settle which may be looked upon as its own property and which ought to be considered as borrowed and adapted.

Everyone knows that the existence of the greater part of the stories current among the various European peoples is accounted for on two different hypotheses—the one supposing that most of them "were common in germ at least to the Aryan tribes before their migration," and that, therefore, "these traditions are as much a portion of the common inheritance of our ancestors as their language unquestionably is:"[1] the other regarding at least a great part of them as foreign importations, Oriental fancies which were originally introduced into Europe, through a series of translations, by the pilgrims and merchants who were always linking the East and the West together or by the emissaries of some of the heretical sects or in the train of such warlike transferrers as the Crusaders or the Arabs who ruled in Spain or the Tartars who so long held the Russia of old times in their grasp. According to the former supposition, "these very stories, these *Mährchen*, which nurses still tell, with almost the same words, in the Thuringian forest and in the Norwegian villages and to which crowds of children listen under the pippal trees of India,"[2] belong "to the common heirloom of the Indo-European race;" according to the latter, the majority of European popular tales are merely naturalised aliens in Europe, being as little the inheritance of its present inhabitants as were the stories and fables which, by a circuitous route, were transmitted from India to Boccaccio or La Fontaine.

On the questions to which these two conflicting hypotheses give rise we will not now dwell. For the present, we will deal with the Russian folktale as we find it, attempting to become acquainted with its principal characteristics to see in what respects it chiefly differs from the stories of the same class which are current among ourselves or in those foreign lands with which we are more familiar than we are with Russia, rather than to explore its birthplace or to divine its original meaning.

We often hear it said, that from the songs and stories of a country we may learn much about the inner life of its people, inasmuch as popular utterances of this kind always bear the stamp of the national character, offer a reflex of

---

1 Dasent's "Popular Tales from the Norse," p. xl.
2 Max Müller, "Chips," vol. ii. p. 226.

the national mind. So far as folksongs are concerned, this statement appears to be well founded but it can be applied to the folktales of Europe only within very narrow limits. Each country possesses certain stories which have special reference to its own manners and customs and by collecting such tales as these, something approximating to a picture of its national life may be labouriously pieced together. But the stories of this class are often nothing more than comparatively modern adaptations of old and foreign themes; nor are they sufficiently numerous, so far as we can judge from existing collections, to render by any means complete the national portrait for which they are expected to supply the materials. In order to fill up the gaps they leave, it is necessary to bring together a number of fragments taken from stories which evidently refer to another clime—fragments which may be looked upon as excrescences or developments due to the novel influences to which the foreign slip or seedling or even full-grown plant, has been subjected since its transportation.

The great bulk of the Russian folktales, and indeed, of those of all the Indo-European nations, is devoted to the adventures of such fairy princes and princesses, such snakes and giants and demons, as are quite out of keeping with ordinary men and women—at all events with the inhabitants of modern Europe since the termination of those internecine struggles between aboriginals and invaders, which some commentators see typified in the combats between the heroes of our popular tales and the whole race of giants, trolls, ogres, snakes, dragons and other monsters. The air we breathe in them is that of Fairyland; the conditions of existence, the relations between the human race and the spiritual world on the one hand the material world on the other, are totally inconsistent with those to which we are now restricted. There is boundless freedom of intercourse between mortals and immortals, between mankind and the brute creation, and although there are certain conventional rules which must always be observed, they are not those which are enforced by any people known to anthropologists. The stories which are common to all Europe differ, no doubt, in different countries but their variations, so far as their matter is concerned, seem to be due less to the moral character than to the geographical distribution of their reciters. The manner in which these tales are told, however, may often be taken as a test of the intellectual capacity of their tellers. For in style the folktale changes greatly as it travels. A story which we find narrated in one country with terseness and precision may be rendered almost unintelligible in another by vagueness or verbiage; by one race it may be elevated into poetic life, by another it may be degraded into the most prosaic dullness.

Now, so far as style is concerned, the Skazkas or Russian folktales, may justly be said to be characteristic of the Russian people. There are numerous points on which the "lower classes" of all the Aryan peoples in Europe closely resemble each other but the Russian peasant has—in common with all his Slavonic brethren—a genuine talent for narrative which distinguishes him from some of his more distant cousins. And the stories which are current among the Russian peasantry are for the most part exceedingly well narrated. Their language is simple and pleasantly quaint, their humour is natural and unobtrusive and their descriptions, whether of persons or of events, are often excellent.[3] A taste for acting is widely spread in Russia and the Russian folktales are full of dramatic positions which offer a wide scope for a display of their reciter's mimetic talents. Every here and there, indeed, a tag of genuine comedy has evidently been attached by the storyteller to a narrative which in its original form was probably devoid of the comic element.

---

3 Take as an illustration of these remarks the close of the story of "Helena the Fair" (No. 34, Chap. IV.). See how light and bright it is (or at least was, before it was translated).

And thus from the Russian tales may be derived some idea of the mental characteristics of the Russian peasantry—one which is very incomplete, but within its narrow limits, sufficiently accurate. And a similar statement may be made with respect to the pictures of Russian peasant life contained in these tales. So far as they go they are true to nature and the notion which they convey to a stranger of the manners and customs of Russian villagers is not likely to prove erroneous but they do not go very far.

On some of the questions which are likely to be of the greatest interest to a foreigner they never touch. There is very little information to be gleaned from them, for instance, with regard to the religious views of the people, none with respect to the relations which, during the times of serfdom, existed between the lord and the thrall. But from the casual references to actual scenes and ordinary occupations which every here and there occur in the descriptions of Fairyland and the narratives of heroic adventure—from the realistic vignettes which are sometimes inserted between the idealised portraits of invincible princes and irresistible princesses—some idea may be obtained of the usual aspect of a Russian village and of the ordinary behaviour of its inhabitants.

Turning from one to another of these accidental illustrations, we by degrees create a mental picture which is not without its peculiar charm. We see the wide sweep of the level corn-land the gloom of the interminable forest, the gleam of the slowly winding river. We pass along the single street of the village and glance at its wooden barn-like huts,[4] so different from the ideal English cottage with its windows set deep in ivy and its porch smiling with roses. We see the land around a Slough of Despond in the spring, an unbroken sea of green in the early summer, a blaze of gold at harvest-time, in the winter

4 I speak only of what I have seen. In some districts of Russia, if one may judge from pictures, the peasants occupy ornamented and ornamental dwellings.

one vast sheet of all but untrodden snow. On Sundays and holidays we accompany the villagers to their white-walled, green-domed church and afterwards listen to the songs which the girls sing in the summer choral dances or take part in the merriment of the social gatherings, which enliven the long nights of winter.

Sometimes the quaint lyric drama of a peasant wedding is performed before our eyes, sometimes we follow a funeral party to one of those dismal and desolate nooks in which the Russian villagers deposit their dead. On working days we see the peasants driving afield in the early morn with their long lines of carts, to till the soil or ply the scythe or sickle or axe, till the day is done and their rude carts come creaking back.

We hear the songs and laughter of the girls beside the stream or pool which ripples pleasantly against its banks in the summertime but in the winter shows no sign of life, except at the spot, much frequented by the wives and daughters of the village, where an "ice-hole" has been cut in its massive pall. And at night we see the homely dwellings of the villagers assume a picturesque aspect to which they are strangers by the tell-tale light of day, their rough lines softened by the mellow splendour of a summer moon or their unshapely forms looming forth mysteriously against the starlit snow of winter. Above all we become familiar with those cottage interiors to which the stories contain so many references.

Sometimes we see the better class of homestead, surrounded by its fence through which we pass between the often-mentioned gates. After a glance at the barns and cattle-sheds and at the garden which supplies the family with fruits and vegetables (on flowers, alas! but little store is set in the northern provinces), we cross the threshold, a spot hallowed by many traditions and pass, through what in more pretentious houses may be called the vestibule, into the "living room."

We become well acquainted with its arrangements, with the cellar beneath its wooden floor, with the "corner of honour" in which are placed the "holy pictures," and with the stove which occupies so large a share of space, within which daily beats, as it were the heart of the house, above which is nightly taken the repose of the family. Sometimes we visit the hut of the poverty-stricken peasant, more like a shed for cattle than a human habitation, with a mud-floor and a tattered roof, through which the smoke makes its devious way.

In these poorer dwellings we witness much suffering; but we learn to respect the patience and resignation with which it is generally borne and in the greater part of the humble homes we visit we become aware of the existence of many domestic virtues, we see numerous tokens of family affection, of filial reverence, of parental love. And when, as we pass along the village street at night, we see gleaming through the utter darkness the faint rays which tell that even in many a poverty-stricken home a lamp is burning before the "holy pictures," we feel that these poor tillers of the soil, ignorant and uncouth though they too often are, may be raised at times by lofty thoughts and noble aspirations far above the low level of the dull and hard lives which they are forced to lead.

From among the stories which contain the most graphic descriptions of Russian village life or which may be regarded as especially illustrative of Russian sentiment and humour those which the present chapter contains have been selected. Any information they may convey will necessarily be of a most fragmentary nature but for all that it may be capable of producing a correct impression. A painter's rough notes and jottings are often more true to nature than the most finished picture into which they may be developed.

The word skazka or folktale, does not very often occur in the Russian popular tales themselves. Still there are occasions on which it appears. The allusions to it are for the most part indirect, as when a princess is said to be more beautiful than anybody ever was, except in a skazka; but sometimes it obtains direct notice. In a story, for instance, of a boy who had been carried off by a Baba Yaga (a species of witch), we are told that when his sister came to his rescue she found him "sitting in an arm-chair, while the cat Jeremiah told him skazkas and sang him songs."[5]

In another story, a *Durak*,—a "ninny" or "gowk"—is sent to take care of the children of a village during the absence of their parents. "Go and get all the children together in one of the cottages and tell them skazkas," are his instructions. He collects the children but as they are "all ever so dirty" he puts them into boiling water by way of cleansing them and so washes them to death.[6] There is a good deal of social life in the Russian villages during the long winter evenings and at some of the gatherings which then take place skazkas are told, though at those in which only the young people participate, songs, games and dances are more popular.

The following skazka has been selected on account of the descriptions of a *vechernitsa* or village *soirée*,[7] and of a rustic courtship, which its opening scene contains. The rest of the story is not remarkable for its fidelity to modern life but it will serve as a good illustration of the class to which it belongs—that of stories about evil spirits, traceable, for the most part, to Eastern sources.

---

5 Khudyakof, vol. ii. p. 65.
6 Khudyakof, vol. ii. p. 115.

7 For a description of such social gatherings see the "Songs of the Russian People," pp. 32–38.

THE FIEND.[8]

The way to deal with an evil one . . .

IN A CERTAIN COUNTRY there lived an old couple who had a daughter called Marusia (Mary). In their village it was customary to celebrate the feast of St. Andrew the First-Called (November 30). The girls used to assemble in some cottage, bake *pampushki,*[9] and enjoy themselves for a whole week or even longer. Well, the girls met together once when this festival arrived and brewed and baked what was wanted. In the evening came the lads with the music, bringing liquor with them and dancing and revelry commenced. All the girls danced well but Marusia the best of all. After a while there came into the cottage such a fine fellow! Marry come up! regular blood and milk and smartly and richly dressed.

"Hail, fair maidens!" says he.

"Hail, good youth!" say they.

"You're merry making?"

"Be so good as to join us."

Thereupon he pulled out of his pocket a purse full of gold, ordered liquor, nuts and gingerbread. All was ready in a trice and he began treating the lads and lasses, giving each a share. Then he took to dancing. Why, it was a treat to look at him! Marusia struck his fancy more than anyone else; so he stuck close to her. The time came for going home.

"Marusia," says he, "come and see me off."

She went to see him off.

"Marusia, sweetheart!" says he, "would you like me to marry you?"

---

8 Afanasief, vi. No. 66.

9 Cakes of unleavened flour flavoured with garlic.

"If you like to marry me, I will gladly marry you. But where do you come from?"

"From such and such a place. I'm the clerk at a merchant's."

Then they bade each other farewell and separated. When Marusia got home, her mother asked her:

"Well, daughter! have you enjoyed yourself?"

"Yes, mother. But I've something pleasant to tell you besides. There was a lad there from the neighbourhood, good-looking and with lots of money and he promised to marry me."

"Harkye Marusia! When you go to where the girls are tomorrow, take a ball of thread with you, make a noose in it, and when you are going to see him off, throw it over one of his buttons and quietly unroll the ball; then, by means of the thread, you will be able to find out where he lives."

Next day Marusia went to the gathering and took a ball of thread with her. The youth came again.

"Good evening, Marusia!" said he.

"Good evening!" said she.

Games began and dances. Even more than before did he stick to Marusia, not a step would he budge from her. The time came for going home.

"Come and see me off, Marusia!" says the stranger.

She went out into the street and while she was taking leave of him she quietly dropped the noose over one of his buttons. He went his way but she remained where she was, unrolling the ball. When she had unrolled the whole of it, she ran after the thread to find out where her betrothed lived.

At first the thread followed the road, then it stretched across hedges and ditches and led Marusia towards the church and right up to the porch. Marusia tried the door; it was locked. She went round the church, found a ladder, set it against a window and climbed up it to see what was going on inside. Having got into the church, she looked—and saw her betrothed standing beside a grave and devouring a dead body—for a corpse had been left for that night in the church.

She wanted to get down the ladder quietly but her fright prevented her from taking proper heed and she made a little noise. Then she ran home—almost beside herself, fancying all the time she was being pursued. She was all but dead before she got in. Next morning her mother asked her:

"Well, Marusia! did you see the youth?"

"I saw him, mother," she replied. But what else she had seen she did not tell.

In the morning Marusia was sitting, considering whether she would go to the gathering or not.

"Go," said her mother. "Amuse yourself while you're young!"

So she went to the gathering; the Fiend[10] was there already. Games, fun, dancing, began anew; the girls knew nothing of what had happened. When they began to separate and go homewards:

"Come, Marusia!" says the Evil One, "see me off."

She was afraid and didn't stir. Then all the other girls opened out upon her.

"What are you thinking about? Have you grown so bashful, forsooth? Go and see the good lad off."

There was no help for it. Out she went, not knowing what would come of it. As soon as they got into the streets he began questioning her:

"You were in the church last night?"

"No."

"And saw what I was doing there?"

"No."

"Very well! Tomorrow your father will die!"

Having said this, he disappeared.

---

10 The Nechistol or unclean. (Chisty = clean, pure, &c.)

Marusia returned home grave and sad. When she woke up in the morning, her father lay dead!

They wept and wailed over him and laid him in the coffin. In the evening her mother went off to the priest's but Marusia remained at home. At last she became afraid of being alone in the house. "Suppose I go to my friends," she thought. So she went and found the Evil One there.

"Good evening, Marusia! why aren't you merry?"

"How can I be merry? My father is dead!"

"Oh! poor thing!"

They all grieved for her. Even the Accursed One himself grieved; just as if it hadn't all been his own doing. By and by they began saying farewell and going home.

"Marusia," says he, "see me off."

She didn't want to.

"What are you thinking of, child?" insist the girls. "What are you afraid of? Go and see him off."

So she went to see him off. They passed out into the street.

"Tell me, Marusia," says he, "were you in the church?"

"No."

"Did you see what I was doing?"

"No."

"Very well! Tomorrow your mother will die."

He spoke and disappeared. Marusia returned home sadder than ever. The night went by; next morning, when she awoke, her mother lay dead! She cried all day long; but when the sun set and it grew dark around, Marusia became afraid of being left alone; so she went to her companions.

"Why, whatever's the matter with you? you're clean out of countenance!"[11] say the girls.

"How am I likely to be cheerful? Yesterday my father died and to-day my mother."

---

11 Literally, "on thee no face is to be seen."

"Poor thing! Poor unhappy girl!" they all exclaim sympathisingly.

Well, the time came to say good-bye. "See me off, Marusia," says the Fiend. So she went out to see him off.

"Tell me; were you in the church?"

"No."

"And saw what I was doing?"

"No."

"Very well! Tomorrow evening you will die yourself!"

Marusia spent the night with her friends; in the morning she got up and considered what she should do. She bethought herself that she had a grandmother—an old, very old woman, who had become blind from length of years. "Suppose I go and ask her advice," she said and then went off to her grandmother's.

"Good-day, granny!" says she.

"Good-day, granddaughter! What news is there with you? How are your father and mother?"

"They are dead, granny," replied the girl and then told her all that had happened.

The old woman listened and said:—

"Oh dear me! my poor unhappy child! Go quickly to the priest and ask him this favour—that if you die, your body shall not be taken out of the house through the doorway but that the ground shall be dug away from under the threshold and that you shall be dragged out through that opening. And also beg that you may be buried at a crossway, at a spot where four roads meet."

Marusia went to the priest, wept bitterly and made him promise to do everything according to her grandmother's instructions. Then she returned home, bought a coffin, lay down in it and straightway expired.

Well, they told the priest and he buried, first her father and mother and then Marusia herself. Her body was passed underneath the threshold and buried at a crossway.

Soon afterwards a seigneur's son happened to drive past Marusia's grave. On that grave he saw growing a wondrous flower, such a one as he had never seen before. Said the young seigneur to his servant:—

"Go and pluck up that flower by the roots. We'll take it home and put it in a flowerpot. Perhaps it will blossom there."

Well, they dug up the flower, took it home, put it in a glazed flowerpot and set it in a window. The flower began to grow larger and more beautiful. One night the servant hadn't gone to sleep somehow and he happened to be looking at the window, when he saw a wondrous thing take place. All of a sudden the flower began to tremble, then it fell from its stem to the ground and turned into a lovely maiden. The flower was beautiful but the maiden was more beautiful still. She wandered from room to room, got herself various things to eat and drink, ate and drank, then stamped upon the ground and became a flower as before, mounted to the window and resumed her place upon the stem. Next day the servant told the young seigneur of the wonders which he had seen during the night.

"Ah, brother!" said the youth, "why didn't you wake me? To-night we'll both keep watch together."

The night came; they slept not but watched. Exactly at twelve o'clock the blossom began to shake, flew from place to place and then fell to the ground and the beautiful maiden appeared, got herself things to eat and drink and sat down to supper. The young seigneur rushed forward and seized her by her white hands. Impossible was it for him sufficiently to look at her, to gaze on her beauty!

Next morning he said to his father and mother, "Please allow me to get married. I've found myself a bride."

His parents gave their consent. As for Marusia, she said:

"Only on this condition will I marry you—that for four years I need not go to church."

"Very good," said he.

Well, they were married and they lived together one year, two years and had a son. But one day they had visitors at their house, who enjoyed themselves and drank and began bragging about their wives. This one's wife was handsome; that one's was handsomer still.

"You may say what you like," says the host, "but a handsomer wife than mine does not exist in the whole world!"

"Handsome, yes!" reply the guests, "but a heathen."

"How so?"

"Why, she never goes to church."

Her husband found these observations distasteful. He waited till Sunday and then told his wife to get dressed for church.

"I don't care what you may say," says he. "Go and get ready directly."

Well, they got ready and went to church. The husband went in—didn't see anything particular. But when she looked round—there was the Fiend sitting at a window.

"Ha! here you are, at last!" he cried. "Remember old times. Were you in the church that night?"

"No."

"And did you see what I was doing there?"

"No."

"Very well! Tomorrow both your husband and your son will die."

Marusia rushed straight out of the church and away to her grandmother. The old woman gave her two phials, the one full of holy water, the other of the water of life and told her what she was to do. Next day both Marusia's husband and her son died. Then the Fiend came flying to her and asked:—

"Tell me; were you in the church?"

"I was."

"And did you see what I was doing?"

"You were eating a corpse."

She spoke and splashed the holy water over him; in a moment he turned into mere dust and ashes, which blew to the winds. Afterwards she sprinkled her husband and her boy with the water of life: straightway they revived. And from that time forward they knew neither sorrow nor separation but they all lived together long and happily.[12]

Another lively sketch of a peasant's lovemaking is given in the introduction to the story of "Ivan the widow's son and Grisha."[13] The tale is one of magic and enchantment, of living clouds and seven-headed snakes; but the opening is a little piece of still-life very quaintly portrayed.

A certain villager, named Trofim, having been unable to find a wife, his Aunt Melania comes to his aid, promising to procure him an interview with a widow who has been left well provided for and whose personal appearance is attractive—"real blood and milk! When she's got on her holiday clothes, she's as fine as a peacock!" Trofim grovels with gratitude at his aunt's feet. "My own dear auntie, Melania Prokhorovna, get me married for heaven's sake! I'll buy you an embroidered kerchief in return, the very best in the whole market."

The widow comes to pay Melania a visit and is induced to believe, on the evidence of beans (frequently used for the purpose of divination), that her destined husband is close at hand. At this propitious moment Trofim appears.

12 I do not propose to comment at any length upon the stories quoted in the present chapter. Some of them will be referred to farther on. Marusia's demon lover will be recognised as akin to Arabian Ghouls or the Rákshasas of Indian mythology. (See the story of Sidi Norman in the "Thousand and One Nights," also Lane's translation, vol. i., p. 32; and the story of Asokadatta and Vijayadatta in the fifth book of the "Kathásaritságara," Brockhaus's translation, 1843, vol. ii. pp. 142-159.) For transformations of a maiden into a flower or tree, see Grimm, No. 76, "Die Nelke," and the notes to that story in vol. iii., p. 125—Hahn, No. 21, "Das Lorbeerkind," etc. "The Water of Life," will meet with due consideration in the fourth chapter. The Holy Water which destroys the Fiend is merely a Christian form of the "Water of Death," viewed in its negative aspect.

13 Chudinsky, No. 3.

Melania makes a little speech to the young couple, ending her recommendation to get married with the words:—

"I can see well enough by the bridegroom's eyes that the bride is to his taste, only I don't know what the bride thinks about taking him."

"I don't mind!" says the widow. "Well, then, glory be to God! Now, stand up, we'll say a prayer before the Holy Pictures; then give each other a kiss and go in Heaven's name and get married at once!" And so the question is settled.

~

From a courtship and a marriage in peasant life we may turn to a death and a burial. There are frequent allusions in the Skazkas to these gloomy subjects, with reference to which we will quote two stories, the one pathetic, the other (unintentionally) grotesque. Neither of them bears any title in the original but we may style the first—

THE DEAD MOTHER.[14]

A power to sustain . . .

IN A CERTAIN VILLAGE there lived a husband and wife—lived happily, lovingly, peaceably. All their neighbours envied them; the sight of them gave pleasure to honest folks. Well, the mistress bore a son but directly after it was born she died. The poor moujik moaned and wept. Above all he was in despair about the babe. How was he to nourish it now? how to bring it up without its mother? He did what was best and hired an old woman to look after it. Only here was a wonder! all day long the babe would take no food and did nothing but cry; there was no soothing it anyhow. But during (a great part of) the night one could fancy it wasn't there at all, so silently and peacefully did it sleep.

"What's the meaning of this?" thinks the old woman; "suppose I keep awake to-night; may be I shall find out."

Well, just at midnight she heard someone quietly open the door and go up to the cradle. The babe became still, just as if it was being suckled.

The next night the same thing took place and the third night, too. Then she told the moujik about it. He called his kinsfolk together and held counsel with them. They determined on this; to keep awake on a certain night and to spy out who it was that came to suckle the babe. So at eventide they all lay down on the floor and beside them they set a lighted taper hidden in an earthen pot.

At midnight the cottage door opened. Someone stepped up to the cradle. The babe became still. At that moment one of

---

14 Afanasief, vi. p. 325. Wolfs "Niederlandische Sagen," No. 326, quoted in Thorpe's "Northern Mythology," i. 292. Note 4.

the kinsfolk suddenly brought out the light. They looked and saw the dead mother, in the very same clothes in which she had been buried, on her knees besides the cradle, over which she bent as she suckled the babe at her dead breast.

The moment the light shone in the cottage she stood up, gazed sadly on her little one and then went out of the room without a sound, not saying a word to anyone. All those who saw her stood for a time terror-struck; and then they found the babe was dead.[15]

~

The second story will serve as an illustration of one of the Russian customs with respect to the dead and also of the ideas about witchcraft, still prevalent in Russia. We may create for it the title of—

15 A number of ghost stories and some remarks about the ideas of the Russian peasants with respect to the dead, will be found in Chap. V. Scott mentions a story in "The Minstrelsy of the Scottish Border," vol. ii. p. 223, of a widower who believed he was haunted by his dead wife. On one occasion the ghost, to prove her identity, gave suck to her surviving infant.

THE DEAD WITCH.[16]

A hot water cure for demons . . .

THERE WAS ONCE AN old woman who was a terrible witch and she had a daughter and a granddaughter. The time came for the old crone to die, so she summoned her daughter and gave her these instructions:

"Mind, daughter! when I'm dead, don't you wash my body with lukewarm water; but fill a cauldron, make it boil its very hottest and then with that boiling water regularly scald me all over."

After saying this, the witch lay ill two or three days and then died. The daughter ran round to all her neighbours, begging them to come and help her to wash the old woman and meantime the little granddaughter was left all alone in the cottage. And this is what she saw there. All of a sudden there crept out from beneath the stove two demons—a big one and a tiny one—and they ran up to the dead witch. The old demon seized her by the feet and tore away at her so that he stripped off all her skin at one pull. Then he said to the little demon:

"Take the flesh for yourself and lug it under the stove."

So the little demon flung his arms round the carcase and dragged it under the stove. Nothing was left of the old woman but her skin. Into it the old demon inserted himself and then he lay down just where the witch had been lying.

Presently the daughter came back, bringing a dozen other women with her and they all set to work laying out the corpse.

"Mammy," says the child, "they've pulled granny's skin off while you were away."

---

16 Afanasief, viii. p. 165.

"What do you mean by telling such lies?"

"It's quite true, Mammy! There was ever such a blackie came from under the stove and he pulled the skin off and got into it himself."

"Hold your tongue, naughty child! you're talking nonsense!" cried the old crone's daughter; then she fetched a big cauldron, filled it with cold water, put it on the stove and heated it till it boiled furiously. Then the women lifted up the old crone, laid her in a trough, took hold of the cauldron and poured the whole of the boiling water over her at once. The demon couldn't stand it. He leaped out of the trough, dashed through the doorway and disappeared, skin and all. The women stared:

"What marvel is this?" they cried. "Here was the dead woman and now she isn't here. There's nobody left to lay out or to bury. The demons have carried her off before our very eyes!"[17]

A Russian peasant funeral is preceded or accompanied by a considerable amount of wailing, which answers in some respect to the Irish "keening." To the *zaplachki*,[18] or laments, which are uttered on such occasions—frequently by hired wailers, who closely resemble the Corsican "vociferators," the modern Greek "myrologists"—allusions are sometimes made in the Skazkas. In the "Fox-wailer,"[19] for example—one of the variants of the well-known "Jack and the Beanstalk" story—an old man puts his wife in a bag and attempts to carry her up the beanstalk to heaven. Becoming tired on the way, he drops the bag and the old woman is killed. After weeping over her dead body he sets out in search of a Wailer. Meeting

---

17 In West-European stories the devil frequently carries off a witch's soul after death. Here the fiend enters the corpse or rather its skin, probably intending to reappear as a vampire. Compare Bleek's "Reynard the Fox in South Africa," No. 24, in which a lion squeezes itself into the skin of a girl it has killed. I have generally rendered by "demon," instead of "devil," the word chort when it occurs in stories of this class, as the spirits to which they refer are manifestly akin to those of oriental demonology.

18 For an account of which, see the "Songs of the Russian People," pp. 333-334. The best Russian work on the subject is Barsof's "Prichitaniya Syevernago Kraya," Moscow, 1872.

19 Afanasief, iv. No. 9.

a bear, he cries, "Wail a bit, Bear, for my old woman! I'll give you a pair of nice white fowls." The bear growls out "Oh, dear granny of mine! how I grieve for thee!" "No, no!" says the old man, "you can't wail." Going a little further he tries a wolf but the wolf succeeds no better than the bear. At last a fox comes by and on being appealed to, begins to cry aloud "Turu-Turu, grandmother! grandfather has killed thee!"—a wail which pleases the widower so much that he hands over the fowls to the fox at once and asks, enraptured, for "that strain again!"[20]

~

One of the most curious of the stories which relate to a village burial,—one in which also the feeling with which the Russian villagers sometimes regard their clergy finds expression—is that called—

20 Professor de Gubernatis justly remarks that this "howling" is more in keeping with the nature of the eastern jackal than with that of its western counterpart, the fox. "Zoological Mythology," ii. 130.

THE TREASURE.[21]

The consequences of greed . . .

IN A CERTAIN KINGDOM there lived an old couple in great poverty. Sooner or later the old woman died. It was in winter, in severe and frosty weather. The old man went round to his friends and neighbours, begging them to help him to dig a grave for the old woman; but his friends and neighbours, knowing his great poverty, all flatly refused. The old man went to the pope,[22] (but in that village they had an awfully grasping pope, one without any conscience) and says he:—

"Lend a hand reverend father, to get my old woman buried."

"But have you got any money to pay for the funeral? if so, friend, pay up beforehand!"

"It's no use hiding anything from you. Not a single copeck have I at home. But if you'll wait a little, I'll earn some and then I'll pay you with interest—on my word I'll pay you!"

The pope wouldn't so much as listen to the old man.

"If you haven't any money, don't you dare to come here," says he.

"What's to be done?" thinks the old man. "I'll go to the graveyard, dig a grave as I best can and bury the old woman myself." So he took an axe and a shovel and went to the graveyard. When he got there he began to prepare a grave. He chopped away the frozen ground on the top with the axe and then he took to the shovel. He dug and dug and at last he dug out a metal pot. Looking into it he saw that it was

21 Afanasief, vii. No. 45.

22 Pope is the ordinary but disrespectful term for a priest (Svyashchennik), as popovich is for a priest's son.

stuffed full of ducats that shone like fire. The old man was immensely delighted and cried, "Glory be to Thee, O Lord! I shall have wherewithal both to bury my old woman and to perform the rites of remembrance."

He did not go on digging the grave any longer but took the pot of gold and carried it home. Well, we all know what money will do—everything went as smooth as oil! In a trice there were found good folks to dig the grave and fashion the coffin. The old man sent his daughter-in-law to purchase meat and drink and different kind of relishes—everything there ought to be at memorial feasts—and he himself took a ducat in his hand and hobbled back again to the pope's. The moment he reached the door, out flew the pope at him.

"You were distinctly told, you old lout, that you were not to come here without money; and now you've slunk back again."

"Don't be angry, batyushka,"[23] said the old man imploringly. "Here's gold for you. If you'll only bury my old woman, I'll never forget your kindness."

The pope took the money and didn't know how best to receive the old man, where to seat him, with what words to smooth him down. "Well now, old friend! Be of good cheer; everything shall be done," said he.

The old man made his bow and went home and the pope and his wife began talking about him.

"There now, the old hunks!" they say. "So poor, forsooth, so poor! And yet he's paid a gold piece. Many a defunct person of quality have I buried in my time but I never got so from anyone before."

The pope got under weigh with all his retinue and buried the old crone in proper style. After the funeral the old man invited him to his house, to take part in the feast in memory of the dead. Well, they entered the cottage and sat down to

---

23 "Father dear," or "reverend father."

table—and there appeared from somewhere or other meat and drink and all sorts of snacks, everything in profusion. The reverend guest sat down, ate for three people, looked greedily at what was not his. The other guests finished their meal and separated to go to their homes; then the pope also rose from the table. The old man went to speed him on his way. As soon as they got into the farmyard and the pope saw they were alone at last, he began questioning the old man: "Listen, friend! confess to me, don't leave so much as a single sin on your soul—it's just the same before me as before God! How have you managed to get on at such a pace? You used to be a poor moujik and now—marry! where did it come from? Confess, friend, whose breath have you stopped? whom have you pillaged?"

"What are you talking about, batyushka? I will tell you the exact truth. I have not robbed, nor plundered, nor killed anyone. A treasure tumbled into my hands of its own accord."

And he told him how it all happened. When the pope heard these words he actually shook all over with greediness. Going home, he did nothing by night and by day but think, "That such a wretched lout of a moujik should have come in for such a lump of money! Is there any way of tricking him now and getting this pot of money out of him?" He told his wife about it and he and she discussed the matter together and held counsel over it.

"Listen, mother," says he; "we've a goat, haven't we?"

"Yes."

"All right, then; we'll wait until it's night and then we'll do the job properly."

Late in the evening the pope dragged the goat indoors, killed it and took off its skin—horns, beard and all complete. Then he pulled the goat's skin over himself and said to his wife:

"Bring a needle and thread, mother and fasten up the skin all round, so that it mayn't slip off."

So she took a strong needle and some tough thread and sewed him up in the goatskin. Well, at the dead of night, the pope went straight to the old man's cottage, got under the window and began knocking and scratching. The old man hearing the noise, jumped up and asked:

"Who's there?"

"The Devil!"

"Ours is a holy spot!"[24] shrieked the moujik and began crossing himself and uttering prayers.

"Listen, old man," says the pope, "From me thou will not escape, although thou may'st pray, although thou may'st cross thyself; much better give me back my pot of money, otherwise I will make thee pay for it. See now, I pitied thee in thy misfortune and I showed thee the treasure, thinking thou wouldst take a little of it to pay for the funeral but thou hast pillaged it utterly."

The old man looked out of window—the goat's horns and beard caught his eye—it was the Devil himself, no doubt of it.

"Let's get rid of him, money and all," thinks the old man; "I've lived before now without money and now I'll go on living without it."

So he took the pot of gold, carried it outside, flung it on the ground and bolted indoors again as quickly as possible.

The pope seized the pot of money and hastened home. When he got back, "Come," says he, "the money is in our hands now. Here, mother, put it well out of sight and take a sharp knife, cut the thread and pull the goatskin off me before anyone sees it."

She took a knife and was beginning to cut the thread at the seam, when forth flowed blood and the pope began to howl:

"Oh! it hurts, mother, it hurts! don't cut mother, don't cut!"

---

24 A phrase often used by the peasants, when frightened by anything of supernatural appearance.

She began ripping the skin open in another place but with just the same result. The goatskin had united with his body all round. And all that they tried and all that they did, even to taking the money back to the old man, was of no avail. The goatskin remained clinging tight to the pope all the same. God evidently did it to punish him for his great greediness.

~

A somewhat less heathenish story with regard to money is the following, which may be taken as a specimen of the Skazkas which bear the impress of the genuine reverence which the peasants feel for their religion, whatever may be the feelings they entertain towards its ministers. While alluding to this subject, by the way, it may be as well to remark that no great reliance can be placed upon the evidence contained in the folktales of any land with respect to the relations between its clergy and their flocks. The local parson of folklore is, as a general rule, merely the innocent inheritor of the bad reputation acquired by some ecclesiastic of another age and clime.

THE CROSS-SURETY.[25]

The power of a promise . . .

ONCE UPON A TIME two merchants lived in a certain town just on the verge of a stream. One of them was a Russian, the other a Tartar; both were rich. But the Russian got so utterly ruined by some business or other that he hadn't a single bit of property left. Everything he had was confiscated or stolen. The Russian merchant had nothing to turn to—he was left as poor as a rat.[26] So he went to his friend the Tartar and besought him to lend him some money.

"Get me a surety," says the Tartar.

"But whom can I get for you, seeing that I haven't a thing belonging to me? Stay, though! there's a surety for you, the life-giving cross on the church!"

"Very good, my friend!" says the Tartar. "I'll trust your cross. Your faith or ours, it's all one to me."

And he gave the Russian merchant fifty thousand roubles. The Russian took the money, bade the Tartar farewell and went back to trade in diverse places.

By the end of two years he had gained a hundred and fifty thousand roubles by the fifty thousand he had borrowed. Now he happened to be sailing one day along the Danube, going with wares from one place to another, when all of a sudden a storm arose and was on the point of sinking the ship he was in. Then the merchant remembered how he had borrowed money and given the life-giving cross as a surety but had not paid his debt. That was doubtless the cause of the storm arising!

---

25 Afanasief, Skazki, vii. No. 49.

26 The Russian expression is gol kak sokòl, "bare as a hawk."

No sooner had he said this to himself than the storm began to subside. The merchant took a barrel, counted out fifty thousand roubles, wrote the Tartar a note, placed it, together with the money, in the barrel and then flung the barrel into the water, saying to himself: "As I gave the cross as my surety to the Tartar, the money will be certain to reach him."

The barrel straightway sank to the bottom; everyone supposed the money was lost. But what happened? In the Tartar's house there lived a Russian kitchen-maid. One day she happened to go to the river for water and when she got there she saw a barrel floating along. So she went a little way into the water and began trying to get hold of it. But it wasn't to be done! When she made for the barrel, it retreated from her: when she turned from the barrel to the shore, it floated after her. She went on trying and trying for some time, then she went home and told her master all that had happened. At first he wouldn't believe her but at last he determined to go to the river and see for himself what sort of barrel it was that was floating there. When he got there—sure enough there was the barrel floating and not far from the shore. The Tartar took off his clothes and went into the water; before he had gone any distance the barrel came floating up to him of its own accord. He laid hold of it, carried it home, opened it and looked inside. There he saw a quantity of money and on top of the money a note. He took out the note and read it and this is what was said in it:—

"Dear friend! I return to you the fifty thousand roubles for which, when I borrowed them from you, I gave the life-giving cross as a surety."

The Tartar read these words and was astounded at the power of the life-giving cross. He counted the money over to see whether the full sum was really there. It was there exactly.

Meanwhile, the Russian merchant, after trading some five years, made a tolerable fortune. Well, he returned to his old home, and thinking that his barrel had been lost, he considered it his first duty to settle with the Tartar. So he went to his house and offered him the money he had borrowed. Then the Tartar told him all that had happened and how he had found the barrel in the river, with the money and the note inside it. Then he showed him the note, saying:

"Is that really your hand?"

"It certainly is," replied the other.

Everyone was astounded at this wondrous manifestation and the Tartar said:

"Then I've no more money to receive from you, brother; take that back again."

The Russian merchant had a service performed as a thank-offering to God and next day the Tartar was baptised with all his household. The Russian merchant was his godfather and the kitchen-maid his godmother. After that they both lived long and happily, survived to a great age and then died peacefully.[27]

~

There is one marked feature in the Russian peasant's character to which the Skazkas frequently refer—his passion for drink. To him strong liquor is a friend, a comforter, a solace amid the ills of life. Intoxication is not so much an evil to be dreaded or remembered with shame, as a joy to be fondly anticipated or classed with the happy memories of the past. By him drunkenness is regarded, like sleep, as the friend of woe—and a friend whose services can be even more readily commanded. On certain occasions he almost believes that to get drunk is a duty he owes either to the Church or to the memory of the Dead; at times without the slightest apparent cause, he is seized by a sudden and irresistible craving for ardent spirits and he commences a drinking-bout which

27 In another story St. Nicolas's picture is the surety

lasts—with intervals of coma—for days or even weeks, after which he resumes his everyday life and his usual sobriety as calmly as if no interruption had taken place. All these ideas and habits of his find expression in his popular tales, giving rise to incidents which are often singularly out of keeping with the rest of the narrative in which they occur. In one of the many variants,[28] for instance, of a widespread and well-known story—that of the three princesses who are rescued from captivity by a hero from whom they are afterwards carried away and who refuse to get married until certain clothes or shoes or other things impossible for ordinary workmen to make are supplied to them—an unfortunate shoemaker is told that if he does not next day produce the necessary shoes (of perfect fit, although no measure has been taken and all set thick with precious stones) he shall be hanged. Away he goes at once to a *traktir* or tavern and sets to work to drown his grief in drink. After awhile he begins to totter. "Now then," he says, "I'll take home a beaker of spirits with me and go to bed. And tomorrow morning, as soon as they come to fetch me to be hanged, I'll toss off half the beakerful. They may hang me then without my knowing anything about it."[29]

In the story of the "Purchased Wife," the Princess Anastasia, the Beautiful, enables the youth Ivan, who ransoms her, to win a large sum of money in the following manner. Having worked a piece of embroidery, she tells him to take it to market. "But if anyone purchases it," says she, "don't take any money from him but ask him to give you liquor enough to make you drunk." Ivan obeys and this is the result. He drank till he was intoxicated and when he left the kabak (or pothouse) he tumbled into a muddy pool. A crowd collected and folks

28 Another variant of this story, under the title of "Norka," will be quoted in full in the next chapter.

29 Afanasief, vii. p. 107.

looked at him and said scoffingly, "Oh, the fair youth! now'd be the time for him to go to church to get married!"

"Fair or foul!" says he, "if I bid her, Anastasia the Beautiful will kiss the crown of my head."

"Don't go bragging like that!" says a rich merchant—"why she wouldn't even so much as look at you," and offers to stake all that he is worth on the truth of his assertion. Ivan accepts the wager. The Princess appears, takes him by the hand kisses him on the crown of his head, wipes the dirt off him and leads him home, still inebriated but no longer impecunious.[30]

Sometimes even greater people than the peasants get drunk. The story of "Semilétka"[31]—a variant of the well-known tale of how a woman's wit enables her to guess all riddles, to detect all deceits and to conquer all difficulties—relates how the heroine was chosen by a Voyvode[32] as his wife, with the stipulation that if she meddled in the affairs of his Voyvodeship she was to be sent back to her father but allowed to take with her whatever thing belonging to her she prized most. The marriage takes place but one day the well-known case comes before him for decision, of the foal of the borrowed mare—does it belong to the owner of the mare or to the borrower in whose possession it was at the time of foaling? The Voyvode adjudges it to the borrower and this is how the story ends:—

"Semilétka heard of this and could not restrain herself but said that he had decided unfairly. The Voyvode waxed wroth and demanded a divorce. After dinner Semilétka was obliged to go back to her father's house. But during the dinner she made the Voyvode drink till he was intoxicated. He drank his fill and went to sleep. While he was sleeping she had him placed in a carriage and then she drove away with him to her

---

30 Afanasief, vii. p. 146.

31 Or "The Seven-year-old." Khudyakof, No. 6. See Grimm, No. 94, "Die kluge Bauerntochter," and iii. 170-2

32 Voevoda, now a general, formerly meant a civil governor, etc.

father's. When they had arrived there the Voyvode awoke and said—

"'Who brought me here?'

"'I brought you,' said Semilétka; 'there was an agreement between us that I might take away with me whatever I prized most. And so I have taken you!'

"The Voyvode marvelled at her wisdom and made peace with her. He and she then returned home and went on living prosperously."

But although drunkenness is very tenderly treated in the Skazkas, as well as in the folksongs, it forms the subject of many a moral lesson, couched in terms of the utmost severity, in the *stikhi* (or poems of a religious character, sung by the blind beggars and other wandering minstrels who sing in front of churches) and also in the "Legends," which are tales of a semi-religious (or rather demi-semi-religious) nature. No better specimen of the stories of this class referring to drunkenness can be offered than the history of—

THE AWFUL DRUNKARD.[33]

Dealing with devils . . .

ONCE THERE WAS AN old man who was such an awful drunkard as passes all description. Well, one day he went to a kabak, intoxicated himself with liquor and then went staggering home blind drunk. Now his way happened to lie across a river. When he came to the river, he didn't stop long to consider but kicked off his boots, hung them round his neck and walked into the water. Scarcely had he got half-way across when he tripped over a stone, tumbled into the water—and there was an end of him.

Now, he left a son called Petrusha.[34] When Peter saw that his father had disappeared and left no trace behind, he took the matter greatly to heart for a time, he wept for awhile, he had a service performed for the repose of his father's soul and he began to act as head of the family. One Sunday he went to church to pray to God. As he passed along the road a woman was pounding away in front of him. She walked and walked, stumbled over a stone and began swearing at it, saying, "What devil shoved you under my feet?"

Hearing these words, Petrusha said:

"Good day, aunt! whither away?"

"To church, my dear, to pray to God."

"But isn't this sinful conduct of yours? You're going to church, to pray to God and yet you think about the Evil One; your foot stumbles and you throw the fault on the Devil!"

Well, he went to church and then returned home. He walked and walked and suddenly, goodness knows whence, there

33 Afanasief. "Legendui," No. 29.

34 Diminutive of Peter.

appeared before him a fine-looking man, who saluted him and said:

"Thanks, Petrusha, for your good word!"

"Who are you and why do you thank me?" asks Petrusha.

"I am the Devil.[35] I thank you because, when that woman stumbled and scolded me without a cause, you said a good word for me." Then he began to entreat him, saying, "Come and pay me a visit, Petrusha. How I will reward you to be sure! With silver and with gold, with everything will I endow you."

"Very good," says Petrusha, "I'll come."

Having told him all about the road he was to take, the Devil straightway disappeared and Petrusha returned home.

Next day Petrusha set off on his visit to the Devil. He walked and walked, for three whole days did he walk and then he reached a great forest, dark and dense—impossible even to see the sky from within it! And in that forest there stood a rich palace. Well, he entered the palace and a fair maiden caught sight of him. She had been stolen from a certain village by the evil spirit. And when she caught sight of him she cried:

"Whatever have you come here for, good youth? here devils abide, they will tear you to pieces."

Petrusha told her how and why he had made his appearance in that palace.

"Well now, mind this," says the fair maiden; "the Devil will begin giving you silver and gold. Don't take any of it but ask him to give you the very wretched horse which the evil spirits use for fetching wood and water. That horse is your father. When he came out of the kabak drunk and fell into the water, the devils immediately seized him and made him their hack and now they use him for fetching wood and water."

Presently there appeared the gallant who had invited Petrusha and began to regale him with all kinds of meat and

---

35 The word employed here is not chort but diavol.

drink. And when the time came for Petrusha to be going homewards, "Come," said the Devil, "I will provide you with money and with a capital horse, so that you will speedily get home."

"I don't want anything," replied Petrusha. "Only, if you wish to make me a present, give me that sorry jade which you use for carrying wood and water."

"What good will that be to you? If you ride it home quickly, I expect it will die!"

"No matter, let me have it. I won't take any other."

So the Devil gave him that sorry jade. Petrusha took it by the bridle and led it away. As soon as he reached the gates there appeared the fair maiden and asked:

"Have you got the horse?"

"I have."

"Well then, good youth, when you get nigh to your village, take off your cross, trace a circle three times about this horse and hang the cross round its neck."

Petrusha took leave of her and went his way. When he came nigh to his village he did everything exactly as the maiden had instructed him. He took off his copper cross, traced a circle three times about the horse and hung the cross round its neck. And immediately the horse was no longer there but in its place there stood before Petrusha his own father. The son looked upon the father, burst into tears and led him to his cottage; and for three days the old man remained without speaking, unable to make use of his tongue. And after that they lived happily and in all prosperity. The old man entirely gave up drinking and to his very last day never took so much as a single drop of spirits.[36]

~

36 Some remarks on the stories of this class, will be found in Chap. VI. The Russian peasants still believe that all people who drink themselves to death are used as carriers of wood and water in the infernal regions.

The Russian peasant is by no means deficient in humour, a fact of which the Skazkas offer abundant evidence. But it is not easy to find stories which can be quoted at full length as illustrations of that humour. The jokes which form the themes of the Russian facetious tales are for the most part common to all Europe. And a similar assertion may be made with regard to the stories of most lands. An unfamiliar joke is but rarely to be discovered in the lower strata of fiction. He who has read the folktales of one country only, is apt to attribute to its inhabitants a comic originality to which they can lay no claim. And so a Russian who knows the stories of his own land but has not studied those of other countries, is very liable to credit the Skazkas with the undivided possession of a number of "merry jests" in which they can claim but a very small share—jests which in reality form the stock-in-trade of rustic wags among the vineyards of France or Germany or on the hills of Greece or beside the fiords of Norway or along the coasts of Brittany or Argyleshire—which for centuries have set beards wagging in Cairo and Ispahan and in the cool of the evening hour have cheered the heart of the villager weary with his day's toil under the burning sun of India.

It is only when the joke hinges upon something which is peculiar to a people that it is likely to be found among that people only. But most of the Russian jests turn upon pivots which are familiar to all the world and have for their themes such common-place topics as the incorrigible folly of man, the inflexible obstinacy of woman. And in their treatments of these subjects they offer very few novel features. It is strange how far a story of this kind may travel and yet how little alteration it may undergo. Take, for instance, the skits against women which are so universally popular. Far away in outlying districts of Russia we find the same time-honoured quips which have so long figured in collections of English facetiæ. There is the good old story, for instance, of the dispute between a husband and wife as to whether a certain rope has been cut with a knife or with scissors, resulting in the murder of the scissors-upholding wife, who is pitched into the river by her knife-advocating husband; but not before she has, in her very death agony, testified to her belief in the scissors hypothesis by a movement of her fingers above the surface of the stream.[37] In a Russian form of the story, told in the Government of Astrakhan, the quarrel is about the husband's beard. He says he has shaved it, his wife declares he has only cut it off. He flings her into a deep pool and calls to her to say "shaved." Utterance is impossible to her but "she lifts one hand above the water and by means of two fingers makes signs to show that it was cut."[38] The story has even settled into a proverb. Of a contradictory woman the Russian peasants affirm that, "If you say 'shaved' she'll say 'cut.'"

In the same way another story shows us in Russian garb our old friend the widower who, when looking for his drowned wife—a woman of a very antagonistic disposition—went up the river instead of down, saying to his astonished companions, "She always did everything contrary-wise, so now, no doubt, she's gone against the stream." A common story again is that of the husband who, having confided a secret to his wife which he justly fears she will reveal, throws discredit on her evidence about things in general by making her believe various absurd stories which she hastens to repeat.[39] The final

---

37 In the sixty-fourth story of Asbjörnsen's "Norske Folke-Eventyr," (Ny Samling, 1871) the dispute between the husband and wife is about a cornfield—as to whether it should be reaped or shorn—and she tumbles into a pool while she is making clipping gestures "under her husband's nose." In the old fabliau of "Le Pré Tondu" (Le Grand d'Aussy, Fabliaux, 1829, iii. 185), the husband cuts out the tongue of his wife, to prevent her from repeating that his meadow has been clipped, whereupon she makes a clipping sign with her fingers. In Poggio's "Facetiæ," the wife is doubly aggravating. For copious information with respect to the use made of this story by the romance-writers, see Liebrecht's translations of Basile's "Pentamerone," ii. 264 and of Dunlop's "History of Literature," p. 516.

38 Afanasief, v. p. 16.

39 Ibid., iii. p. 87.

paragraph of one of the variants of this time-honoured jest is quaint, concluding as it does, by way of sting, with a highly popular Russian saw. The wife has gone to the seigneur of the village and accused her husband of having found a treasure and kept it for his own use. The charge is true but the wife is induced to talk such nonsense and the husband complains so bitterly of her, that "the seigneur pitied the moujik for being so unfortunate, so he set him at liberty; and he had him divorced from his wife and married to another, a young and good-looking one. Then the moujik immediately dug up his treasure and began living in the best manner possible." Sure enough the proverb doesn't say without reason: "Women have long hair and short wits."[40]

There is another story of this class which is worthy of being mentioned, as it illustrates a custom in which the Russians differ from some other peoples.

A certain man had married a wife who was so capricious that there was no living with her. After trying all sorts of devices her dejected husband at last asked her how she had been brought up and learnt that she had received an education almost entirely German and French, with scarcely any Russian in it; she had not even been wrapped in swaddling-clothes when a baby, nor swung in a *liulka*.[41] Thereupon her husband determined to remedy the short-comings of her early education and "whenever she showed herself capricious or took to squalling, he immediately had her swaddled and placed in a *liulka* and began swinging her to and fro." By the end of a half year she became "quite silky"—all her caprices had been swung out of her.

---

40 Chudinsky, No. 8. The proverb is dear to the Tartars also.

41 Ibid. No. 23. The liulka or Russian cradle, is suspended and swung, instead of being placed on the floor and rocked. Russian babies are usually swaddled tightly, like American papooses.

But instead of giving mere extracts from anymore of the numerous stories to which the fruitful subject of woman's caprice has given rise, we will quote a couple of such tales at length. The first is the Russian variant of a story which has a long family tree, with ramifications extending over a great part of the world. Dr. Benfey has devoted to it no less than sixteen pages of his introduction to the Panchatantra,[42] tracing it from its original Indian home and its subsequent abode in Persia, into almost every European land.

42 "Panchatantra," 1859, vol. i. § 212, pp. 519-524. I gladly avail myself of this opportunity of gratefully acknowledging my obligations to Dr. Benfey's invaluable work

THE BAD WIFE.[43]

The tricking of a wife and a demon . . .

A BAD WIFE LIVED on the worst of terms with her husband and never paid any attention to what he said. If her husband told her to get up early, she would lie in bed three days at a stretch; if he wanted her to go to sleep, she couldn't think of sleeping. When her husband asked her to make pancakes, she would say: "You thief, you don't deserve a pancake!"

If he said:

"Don't make any pancakes, wife, if I don't deserve them," she would cook a two-gallon pot full and say,

"Eat away, you thief, till they're all gone!"

"Now then, wife," perhaps he would say, "I feel quite sorry for you; don't go toiling and moiling and don't go out to the hay cutting."

"No, no, you thief!" she would reply, "I shall go and do you follow after me!"

One day, after having had his trouble and bother with her he went into the forest to look for berries and distract his grief and he came to where there was a currant bush and in the middle of that bush he saw a bottomless pit. He looked at it for some time and considered, "Why should I live in torment with a bad wife? can't I put her into that pit? can't I teach her a good lesson?"

So when he came home, he said:

"Wife, don't go into the woods for berries."

"Yes, you bugbear, I shall go!"

---

43 Afanasief, i. No. 9. Written down in the Novgorod Government. Its dialect renders it somewhat difficult to read.

"I've found a currant bush; don't pick it."

"Yes I will; I shall go and pick it clean; but I won't give you a single currant!"

The husband went out, his wife with him. He came to the currant bush and his wife jumped into it, crying out at the top her voice:

"Don't you come into the bush, you thief or I'll kill you!"

And so she got into the middle of the bush and went flop into the bottomless pit.

The husband returned home joyfully and remained there three days; on the fourth day he went to see how things were going on. Taking a long cord, he let it down into the pit and out from thence he pulled a little demon. Frightened out of his wits, he was going to throw the imp back again into the pit but it shrieked aloud and earnestly entreated him, saying:

"Don't send me back again, O peasant! let me go out into the world! A bad wife has come and absolutely devoured us all, pinching us and biting us—we're utterly worn out with it. I'll do you a good turn, if you will."

So the peasant let him go free—at large in Holy Russia. Then the imp said:

"Now then, peasant, come along with me to the town of Vologda. I'll take to tormenting people and you shall cure them."

Well, the imp went to where there were merchant's wives and merchant's daughters; and when they were possessed by him, they fell ill and went crazy. Then the peasant would go to a house where there was illness of this kind, and as soon as he entered, out would go the enemy; then there would be blessing in the house and everyone would suppose that the peasant was a doctor indeed and would give him money and treat him to pies. And so the peasant gained an incalculable sum of money. At last the demon said:

"You've plenty now, peasant; aren't you content? I'm going now to enter into the Boyar's daughter. Mind you don't go curing her. If you do, I shall eat you."

The Boyar's daughter fell ill and went so crazy that she wanted to eat people. The Boyar ordered his people to find out the peasant—(that is to say) to look for such and such a physician. The peasant came, entered the house and told Boyar to make all the townspeople and the carriages with coachmen, stand in the street outside. Moreover, he gave orders that all the coachmen should crack their whips and cry at the top of their voices: "The Bad Wife has come! the Bad Wife has come!" and then he went into the inner room. As soon as he entered it, the demon rushed at him crying, "What do you mean, Russian? what have you come here for? I'll eat you!"

"What do *you* mean?" said the peasant, "why I didn't come here to turn you out. I came, out of pity to you, to say that the Bad Wife has come here."

The Demon rushed to the window, stared with all his eyes and heard everyone shouting at the top of his voice the words, "The Bad Wife!"

"Peasant," cries the Demon, "wherever can I take refuge?"

"Run back into the pit. She won't go there anymore."

The Demon went back to the pit—and to the Bad Wife too.

In return for his services, the Boyar conferred a rich guerdon on the peasant, giving him his daughter to wife and presenting him with half his property.

But the Bad Wife sits to this day in the pit—in Tartarus.[44]

~

44 This story is known to the Finns but with them the Russian Demon, (chortenok = a little chort or devil), has become the Plague. In the original Indian story the demon is one which had formerly lived in a Brahman's house but had been frightened away by his cantankerous wife. In the Servian version (Karajich, No. 37), the opening consists of the "Scissors-story," to which allusion has already been made. The vixen falls into a hole which she does not see, so bent is she on controverting her husband.

Our final illustration of the Skazkas which satirize women is the story of the *Golovikha*. It is all the more valuable, inasmuch as it is one of the few folktales which throw any light on the working of Russian communal institutions. The word *Golovikha* means, in its strict sense, the wife of a *Golova* or elected chief [*Golova* = head] of a *Volost* or association of village communities; but here it is used for a "female *Golova*," a species of "mayoress."

THE GOLOVIKHA.[45]

A comeuppance for greedy ambition . . .

A CERTAIN WOMAN WAS very bumptious. Her husband came from a village council one day and she asked him:

"What have you been deciding over there?"

"What have we been deciding? why choosing a Golova."

"Whom have you chosen?"

"No one as yet."

"Choose me," says the woman.

So as soon as her husband went back to the council (she was a bad sort; he wanted to give her a lesson) he told the elders what she had said. They immediately chose her as Golova.

Well the woman got along, settled all questions, took bribes and drank spirits at the peasant's expense. But the time came to collect the poll-tax. The Golova couldn't do it, wasn't able to collect it in time. There came a Cossack and asked for the Golova; but the woman had hidden herself. As soon as she learnt that the Cossack had come, off she ran home.

"Where, oh where can I hide myself?" she cries to her husband. "Husband dear! tie me up in a bag and put me out there where the corn-sacks are."

Now there were five sacks of seed-corn outside, so her husband tied up the Golova and set her in the midst of them. Up came the Cossack and said:

"Ho! so the Golova's in hiding."

Then he took to slashing at the sacks one after another with his whip and the woman began howling at the top of her voice:

---

45 Afanasief, ii. No. 12. Written down by a "Crown Serf," in the government of Perm.

"Oh, my father! I won't be a Golova, I won't be a Golova."

At last the Cossack left off beating the sacks and rode away. But the woman had had enough of Golova-ing; from that time forward she took to obeying her husband.

~

Before passing on to another subject, it may be advisable to quote one of the stories in which the value of a good and wise wife is fully acknowledged. I have chosen for that purpose one of the variants of a tale from which, in all probability, our own (English) story of "Whittington and his Cat" has been derived. With respect to its origin, there can be very little doubt, such a feature as that of the incense-burning pointing directly to a Buddhist source. It is called—

THE THREE COPECKS.[46]

A morality tale of reward in return for humility . . .

THERE ONCE WAS A poor little orphan-lad who had nothing at all to live on; so he went to a rich moujik and hired himself out to him, agreeing to work for one copeck a year. And when he had worked for a whole year and had received his copeck, he went to a well and threw it into the water, saying, "If it don't sink, I'll keep it. It will be plain enough I've served my master faithfully."

But the copeck sank. Well, he remained in service a second year and received a second copeck. Again he flung it into the well and again it sank to the bottom. He remained a third year; worked and worked, till the time came for payment. Then his master gave him a rouble. "No," says the orphan, "I don't want your money; give me my copeck." He got his copeck and flung it into the well. Lo and behold! there were all three copecks floating on the surface of the water. So he took them and went into the town.

Now as he went along the street, it happened that some small boys had got hold of a kitten and were tormenting it. And he felt sorry for it and said:

"Let me have that kitten, my boys?"

"Yes, we'll sell it you."

"What do you want for it?"

"Three copecks."

Well the orphan bought the kitten and afterwards hired himself to a merchant, to sit in his shop.

46 Afanasief, viii. No. 20. A copeck is worth about a third of a penny.

That merchant's business began to prosper wonderfully. He couldn't supply goods fast enough; purchasers carried off everything in a twinkling. The merchant got ready to go to sea, freighted a ship and said to the orphan:

"Give me your cat; maybe it will catch mice on board and amuse me."

"Pray take it, master! only if you lose it, I shan't let you off cheap."

The merchant arrived in a far off land and put up at an inn. The landlord saw that he had a great deal of money, so he gave him a bedroom which was infested by countless swarms of rats and mice, saying to himself, "If they should happen to eat him up, his money will belong to me." For in that country they knew nothing about cats and the rats and mice had completely got the upper hand. Well the merchant took the cat with him to his room and went to bed. Next morning the landlord came into the room. There was the merchant alive and well, holding the cat in his arms and stroking its fur; the cat was purring away, singing its song and on the floor lay a perfect heap of dead rats and mice!

"Master merchant, sell me that beastie," says the landlord.

"Certainly."

"What do you want for it?"

"A mere trifle. I'll make the beastie stand on his hind legs while I hold him up by his forelegs and you shall pile gold pieces around him, so as just to hide him—I shall be content with that!"

The landlord agreed to the bargain. The merchant gave him the cat, received a sackful of gold and as soon as he had settled his affairs, started on his way back. As he sailed across the seas, he thought:

"Why should I give the gold to that orphan? Such a lot of money in return for a mere cat! that would be too much of a good thing. No, much better keep it myself."

The moment he had made up his mind to the sin, all of a sudden there arose a storm—such a tremendous one! the ship was on the point of sinking.

"Ah, accursed one that I am! I've been longing for what doesn't belong to me; O Lord, forgive me a sinner! I won't keep back a single copeck."

The moment the merchant began praying the winds were stilled, the sea became calm and the ship went sailing on prosperously to the quay.

"Hail, master!" says the orphan. "But where's my cat?"

"I've sold it," answers the merchant; "There's your money, take it in full."

The orphan received the sack of gold, took leave of the merchant and went to the strand where the shipmen were. From them he obtained a shipload of incense in exchange for his gold and he strewed the incense along the strand and burnt it in honour of God. The sweet savour spread through all that land and suddenly an old man appeared and he said to the orphan:

"Which desirest thou—riches or a good wife?"

"I know not, old man."

"Well then, go afield. Three brothers are ploughing over there. Ask them to tell thee."

The orphan went afield. He looked and saw peasants tilling the soil.

"God lend you aid!" says he.

"Thanks, good man!" say they. "What dost thou want?"

"An old man has sent me here and told me to ask you which of the two I shall wish for—riches or a good wife?"

"Ask our elder brother; he's sitting in that cart there."

The orphan went to the cart and saw a little boy—one that seemed about three years old.

"Can this be their elder brother?" thought he—however he asked him:

"Which dost thou tell me to choose—riches or a good wife?"

"Choose the good wife."

So the orphan returned to the old man.

"I'm told to ask for the wife," says he.

"That's all right!" said the old man and disappeared from sight. The orphan looked round; by his side stood a beautiful woman.

"Hail, good youth!" says she. "I am thy wife; let us go and seek a place where we may live."[47]

~

One of the sins to which the Popular Tale shows itself most hostile is that of avarice. The folktales of all lands delight to gird at misers and skinflints, to place them in unpleasant positions and to gloat over the sufferings which attend their death and embitter their ghostly existence. As a specimen of the manner in which the humour of the Russian peasant has manipulated the stories of this class, most of which probably reached him from the East, we may take the following tale of—

47 The story is continued very little further by Afanasief, its conclusion being the same as that of "The Wise Wife," in Book vii. No. 22, a tale of magic. For a Servian version of the tale see Vuk Karajich, No. 7.

THE MISER.[48]

There is never enough loose change to return a copeck . . .

THERE ONCE WAS A rich merchant named Marko—a stingier fellow never lived! One day he went out for a stroll. As he went along the road he saw a beggar—an old man, who sat there asking for alms—"Please to give, O ye Orthodox, for Christ's sake!"

Marko the Rich passed by. Just at that time there came up behind him a poor moujik, who felt sorry for the beggar and gave him a copeck. The rich man seemed to feel ashamed, for he stopped and said to the moujik:

"Harkye, neighbour, lend me a copeck. I want to give that poor man something but I've no small change."

The moujik gave him one and asked when he should come for his money. "Come tomorrow," was the reply. Well next day the poor man went to the rich man's to get his copeck. He entered his spacious courtyard and asked:

"Is Marko the Rich at home?"

"Yes. What do you want?" replied Marko.

"I've come for my copeck."

"Ah, brother! come again. Really I've no change just now."

The poor man made his bow and went away.

"I'll come tomorrow," said he.

On the morrow he came again but it was just the same story as before.

"I haven't a single copper. If you like to change me a note for a hundred—No? well then come again in a fortnight."

48 Afanasief, v. No. 3. From the Novgorod Government.

At the end of the fortnight the poor man came again but Marko the Rich saw him from the window and said to his wife:

"Harkye, wife! I'll strip myself naked and lie down under the holy pictures. Cover me up with a cloth and sit down and cry, just as you would over a corpse. When the moujik comes for his money, tell him I died this morning."

Well the wife did everything exactly as her husband directed her. While she was sitting there drowned in bitter tears, the moujik came into the room.

"What do you want?" says she.

"The money Marko the Rich owes me," answers the poor man.

"Ah, moujik, Marko the Rich has wished us farewell;[49] he's only just dead."

"The kingdom of heaven be his! If you'll allow me, mistress, in return for my copeck I'll do him a last service—just give his mortal remains a wash."

So saying he laid hold of a pot full of boiling water and began pouring its scalding contents over Marko the Rich. Marko, his brows knit, his legs contorted, was scarcely able to hold out.[50]

"Writhe away or not as you please," thought the poor man, "but pay me my copeck!"

When he had washed the body and laid it out properly, he said:

"Now then, mistress, buy a coffin and have it taken into the church; I'll go and read psalms over it."

So Marko the Rich was put in a coffin and taken into the church and the moujik began reading psalms over him. The darkness of night came on. All of a sudden a window opened and a party of robbers crept through it into the church. The

---

49 Literally, "has bid to live long," a conventional euphemism for "has died." "Remember what his name was," is sometimes added.

50 It will be observed that the miser holds out against the pain which the scalded demon was unable to bear. See above, p. 21.

moujik hid himself behind the altar. As soon as the robbers had come in they began dividing their booty and after everything else was shared there remained over and above a golden sabre—each one laid hold of it for himself, no one would give up his claim to it. Out jumped the poor man, crying:

"What's the good of disputing that way? Let the sabre belong to him who will cut this corpse's head off!"

Up jumped Marko the Rich like a madman. The robbers were frightened out of their wits, flung away their spoil and scampered off.

"Here, Moujik," says Marko, "let's divide the money."

They divided it equally between them: each of the shares was a large one.

"But how about the copeck?" asks the poor man.

"Ah, brother!" replies Marko, "surely you can see I've got no change!"

And so Marko the Rich never paid the copeck after all.

~

We may take next the large class of stories about simpletons, so dear to the public in all parts of the world. In the Skazkas a simpleton is known as a *duràk*, a word which admits of a variety of explanations. Sometimes it means an idiot, sometimes a fool in the sense of a jester. In the stories of village life its signification is generally that of a "ninny;" in the "fairy stories" it is frequently applied to the youngest of the well-known "Three Brothers," the "Boots" of the family as Dr. Dasent has called him. In the latter case, of course, the hero's *durachestvo* or foolishness, is purely subjective. It exists only in the false conceptions of his character which his family or his neighbours have formed.[51] But the *duràk* of the following tale is represented as being really "daft." The story begins with one of the conventional openings of the

51 Professor de Gubernatis remarks that he may sometimes be called "the first Brutus of popular tradition." "Zoological Mythology," vol. i. p. 199.

Skazka—"In a certain *tsarstvo*, in a certain *gosudarstvo*,"—but the two synonyms for "kingdom" or "state" are used only because they rhyme.

THE FOOL AND THE BIRCH-TREE.[52]

An ox, a treasure, a murder and a goat . . .

IN A CERTAIN COUNTRY there once lived an old man who had three sons. Two of them had their wits about them but the third was a fool. The old man died and his sons divided his property among themselves by lot. The sharp-witted ones got plenty of all sorts of good things but nothing fell to the share of the Simpleton but one ox—and that such a skinny one!

Well, fair-time came round and the clever brothers got ready to go and transact business. The Simpleton saw this and said:

"I'll go, too, brothers and take my ox for sale."

So he fastened a cord to the horn of the ox and drove it to the town. On his way he happened to pass through a forest and in the forest there stood an old withered Birch-tree. Whenever the wind blew the Birch-tree creaked.

"What is the Birch creaking about?" thinks the Simpleton. "Surely it must be bargaining for my ox. Well," says he, "if you want to buy it, why buy it. I'm not against selling it. The price of the ox is twenty roubles. I can't take less. Out with the money!"

The Birch made no reply, only went on creaking. But the Simpleton fancied that it was asking for the ox on credit. "Very good," says he, "I'll wait till tomorrow!" He tied the ox to the Birch, took leave of the tree and went home. Presently in came the clever brothers and began questioning him:

"Well, Simpleton! sold your ox?"

52 Afanasief, v. No. 53.

"I've sold it."

"For how much?"

"For twenty roubles."

"Where's the money?"

"I haven't received the money yet. It was settled I should go for it tomorrow."

"There's simplicity for you!" say they.

Early next morning the Simpleton got up, dressed himself and went to the Birch-tree for his money. He reached the wood; there stood the Birch, waving in the wind but the ox was not to be seen. During the night the wolves had eaten it.

"Now, then, neighbour!" he exclaimed, "pay me my money. You promised you'd pay me to-day."

The wind blew, the Birch creaked and the Simpleton cried:

"What a liar you are! Yesterday you kept saying, 'I'll pay you tomorrow,' and now you make just the same promise. Well, so be it, I'll wait one day more but not a bit longer. I want the money myself."

When he returned home, his brothers again questioned him closely:

"Have you got your money?"

"No, brothers; I've got to wait for my money again."

"Whom have you sold it to?"

"To the withered Birch-tree in the forest."

"Oh, what an idiot!"

On the third day the Simpleton took his hatchet and went to the forest. Arriving there, he demanded his money; but the Birch-tree only creaked and creaked. "No, no, neighbour!" says he. "If you're always going to treat me to promises,[53] there'll be no getting anything out of you. I don't like such joking; I'll pay you out well for it!"

---

53 Zavtrakami podchivat = to dupe; zavtra = tomorrow; zavtrak = breakfast.

With that he pitched into it with his hatchet, so that its chips flew about in all directions. Now, in that Birch-tree there was a hollow and in that hollow some robbers had hidden a pot full of gold. The tree split asunder and the Simpleton caught sight of the gold. He took as much of it as the skirts of his caftan would hold and toiled home with it. There he showed his brothers what he had brought.

"Where did you get such a lot, Simpleton?" said they.

"A neighbour gave it me for my ox. But this isn't anything like the whole of it; a good half of it I didn't bring home with me! Come along, brothers, let's get the rest!"

Well, they went into the forest, secured the money and carried it home.

"Now mind, Simpleton," say the sensible brothers, "don't tell anyone that we've such a lot of gold."

"Never fear, I won't tell a soul!"

All of a sudden they run up against a Diachok,[54] and says he:—

"What's that, brothers, you're bringing from the forest?"

The sharp ones replied, "Mushrooms." But the Simpleton contradicted them, saying:

"They're telling lies! we're carrying money; here, just take a look at it."

The Diachok uttered such an "Oh!"—then he flung himself on the gold and began seizing handfuls of it and stuffing them into his pocket. The Simpleton grew angry, dealt him a blow with his hatchet and struck him dead.

"Heigh, Simpleton! what have you been and done!" cried his brothers. "You're a lost man and you'll be the cause of our destruction, too! Wherever shall we put the dead body?"

---

54 One of the inferior members of the Russian clerical body, though not of the clergy. But in one of the variants of the story it is a "pope" or priest, who appears and he immediately claims a share in the spoil. Whereupon the Simpleton makes use of his hatchet. Priests are often nicknamed goats by the Russian peasantry, perhaps on account of their long beards.

They thought and thought and at last they dragged it to an empty cellar and flung it in there. But later on in the evening the eldest brother said to the second one:—

"This piece of work is sure to turn out badly. When they begin looking for the Diachok, you'll see that Simpleton will tell them everything. Let's kill a goat and bury it in the cellar and hide the body of the dead man in some other place."

Well, they waited till the dead of night; then they killed a goat and flung it into the cellar but they carried the Diachok to another place and there hid him in the ground. Several days passed and then people began looking everywhere for the Diachok, asking everyone about him.

"What do you want him for?" said the Simpleton, when he was asked. "I killed him some time ago with my hatchet and my brothers carried him into the cellar."

Straightway they laid hands on the Simpleton, crying, "Take us there and show him to us."

The Simpleton went down into the cellar, got hold of the goat's head and asked:—

"Was your Diachok dark-haired?"

"He was."

"And had he a beard?"

"Yes, he'd a beard."

"And horns?"

"What horns are you talking about, Simpleton?"

"Well, see for yourselves," said he, tossing up the head to them. They looked, saw it was a goat's, spat in the Simpleton's face and went their ways home.

~

One of the most popular simpleton-tales in the world is that of the fond parents who harrow their feelings by conjuring up the misfortunes which may possibly await their as yet unborn grandchildren. In Scotland it is told, in a slightly different form, of two old maids who were once found bathed in tears and who were obliged to confess that they had been day-dreaming and supposing—if they had been married and one had had a boy and the other a girl; and if the children, when they grew up, had married and had had a little child; and if it had tumbled out of the window and been killed—what a dreadful thing it would have been. At which terrible idea they both gave way to not unnatural tears.

In one of its Russian forms, it is told of the old parents of a boy named Lutonya, who weep over the hypothetical death of an imaginary grandchild, thinking how sad it would have been if a log which the old woman has dropped had killed that as yet merely potential infant. The parent's grief appears to Lutonya so uncalled for that he leaves home, declaring that he will not return until he has found people more foolish than they. He travels long and far and witnesses several foolish doings, most of which are familiar to us. In one place, a cow is being hoisted on to a roof in order that it may eat the grass growing thereon; in another a horse is being inserted into its collar by sheer force; in a third, a woman is fetching milk from the cellar, a spoonful at a time. But the story comes to an end before its hero has discovered the surpassing stupidity of which he is in quest. In another Russian story of a similar nature Lutonya goes from home in search of someone more foolish than his mother, who has been tricked by a cunning sharper. First he finds carpenters attempting to stretch a beam which is not long enough and earns their gratitude by showing them how to add a piece to it. Then he comes to a place where sickles are unknown and harvesters are in the habit of biting off the ears of corn, so he makes a sickle for them, thrusts it into a sheaf and leaves it there. They take it for a monstrous worm, tie a cord to it and drag it away to the bank of the river. There they fasten one of their number to a log and set him afloat, giving him the end of the cord, in order that he may drag the "worm" after him into the water. The log turns over and the moujik with it, so that his head is under water while his legs appear above it. "Why, brother!" they call to him from the bank, "why are you so particular about your leggings? If they do get wet, you can dry them at the fire." But he makes no reply, only drowns. Finally Lutonya meets the counterpart of the well-known Irishman who, when counting the party to which he belongs, always forgets to count himself and so gets into numerical difficulties. After which he returns home.[55]

It would be easy to multiply examples of this style of humour—to find in the folktales current all over Russia the equivalents of our own facetious narratives about the wise men of Gotham, the old woman whose petticoats were cut short by the pedlar whose name was Stout and a number of other inhabitants of Fool-land to whom the heart of childhood is still closely attached and also of the exaggeration-stories, the German *Lügenmährchen*, on which was founded the narrative of Baron Munchausen's surprising adventures. But instead of doing this, before passing on to the more important groups of the Skazkas, I will quote, as this chapter's final illustrations of the Russian storyteller's art, an "animal story" and a "legend." Here is the former:—

55 Afanasief, ii. No. 8, v. No. 5. See also Khudyakof, No. 76. Cf. Grimm, No. 34, "Die kluge Else." Haltrich, No. 66. Asbjörnsen and Moe, No. 10. (Dasent No. 24, "Not a Pin to choose between them.")

THE MIZGIR.[56]

A spider's cunning and a little snuff . . .

IN THE OLDEN YEARS, long long ago, with the spring-tide fair and the summer's heat there came on the world distress and shame. For gnats and flies began to swarm, biting folks and letting their warm blood flow.

Then the Spider[57] appeared, the hero bold, who, with waving arms, weaved webs around the highways and byways in which the gnats and flies were most to be found.

A ghastly Gadfly, coming that way, stumbled straight into the Spider's snare. The Spider, tightly squeezing her throat, prepared to put her out of the world. From the Spider the Gadfly mercy sought.

"Good father Spider! please not to kill me. I've ever so many little ones. Without me they'll be orphans left and from door to door have to beg their bread and squabble with dogs."

Well, the Spider released her. Away she flew and everywhere humming and buzzing about, told the flies and gnats of what had occurred.

"Ho, ye gnats and flies! Meet here beneath this ash-tree's roots. A spider has come, and with waving of arms and weaving of nets, has set his snares in all the ways to which the flies and gnats resort. He'll catch them, every single one!"

They flew to the spot; beneath the ash-tree's roots they hid and lay there as though they were dead. The Spider came and there he found a cricket, a beetle and a bug.

"O Cricket!" he cried, "upon this mound sit and take snuff! Beetle, do thou beat a drum. And do thou crawl, O Bug, the

---

56 Afanasief, ii. No. 5. Written down by a crown-peasant in the government of Perm.
57 Mizgir, a venomous spider, like the Tarantula, found in the Kirghiz Steppes.

bun-like, beneath the ash and spread abroad this news of me, the Spider, the wrestler, the hero bold—that the Spider, the wrestler, the hero bold, no longer in the world exists; that they have sent him to Kazan; that in Kazan, upon a block, they've chopped his head off and the block destroyed."

On the mound sat the Cricket and took snuff. The Beetle smote upon the drum. The Bug crawled in among the ash-tree's roots and cried:—

"Why have ye fallen? Wherefore as in death do ye lie here? Truly no longer lives the Spider, the wrestler, the hero bold. They've sent him to Kazan and in Kazan they've chopped his head off on a block and afterwards destroyed the block."

The gnats and flies grew blithe and merry. Thrice they crossed themselves, then out they flew—and straight into the Spider's snares. Said he:—

"But seldom do ye come! I would that ye would far more often come to visit me! to quaff my wine and beer and pay me tribute!"[58]

~

This story is especially interesting in the original, inasmuch as it is rhymed throughout, although printed as prose. A kind of lilt is perceptible in many of the Skazkas and traces of rhyme are often to be detected in them but "The Mizgir's" mould is different from theirs. Many stories also exist in an artificially versified form but their movement differs entirely from that of the naturally cadenced periods of the ordinary Skazka or of such rhymed prose as that of "The Mizgir."

The following legend is not altogether new in "motive," but a certain freshness is lent to it by its simple style, its unstrained humour and its genial tone.

---

58 In another story bearing the same title (v. 39) the spider lies on its back awaiting its prey. Up comes "the honourable widow," the wasp and falls straight into the trap. The spider beheads her. Then the gnats and flies assemble, perform a funeral service over her remains and carry them off on their shoulders to the village of Komarovo (komar = gnat). For specimens of the Russian "Beast-Epos" the reader is referred (as I have stated in the preface) to Professor de Gubernatis's "Zoological Mythology."

THE SMITH AND THE DEMON.[59]

And if they haven't dies, they are ling still . . .

ONCE UPON A TIME there was a Smith and he had one son, a sharp, smart, six-year-old boy. One day the old man went to church and as he stood before a picture of the Last Judgment he saw a Demon painted there—such a terrible one!—black, with horns and a tail.

"O my!" says he to himself. "Suppose I get just such another painted for the smithy." So he hired an artist and ordered him to paint on the door of the smithy exactly such another demon as he had seen in the church. The artist painted it. Thenceforward the old man, every time he entered the smithy, always looked at the Demon and said, "Good morning, fellow countryman!" And then he would lay the fire in the furnace and begin his work.

Well, the Smith lived in good accord with the Demon for some ten years. Then he fell ill and died. His son succeeded to his place as head of the household and took the smithy into his own hands. But he was not disposed to show attention to the Demon as the old man had done. When he went into the smithy in the morning, he never said "Good morrow" to him; instead of offering him a kindly word, he took the biggest hammer he had handy and thumped the Demon with it three times right on the forehead and then he would go to his work. And when one of God's holy days came round, he would go to church and offer each saint a taper; but he would go up to the Demon and spit in his face. Thus three years went by, he all the while favouring the Evil One every morning either

59 Afanasief, "Legendui," No. 31. Taken from Dahl's collection. Some remarks on the Russian "legends" are given in Chap. VI.

with a spitting or with a hammering. The Demon endured it and endured it and at last found it past all endurance. It was too much for him.

"I've had quite enough of this insolence from him!" thinks he. "Suppose I make use of a little diplomacy and play him some sort of a trick!"

So the Demon took the form of a youth and went to the smithy.

"Good day, uncle!" says he.

"Good day!"

"What should you say, uncle, to taking me as an apprentice? At all events, I could carry fuel for you and blow the bellows."

The Smith liked the idea. "Why shouldn't I?" he replied. "Two are better than one."

The Demon began to learn his trade; at the end of a month he knew more about smith's work than his master did himself, was able to do everything that his master couldn't do. It was a real pleasure to look at him! There's no describing how satisfied his master was with him, how fond he got of him. Sometimes the master didn't go into the smithy at all himself but trusted entirely to his journeyman, who had complete charge of everything.

Well, it happened one day that the master was not at home and the journeyman was left all by himself in the smithy. Presently he saw an old lady[60] driving along the street in her carriage, whereupon he popped his head out of doors and began shouting:—

"Heigh, sirs! Be so good as to step in here! We've opened a new business here; we turn old folks into young ones."

Out of her carriage jumped the lady in a trice and ran into the smithy.

"What's that you're bragging about? Do you mean to say it's true? Can you really do it?" she asked the youth.

---

60 *Baruinya*, the wife of a *barin* or seigneur.

"We haven't got to learn our business!" answered the Demon. "If I hadn't been able to do it, I wouldn't have invited people to try."

"And how much does it cost?" asked the lady.

"Five hundred roubles altogether."

"Well, then, there's your money; make a young woman of me."

The Demon took the money; then he sent the lady's coachman into the village.

"Go," says he, "and bring me here two buckets full of milk."

After that he took a pair of tongs, caught hold of the lady by the feet, flung her into the furnace and burnt her up; nothing was left of her but her bare bones.

When the buckets of milk were brought, he emptied them into a large tub, then he collected all the bones and flung them into the milk. Just fancy! at the end of about three minutes the lady emerged from the milk—alive and young and beautiful!

Well, she got into her carriage and drove home. There she went straight to her husband and he stared hard at her but didn't know she was his wife.

"What are you staring at?" says the lady. "I'm young and elegant, you see and I don't want to have an old husband! Be off at once to the smithy and get them to make you young; if you don't, I won't so much as acknowledge you!"

There was no help for it; off set the seigneur. But by that time the Smith had returned home and had gone into the smithy. He looked about; the journeyman wasn't to be seen. He searched and searched, he enquired and enquired, never a thing came of it; not even a trace of the youth could be found. He took to his work by himself and was hammering away, when at that moment up drove the seigneur and walked straight into the smithy.

"Make a young man of me," says he.

"Are you in your right mind, Barin? How can one make a young man of you?"

"Come, now! you know all about that."

"I know nothing of the kind."

"You lie, you scoundrel! Since you made my old woman young, make me young too; otherwise, there will be no living with her for me."

"Why I haven't so much as seen your good lady."

"Your journeyman saw her and that's just the same thing. If he knew how to do the job, surely you, an old hand must have learnt how to do it long ago. Come, now, set to work at once. If you don't, it will be the worse for you. I'll have you rubbed down with a birch-tree towel."

The Smith was compelled to try his hand at transforming the seigneur. He held a private conversation with the coachman as to how his journeyman had set to work with the lady and what he had done to her and then he thought:—

"So be it! I'll do the same. If I fall on my feet, good; if I don't, well, I must suffer all the same!"

So he set to work at once, stripped the seigneur naked, laid hold of him by the legs with the tongs, popped him into the furnace and began blowing the bellows. After he had burnt him to a cinder, he collected his remains, flung them into the milk and then waited to see how soon a youthful seigneur would jump out of it. He waited one hour, two hours. But nothing came of it. He made a search in the tub. There was nothing in it but bones and those charred ones.

Just then the lady sent messengers to the smithy, to ask whether the seigneur would soon be ready. The poor Smith had to reply that the seigneur was no more.

When the lady heard that the Smith had only turned her husband into a cinder, instead of making him young, she was tremendously angry and she called together her trusty servants and ordered them to drag him to the gallows. No sooner said than done. Her servants ran to the Smith's house, laid hold of him, tied his hands together and dragged him off to the gallows. All of a sudden there came up with them the youngster who used to live with the Smith as his journeyman, who asked him:—

"Where are they taking you, master?"

"They're going to hang me," replied the Smith and straightway related all that had happened to him.

"Well, uncle!" said the Demon, "swear that you will never strike me with your hammer but that you will pay me the same respect your father always paid and the seigneur shall be alive and young, too, in a trice."

The Smith began promising and swearing that he would never again lift his hammer against the Demon but would always pay him every attention. Thereupon the journeyman hastened to the smithy and shortly afterwards came back again, bringing the seigneur with him and crying to the servants:

"Hold! hold! Don't hang him! Here's your master!"

Then they immediately untied the cords and let the Smith go free.

From that time forward the Smith gave up spitting at the Demon and striking him with his hammer. The journeyman disappeared and was never seen again. But the seigneur and his lady entered upon a prosperous course of life and if they haven't died, they're living still.[61]

---

61 The chort of this legend is evidently akin to the devil himself, whom traditions frequently connect with blacksmiths; but his prototype, in the original form of this story, was doubtless a demigod or demon. His part is played by St. Nicholas in the legend of "The Priest with the Greedy Eyes," for which and for further comment on the story, see Chap. VI.

PART II

Mythological

On the " Mythical Skazkas "—Male embodiments of Evil : 1. The Snake as the Stealer of Daylight; 2. Norkathe Beast, Lord of the Lower World ; 3. Koshchei the Deathless, The Stealer of Fair Princesses—his connexion with Punchkin and " the Giant who had no?Ieart in his Body "—Excursus on Bluebeard's Chamber ; 4. The Water King or Subaqueous Demon—Female Embodiments of Evil : 1. The Baba Yaga or Hag, and 2. The Witch, feminine counterparts of the Snake

THE PRESENT CHAPTER IS devoted to specimens of those skazkas which most Russian critics assert to be distinctly mythical. The stories of this class are so numerous, that the task of selection has been by no means easy. But I have done my best to choose such examples as are most characteristic of that species of the "mythical" folktale which prevails in Russia and to avoid, as far as possible, the repetition of narratives which have already been made familiar to the English reader by translations of German and Scandinavian stories.

There is a more marked individuality in the Russian tales of this kind, as compared with those of Western Europe, than is to be traced in the stories (especially those of a humorous cast) which relate to the events that chequer an ordinary existence. The actors in the *comediettas* of European peasant-life vary but little, either in title or in character, wherever the scene may be laid; just as in the European beast-epos the Fox, the Wolf and the Bear play parts which change but slightly with the regions they inhabit. But the supernatural beings which people the Fairyland peculiar to each race, though closely resembling each other in many respects, differ conspicuously in others. They may, it is true, be nothing more than various developments of the same original type; they may be traceable to germs common to the prehistoric ancestors of the now widely separated Aryan peoples; their peculiarities may simply be due to the accidents to which travellers from distant lands are liable. But at all events each family now has features of its own, typical characteristics by which it may be readily distinguished from its neighbours. My chief aim at present is to give an idea of those characteristics which lend individuality to the "mythical beings" in the Skazkas; in order to effect this, I shall attempt a delineation of those supernatural figures, to some extent peculiar to Slavonic Fairyland which make their appearance in the Russian folktales. I have given a brief sketch of them elsewhere.[62] I now propose to deal with them more fully, quoting at length, instead of merely mentioning, some of the evidence on which the proof of their existence depends.

For the sake of convenience, we may select from the great mass of the mythical skazkas those which are supposed most manifestly to typify the conflict of opposing elements—whether of Good and Evil or of Light and Darkness or of Heat and Cold or of any other pair of antagonistic forces or phenomena. The typical hero of this class of stories, who represents the cause of right and who is resolved by mythologists into so many different essences, presents almost identically the same appearance in most of the countries wherein he has become naturalised. He is endowed with supernatural powers but he remains a man, for all that. Whether as prince or peasant, he alters but very little in his wanderings among the Aryan races of Europe.

---

62 "Songs of the Russian People," pp. 160–185.

And a somewhat similar statement may be made about his feminine counterpart—for all the types of Fairyland life are of an epicene nature, admitting of a feminine as well as a masculine development—the heroine who in the Skazkas, as well as in other folktales, braves the wrath of female demons in quest of means whereby to lighten the darkness of her home or rescues her bewitched brothers from the thraldom of an enchantress or liberates her captive husband from a dungeon's gloom.

But their antagonists—the dark or evil beings whom the hero attacks and eventually destroys or whom the heroine overcomes by her virtues, her subtlety or her skill—vary to a considerable extent with the region they occupy or rather with the people in whose memories they dwell. The Giants by killing whom our own Jack gained his renown, the Norse Trolls, the Ogres of southern romance, the Drakos and Lamia of modern Greece, the Lithuanian Laume—these and all the other groups of monstrous forms under which the imagination of each race has embodied its ideas about (according to one hypothesis) the Powers of Darkness it feared or (according to another) the Aborigines it detested, differ from each other to a considerable and easily recognizable extent. An excellent illustration of this statement is offered by the contrast between the Slavonic group of supernatural beings of this class and their equivalents in lands tenanted by non-Slavonic members of the Indo-European family. A family likeness will, of course, be traced between all these conceptions of popular fancy but the gloomy figures with which the folktales of the Slavonians render us familiar may be distinguished at a glance among their kindred monsters of Latin, Hellenic, Teutonic or Celtic extraction. Of those among the number to which the Russian skazkas relate I will now proceed to give a sketch, allowing the stories, so far as is possible, to speak for themselves.

If the powers of darkness in the "mythical" skazkas are divided into two groups—the one male, the other female—there stand out as the most prominent figures in the former set, the Snake (or some other illustration of "Zoological Mythology"), Koshchei the Deathless and the Morskoi Tsar or King of the Waters. In the latter group the principal characters are the Baba Yaga or Hag, her close connection the Witch and the Female Snake. On the forms and natures of the less conspicuous characters to be found in either class we will not at present dwell. An opportunity for commenting on some of them will be afforded in another chapter.

To begin with the Snake. His outline, like that of the cloud with which he is so frequently associated and which he is often supposed to typify, is seldom well-defined. Now in one form and now in another, he glides a shifting shape, of which it is difficult to obtain a satisfactory view. Sometimes he retains throughout the story an exclusively reptilian character; sometimes he is of a mixed nature, partly serpent and partly man. In one story we see him riding on horseback, with hawk on wrist (or raven on shoulder) and hound at heel; in another he figures as a composite being with a human body and a serpent's head; in a third he flies as a fiery snake into his mistress's bower, stamps with his foot on the ground and becomes a youthful gallant. But in most cases he is a serpent which in outward appearance seems to differ from other ophidians only in being winged and polycephalous—the number of his heads generally varying from three to twelve.[63]

He is often known by the name of *Zméï* [snake] Goruinuich [son of the *gora* or mountain] and sometimes he is supposed to dwell in the mountain caverns. To his abode, whether in the bowels of the earth or in the open light of day—whether

63 In one story (Khudyakof, No. 117) there are snakes with twenty-eight and twenty-nine heads but this is unusual.

it be a sumptuous palace or "an *izba* on fowl's legs," a hut upheld by slender supports on which it turns as on a pivot—he carries off his prey.

In one story he appears to have stolen or in some way concealed, the daylight; in another the bright moon and the many stars come forth from within him after his death. But as a general rule it is some queen or princess whom he tears away from her home, as Pluto carried off Proserpina and who remains with him reluctantly and hails as her rescuer the hero who comes to give him battle. Sometimes, however, the snake is represented as having a wife of his own species and daughters who share their parent's tastes and powers. Such is the case in the (South-Russian) story of:—

IVAN POPYALOF.[64]

Ivan deals with many-headed snakes . . .

ONCE UPON A TIME there was an old couple and they had three sons. Two of these had their wits about them but the third was a simpleton, Ivan by name, surnamed Popyalof.

For twelve whole years Ivan lay among the ashes from the stove; but then he arose and shook himself, so that six poods of ashes[65] fell off from him.

Now in the land in which Ivan lived there was never any day but always night. That was a Snake's doing. Well, Ivan undertook to kill that Snake, so he said to his father, "Father, make me a mace five poods in weight." And when he had got the mace, he went out into the fields and flung it straight up in the air and then he went home. The next day he went out into the fields to the spot from which he had flung the mace on high and stood there with his head thrown back. So when the mace fell down again it hit him on the forehead. And the mace broke in two.

Ivan went home and said to his father, "Father, make me another mace, a ten pood one." And when he had got it he went out into the fields and flung it aloft. And the mace went flying through the air for three days and three nights. On the fourth day Ivan went out to the same spot and when the mace came tumbling down, he put his knee in the way and the mace broke over it into three pieces.

64 Afanasief, ii. No. 30. From the Chernigof Government. The accent falls on the second syllable of Ivan, on the first of Popyalof.

65 Popyal, provincial word for pepel = ashes, cinders, whence the surname Popyalof. A pood is about 40lbs.

Ivan went home and told his father to make him a third mace, one of fifteen poods weight. And when he had got it, he went out into the fields and flung it aloft. And the mace was up in the air six days. On the seventh Ivan went to the same spot as before. Down fell the mace and when it struck Ivan's forehead, the forehead bowed under it. Thereupon he said, "This mace will do for the Snake!"

So when he had got everything ready, he went forth with his brothers to fight the Snake. He rode and rode and presently there stood before him a hut on fowl's legs,[66] and in that hut lived the Snake. There all the party came to a standstill. Then Ivan hung up his gloves and said to his brothers, "Should blood drop from my gloves, make haste to help me." When he had said this he went into the hut and sat down under the boarding.[67]

Presently there rode up a Snake with three heads. His steed stumbled, his hound howled, his falcon clamoured.68 Then cried the Snake:

"Wherefore hast thou stumbled, O Steed! hast thou howled, O Hound! hast thou clamoured, O Falcon?"

"How can I but stumble," replied the Steed, "when under the boarding sits Ivan Popyalof?"

Then said the Snake, "Come forth, Ivanushka! Let us try our strength together." Ivan came forth and they began to fight. And Ivan killed the Snake and then sat down again beneath the boarding.

Presently there came another Snake, a six-headed one and him, too, Ivan killed. And then there came a third, which had twelve heads. Well, Ivan began to fight with him and lopped off nine of his heads. The Snake had no strength left in him.

Just then a raven came flying by and it croaked:

---

66 On slender supports.

67 Pod mostom, *i.e.*, says Afanasief (vol. v. p. 243), under the raised flooring which, in an izba, serves as a sleeping place.

68 Zatvelyef, apparently a provincial word.

"Krof? Krof!"[69]

Then the Snake cried to the Raven, "Fly and tell my wife to come and devour Ivan Popyalof."

But Ivan cried: "Fly and tell my brothers to come and then we will kill this Snake and give his flesh to thee."

And the Raven gave ear to what Ivan said and flew to his brothers and began to croak above their heads. The brothers awoke and when they heard the cry of the Raven, they hastened to their brother's aid. And they killed the Snake and then, having taken his heads, they went into his hut and destroyed them. And immediately there was bright light throughout the whole land.

After killing the Snake, Ivan Popyalof and his brothers set off on their way home. But he had forgotten to take away his gloves, so he went back to fetch them, telling his brothers to wait for him meanwhile. Now when he had reached the hut and was going to take away his gloves, he heard the voices of the Snake's wife and daughters, who were talking with each other. So he turned himself into a cat and began to mew outside the door. They let him in and he listened to everything they said. Then he got his gloves and hastened away.

As soon as he came to where his brothers were, he mounted his horse and they all started afresh. They rode and rode; presently they saw before them a green meadow and on that meadow lay silken cushions. Then the elder brothers said, "Let's turn out our horses to graze here, while we rest ourselves a little."

But Ivan said, "Wait a minute, brothers!" and he seized his mace and struck the cushions with it. And out of those cushions there streamed blood.

So they all went on further. They rode and rode; presently there stood before them an apple-tree and upon it were gold

---

69 The Russian word krof also signifies blood.

and silver apples. Then the elder brothers said, "Let's eat an apple apiece." But Ivan said, "Wait a minute, brothers; I'll try them first," and he took his mace and struck the apple-tree with it. And out of the tree streamed blood.

So they went on further. They rode and rode and by and by they saw a spring in front of them. And the elder brothers cried, "Let's have a drink of water." But Ivan Popyalof cried: "Stop, brothers!" and he raised his mace and struck the spring and its waters became blood.

For the meadow, the silken cushions, the apple-tree and the spring, were all of them daughters of the Snake.

After killing the Snake's daughters, Ivan and his brothers went on homewards. Presently came the Snake's Wife flying after them and she opened her jaws from the sky to the earth and tried to swallow up Ivan. But Ivan and his brothers threw three poods of salt into her mouth. She swallowed the salt, thinking it was Ivan Popyalof but afterwards—when she had tasted the salt and found out it was not Ivan—she flew after him again.

Then he perceived that danger was at hand and so he let his horse go free and hid himself behind twelve doors in the forge of Kuzma and Demian. The Snake's Wife came flying up and said to Kuzma and Demian, "Give me up Ivan Popyalof." But they replied:

"Send your tongue through the twelve doors and take him." So the Snake's Wife began licking the doors. But meanwhile they all heated iron pincers and as soon as she had sent her tongue through into the smithy, they caught tight hold of her by the tongue and began thumping her with hammers. And when the Snake's Wife was dead they consumed her with fire and scattered her ashes to the winds. And then they went home and there they lived and enjoyed themselves, feasting and revelling and drinking mead and wine.

I was there, too and had liquor to drink; it didn't go into my mouth but only ran down my beard.[70]

~

The skazka of Ivan Buikovich (Bull's son)[71] contains a variant of part of this story but the dragon which the Slavonic St. George kills is called, not a snake but a Chudo-Yudo.[72] Ivan watches one night while his brothers sleep. Presently up rides "a six-headed Chudo-Yudo" which he easily kills. The next night he slays but with more difficulty, a nine-headed specimen of the same family. On the third night appears "a twelve-headed Chudo-Yudo," mounted on a horse "with twelve wings, its coat of silver, its mane and tail of gold." Ivan lops off three of the monster's heads but they, like those of the Lernæan Hydra, become re-attached to their necks at the touch of their owner's "fiery finger." Ivan, whom his foe has driven into the ground up to his knees, hurls one of his gloves at the hut in which his brothers are sleeping. It smashes the windows but the sleepers slumber on and take no heed. Presently Ivan smites off six of his antagonist's heads but they grow again as before.[73] Half buried in the ground by the monster's strength, Ivan hurls his other glove at the hut, piercing its roof this time. But still his brothers slumber on. At last, after fruitlessly shearing off nine of the Chudo-Yudo's

---

70 The last sentence of the story forms one of the conventional and meaningless "tags" frequently attached to the skazkas. In future I shall omit them. Kuzma and Demian (SS. Cosmas and Damian) figure in Russian folklore as saintly and supernatural smiths, frequently at war with snakes, which they maltreat in various ways. See A. de Gubernatis, "Zoological Mythology," vol. ii. p. 397.

71 Afanasief, Skazki, vol. vii. p. 3.

72 Chudo = prodigy. Yudo may be a remembrance of Judas or it may be used merely for the sake of the rhyme

73 In an Indian story ("Kathásaritságara," book vii. chap. 42), Indrasena comes to a place in which sits a Rákshasa on a throne between two fair ladies. He attacks the demon with a magic sword and soon cuts off his head. But the head always grows again, until at last the younger of the ladies gives him a sign to split in half the head he has just chopped off. Thereupon the demon dies and the two ladies greet the conqueror rapturously. The younger is the demon's sister, the elder is a king's daughter whom the demon has carried off from her home, after eating her father and all his followers. See Professor Brockhaus's summary in the "Berichte der phil. hist. Classe der K. Sächs. Gesellschaft der Wissenschaften," 1861. pp. 241-2.

heads and finding himself embedded in the ground up to his armpits, Ivan flings his cap at the hut. The hut reels under the blow and its beams fall asunder; his brothers awake and hasten to his aid and the Chudo-Yudo is destroyed. The "Chudo-Yudo wives" as the widows of the three monsters are called, then proceed to play the parts attributed in "Ivan Popyalof" to the Snake's daughters.

"I will become an apple-tree with golden and silver apples," says the first; "whoever plucks an apple will immediately burst." Says the second, "I will become a spring—on the water will float two cups, the one golden, the other of silver; whoever touches one of the cups, him will I drown." And the third says, "I will become a golden bed; whoever lies down upon that bed will be consumed with fire." Ivan, in a sparrow's form, overhears all this and acts as in the preceding story. The three widows die but their mother, "an old witch," determines on revenge. Under the form of a beggar-woman she asks alms from the retreating brothers. Ivan tenders her a ducat. She seizes, not the ducat but his outstretched hand and in a moment whisks him off underground to her husband an Aged One, whose appearance is that of the mythical being whom the Servians call the Vy. He "lies on an iron couch and sees nothing; his long eyelashes and thick eyebrows completely hide his eyes," but he sends for "twelve mighty heroes," and orders them to take iron forks and lift up the hair about his eyes and then he gazes at the destroyer of his family. The glance of the Servian Vy is supposed to be as deadly as that of a basilisk but the patriarch of the Russian story does not injure his captive. He merely sends him on an errand which leads to a fresh set of adventures, of which we need not now take notice.

In a third variant of the story,[74] they are snakes which are killed by the hero, Ivan Koshkin (Cat's son) and it is a Baba

74 Khudyakof, No. 46.

Yaga or Hag, who undertakes to revenge their deaths and those of their wives, her daughters. Accordingly she pursues the three brothers and succeeds in swallowing two of them. The third, Ivan Koshkin, takes refuge in a smithy, and as before, the monster's tongue is seized and she is beaten with hammers until she disgorges her prey, none the worse for their temporary imprisonment.

We have seen, in the story about the Chudo-Yudo, that the place usually occupied by the Snake is at times filled by some other magical being. This frequently occurs in that class of stories which relates how three brothers set out to apprehend a trespasser or to seek a mother or sister who has been mysteriously spirited away. They usually come either to an opening which leads into the underground world or to the base of an apparently inaccessible hill. The youngest brother descends or ascends as the case may be and after a series of adventures which generally lead him through the kingdoms of copper, of silver and of gold, returns in triumph to where his brothers are awaiting him. And he is almost invariably deserted by them, as soon as they have secured the beautiful princesses who accompany him—as may be read in the following (South-Russian) history of—

THE NORKA.[75]

Ivan achieves three weddings . . .

ONCE UPON A TIME there lived a king and queen. They had three sons, two of them with their wits about them but the third a simpleton. Now the King had a deer-park in which were quantities of wild animals of different kinds. Into that park there used to come a huge beast—Norka was its name—and do fearful mischief, devouring some of the animals every night. The King did all he could but he was unable to destroy it. So at last he called his sons together and said: "Whoever will destroy the Norka, to him will I give the half of my kingdom."

Well, the eldest son undertook the task. As soon as it was night, he took his weapons and set out. But before he reached the park, he went into a *traktir* (or tavern) and there he spent the whole night in revelry. When he came to his senses it was too late; the day had already dawned. He felt himself disgraced in the eyes of his father but there was no help for it. The next day the second son went and did just the same. Their father scolded them both soundly and there was an end of it.

Well, on the third day the youngest son undertook the task. They all laughed him to scorn, because he was so stupid, feeling sure he wouldn't do anything. But he took his arms and went straight into the park and sat down on the grass in such a position that, the moment he went asleep, his weapons would prick him and he would awake.

75 Afanasief, vol. i. No. 6. From the Chernigof Government. The Norka-Zvyer' (Norka-Beast) of this story is a fabulous creature but zoologically the name of Norka (from nora = a hole) belongs to the Otter.

Presently the midnight hour sounded. The earth began to shake and the Norka came rushing up and burst right through the fence into the park, so huge was it. The Prince pulled himself together, leapt to his feet, crossed himself and went straight at the beast. It fled back and the Prince ran after it. But he soon saw that he couldn't catch it on foot, so he hastened to the stable, laid his hands on the best horse there and set off in pursuit. Presently he came up with the beast and they began a fight. They fought and fought; the Prince gave the beast three wounds. At last they were both utterly exhausted, so they lay down to take a short rest. But the moment the Prince closed his eyes, up jumped the Beast and took to flight. The Prince's horse awoke him; up he jumped in a moment and set off again in pursuit, caught up the Beast and again began fighting with it. Again the Prince gave the Beast three wounds and then he and the Beast lay down again to rest. Thereupon away fled the Beast as before. The Prince caught it up and again gave it three wounds. But all of a sudden, just as the Prince began chasing it for the fourth time, the Beast fled to a great white stone, tilted it up and escaped into the other world,[76] crying out to the Prince: "Then only will you overcome me, when you enter here."

The Prince went home, told his father all that had happened and asked him to have a leather rope plaited, long enough to reach to the other world. His father ordered this to be done. When the rope was made, the Prince called for his brothers and he and they, having taken servants with them and everything that was needed for a whole year, set out for the place where the Beast had disappeared under the stone. When they got there, they built a palace on the spot and lived in it for some time. But when everything was ready, the youngest brother said to the others: "Now, brothers, who is going to lift this stone?"

---

76 Literally "into that world" as opposed to this in which we live.

Neither of them could so much as stir it but as soon as he touched it, away it flew to a distance, though it was ever so big—big as a hill. And when he had flung the stone aside, he spoke a second time to his brothers, saying:

"Who is going into the other world, to overcome the Norka?"

Neither of them offered to do so. Then he laughed at them for being such cowards and said:

"Well, brothers, farewell! Lower me into the other world and don't go away from here but as soon as the cord is jerked, pull it up."

His brothers lowered him accordingly and when he had reached the other world, underneath the earth, he went on his way. He walked and walked. Presently he espied a horse with rich trappings and it said to him:

"Hail, Prince Ivan! Long have I awaited thee!"

He mounted the horse and rode on—rode and rode, until he saw standing before him, a palace made of copper. He entered the courtyard, tied up his horse and went indoors. In one of the rooms a dinner was laid out. He sat down and dined and then went into a bedroom. There he found a bed, on which he lay down to rest. Presently there came in a lady, more beautiful than can be imagined anywhere but in a skazka, who said:

"Thou who art in my house, name thyself! If thou art an old man, thou shall be my father; if a middle-aged man, my brother; but if a young man, thou shalt be my husband dear. And if thou art a woman and an old one, thou shalt be my grandmother; if middle-aged, my mother; and if a girl, thou shalt be my own sister."[77]

Thereupon he came forth. And when she saw him, she was delighted with him and said:

77 This address is a formula, of frequent occurrence under similar circumstances.

"Wherefore, O Prince Ivan—my husband dear shalt thou be!—wherefore hast thou come hither?"

Then he told her all that had happened and she said:

"That beast which thou wishest to overcome is my brother. He is staying just now with my second sister, who lives not far from here in a silver palace. I bound up three of the wounds which thou didst give him."

Well, after this they drank and enjoyed themselves and held sweet converse together and then the prince took leave of her and went on to the second sister, the one who lived in the silver palace and with her also he stayed awhile. She told him that her brother Norka was then at her youngest sister's. So he went on to the youngest sister, who lived in a golden palace. She told him that her brother was at that time asleep on the blue sea and she gave him a sword of steel and a draught of the Water of Strength and she told him to cut off her brother's head at a single stroke. And when he had heard these things, he went his way.

And when the Prince came to the blue sea, he looked—there slept Norka on a stone in the middle of the sea; and when it snored, the water was agitated for seven versts around. The Prince crossed himself, went up to it and smote it on the head with his sword. The head jumped off, saying the while, "Well, I'm done for now!" and rolled far away into the sea.

After killing the Beast, the Prince went back again, picking up all the three sisters by the way, with the intention of taking them out into the upper world: for they all loved him and would not be separated from him. Each of them turned her palace into an egg—for they were all enchantresses—and they taught him how to turn the eggs into palaces and back again and they handed over the eggs to him. And then they all went to the place from which they had to be hoisted into the upper world. And when they came to where the rope was, the

Prince took hold of it and made the maidens fast to it.[78] Then he jerked away at the rope and his brothers began to haul it up. And when they had hauled it up and had set eyes on the wondrous maidens, they went aside and said: "Let's lower the rope, pull our brother part of the way up and then cut the rope. Perhaps he'll be killed; but then if he isn't, he'll never give us these beauties as wives."

So when they had agreed on this, they lowered the rope. But their brother was no fool; he guessed what they were at, so he fastened the rope to a stone and then gave it a pull. His brothers hoisted the stone to a great height and then cut the rope. Down fell the stone and broke in pieces; the Prince poured forth tears and went away. Well, he walked and walked. Presently a storm arose; the lightning flashed, the thunder roared, the rain fell in torrents. He went up to a tree in order to take shelter under it and on that tree he saw some young birds which were being thoroughly drenched. So he took off his coat and covered them over with it and he himself sat down under the tree. Presently there came flying a bird—such a big one, that the light was blotted out by it. It had been dark there before but now it became darker still. Now this was the mother of those small birds which the Prince had covered up. And when the bird had come flying up, she perceived that her little ones were covered over and she said, "Who has wrapped up my nestlings?" and presently, seeing the Prince, she added: "Didst thou do that? Thanks! In return, ask of me any thing thou desirest. I will do anything for thee."

"Then carry me into the other world," he replied.

"Make me a large *zasyek*[79] with a partition in the middle," she said; "catch all sorts of game and put them into one half

78 Literally "seated the maidens and pulled the rope.
79 Some sort of safe or bin.

of it and into the other half pour water; so that there may be meat and drink for me."

All this the Prince did. Then the bird—having taken the *zasyek* on her back, with the Prince sitting in the middle of it—began to fly. And after flying some distance she brought him to his journey's end, took leave of him and flew away back. But he went to the house of a certain tailor and engaged himself as his servant. So much the worse for wear was he, so thoroughly had he altered in appearance, that nobody would have suspected him of being a Prince.

Having entered into the service of this master, the Prince began to ask what was going on in that country. And his master replied: "Our two princes—for the third one has disappeared—have brought away brides from the other world and want to marry them but those brides refuse. For they insist on having all their wedding-clothes made for them first, exactly like those which they used to have in the other world and that without being measured for them. The King has called all the workmen together but not one of them will undertake to do it."

The Prince, having heard all this, said, "Go to the King, master and tell him that you will provide everything that's in your line."

"However can I undertake to make clothes of that sort; I work for quite common folks," says his master.

"Go along, master! I will answer for everything," says the Prince.

So the tailor went. The King was delighted that at least one good workman had been found and gave him as much money as ever he wanted. When the tailor had settled everything, he went home. And the Prince said to him:

"Now then, pray to God and lie down to sleep; tomorrow all will be ready." And the tailor followed his lad's advice and went to bed.

Midnight sounded. The Prince arose, went out of the city into the fields, took out of his pocket the eggs which the maidens had given him and as they had taught him, turned them into three palaces. Into each of these he entered, took the maidens' robes, went out again, turned the palaces back into eggs and went home. And when he got there he hung up the robes on the wall and lay down to sleep.

Early in the morning his master awoke and behold! there hung such robes as he had never seen before, all shining with gold and silver and precious stones. He was delighted and he seized them and carried them off to the King. When the princesses saw that the clothes were those which had been theirs in the other world, they guessed that Prince Ivan was in this world, so they exchanged glances with each other but they held their peace. And the master, having handed over the clothes, went home but he no longer found his dear journeyman there. For the Prince had gone to a shoemaker's and him too he sent to work for the King; and in the same way he went the round of all the artificers and they all proffered him thanks, inasmuch as through him they were enriched by the King.

By the time the princely workman had gone the round of all the artificers, the princesses had received what they had asked for; all their clothes were just like what they had been in the other world. Then they wept bitterly because the Prince had not come and it was impossible for them to hold out any longer, it was necessary that they should be married. But when they were ready for the wedding, the youngest bride said to the King:

"Allow me, my father, to go and give alms to the beggars."

He gave her leave and she went and began bestowing alms upon them and examining them closely. And when she had come to one of them and was going to give him some money, she caught sight of the ring which she had given to the Prince in the other world and her sisters' rings too—for it really was he. So she seized him by the hand and brought him into the hall and said to the King:

"Here is he who brought us out of the other world. His brothers forbade us to say that he was alive, threatening to slay us if we did."

Then the King was wroth with those sons and punished them as he thought best. And afterwards three weddings were celebrated.

~

[The conclusion of this story is somewhat obscure. Most of the variants represent the Prince as forgiving his brothers and allowing them to marry two of the three princesses but the present version appears to keep closer to its original, in which the prince doubtless married all three. With this story may be compared: Grimm, No. 166, "Der starke Hans," and No. 91, "Dat Erdmänneken." See also vol. iii. p. 165, where a reference is given to the Hungarian story in Gaal, No. 5—Dasent, No. 55, "The Big Bird Dan," and No. 56, "Soria Moria Castle" (Asbjörnsen and Moe, Nos. 3 and 2. A somewhat similar story, only the palaces are in the air, occurs in Asbjörnsen's "Ny Samling," No. 72)—Campbell's "Tales of the West Highlands," No. 58—Schleicher's "Litauische Märchen," No. 38—The Polish story, Wojcicki, Book iii. No. 6, in which Norka is replaced by a witch who breaks the windows of a church and is wounded, in falcon-shape, by the youngest brother—Hahn, No. 70, in which a Drakos, as a cloud, steals golden apples, a story closely resembling the Russian skazka. See also No. 26, very similar to which is the Servian Story in "Vuk Karajich," No. 2—and a very interesting Tuscan story printed for the first time by A. de Gubernatis, "Zoological Mythology," vol. ii. p. 187. See also ibid. p. 391.

But still more important than these are the parallels offered by Indian fiction. Take, for instance, the story of Sringabhuja, in chap. xxxix. of book vii. of the "Kathásaritságara." In it the elder sons of a certain king wish to get rid of their younger half-brother. One day a Rákshasa appears in the form of a gigantic crane. The other princes shoot at it in vain but the youngest wounds it and then sets off in pursuit of it and of the valuable arrow which is fixed in it. After long wandering he comes to a castle in a forest. There he finds a maiden who tells him she is the daughter of the Rákshasa whom, in the form of a crane, he has wounded. She at once takes his part against her demon father and eventually flies with him to his own country. The perils which the fugitives have to encounter will be mentioned in the remarks on Skazka XIX. See Professor Brockhaus's summary of the story in the "Berichte der phil. hist. Classe der K. Sächs. Gesellschaft der Wissenschaften," 1861, pp. 223-6. Also Professor Wilson's version in his "Essays on Sanskrit Literature," vol. ii. pp. 134-5.

In two other stories in the same collection the hero gives chase to a boar of gigantic size. It takes refuge in a cavern into which he follows it. Presently he finds himself in a different world, wherein he meets a beauteous maiden who explains everything to him. In the first of these two stories the lady is the daughter of a Rákshasa, who is invulnerable except in the palm of the left hand for which reason, our hero, Chandasena has been unable to wound him when in his boar disguise. She instructs Chandasena how to kill her father, who accordingly falls a victim to a well-aimed shaft. (Brockhaus's "Mährchensammlung des Somadeva Bhatta," 1843, vol. i. pp. 110-13). In the other story, the lady turns out to be a princess whom "a demon with fiery eyes" had carried off and imprisoned. She tells the hero, Saktideva, that the demon has just died from a wound inflicted upon him, while transformed into a boar, by a bold archer. Saktideva informs her that he is that archer. Whereupon she immediately requests him to marry her (ibid. vol. ii. p. 175). In both stories the boar is described as committing great ravages in the upper world until the hero attacks it.]

The Adventures of a prince, the youngest of three brothers, who has been lowered into the underground world or who has ascended into an enchanted upper realm, form the theme of numerous skazkas, several of which are variants of the story of Norka. The prince's elder brothers almost always attempt to kill him, when he is about to ascend from the gulf or descend from the steeps which separate him from them. In one instance, the following excuse is offered for their conduct. The hero has killed a Snake in the underground world and is carrying its head on a lance, when his brothers begin to hoist him up. "His brothers were frightened at the sight of that head and thinking the Snake itself was coming, they let Ivan fall back into the pit."[80] But this apology for their behaviour seems to be due to the storyteller's imagination. In some instances their unfraternal conduct may be explained in the following manner. In oriental tales the hero is often the son of a king's youngest wife and he is not unnaturally hated by his half-brothers, the sons of an older queen, whom the hero's mother has supplanted in their royal father's affections. Accordingly they do their best to get rid of him. Thus, in one of the Indian stories which correspond to that of Norka, the hero's success at court "excited the envy and jealousy of his brothers [doubtless half-brothers] and they were not satisfied until they had devised a plan to effect his removal, and as they hoped, accomplish his destruction."[81] We know also that "Israel loved Joseph more than all his children," because he was the son "of his old age," and the result was that "when his brethren [who were only his half-brothers] saw that their father loved him more than all his brethren, they hated him."[82] When such tales as these came west in Christian times, their references to polygamy were constantly suppressed and their distinctions between brothers and half-brothers disappeared. In the same way the elder and jealous wife, who had behaved

80 Khudyakof, ii. p. 17.
81 "Kathásaritságara," bk. vii. c. xxxix. Wilson's translation.
82 Genesis, xxxvii. 3, 4.

with cruelty in the original stories to the offspring of her rival, often became turned, under Christian influences, into a stepmother who hated her husband's children by a previous marriage.

There may, however, be a mythological explanation of the behaviour of the two elder brothers. Professor de Gubernatis is of opinion that "in the Vedic hymns, Tritas, the third brother and the ablest as well as best, is persecuted by his brothers," who, "in a fit of jealousy, on account of his wife, the aurora and the riches she brings with her from the realm of darkness, the cistern or well [into which he has been lowered], detain their brother in the well,"[83] and he compares this form of the myth with that which it assumes in the following Hindoo tradition. "Three brothers, *Ekata* (*i.e.* the first), *Dwita* (*i.e.* the second) and *Trita* (*i.e.* the third) were travelling in a desert and being distressed with thirst, came to a well, from which the youngest, Trita, drew water and gave it to his brothers; in requital, they drew him into the well, in order to appropriate his property and having covered the top with a cart-wheel, left him in the well. In this extremity he prayed to the gods to extricate him and by their favour he made his escape."[84] This myth may, perhaps, be the germ from which have sprung the numerous folktales about the desertion of a younger brother in some pit or chasm, into which his brothers have lowered him.[85]

It may seem more difficult to account for the willingness of Norka's three sisters to aid in his destruction—unless, indeed, the whole story be considered to be mythological, as its Indian equivalents undoubtedly are. But in many versions of the same tale the difficulty does not arise. The princesses of the

83 "Zoological Mythology," i. 25.

84 Quoted from the "Nitimanjari," by Wilson, in his translation of the "Rig-Veda-Sanhita," vol. i. p. 142

85 See also Jülg's "Kalmukische Märchen," p. 19, where Massang, the Calmuck Minotaur, is abandoned in the pit by his companions.

copper, silver and golden realms, are usually represented as united by no ties of consanguinity with the snake or other monster whom the hero comes to kill. In the story of "Usuinya,"[86] for instance, there appears to be no relationship between these fair maidens and the "Usuinya-Bird," which steals the golden apples from a monarch's garden and is killed by his youngest son Ivan. That monster is not so much a bird as a flying dragon. "This Usuinya-bird is a twelve-headed snake," says one of the fair maidens. And presently it arrives—its wings stretching afar, while along the ground trail its moustaches [*usui*, whence its name]. In a variant of the same story in another collection,[87] the part of Norka is played by a white wolf. In that of Ivan Suchenko[88] it is divided among three snakes who have stolen as many princesses. For the snake is much given to abduction, especially when he appears under the terrible form of "Koshchei, the Deathless."

Koshchei is merely one of the many incarnations of the dark spirit which takes so many monstrous shapes in the folktales of the class with which we are now dealing. Sometimes he is described as altogether serpent-like in form; sometimes he seems to be of a mixed nature, partly human and partly ophidian but in some of the stories he is apparently framed after the fashion of a man. His name is by some mythologists derived from *kost*, a bone whence comes a verb signifying to become ossified, petrified or frozen; either because he is bony of limb or because he produces an effect akin to freezing or petrifaction.[89]

---

86 Khudyakof, No. 42.

87 Erlenvein, No. 41. A king's horses disappear. His youngest son keeps watch and discovers that the thief is a white wolf. It escapes into a hole. He kills his horse at its own request and makes from its hide a rope by which he is lowered into the hole, etc.

88 Afanasief, v. 54.

89 The word koshchei, says Afanasief, may fairly be derived from kost', a bone, for changes between st and shch are not uncommon—as in the cases of pustoi, waste, pushcha, a wild wood or of gustoi, thick, gushcha, sediment, etc. The verb okostenyet', to grow numb, describes the state into which a skazka represents the realm of the "Sleeping Beauty," as being thrown by Koshchei. Buslaef remarks in his "Influence of Christianity on Slavonic

He is called "Immortal" or "The Deathless,"[90] because of his superiority to the ordinary laws of existence. Sometimes, like Baldur, he cannot be killed except by one substance; sometimes his "death"—that is, the object with which his life is indissolubly connected—does not exist within his body. Like the vital centre of "the giant who had no heart in his body" in the well-known Norse tale, it is something extraneous to the being whom it affects and until it is destroyed he may set all ordinary means of annihilation at defiance. But this is not always the case, as may be learnt from one of the best of the skazkas in which he plays a leading part, the history of—

Language," p. 103, that one of the Gothic words used by Ulfilas to express the Greek δαιμόνιον is *skôhsl*, which "is purely Slavonic, being preserved in the Czekh kauzlo, sorcery; in the Lower-Lusatian-Wendish, kostlar means a sorcerer. (But see Grimm's "Deutsche Mythologie," pp. 454-5, where skôhsl is supposed to mean a forest-sprite, also p. 954.) Kost' changes into koshch whence our Koshchei." There is also a provincial word, kostit', meaning to revile or scold.

90 Bezsmertny (bez = without, smert' = death).

MARYA MOREVNA.[91]

Even chopped in pieces, Ivan pursues his love . . .

IN A CERTAIN KINGDOM there lived a Prince Ivan. He had three sisters. The first was the Princess Marya, the second the Princess Olga, the third the Princess Anna. When their father and mother lay at the point of death, they had thus enjoined their son:—"Give your sisters in marriage to the very first suitors who come to woo them. Don't go keeping them by you!"

They died and the Prince buried them and then, to solace his grief, he went with his sisters into the garden green to stroll. Suddenly the sky was covered by a black cloud; a terrible storm arose.

"Let us go home, sisters!" he cried.

Hardly had they got into the palace, when the thunder pealed, the ceiling split open and into the room where they were, came flying a falcon bright. The Falcon smote upon the ground, became a brave youth and said:

"Hail, Prince Ivan! Before I came as a guest but now I have come as a wooer! I wish to propose for your sister, the Princess Marya."

"If you find favour in the eyes of my sister, I will not interfere with her wishes. Let her marry you in God's name!"

The Princess Marya gave her consent; the Falcon married her and bore her away into his own realm.

Days follow days, hours chase hours; a whole year goes by. One day Prince Ivan and his two sisters went out to stroll in the garden green. Again there arose a storm cloud with whirlwind and lightning.

---

91 Afanasief, viii. No. 8. Morevna means daughter of More, (the Sea or any great water).

"Let us go home, sisters!" cried the Prince. Scarcely had they entered the palace, when the thunder crashed, the roof burst into a blaze, the ceiling split in twain and in flew an eagle. The Eagle smote upon the ground and became a brave youth.

"Hail, Prince Ivan! Before I came as a guest but now I have come as a wooer!"

And he asked for the hand of the Princess Olga. Prince Ivan replied:

"If you find favour in the eyes of the Princess Olga, then let her marry you. I will not interfere with her liberty of choice."

The Princess Olga gave her consent and married the Eagle. The Eagle took her and carried her off to his own kingdom.

Another year went by. Prince Ivan said to his youngest sister:

"Let us go out and stroll in the garden green!"

They strolled about for a time. Again there arose a storm cloud, with whirlwind and lightning.

"Let us return home, sister!" said he.

They returned home but they hadn't had time to sit down when the thunder[92] crashed, the ceiling split open and in flew a raven. The Raven smote upon the floor and became a brave youth. The former youths had been handsome but this one was handsomer still.

"Well, Prince Ivan! Before I came as a guest but now I have come as a wooer. Give me the Princess Anna to wife."

"I won't interfere with my sister's freedom. If you gain her affections, let her marry you."

So the Princess Anna married the Raven and he bore her away to his own realm. Prince Ivan was left alone. A whole year he lived without his sisters; then he grew weary and said:—

"I will set out in search of my sisters."

---

92 Grom. It is the thunder, rather than the lightning, which the Russian peasants look upon as the destructive agent in a storm. They let the flash pass unheeded but they take the precaution of crossing themselves when the roar follows.

He got ready for the journey, he rode and rode and one day he saw a whole army lying dead on the plain. He cried aloud, "If there be a living man there, let him make answer! who has slain this mighty host?"

There replied unto him a living man:

"All this mighty host has been slain by the fair Princess Marya Morevna."

Prince Ivan rode further on and came to a white tent and forth came to meet him the fair Princess Marya Morevna.

"Hail Prince!" says she, "whither does God send you? and is it of your free will or against your will?"

Prince Ivan replied, "Not against their will do brave youths ride!"

"Well, if your business be not pressing, tarry awhile in my tent."

Thereat was Prince Ivan glad. He spent two nights in the tent and he found favour in the eyes of Marya Morevna and she married him. The fair Princess, Marya Morevna, carried him off into her own realm.

They spent some time together and then the Princess took it into her head to go a warring. So she handed over all the housekeeping affairs to Prince Ivan and gave him these instructions:

"Go about everywhere, keep watch over everything, only do not venture to look into that closet there."

He couldn't help doing so. The moment Marya Morevna had gone he rushed to the closet, pulled open the door and looked in—there hung Koshchei the Deathless, fettered by twelve chains. Then Koshchei entreated Prince Ivan, saying,—

"Have pity upon me and give me to drink! Ten years long have I been here in torment, neither eating or drinking; my throat is utterly dried up."

The Prince gave him a bucketful of water; he drank it up and asked for more, saying:

"A single bucket of water will not quench my thirst; give me more!"

The Prince gave him a second bucketful. Koshchei drank it up and asked for a third and when he had swallowed the third bucketful, he regained his former strength, gave his chains a shake and broke all twelve at once.

"Thanks, Prince Ivan!" cried Koshchei the deathless, "now you will sooner see your own ears than Marya Morevna!" and out of the window he flew in the shape of a terrible whirlwind. And he came up with the fair Princess Marya Morevna as she was going her way, laid hold of her and carried her off home with him. But Prince Ivan wept full sore and he arrayed himself and set out a wandering, saying to himself: "Whatever happens, I will go and look for Marya Morevna!"

One day passed, another day passed: at the dawn of the third day he saw a wondrous palace and by the side of the palace stood an oak and on the oak sat a falcon bright. Down flew the Falcon from the oak, smote upon the ground, turned into a brave youth and cried aloud:

"Ha, dear brother-in-law! how deals the Lord with you?"

Out came running the Princess Marya, joyfully greeted her brother Ivan and began enquiring after his health and telling him all about herself. The Prince spent three days with them, then he said:

"I cannot abide with you; I must go in search of my wife the fair Princess Marya Morevna."

"Hard will it be for you to find her," answered the Falcon. "At all events leave with us your silver spoon. We will look at it and remember you." So Prince Ivan left his silver spoon at the Falcon's and went on his way again.

On he went one day, on he went another day and by the dawn of the third day he saw a palace still grander than the former one and hard by the palace stood an oak and on the oak sat an eagle. Down flew the eagle from the oak, smote upon the ground, turned into a brave youth and cried aloud:

"Rise up, Princess Olga! Hither comes our brother dear!"

The Princess Olga immediately ran to meet him and began kissing him and embracing him, asking after his health and telling him all about herself. With them Prince Ivan stopped three days; then he said:

"I cannot stay here any longer. I am going to look for my wife, the fair Princess Marya Morevna."

"Hard will it be for you to find her," replied the Eagle, "Leave with us a silver fork. We will look at it and remember you."

He left a silver fork behind and went his way. He travelled one day, he travelled two days; at daybreak on the third day he saw a palace grander than the first two and near the palace stood an oak and on the oak sat a raven. Down flew the Raven from the oak, smote upon the ground, turned into a brave youth and cried aloud:

"Princess Anna, come forth quickly! our brother is coming!"

Out ran the Princess Anna, greeted him joyfully and began kissing and embracing him, asking after his health and telling him all about herself. Prince Ivan stayed with them three days; then he said:

"Farewell! I am going to look for my wife, the fair Princess Marya Morevna."

"Hard will it be for you to find her," replied the Raven, "Anyhow, leave your silver snuffbox with us. We will look at it and remember you."

The Prince handed over his silver snuffbox, took his leave and went his way. One day he went, another day he went and on the third day he came to where Marya Morevna was. She caught sight of her love, flung her arms around his neck, burst into tears and exclaimed:

"Oh, Prince Ivan! why did you disobey me and go looking into the closet and letting out Koshchei the Deathless?"

"Forgive me, Marya Morevna! Remember not the past; much better fly with me while Koshchei the Deathless is out of sight. Perhaps he won't catch us."

So they got ready and fled. Now Koshchei was out hunting. Towards evening he was returning home, when his good steed stumbled beneath him.

"Why stumblest thou, sorry jade? scentest thou some ill?"

The steed replied:

"Prince Ivan has come and carried off Marya Morevna."

"Is it possible to catch them?"

"It is possible to sow wheat, to wait till it grows up, to reap it and thresh it, to grind it to flour, to make five pies of it, to eat those pies and then to start in pursuit—and even then to be in time."

Koshchei galloped off and caught up Prince Ivan.

"Now," says he, "this time I will forgive you, in return for your kindness in giving me water to drink. And a second time I will forgive you; but the third time beware! I will cut you to bits."

Then he took Marya Morevna from him and carried her off. But Prince Ivan sat down on a stone and burst into tears. He wept and wept—and then returned back again to Marya Morevna. Now Koshchei the Deathless happened not to be at home.

"Let us fly, Marya Morevna!"

"Ah, Prince Ivan! he will catch us."

"Suppose he does catch us. At all events we shall have spent an hour or two together."

So they got ready and fled. As Koshchei the Deathless was returning home, his good steed stumbled beneath him.

"Why stumblest thou, sorry jade? scentest thou some ill?"

"Prince Ivan has come and carried off Marya Morevna."

"Is it possible to catch them?"

"It is possible to sow barley, to wait till it grows up, to reap it and thresh it, to brew beer, to drink ourselves drunk on it, to sleep our fill and then to set off in pursuit—and yet to be in time."

Koshchei galloped off, caught up Prince Ivan:

"Didn't I tell you that you should not see Marya Morevna anymore than your own ears?"

And he took her away and carried her off home with him.

Prince Ivan was left there alone. He wept and wept; then he went back again after Marya Morevna. Koshchei happened to be away from home at that moment.

"Let us fly, Marya Morevna."

"Ah, Prince Ivan! He is sure to catch us and hew you in pieces."

"Let him hew away! I cannot live without you."

So they got ready and fled.

Koshchei the Deathless was returning home when his good steed stumbled beneath him.

"Why stumblest thou? scentest thou any ill?"

"Prince Ivan has come and has carried off Marya Morevna."

Koshchei galloped off, caught Prince Ivan, chopped him into little pieces, put them in a barrel, smeared it with pitch and bound it with iron hoops and flung it into the blue sea. But Marya Morevna he carried off home.

At that very time, the silver turned black which Prince Ivan had left with his brothers-in-law.

"Ah!" said they, "the evil is accomplished sure enough!"

Then the Eagle hurried to the blue sea, caught hold of the barrel and dragged it ashore; the Falcon flew away for the Water of Life and the Raven for the Water of Death.

Afterwards they all three met, broke open the barrel, took out the remains of Prince Ivan, washed them and put them together in fitting order. The Raven sprinkled them with the Water of Death—the pieces joined together, the body became whole. The Falcon sprinkled it with the Water of Life—Prince Ivan shuddered, stood up and said:

"Ah! what a time I've been sleeping!"

"You'd have gone on sleeping a good deal longer, if it hadn't been for us," replied his brothers-in-law. "Now come and pay us a visit."

"Not so, brothers; I shall go and look for Marya Morevna."

And when he had found her, he said to her:

"Find out from Koshchei the Deathless whence he got so good a steed."

So Marya Morevna chose a favourable moment and began asking Koshchei about it. Koshchei replied:

"Beyond thrice nine lands, in the thirtieth kingdom, on the other side of the fiery river, there lives a Baba Yaga. She has so good a mare that she flies right round the world on it every day. And she has many other splendid mares. I watched her herds for three days without losing a single mare and in return for that the Baba Yaga gave me a foal."

"But how did you get across the fiery river?"

"Why, I've a handkerchief of this kind—when I wave it thrice on the right hand there springs up a very lofty bridge and the fire cannot reach it."

Marya Morevna listened to all this and repeated it to Prince Ivan and she carried off the handkerchief and gave it to him. So he managed to get across the fiery river and then went on to the Baba Yaga's. Long went he on without getting anything either to eat or to drink. At last he came across an outlandish[93] bird and its young ones. Says Prince Ivan:

"I'll eat one of these chickens."

"Don't eat it, Prince Ivan!" begs the outlandish bird; "some time or other I'll do you a good turn."

He went on farther and saw a hive of bees in the forest.

93 Zamorskaya, from the other side of the water, strange, splendid.

"I'll get a bit of honeycomb," says he.

"Don't disturb my honey, Prince Ivan!" exclaims the queen bee; "some time or other I'll do you a good turn."

So he didn't disturb it but went on. Presently there met him a lioness with her cub.

"Anyhow I'll eat this lion cub," says he; "I'm so hungry, I feel quite unwell!"

"Please let us alone, Prince Ivan," begs the lioness; "some time or other I'll do you a good turn."

"Very well; have it your own way," says he.

Hungry and faint he wandered on, walked farther and farther and at last came to where stood the house of the Baba Yaga. Round the house were set twelve poles in a circle and on each of eleven of these poles was stuck a human head, the twelfth alone remained unoccupied.

"Hail, granny!"

"Hail, Prince Ivan! wherefore have you come? Is it of your own accord or on compulsion?"

"I have come to earn from you a heroic steed."

"So be it, Prince, you won't have to serve a year with me but just three days. If you take good care of my mares, I'll give you a heroic steed. But if you don't—why then you mustn't be annoyed at finding your head stuck on top of the last pole up there."

Prince Ivan agreed to these terms. The Baba Yaga gave him food and drink and bid him set about his business. But the moment he had driven the mares afield, they cocked up their tails and away they tore across the meadows in all directions. Before the Prince had time to look round, they were all out of sight. Thereupon he began to weep and to disquiet himself and then he sat down upon a stone and went to sleep. But when the sun was near its setting, the outlandish bird came flying up to him and awakened him saying:—

"Arise, Prince Ivan! the mares are at home now."

The Prince arose and returned home. There the Baba Yaga was storming and raging at her mares and shrieking:—

"Whatever did ye come home for?"

"How could we help coming home?" said they. "There came flying birds from every part of the world and all but pecked our eyes out."

"Well, well! tomorrow don't go galloping over the meadows but disperse amid the thick forests."

Prince Ivan slept all night. In the morning the Baba Yaga says to him:—

"Mind, Prince! if you don't take good care of the mares, if you lose merely one of them—your bold head will be stuck on that pole!"

He drove the mares afield. Immediately they cocked up their tails and dispersed among the thick forests. Again did the Prince sit down on the stone, weep and weep and then go to sleep. The sun went down behind the forest. Up came running the lioness.

"Arise, Prince Ivan! The mares are all collected."

Prince Ivan arose and went home. More than ever did the Baba Yaga storm at her mares and shriek:—

"Whatever did ye come back home for?"

"How could we help coming back? Beasts of prey came running at us from all parts of the world, all but tore us utterly to pieces."

"Well, tomorrow run off into the blue sea."

Again did Prince Ivan sleep through the night. Next morning the Baba Yaga sent him forth to watch the mares:

"If you don't take good care of them," says she, "your bold head will be stuck on that pole!"

He drove the mares afield. Immediately they cocked up their tails, disappeared from sight and fled into the blue sea. There they stood, up to their necks in water. Prince Ivan sat down on the stone, wept and fell asleep. But when the sun had set behind the forest, up came flying a bee and said:—

"Arise, Prince! The mares are all collected. But when you get home, don't let the Baba Yaga set eyes on you but go into the stable and hide behind the mangers. There you will find a sorry colt rolling in the muck. Do you steal it and at the dead of night ride away from the house."

Prince Ivan arose, slipped into the stable and lay down behind the mangers, while the Baba Yaga was storming away at her mares and shrieking:—

"Why did ye come back?"

"How could we help coming back? There came flying bees in countless numbers from all parts of the world and began stinging us on all sides till the blood came!"

The Baba Yaga went to sleep. In the dead of the night Prince Ivan stole the sorry colt, saddled it, jumped on its back and galloped away to the fiery river. When he came to that river he waved the handkerchief three times on the right hand and suddenly, springing goodness knows whence, there hung across the river, high in the air, a splendid bridge. The Prince rode across the bridge and waved the handkerchief twice only on the left hand; there remained across the river a thin—ever so thin a bridge!

When the Baba Yaga got up in the morning, the sorry colt was not to be seen! Off she set in pursuit. At full speed did she fly in her iron mortar, urging it on with the pestle, sweeping away her traces with the broom. She dashed up to the fiery river, gave a glance and said, "A capital bridge!" She drove on to the bridge but had only got half-way when the bridge broke in two and the Baba Yaga went flop into the river. There truly did she meet with a cruel death!

Prince Ivan fattened up the colt in the green meadows and it turned into a wondrous steed. Then he rode to where Marya

Morevna was. She came running out and flung herself on his neck, crying:—

"By what means has God brought you back to life?"

"Thus and thus," says he. "Now come along with me."

"I am afraid, Prince Ivan! If Koshchei catches us, you will be cut in pieces again."

"No, he won't catch us! I have a splendid heroic steed now; it flies just like a bird." So they got on its back and rode away.

Koshchei the Deathless was returning home when his horse stumbled beneath him.

"What art thou stumbling for, sorry jade? dost thou scent any ill?"

"Prince Ivan has come and carried off Marya Morevna."

"Can we catch them?"

"God knows! Prince Ivan has a horse now which is better than I."

"Well, I can't stand it," says Koshchei the Deathless. "I will pursue."

After a time he came up with Prince Ivan, lighted on the ground and was going to chop him up with his sharp sword. But at that moment Prince Ivan's horse smote Koshchei the Deathless full swing with its hoof and cracked his skull and the Prince made an end of him with a club. Afterwards the Prince heaped up a pile of wood, set fire to it, burnt Koshchei the Deathless on the pyre and scattered his ashes to the wind. Then Marya Morevna mounted Koshchei's horse and Prince Ivan got on his own and they rode away to visit first the Raven and then the Eagle and then the Falcon. Wherever they went they met with a joyful greeting.

"Ah, Prince Ivan! why, we never expected to see you again. Well, it wasn't for nothing that you gave yourself so much trouble. Such a beauty as Marya Morevna one might search for all the world over—and never find one like her!"

And so they visited and they feasted; and afterwards they went off to their own realm.[94]

~

With the Baba Yaga, the feminine counterpart of Koshchei and the Snake, we shall deal presently and the Waters of Life and Death will find special notice elsewhere.[95] A magic water, which brings back the dead to life, plays a prominent part in the folklore of all lands but the two waters, each performing one part only of the cure, render very noteworthy the Slavonic stories in which they occur.

The Princess, Marya Morevna, who slaughters whole armies before she is married and then becomes mild and gentle, belongs to a class of heroines who frequently occur both in the stories and in the "metrical romances," and to whom may be applied the remarks made by Kemble with reference to a similar Amazon.[96] In one of the variants of the story the representative of Marya Morevna fights the hero before she marries him.[97] The Bluebeard incident of the forbidden closet is one which often occurs in the Skazkas, as we shall see further on; and the same may be said about the gratitude of the Bird, Bee and Lioness.

The story of Immortal Koshchei is one of very frequent occurrence, the different versions maintaining a unity of

---

94 In Afanasief, iv. No. 39, a father marries his three daughters to the Sun, the Moon and the Raven. In Hahn, No. 25, a younger brother gives his sisters in marriage to a Lion, a Tiger and an Eagle, after his elder brothers have refused to do so. By their aid he recovers his lost bride. In Schott, No. 1 and Vuk Karajich, No. 5, the three sisters are carried off by Dragons, which their subsequently-born brother kills. (See also Basile, No. 33, referred to by Hahn and Valjavec, p. 1, Stier, No. 13 and Bozena Nêmcova, pp. 414-432 and a German story in Musæus, all referred to by Afanasief, viii. p. 662.)

95 See Chap. IV.

96 "Being by the advice of her father Hæreð given in marriage to Offa, she left off her violent practices; and accordingly she appears in Hygelác's court, exercising the peaceful duties of a princess. Now this whole representation can hardly be other than the modern, altered and Christian one of a Wælcyrie or Swan-Maiden; and almost in the same words the Nibelungen Lied relates of Brynhild, the flashing shield-may of the Edda, that with her virginity she lost her mighty strength and warlike habits."—Kemble's Beowulf, p. xxxv.

97 Khudyakof, ii, p. 90.

idea but varying considerably in detail. In one of them,[98] in which Koshchei's part is played by a Snake, the hero's sisters are carried off by their feathered admirers without his leave being asked—an omission for which a full apology is afterwards made; in another, the history of "Fedor Tugarin and Anastasia the Fair,"[99] the hero's three sisters are wooed and won, not by the Falcon, the Eagle and the Raven but by the Wind, the Hail and the Thunder. He himself marries the terrible heroine Anastasia the Fair, in the forbidden chamber of whose palace he finds a snake "hung up by one of its ribs." He gives it a lift and it gets free from its hook and flies away, carrying off Anastasia the Fair. Fedor eventually finds her, escapes with her on a magic foal which he obtains, thanks to the aid of grateful wolves, bees and crayfish and destroys the snake by striking it "on the forehead" with the stone which was destined to be its death. In a third version of the story,[100] the hero finds in the forbidden chamber "Koshchei the Deathless, in a cauldron amid flames, boiling in pitch." There he has been, he declares, for fifteen years, having been lured there by the beauty of Anastasia the Fair. In a fourth,[101] in which the hero's three sisters marry three beggars, who turn out to be snakes with twenty, thirty and forty heads apiece, Koshchei is found in the forbidden chamber, seated on a horse which is chained to a cauldron. He begs the hero to unloose the horse, promising, in return, to save him from three deaths.

[Into the mystery of the forbidden chamber I will not enter fully at present. Suffice to say that there can be little doubt as to its being the same as that in which Bluebeard kept the corpses of his dead wives. In the Russian, as well as in the Oriental stories, it is generally the curiosity of a man, not of a woman, which leads

98 Khudyakof, No. 20.
99 Afanasief, i. No. 14.
100 Khudyakof, No. 62.
101 Erlenvein, No. 31.

to the opening of the prohibited room. In the West of Europe the fatal inquisitiveness is more frequently ascribed to a woman. For parallels see the German stories of "Marienkind," and "Fitchers Vogel." (Grimm, KM., Nos. 3 and 46, also the notes in Bd. iii. pp. 8, 76, 324.) Less familiar than these is, probably, the story of "Die eisernen Stiefel" (Wolf's "Deutsche Hausmärchen," 1851, No. 19), in which the hero opens a forbidden door—that of a summer-house—and sees "deep down below him the earth and on the earth his father's palace," and is seized by a sudden longing after his former home. The Wallachian story of "The Immured Mother" (Schott, No. 2) resembles Grimm's "Marienkind" in many points. But its forbidden chamber differs from that of the German tale. In the latter the rash intruder sees "die Dreieinigkeit im Feuer und Glanz sitzen;" in the former, "the Holy Mother of God healing the wounds of her Son, the Lord Christ." In the Neapolitan story of "Le tre Corune" (Pentamerone, No. 36), the forbidden chamber contains "three maidens, clothed all in gold, sitting and seeming to slumber upon as many thrones" (Liebrecht's translation, ii. 76). The Esthonian tale of the "Wife-murderer" (Löwe's "Ehstnische Märchen," No. 20) is remarkably—not to say suspiciously—like that French story of Blue Beard which has so often made our young blood run cold. Sister Anne is represented and so are the rescuing brothers, the latter in the person of the heroine's old friend and playmate, Tönnis the gooseherd. Several very curious Gaelic versions of the story are given by Mr. Campbell ("Tales of the West Highlands," No. 41, ii. 265-275). Two of the three daughters of a poor widow look into a forbidden chamber, find it "full of dead gentlewomen," get stained knee-deep in blood and refuse to give a drop of milk to a cat which offers its services. So their heads are chopped off. The third daughter makes friends with the cat, which licks off the tell-tale blood, so she escapes detection. In a Greek story (Hahn, ii. p. 197) the hero discovers in the one-and-fortieth room of a castle belonging to a Drakos, who had given him leave to enter forty only, a magic horse and before the door of the room he finds a pool of gold in which he becomes gilded. In another (Hahn, No. 15) a prince finds in the forbidden fortieth a lake in which fairies of the swan-maiden species are bathing. In a third (No. 45) the fortieth room contains a golden horse and a golden dog which assist their bold releaser. In a fourth (No. 68) it imprisons "a fair maiden, shining like the sun," whom the demon proprietor of the castle has hung up within it by her hair.

As usual, all these stories are hard to understand. But one of the most important of their Oriental equivalents is perfectly intelligible. When Saktideva, in the fifth book of the "Kathásaritságara," comes after long travel to the Golden City and is welcomed as her destined husband by its princess, she warns him not to ascend the central terrace of her palace. Of course he does so and finds three chambers, in each of which lies the lifeless form of a fair maiden. After gazing at these seeming corpses, in one of which he recognizes his first love, he approaches a horse which is grazing beside a lake. The horse kicks him into the water; he sinks deep—and comes up again in his native land. The whole of the story is, towards its termination, fully explained by one of its principal characters—one of the four maidens whom Saktideva simultaneously marries. With the version of this romance in the "Arabian Nights" ("History of the Third Royal Mendicant," Lane, i. 160-173), everyone is doubtless acquainted.

A less familiar story is that of Kandarpaketu, in the second book of the "Hitopadesa," who lives happily for a time as the husband of the beautiful semi-divine queen of the Golden City. At last, contrary to her express commands, he ventures to touch a picture of a Vidyádharí. In an instant the pictured demigoddess gives him a kick which sends him flying back into his own country.

For an explanation of the myth which lies at the root of all these stories, see Cox's "Mythology of the Aryan Nations," ii. 36, 330. See also Professor de Gubernatis's "Zoological Mythology," i. 168.]

We will now take one of those versions of the story which describe how Koshchei's death is brought about by the destruction of that extraneous object on which his existence depends. The incident is one which occupies a prominent place in the stories of this class current in all parts of Europe and Asia and its result is almost always the same. But the means by which that result is brought about differ considerably in different lands. In the Russian tales the "death" of the Evil Being with whom the hero contends—the substance, namely, the destruction of which involves his death—is usually the last of a sequence of objects either identical with or closely resembling, those mentioned in the following story of—

KOSHCHEI THE DEATHLESS.[102]

With the help of friends, even death may be conquered . . .

IN A CERTAIN COUNTRY there once lived a king and he had three sons, all of them grown up. All of a sudden Koshchei the Deathless carried off their mother. Then the eldest son craved his father's blessing, that he might go and look for his mother. His father gave him his blessing and he went off and disappeared, leaving no trace behind. The second son waited and waited, then he too obtained his father's blessing—and he also disappeared. Then the youngest son, Prince Ivan, said to his father, "Father, give me your blessing and let me go and look for my mother."

But his father would not let him go, saying, "Your brothers are no more; if you likewise go away, I shall die of grief."

"Not so, father. But if you bless me I shall go; and if you do not bless me I shall go."

So his father gave him his blessing.

Prince Ivan went to choose a steed but everyone that he laid his hand upon gave way under it. He could not find a steed to suit him, so he wandered with drooping brow along the road and about the town. Suddenly there appeared an old woman, who asked:

"Why hangs your brow so low, Prince Ivan?"

"Be off, old crone," he replied. "If I put you on one of my hands and give it a slap with the other, there'll be a little wet left, that's all."[103]

---

102 Afanasief, ii. No. 24. From the Perm Government.

103 A conventional expression of contempt which frequently occurs in the Skazkas.

The old woman ran down a by-street, came to meet him a second time and said:

"Good day, Prince Ivan! why hangs your brow so low?"

Then he thought:

"Why does this old woman ask me? Mightn't she be of use to me?"—and he replied:

"Well, mother! because I cannot get myself a good steed."

"Silly fellow!" she cried, "to suffer and not to ask the old woman's help! Come along with me."

She took him to a hill, showed him a certain spot and said:

"Dig up that piece of ground."

Prince Ivan dug it up and saw an iron plate with twelve padlocks on it. He immediately broke off the padlocks, tore open a door and followed a path leading underground. There, fastened with twelve chains, stood a heroic steed which evidently heard the approaching steps of a rider worthy to mount it and so began to neigh and to struggle, until it broke all twelve of its chains. Then Prince Ivan put on armour fit for a hero and bridled the horse and saddled it with a Circassian saddle. And he gave the old woman money and said to her:

"Forgive me, mother and bless me!" then he mounted his steed and rode away.

Long time did he ride; at last he came to a mountain—a tremendously high mountain and so steep that it was utterly impossible to get up it. Presently his brothers came that way. They all greeted each other and rode on together, till they came to an iron rock[104] a hundred and fifty poods in weight and on it was this inscription, "Whosoever will fling this rock against the mountain, to him will a way be opened." The two elder brothers were unable to lift the rock but Prince Ivan at the first try flung it against the mountain—and immediately there appeared a ladder leading up the mountain side.

---

104 *Do chiguimova kaimtya*, to an iron stone.

Prince Ivan dismounted, let some drops of blood run from his little finger into a glass, gave it to his brothers and said:

"If the blood in this glass turns black, tarry here no longer: that will mean that I am about to die." Then he took leave of them and went his way.

He mounted the hill. What did not he see there? All sorts of trees were there, all sorts of fruits, all sorts of birds! Long did Prince Ivan walk on; at last he came to a house, a huge house! In it lived a king's daughter who had been carried off by Koshchei the Deathless. Prince Ivan walked round the enclosure but could not see any doors. The king's daughter saw there was someone there, came on to the balcony and called out to him, "See, there is a chink in the enclosure; touch it with your little finger and it will become a door."

What she said turned out to be true. Prince Ivan went into the house and the maiden received him kindly, gave him to eat and to drink and then began to question him. He told her how he had come to rescue his mother from Koshchei the Deathless. Then the maiden said:

"It will be difficult for you to get at your mother, Prince Ivan. You see, Koshchei is not mortal: he will kill you. He often comes here to see me. There is his sword, fifty poods in weight. Can you lift it? If so, you may venture to go."

Not only did Prince Ivan lift the sword but he tossed it high in the air. So he went on his way again.

By-and-by he came to a second house. He knew now where to look for the door and he entered in. There was his mother. With tears did they embrace each other.

Here also did he try his strength, heaving aloft a ball which weighed some fifteen hundred poods. The time came for Koshchei the Deathless to arrive. The mother hid away her son. Suddenly Koshchei the Deathless entered the house and cried out, "Phou, Phou! A Russian bone[105] one usen't to hear with one's ears or see with one's eyes but now a Russian bone has come to the house! Who has been with you? Wasn't it your son?"

"What are you talking about, God bless you! You've been flying through Russia and got the air up your nostrils, that's why you fancy it's here," answered Prince Ivan's mother and then she drew nigh to Koshchei, addressed him in terms of affection, asked him about one thing and another and at last said:

"Whereabouts is your death, O Koshchei?"

"My death," he replied, "is in such a place. There stands an oak and under the oak is a casket and in the casket is a hare and in the hare is a duck and in the duck is an egg and in the egg is my death."

Having thus spoken, Koshchei the Deathless tarried there a little longer and then flew away.

The time came—Prince Ivan received his mother's blessing and went to look for Koshchei's death. He went on his way a long time without eating or drinking; at last he felt mortally hungry and thought, "If only something would come my way!" Suddenly there appeared a young wolf; he determined to kill it. But out from a hole sprang the she wolf and said, "Don't hurt my little one; I'll do you a good turn." Very good! Prince Ivan let the young wolf go. On he went and saw a crow. "Stop a bit," he thought, "here I shall get a mouthful." He loaded his gun and was going to shoot but the crow exclaimed, "Don't hurt me; I'll do you a good turn."

Prince Ivan thought the matter over and spared the crow. Then he went farther and came to a sea and stood still on the shore. At that moment a young pike suddenly jumped out of the water and fell on the strand. He caught hold of it and thought—for he was half dead with hunger—"Now I shall

---

105 "Russkaya kost'." I have translated literally but the words mean nothing more than "a man," "something human." Cf. Radloff, iii. III. 301.

ave something to eat." All of a sudden appeared a pike and said, "Don't hurt my little one, Prince Ivan; I'll do you a good turn." And so he spared the little pike also.

But how was he to cross the sea? He sat down on the shore and meditated. But the pike knew quite well what he was thinking about and laid herself right across the sea. Prince Ivan walked along her back, as if he were going over a bridge and came to the oak where Koshchei's death was. There he found the casket and opened it—out jumped the hare and ran away. How was the hare to be stopped?

Prince Ivan was terribly frightened at having let the hare escape and gave himself up to gloomy thoughts; but a wolf, the one he had refrained from killing, rushed after the hare, caught it and brought it to Prince Ivan. With great delight he seized the hare, cut it open—and had such a fright! Out popped the duck and flew away. He fired after it but shot all on one side, so again he gave himself up to his thoughts. Suddenly there appeared the crow with her little crows and set off after the duck and caught it and brought it to Prince Ivan. The Prince was greatly pleased and got hold of the egg. Then he went on his way. But when he came to the sea, he began washing the egg and let it drop into the water. However was he to get it out of the water? an immeasurable depth! Again the Prince gave himself up to dejection.

Suddenly the sea became violently agitated and the pike brought him the egg. Moreover it stretched itself across the sea. Prince Ivan walked along it to the other side and then he set out again for his mother's. When he got there, they greeted each other lovingly and then she hid him again as before. Presently in flew Koshchei the Deathless and said:

"Phoo, Phoo! No Russian bone can the ear hear nor the eye see but there's a smell of Russia here!"

"What are you talking about, Koshchei? There's no one with me," replied Prince Ivan's mother.

A second time spake Koshchei and said, "I feel rather unwell."

Then Prince Ivan began squeezing the egg and thereupon Koshchei the Deathless bent double. At last Prince Ivan came out from his hiding-place, held up the egg and said, "There is your death, O Koshchei the Deathless!"

Then Koshchei fell on his knees before him, saying, "Don't kill me, Prince Ivan! Let's be friends! All the world will lie at our feet."

But these words had no weight with Prince Ivan. He smashed the egg and Koshchei the Deathless died.

Ivan and his mother took all they wanted and started homewards. On their way they came to where the King's daughter was whom Ivan had seen on his way and they took her with them too. They went further and came to the hill where Ivan's brothers were still waiting for him. Then the maiden said, "Prince Ivan! do go back to my house. I have forgotten a marriage robe, a diamond ring and a pair of seamless shoes."

He consented to do so but in the meantime he let his mother go down the ladder, as well as the Princess—whom it had been settled he was to marry when they got home. They were received by his brothers, who then set to work and cut away the ladder, so that he himself would not be able to get down. And they used such threats to his mother and the Princess, that they made them promise not to tell about Prince Ivan when they got home. And after a time they reached their native country. Their father was delighted at seeing his wife and his two sons but still he was grieved about the other one, Prince Ivan.

But Prince Ivan returned to the home of his betrothed and got the wedding dress and the ring and the seamless shoes. Then he came back to the mountain and tossed the ring from one hand to the other. Immediately there appeared twelve strong youths, who said:

"What are your commands?"

"Carry me down from this hill."

The youths immediately carried him down. Prince Ivan put the ring on his finger—they disappeared.

Then he went on to his own country and arrived at the city in which his father and brothers lived.

There he took up his quarters in the house of an old woman and asked her:

"What news is there, mother, in your country?"

"What news, lad? You see our queen was kept in prison by Koshchei the Deathless. Her three sons went to look for her and two of them found her and came back but the third, Prince Ivan, has disappeared and no one knows where he is. The King is very unhappy about him. And those two Princes and their mother brought a certain Princess back with them; and the eldest son wants to marry her but she declares he must fetch her betrothal ring first or get one made just as she wants it. But although they have made a public proclamation about it, no one has been found to do it yet."

"Well, mother, go and tell the King that you will make one. I'll manage it for you," said Prince Ivan.

So the old woman immediately dressed herself and hastened to the King and said:

"Please, your Majesty, I will make the wedding ring."

"Make it, then, make it, mother! Such people as you are welcome," said the king. "But if you don't make it, off goes your head!"

The old woman was dreadfully frightened; she ran home and told Prince Ivan to set to work at the ring. But Ivan lay down to sleep, troubling himself very little about it. The ring was there all the time. So he only laughed at the old woman but she was trembling all over and crying and scolding him.

"As for you," she said, "you're out of the scrape; but you've done for me, fool that I was!"

The old woman cried and cried until she fell asleep. Early in the morning Prince Ivan got up and awakened her, saying:

"Get up, mother and go out! take them the ring and mind, don't accept more than one ducat for it. If anyone asks who made the ring, say you made it yourself; don't say a word about me."

The old woman was overjoyed and carried off the ring. The bride was delighted with it.

"Just what I wanted," she said. So they gave the old woman a dish full of gold but she took only one ducat.

"Why do you take so little?" said the king.

"What good would a lot do me, your Majesty? if I want some more afterwards, you'll give it me."

Having said this the old woman went away.

Time passed and the news spread abroad that the bride had told her lover to fetch her wedding-dress or else to get one made, just such a one as she wanted. Well, the old woman, thanks to Prince Ivan's aid, succeeded in this matter too and took her the wedding-dress. And afterwards she took her the seamless shoes also and would only accept one ducat each time and always said that she had made the things herself.

Well, the people heard that there would be a wedding at the palace on such-and-such a day. And the day they all anxiously awaited came at last. Then Prince Ivan said to the old woman:

"Look here, mother! when the bride is just going to be married, let me know."

The old woman didn't let the time go by unheeded.

Then Ivan immediately put on his princely raiment and went out of the house.

"See, mother, this is what I'm really like!" says he.

The old woman fell at his feet.

"Pray forgive me for scolding you," said she.

"God be with you," said he.[106]

So he went into the church and finding his brothers had not yet arrived, he stood up alongside of the bride and got married to her. Then he and she were escorted back to the palace and as they went along, the proper bridegroom, his eldest brother, met them. But when he saw that his bride and Prince Ivan were being escorted home together, he turned back again ignominiously.

As to the king, he was delighted to see Prince Ivan again and when he had learnt all about the treachery of his brothers, after the wedding feast had been solemnised, he banished the two elder princes but he made Ivan heir to the throne.

~

In the story of "Prince Arikad,"[107] the Queen-Mother is carried off by the Whirlwind,[108] instead of by Koshchei. Her youngest son climbs the hill by the aid of iron hooks, kills Vikhor and lowers his mother and three other ladies whom he has rescued, by means of a rope made of strips of hide. This his brothers cut to prevent him from descending.[109] They then oblige the ladies to swear not to betray them, the taking of the oath being accompanied by the eating of earth.[110] The same formality is observed in another story in which an oath of a like kind is exacted.[111]

---

106 Bog prostit = God will forgive. This sounds to the English ear like an ungracious reply but it is the phrase ordinarily used by a superior when an inferior asks his pardon. Before taking the sacrament at Easter, the servants in a Russian household ask their employers to forgive them for any faults of which they may have been guilty. "God will forgive," is the proper reply.

107 Khudyakof, No. 43.

108 Vikhor' (vit' = to whirl), an agent often introduced for the purpose of abduction. The sorcerers of the present day are supposed to be able to direct whirlwinds and a not uncommon form of imprecation in some parts of Russia is "May the whirlwind carry thee off!" See Afanasief, P.V.S. i. 317 and "Songs of the Russian People," p. 382.

109 This story is very like that of the "Rider of Grianaig," "Tales of the West Highlands," iii. No. 58.

110 Cf. Herodotus, bk. iv. chap. 172.

111 Khudyakof, No. 44.

The sacred nature of such an obligation may account for the singular reticence so often maintained, under similar circumstances, in stories of this class.

In one of the descriptions of Koshchei's death, he is said to be killed by a blow on the forehead inflicted by the mysterious egg—that last link in the magic chain by which his life is darkly bound.[112] In another version of the same story but told of a Snake, the fatal blow is struck by a small stone found in the yolk of an egg, which is inside a duck, which is inside a hare, which is inside a stone, which is on an island [*i.e.*, the fabulous island Buyan].[113] In another variant[114] Koshchei attempts to deceive his fair captive, pretending that his "death" resides in a besom or in a fence, both of which she adorns with gold in token of her love. Then he confesses that his "death" really lies in an egg, inside a duck, inside a log which is floating on the sea. Prince Ivan gets hold of the egg and shifts it from one hand to the other. Koshchei rushes wildly from side to side of the room. At last the prince breaks the egg. Koshchei falls on the floor and dies.

This heart-breaking episode occurs in the folktales of many lands.[115] It may not be amiss to trace it through some of its forms. In a Norse story[116] a Giant's heart lies in an egg, inside a duck, which swims in a well, in a church, on an island. With this may be compared another Norse tale,[117] in which a *Haugebasse* or Troll, who has carried off a princess, informs her that he and all his companions will burst asunder when above them passes "the grain of sand that lies under the ninth

---

112 Erlenvein, No. 12, p. 67. A popular tradition asserts that the Devil may be killed if shot with an egg laid on Christmas Eve. See Afanasief, P.V.S. ii. 603.
113 Afanasief, i. No. 14, p. 92. For an account of Buyan, see "Songs of the Russian People," p. 374.
114 Afanasief, vii. No. 6, p. 83.
115 Some of these have been compared by Mr. Cox, in his "Mythology of the Aryan Nations," i. 135-142. Also by Professor A. de Gubernatis, who sees in the duck the dawn, in the hare "the moon sacrificed in the morning," and in the egg the sun. "Zoological Mythology," i. 269.
116 Asbjörnsen and Moe, No. 36, Dasent, No. 9, p. 71.
117 Asbjörnsen's "New Series," No. 70, p. 39.

tongue in the ninth head" of a certain dead dragon. The grain of sand is found and brought and the result is that the whole of the monstrous brood of Trolls or *Haugebasser* is instantaneously destroyed. In a Transylvanian-Saxon story[118] a Witch's "life" is a light which burns in an egg, inside a duck, which swims on a pond, inside a mountain and she dies when it is put out. In the Bohemian story of "The Sun-horse"[119] a Warlock's "strength" lies in an egg, which is within a duck, which is within a stag, which is under a tree. A Seer finds the egg and sucks it. Then the Warlock becomes as weak as a child, "for all his strength had passed into the Seer." In the Gaelic story of "The Sea-Maiden,"[120] the "great beast with three heads" which haunts the loch cannot be killed until an egg is broken, which is in the mouth of a trout, which springs out of a crow, which flies out of a hind, which lives on an island in the middle of the loch. In a Modern Greek tale the life of a dragon or other baleful being comes to an end simultaneously with the lives of three pigeons which are shut up in an all but inaccessible chamber,[121] or enclosed within a wild boar.[122] Closely connected with the Greek tale is the Servian story of the dragon[123] whose "strength" (*snaga*) lies in a sparrow, which is inside a dove, inside a hare, inside a boar, inside a dragon (*ajdaya*) which is in a lake, near a royal city. The hero of the story fights the dragon of the lake and after a long struggle, being invigourated at the critical moment by a kiss which the heroine imprints on his forehead—he flings it high in the air. When it falls to the ground it breaks in pieces and

118 Haltrich's "Deutsche Volksmärchen aus dem Sachsenlande in Siebenbürgen," p. 188.

119 Wenzig's "Westslawischer Märchenschatz," No. 37, p. 190.

120 Campbell's "Tales of the West Highlands," i. No. 4, p. 81.

121 Hahn, No. 26, i. 187.

122 Ibid., vol. ii. pp. 215, 294-5.

123 Vuk Karajich, No. 8. The monster is called in the Servian text an *Ajdaya*, a word meaning a dragon or snake. It is rendered by *Drache* in the German translation of his collection of tales made by his daughter but the word is evidently akin to the Sanskrit *ahi*, the Greek έχιρ έχιδνα, the Latin *anguis*, the Russian *ujak*, the Luthanian *angis*, etc. The Servian word *snaga* answers to the Russian *sila*, strength.

out comes the boar. Eventually the hero seizes the sparrow and wrings its neck but not before he has obtained from it the charm necessary for the recovery of his missing brothers and a number of other victims of the dragon's cruelty.

To these European tales a very interesting parallel is afforded by the Indian story of "Punchkin,"[124] whose life depends on that of a parrot, which is in a cage placed beneath the lowest of six jars of water, piled one on the other and standing in the midst of a desolate country covered with thick jungle. When the parrot's legs and wings are pulled off, Punchkin loses his legs and arms; and when its neck is wrung, his head twists round and he dies.

One of the strangest of the stories which turn on this idea of an external heart is the Samoyed tale,[125] in which seven brothers are in the habit, every night, of taking out their hearts and sleeping without them. A captive damsel whose mother they have killed, receives the extracted hearts and hangs them on the tent-pole, where they remain till the following morning. One night her brother contrives to get the hearts into his possession. Next morning he takes them into the tent, where he finds the brothers at the point of death. In vain do they beg for their hearts, which he flings on the floor. "And as he flings down the hearts the brothers die."

The legend to which I am now about to refer will serve as a proof of the venerable antiquity of the myth from which the folktales, which have just been quoted, appear to have sprung. A papyrus, which is supposed to be "of the age of the nineteenth dynasty, about B.C. 1300," has preserved an Egyptian tale about two brothers. The younger of these, Satou, leaves the elder, Anepou (Anubis) and retires to the Valley of the Acacia. But before setting off, Satou states that he shall take his heart and place it "in the flowers of the acacia-tree,"

---

124 Miss Frere's "Old Deccan Days," pp. 13-16.
125 Castren's "Ethnologische Vorlesungen über die Altaischen Völker," p. 174.

so that, if the tree is cut down, his heart will fall to the ground and he will die. Having given Anepou instructions what to do in such a case, he seeks the valley. There he hunts wild animals by day and at night he sleeps under the acacia-tree on which his heart rests. But at length Noum, the Creator, forms a wife for him and all the other gods endow her with gifts. To this Egyptian Pandora Satou confides the secret of his heart. One day a tress of her perfumed hair floats down the river and is taken to the King of Egypt. He determines to make its owner his queen and she, like Rhodope or Cinderella, is sought for far and wide. When she has been found and brought to the king, she recommends him to have the acacia cut down, so as to get rid of her lawful husband. Accordingly the tree is cut down, the heart falls and Satou dies.

About this time Anepou sets out to pay his long-lost brother a visit. Finding him dead, he searches for his heart but searches in vain for three years. In the fourth year, however, it suddenly becomes desirous of returning to Egypt and says, "I will leave this celestial sphere." Next day Anepou finds it under the acacia and places it in a vase which contains some mystic fluid. When the heart has become saturated with the moisture, the corpse shudders and opens its eyes. Anepou pours the rest of the fluid down its throat, the heart returns to its proper place and Satou is restored to life.[126]

In one of the Skazkas, a *volshebnitsa* or enchantress is introduced, whose "death," like that of Koshchei, is spoken of as something definite and localised. A prince

---

126 The story has been translated by M. de Rougé in the "Revue Archéologique," 1852-3, p. 391 (referred to by Professor Benfey, "Panchatantra," i. 426) and summarised by Mr. Goodwin in the "Cambridge Essays" for 1858, pp. 232-7 and by Dr. Mannhardt in the "Zeitschrift für deutsche Mythologie," &c., vol. iv. pp. 232-59. For other versions of the story of the Giant's heart or Koshchei's death, see Professor R. Köhler's remarks on the subject in "Orient und Occident," ii. pp. 99-103. A singular parallel to part of the Egyptian myth is offered by the Hottentot story in which the heart of a girl whom a lion has killed and eaten, is extracted from the lion and placed in a calabash filled with milk. "The calabash increased in size and in proportion to this, the girl grew again inside it." Bleek's "Reynard the Fox in South Africa," p. 55. Cf. Radloff, i. 75; ii. 237-8, 532-3.

has loved and lost a princess, who is so beautiful that no man can look at her without fainting. Going in search of her, he comes to the home of an enchantress, who invites him to tea and gives him leave to inspect her house. As he wanders about he comes to a cellar in which "he sees that beautiful one whom he loves, in fire." She tells him her love for him has brought her there; and he learns that there is no hope of freeing her unless he can find out "where lies the death of the enchantress." So that evening he asks his hostess about it and she replies:

"In a certain lake stands a blue rose-tree. It is in a deep place and no man can reach unto it. My death is there."

He sets out in search of it, and aided by a magic ring, reaches the lake, "and sees there the blue rose-tree and around it a blue forest." After several failures, he succeeds in plucking up the rose-tree by the roots, whereupon the enchantress straightway sickens. He returns to her house, finds her at the point of death and throws the rose-bush into the cellar where his love is crying, "Behold her death!" and immediately the whole building shakes to its foundations—"and becomes an island on which are people who had been sitting in Hell and who offer up thanks to Prince Ivan."[127]

In another Russian story,[128] a prince is grievously tormented by a witch who has got hold of his heart and keeps it perpetually seething in a magic cauldron. In a third,[129] a "Queen-Maiden" falls in love with the young Ivan, and after being betrothed to him, would fain take him away to her own land and marry him. But his stepmother throws him into a magic slumber and the Queen-Maiden has to return home without him. When

---

127 Khudyakof, No. 109.
128 Khudyakof, No. 110.
129 Afanasief, v. No. 42. See also the Zagovor or spell, "to give a good youth a longing for a fair maiden," ("Songs of the Russian People," p. 369,) in which "the Longing" is described as lying under a plank in a hut, weeping and sobbing and "waiting to get at the white light," and is desired to gnaw its way into the youth's heart.

he awakes and learns that she has gone, he sorrows greatly and sets out in search of her. At last he learns from a friendly witch that his betrothed no longer cares for him, "her love is hidden far away." It seems "that on the other side of the ocean stands an oak and on the oak a coffer and in the coffer a hare and in the hare a duck and in the duck an egg and in the egg the love of the Queen-Maiden." Ivan gets possession of the egg and the friendly witch contrives to have it placed before the Queen-Maiden at dinner. She eats it and immediately her love for Ivan returns in all its pristine force. He appears and she, overjoyed, carries him off to her own land and there marries him.

* * * * *

After this digression we will now return to our Snakes. All the monstrous forms which figure in the stories we have just been considering appear to be merely different species of the great serpent family. Such names as Koshchei, Chudo Yudo, Usuinya and the like, seem to admit of exchange at the will of the storyteller with that of Zméï Goruinuich, the many-headed Snake, who in Russian storyland is represented as the type of all that is evil. But in the actual Russia of to-day, snakes bear by no means so bad a character. Their presence in a cottage is considered a good omen by the peasants, who leave out milk for them to drink and who think that to kill such visitors would be a terrible sin.[130] This is probably a result of some remembrance of a religious cultus paid to the household gods under the form of snakes, such as existed of old, according to Kromer, in Poland and Lithuania. The following story is more in keeping with such ideas as these, than with those which are expressed in the tales about Koshchei and his kin.

---

130 For stories about house snakes, &c., see Grimm "Deutsche Mythologie," p. 650 and Tylor, "Primitive Culture," ii. pp. 7, 217-220.

THE WATER SNAKE.[131]

Selfishness destroys the life and love of another . . .

THERE WAS ONCE AN old woman who had a daughter; and her daughter went down to the pond one day to bathe with the other girls. They all stripped off their shifts and went into the water. Then there came a snake out of the water and glided on to the daughter's shift. After a time the girls all came out and began to put on their shifts and the old woman's daughter wanted to put on hers but there was the snake lying on it. She tried to drive him away but there he stuck and would not move. Then the snake said:

"If you'll marry me, I'll give you back your shift."

Now she wasn't at all inclined to marry him but the other girls said:

"As if it were possible for you to be married to him! Say you will!" So she said, "Very well, I will." Then the snake glided off from the shift and went straight into the water. The girl dressed and went home. And as soon as she got there, she said to her mother,

"Mammie, mammie, thus and thus, a snake got upon my shift and says he, 'Marry me or I won't let you have your shift;' and I said, 'I will.'"

"What nonsense are you talking, you little fool! as if one could marry a snake!"

And so they remained just as they were and forgot all about the matter.

A week passed by and one day they saw ever so many snakes, a huge troop of them, wriggling up to their cottage. "Ah,

131 Or Ujak. Erlenvein, No. 2. From the Tula Government.

mammie, save me, save me!" cried the girl and her mother slammed the door and barred the entrance as quickly as possible. The snakes would have rushed in at the door but the door was shut; they would have rushed into the passage but the passage was closed. Then in a moment they rolled themselves into a ball, flung themselves at the window, smashed it to pieces and glided in a body into the room. The girl got upon the stove but they followed her, pulled her down and bore her out of the room and out of doors. Her mother accompanied her, crying like anything.

They took the girl down to the pond and dived right into the water with her. And there they all turned into men and women. The mother remained for some time on the dike, wailed a little and then went home.

Three years went by. The girl lived down there and had two children, a son and a daughter. Now she often entreated her husband to let her go to see her mother. So at last one day he took her up to the surface of the water and brought her ashore. But she asked him before leaving him,

"What am I to call out when I want you?"

"Call out to me, 'Osip, [Joseph] Osip, come here!' and I will come," he replied.

Then he dived under water again and she went to her mother's, carrying her little girl on one arm and leading her boy by the hand. Out came her mother to meet her—was so delighted to see her!

"Good day, mother!" said the daughter.

"Have you been doing well while you were living down there?" asked her mother.

"Very well indeed, mother. My life there is better than yours here."

They sat down for a bit and chatted. Her mother got dinner ready for her and she dined.

"What's your husband's name?" asked her mother.

"Osip," she replied.

"And how are you to get home?"

"I shall go to the dike and call out, 'Osip, Osip, come here!' and he'll come."

"Lie down, daughter and rest a bit," said the mother.

So the daughter lay down and went to sleep. The mother immediately took an axe and sharpened it and went down to the dike with it. And when she came to the dike, she began calling out,

"Osip, Osip, come here!"

No sooner had Osip shown his head than the old woman lifted her axe and chopped it off. And the water in the pond became dark with blood.

The old woman went home. And when she got home her daughter awoke.

"Ah! mother," says she, "I'm getting tired of being here; I'll go home."

"Do sleep here to-night, daughter; perhaps you won't have another chance of being with me."

So the daughter stayed and spent the night there. In the morning she got up and her mother got breakfast ready for her; she breakfasted and then she said good-bye to her mother and went away, carrying her little girl in her arms, while her boy followed behind her. She came to the dike and called out:

"Osip, Osip, come here!"

She called and called but he did not come.

Then she looked into the water and there she saw a head floating about. Then she guessed what had happened.

"Alas! my mother has killed him!" she cried.

There on the bank she wept and wailed. And then to her girl she cried:

"Fly about as a wren, henceforth and evermore!"

And to her boy she cried:

"Fly about as a nightingale, my boy, henceforth and evermore!"

"But I," she said, "will fly about as a cuckoo, crying 'Cuckoo!' henceforth and evermore!"

~

[Stories about serpent-spouses are by no means uncommon but I can find no parallel to the above so far as the termination is concerned. Benfey quotes or refers to a great number of the transformation tales in which a husband or a wife appears at times in the form of a snake (Panchatantra, i. pp. 254-7 266-7). Sometimes, when a husband of this kind has doffed his serpent's skin, his wife seizes it and throws it into the fire. Her act generally proves to be to her advantage, as well as to his but not always. On a story of this kind was doubtless founded the legend handed down to us by Appuleius of Cupid and Psyche. Among its wildest versions are the Albanian "Schlangenkind" (Hahn, No. 100), a very similar Roumanian tale (Ausland 1857, No. 43, quoted by Benfey), the Wallachian Trandafíru (Schott, No. 23, in which the husband is a pumpkin (Kürbiss) by day) and the second of the Servian tales of the Snake-Husband (Vuk Karajich, No. 10).]

The snakes which figure in this weird story, the termination of which is so unusually tragic, bear a strong resemblance to the Indian Nágas, the inhabitants of Patala or the underground world, serpents which take at will the human shape and often mix with mortals. They may, also, be related to the mermen and mermaids of the sea-coasts and to the similar beings with which, under various names, tradition peoples the lakes and streams and fountains of Europe. The South-Russian peasantry have from immemorial times maintained a firm belief in the existence of water-nymphs, called Rusalkas, closely resembling the Nereids of Modern Greece, the female Nixies of the North of Europe and throughout the whole of Russia, at least in outlying districts, there still lingers a sort of cultus of certain male water-sprites who bear the name of Vodyanies and who are almost identical with the beings who haunt the waters of various countries—such as the German *Nix*, the Swedish *Nek*, the Finnish *Näkke*, etc.[132]

In the Skazkas we find frequent mention of beauteous maidens who usually live beneath the wave but who can transform themselves into birds and fly wherever they please. We may perhaps be allowed to designate them by the well-known name of Swan-Maidens, though they do not always assume, together with their plumage-robes, the form of swans but sometimes appear as geese, ducks, spoonbills or aquatic birds of some other species. They are, for the most part, the daughters of the Morskoi Tsar or Water King—a being who plays an important part in Slavonic popular fiction. He is of a somewhat shadowy form and his functions are not very clearly defined, for the part he usually fills is sometimes allotted to Koshchei or to the Snake but the stories generally represent him as a patriarchal monarch, living in subaqueous halls of light and splendour, whence he emerges at times to seize a human victim. It is generally a boy whom he gets into his power and who eventually obtains the hand of one of his daughters and escapes with her to the upper world, though not without considerable difficulty. Such are, for instance, the leading incidents in the following skazka, many features of which closely resemble those of various well-known West-European folktales.

---

132 Grimm, "Deutsche Mythologie," 456. For a description of the Rusalka and the Vodyany, see "Songs of the Russian People," pp. 139-146.

THE WATER KING AND VASILISSA THE WISE.[133]

Husbandly forgetfulness can be cured, it seems . . .

ONCE UPON A TIME there lived a King and Queen and the King was very fond of hunting and shooting. Well one day he went out hunting and he saw an Eaglet sitting on an oak. But just as he was going to shoot at it the Eaglet began to entreat him, crying:—

"Don't shoot me, my lord King! better take me home with you; some time or other I shall be of service to you."

The King reflected awhile and said, "How can you be of use to me?" and again he was going to shoot.

Then the Eaglet said to him a second time:—

"Don't shoot me, my lord King! better take me home with you; some time or other I shall be of use to you."

The King thought and thought but couldn't imagine a bit the more what use the Eaglet could be to him and so he determined to shoot it. Then a third time the Eaglet exclaimed:—

"Don't shoot me, my lord King! better take me home with you and feed me for three years. Some time or other I shall be of service to you!"

The King relented, took the Eaglet home with him and fed it for a year, for two years. But it ate so much that it devoured all his cattle. The King had neither a cow nor a sheep left. At length the Eagle said:—

"Now let me go free!"

The King set it at liberty; the Eagle began trying its wings. But no, it could not fly yet! So it said:—

133 Afanasief, v. No. 23. From the Voroneje Government.

"Well, my lord King! you have fed me two years; now, whether you like it or no, feed me for one year more. Even if you have to borrow, at all events feed me; you won't lose by it!"

Well, this is what the King did. He borrowed cattle from everywhere round about and he fed the Eagle for the space of a whole year and afterwards he set it at liberty. The Eagle rose ever so high, flew and flew, then dropped down again to the earth and said:—

"Now then, my lord King! Take a seat on my back! we'll have a fly together?"

The King got on the Eagle's back. Away they went flying. Before very long they reached the blue sea. Then the Eagle shook off the King, who fell into the sea and sank up to his knees. But the Eagle didn't let him drown! it jerked him on to its wing and asked:—

"How now, my lord King! were you frightened, perchance?"

"I was," said the King; "I thought I was going to be drowned outright!"

Again they flew and flew till they reached another sea. The Eagle shook off the King right in the middle of the sea; the King sank up to his girdle. The Eagle jerked him on to its wing again and asked:—

"Well, my lord King, were you frightened, perchance?"

"I was," he replied, "but all the time I thought, 'Perhaps, please God, the creature will pull me out.'"

Away they flew again, flew and arrived at a third sea. The Eagle dropped the King into a great gulf, so that he sank right up to his neck. And the third time the Eagle jerked him on to its wing and asked:—

"Well, my lord King! Were you frightened, perchance?"

"I was," says the King, "but still I said to myself, 'Perhaps it will pull me out.'"

"Well, my lord King! now you have felt what the fear of death is like! What I have done was in payment of an old score. Do you remember my sitting on an oak and your wanting to shoot me? Three times you were going to let fly but I kept on entreating you not to shoot, saying to myself all the time, 'Perhaps he won't kill me; perhaps he'll relent and take me home with him!'"

Afterwards they flew beyond thrice nine lands: long, long did they fly. Says the Eagle, "Look, my lord King! what is above us and what below us?"

The King looked.

"Above us," he says, "is the sky, below us the earth."

"Look again; what is on the right hand and on the left?"

"On the right hand is an open plain, on the left stands a house."

"We will fly thither," said the Eagle; "my youngest sister lives there."

They went straight into the courtyard. The sister came out to meet them, received her brother cordially and seated him at the oaken table. But on the King she would not so much as look but left him outside, loosed greyhounds and set them at him. The Eagle was exceedingly wroth, jumped up from table, seized the King and flew away with him again.

Well, they flew and flew. Presently the Eagle said to the King, "Look round; what is behind us?"

The King turned his head, looked and said, "Behind us is a red house."

"That is the house of my youngest sister—on fire, because she did not receive you but set greyhounds at you."

They flew and flew. Again the Eagle asked:

"Look again, my lord King; what is above us and what below us?"

"Above us is the sky, below us the earth."

"Look and see what is on the right hand and on the left."

"On the right is the open plain, on the left there stands a house."

"There lives my second sister; we'll go and pay her a visit."

They stopped in a wide courtyard. The second sister received her brother cordially and seated him at the oaken table; but the King was left outside and she loosed greyhounds and set them at him. The Eagle flew into a rage, jumped up from table, caught up the King and flew away farther with him. They flew and flew. Says the Eagle:

"My lord King! look round! what is behind us?"

The King looked back.

"There stands behind us a red house."

"That's my second sister's house burning!" said the Eagle. "Now we'll fly to where my mother and my eldest sister live."

Well, they flew there. The Eagle's mother and eldest sister were delighted to see them and received the King with cordiality and respect.

"Now, my lord King," said the Eagle, "tarry awhile with us and afterwards I will give you a ship and will repay you for all I ate in your house and then—God speed you home again!"

So the Eagle gave the King a ship and two coffers—the one red, the other green—and said:

"Mind now! don't open the coffers until you get home. Then open the red coffer in the back court and the green coffer in the front court."

The King took the coffers, parted with the Eagle and sailed along the blue sea. Presently he came to a certain island and there his ship stopped. He landed on the shore and began thinking about the coffers and wondering whatever there could be in them and why the Eagle had told him not to open them. He thought and thought and at last couldn't hold out anymore—he longed so awfully to know all about it. So he took the red coffer, set it on the ground and opened it—and out of it came such a quantity of different kinds of cattle that there was no counting them: the island had barely room enough for them.

When the King saw that, he became exceedingly sorrowful and began to weep and therewithal to say:

"What is there now left for me to do? how shall I get all these cattle back into so little a coffer?"

Lo! there came out of the water a man—came up to him and asked:

"Wherefore are you weeping so bitterly, O lord King?"

"How can I help weeping!" answers the King. "How shall I be able to get all this great herd into so small a coffer?"

"If you like, I will set your mind at rest. I will pack up all your cattle for you. But on one condition only. You must give me whatever you have at home that you don't know of."

The King reflected.

"Whatever is there at home that I don't know of?" says he. "I fancy I know about everything that's there."

He reflected and consented. "Pack them up," says he. "I will give you whatever I have at home that I know nothing about."

So that man packed away all his cattle for him in the coffer. The King went on board ship and sailed away homewards.

When he reached home, then only did he learn that a son had been born to him. And he began kissing the child, caressing it and at the same time bursting into such floods of tears!

"My lord King!" says the Queen, "tell me wherefore thou droppest bitter tears?"

"For joy!" he replies.

He was afraid to tell her the truth, that the Prince would have to be given up. Afterwards he went into the back court, opened the red coffer and thence issued oxen and cows, sheep and rams; there were multitudes of all sorts of cattle, so that all the sheds and pastures were crammed full. He went into the front court, opened the green coffer and there appeared a great and glorious garden. What trees there were in it to be sure! The King was so delighted that he forgot all about giving up his son.

Many years went by. One day the King took it into his head to go for a stroll and he came to a river. At that moment the same man he had seen before came out of the water and said:

"You've pretty soon become forgetful, lord King! Think a little! surely you're in my debt!"

The King returned home full of grief and told all the truth to the Queen and the Prince. They all mourned and wept together but they decided that there was no help for it, the Prince must be given up. So they took him to the mouth of the river and there they left him alone.

The Prince looked around, saw a footpath and followed trusting God would lead him somewhere. He walked and walked and came to a dense forest: in the forest stood a hut, in the hut lived a Baba Yaga.

"Suppose I go in," thought the Prince and went in.

"Good day, Prince!" said the Baba Yaga. "Are you seeking work or shunning work?"

"Eh, granny! First give me to eat and to drink and then ask me questions."

So she gave him food and drink and the Prince told her everything as to whither he was going and with what purpose.

Then the Baba Yaga said: "Go, my child, to the seashore; there will fly thither twelve spoonbills, which will turn into fair maidens and begin bathing; do you steal quietly up and lay your hands on the eldest maiden's shift. When you have come to terms with her, go to the Water King and there will meet you on the way Obédalo and Opivalo and also MorozTreskum[134]—take all of them with you; they will do you good service."

---

134 Three of the well-known servants of Fortunatus. The eater-up (ob'egedat' = to devour), the drinker-up (pit' = to drink, opivat'sya, to drink oneself to death) and "Crackling Frost."

The Prince bid the Yaga farewell, went to the appointed spot on the seashore and hid behind the bushes. Presently twelve spoonbills came flying thither, struck the moist earth, turned into fair maidens and began to bathe. The Prince stole the eldest one's shift and sat down behind a bush—didn't budge an inch. The girls finished bathing and came out on the shore: eleven of them put on their shifts, turned into birds and flew away home. There remained only the eldest, Vasilissa the Wise. She began praying and begging the good youth:

"Do give me my shift!" she says. "You are on your way to the house of my father, the Water King. When you come I will do you good service."

So the Prince gave her back her shift and she immediately turned into a spoonbill and flew away after her companions. The Prince went further on; there met him by the way three heroes—Obédalo, Opivalo and Moroz Treskum; he took them with him and went on to the Water King's.

The Water King saw him and said:

"Hail, friend! why have you been so long in coming to me? I have grown weary of waiting for you. Now set to work. Here is your first task. Build me in one night a great crystal bridge, so that it shall be ready for use tomorrow. If you don't build it—off goes your head!"

The Prince went away from the Water King and burst into a flood of tears. Vasilissa the Wise opened the window of her upper chamber and asked:

"What are you crying about, Prince?"

"Ah! Vasilissa the Wise! how can I help crying? Your father has ordered me to build a crystal bridge in a single night and I don't even know how to handle an axe."

"No matter! lie down and sleep; the morning is wiser than the evening."

She ordered him to sleep but she herself went out on the steps and called aloud with a mighty whistling cry. Then from all sides there ran together carpenters and workmen; one levelled the ground, another carried bricks. Soon had they built a crystal bridge and traced cunning devices on it; and then they dispersed to their homes.

Early next morning Vasilissa the Wise awoke the Prince:

"Get up, Prince! the bridge is ready: my father will be coming to inspect it directly."

Up jumped the Prince, seized a broom, took his place on the bridge and began sweeping here, clearing up there.

The Water King bestowed praise upon him:

"Thanks!" says he. "You've done me one service: now do another. Here is your task. Plant me by tomorrow a garden green—a big and shady one; and there must be birds singing in the garden and flowers blossoming on the trees and ripe apples and pears hanging from the boughs."

Away went the Prince from the Water King, all dissolved in tears. Vasilissa the Wise opened her window and asked:

"What are you crying for, Prince?"

"How can I help crying? Your father has ordered me to plant a garden in one night!"

"That's nothing! lie down and sleep: the morning is wiser than the evening."

She made him go to sleep but she herself went out on the steps, called and whistled with a mighty whistle. From every side there ran together gardeners of all sorts and they planted a garden green and in the garden birds sang, on the trees flowers blossomed, from the boughs hung ripe apples and pears.

Early in the morning Vasilissa the Wise awoke the Prince:

"Get up, Prince! the garden is ready: Papa is coming to see it."

The Prince immediately snatched up a broom and was off to the garden. Here he swept a path, there he trained a twig. The Water King praised him and said:

"Thanks, Prince! You've done me right trusty service. So choose yourself a bride from among my twelve daughters. They are all exactly alike in face, in hair and in dress. If you can pick out the same one three times running, she shall be your wife; if you fail to do so, I shall have you put to death."

Vasilissa the Wise knew all about that, so she found time to say to the Prince:

"The first time I will wave my handkerchief, the second I will be arranging my dress, the third time you will see a fly above my head."

And so the Prince guessed which was Vasilissa the Wise three times running. And he and she were married and a wedding feast was got ready.

Now the Water King had prepared much food of all sorts more than a hundred men could get through. And he ordered his son-in-law to see that everything was eaten. "If anything remains over, the worse for you!" says he.

"My Father," begs the Prince, "there's an old fellow of mine here; please let him take a snack with us."

"Let him come!"

Immediately appeared Obédalo—ate up everything and wasn't content then! The Water King next set out two score tubs of all kinds of strong drinks and ordered his son-in-law to see that they were all drained dry.

"My Father!" begs the Prince again, "there's another old man of mine here, let him, too, drink your health."

"Let him come!"

Opivalo appeared, emptied all the forty tubs in a twinkling and then asked for a drop more by way of stirrup-cup.[135]

The Water King saw that there was nothing to be gained that way, so he gave orders to prepare a bathroom for the young couple—an iron bathroom—and to heat it as hot as

135 Opokhmyelit'sya, which may be rendered, "in order to drink off the effects of the debauch."

possible. So the iron bathroom was made hot. Twelve loads of firewood were set alight and the stove and the walls were made red-hot—impossible to come within five versts of it.

"My Father!" says the Prince; "let an old fellow of ours have a scrub first, just to try the bathroom."

"Let him do so!"

Moroz Treskum went into the bath room, blew into one corner, blew in another—in a moment icicles were hanging there. After him the young couple also went into the bathroom, were lathered and scrubbed,[136] and then went home.

After a time Vasilissa said to the Prince, "Let us get out of my father's power. He's tremendously angry with you; perhaps he'll be doing you some hurt."

"Let us go," says the Prince.

Straightway they saddled their horses and galloped off into the open plain. They rode and rode; many an hour went by.

"Jump down from your horse, Prince and lay your ear close to the earth," said Vasilissa. "Cannot you hear a sound as of pursuers?"

The prince bent his ear to the ground but he could hear nothing. Then Vasilissa herself lighted down from her good steed, laid herself flat on the earth and said: "Ah Prince! I hear a great noise as of chasing after us." Then she turned the horses into a well and herself into a bowl and the Prince into an old, very old man. Up came the pursuers.

"Heigh, old man!" say they, "haven't you seen a youth and a maiden pass by?"

"I saw them, my friends! only it was a long while ago. I was a youngster at the time when they rode by."

The pursuers returned to the Water King.

---

136 The Russian bath somewhat resembles the Turkish. The word here translated "to scrub," properly means to rub and flog with the soft twig used in the baths for that purpose. At the end of the ceremonies attended on a Russian peasant wedding, the young couple always go to the bath.

"There is no trace of them," they said, "no news: all we saw was an old man beside a well and a bowl floating on the water."

"Why did not ye seize them?" cried the Water King, who thereupon put the pursuers to a cruel death and sent another troop after the Prince and Vasilissa the Wise.

The fugitives in the meantime had ridden far, far away. Vasilissa the Wise heard the noise made by the fresh set of pursuers, so she turned the Prince into an old priest and she herself became an ancient church. Scarcely did its walls hold together, covered all over with moss. Presently up came the pursuers.

"Heigh, old man! haven't you seen a youth and a maiden pass by?"

"I saw them, my own! only it was long, ever so long ago. I was a young man when they rode by. It was just while I was building this church."

So the second set of pursuers returned to the Water King, saying:

"There is neither trace nor news of them, your Royal Majesty. All that we saw was an old priest and an ancient church."

"Why did not ye seize them?" cried the Water King louder than before and having put the pursuers to a cruel death, he galloped off himself in pursuit of the Prince and Vasilissa the Wise. This time Vasilissa turned the horses into a river of honey with *kissel*[137] banks and changed the Prince into a Drake and herself into a grey duck. The Water King flung himself on the *kissel* and honey-water and ate and ate and drank and drank until he burst! And so he gave up the ghost.

The Prince and Vasilissa rode on and at length they drew nigh to the home of the Prince's parents. Then said Vasilissa,

137 A sort of pudding or jelly.

"Go on in front, Prince and report your arrival to your father and mother. But I will wait for you here by the wayside. Only remember these words of mine: kiss everyone else, only don't kiss your sister; if you do, you will forget me."

The Prince reached home, began saluting everyone, kissed his sister too—and no sooner had he kissed her than from that very moment he forgot all about his wife, just as if she had never entered into his mind.

Three days did Vasilissa the Wise await him. On the fourth day she clad herself like a beggar, went into the capital and took up her quarters in an old woman's house. But the Prince was preparing to marry a rich Princess and orders were given to proclaim throughout the kingdom, that all Christian people were to come to congratulate the bride and bridegroom, each one bringing a wheaten pie as a present. Well, the old woman with whom Vasilissa lodged, prepared, like everyone else, to sift flour and make a pie.

"Why are you making a pie, granny?" asked Vasilissa.

"Is it why? you evidently don't know then. Our King is giving his son in marriage to a rich princess: one must go to the palace to serve up the dinner to the young couple."

"Come now! I, too, will bake a pie and take it to the palace; may be the King will make me some present."

"Bake away in God's name!" said the old woman.

Vasilissa took flour, kneaded dough and made a pie. And inside it she put some curds and a pair of live doves.

Well, the old woman and Vasilissa the Wise reached the palace just at dinnertime. There a feast was in progress, one fit for all the world to see. Vasilissa's pie was set on the table but no sooner was it cut in two than out of it flew the two doves. The hen bird seized a piece of curd and her mate said to her:

"Give me some curds, too, Dovey!"

"No I won't," replied the other dove: "else you'd forget me, as the Prince has forgotten his Vasilissa the Wise."

Then the Prince remembered about his wife. He jumped up from table, caught her by her white hands and seated her close by his side. From that time forward they lived together in all happiness and prosperity.

~

[With this story may be compared a multitude of tales in very many languages. In German for instance, "Der König vom goldenen Berg," (Grimm, KM. No. 92. See also Nos. 51, 56, 113, 181 and the opening of No. 31), "Der Königssohn und die Teufelstochter," (Haltrich, No. 26) and "Grünus Kravalle" (Wolf's "Deutsche Hausmärchen," No. 29)—the Norse "Mastermaid," (Asbjörnsen and Moe, No. 46, Dasent, No. 11) and "The Three Princesses of Whiteland," (A. and M. No. 9, Dasent, No. 26)—the Lithuanian story (Schleicher, No. 26, p. 75) in which a "field-devil" exacts from a farmer the promise of a child—the Wallachian stories (Schott, Nos. 2 and 15) in which a devil obtains a like promise from a woodcutter and a fisherman—the Modern Greek (Hahn, Nos. 4, 5, 54 and 68) in which a child is promised to a Dervish, a Drakos, the Devil and a Demon—and the Gaelic tales of "The Battle of the Birds" and "The Sea-maiden," (Campbell, Nos. 2 and 4) in the former of which the child is promised to a Giant, in the latter to a Mermaid. The likeness between the Russian story and the "Battle of the Birds" is very striking. References to a great many other similar tales will be found in Grimm (KM. iii. pp. 96-7 and 168-9). The group to which all these stories belong is linked with a set of tales about a father who apprentices his son to a wizard, sometimes to the Devil, from whom the youth escapes with great difficulty. The principal Russian representative of the second set is called "Eerie Art," "Khitraya Nauka," (Afanasief, v. No. 22, vi. No. 45, viii. p. 339).

To the hero's adventures while with the Water King and while escaping from him, an important parallel is offered by the end of the already mentioned (at p. 92) Indian story of Sringabhuja. That prince asks Agnisikha, the Rákshasa whom, in his crane-form, he has wounded, to bestow upon him the hand of his daughter—the maiden who had met him on his arrival at the Rákshasa's palace. The demon pretends to consent but only on condition that the prince is able to pick out his love from among her numerous sisters. This

Sringabhuja is able to do in spite of all the demon's daughters being exactly alike, as she has told him beforehand she will wear her pearls on her brow instead of round her neck. Her father will not remark the change, she says, for being of the demon race, he is not very sharp witted. The Rákshasa next sets the prince two of the usual tasks. He is to plough a great field and sow a hundred bushels of corn. When this, by the daughter's help, is done, he is told to gather up the seed again. This also the demon's daughter does for him, sending to his aid a countless swarm of ants. Lastly he is commanded to visit the demon's brother and invite him to the wedding. He does so and is pursued by the invited guest, from whom he escapes only by throwing behind him earth, water, thorns and lastly fire, with all of which he has been provided by his love. They produce corresponding obstacles which enable him to get away from the uncle of his bride. The demon now believes that his proposed son-in-law must be a god in disguise, so he gives his consent to the marriage. All goes well for a time but at last the prince wants to go home, so he and his wife fly from her father's palace. Agnisikha pursues them. She makes her husband invisible, while she assumes the form of a woodman. Up comes her angry sire and asks for news of the fugitives. She replies she has seen none, her eyes being full of tears caused by the death of the Rákshasa prince Agnisikha. The slow-witted demon immediately flies home to find out whether he is really dead. Discovering that he is not, he renews the pursuit. Again his daughter renders her husband invisible and assumes the form of a messenger carrying a letter. When her father arrives and repeats his question, she says she has seen no one: she is going with a letter to his brother from Agnisikha, who has just been mortally wounded. Back again home flies the demon in great distress, anxious to find out whether he has really been wounded to death or not. After settling this question, he leaves his daughter and her husband in peace. See Professor Brockhaus in the "Berichte der phil. hist. Classe der K. Sächs. Gesellschaft der Wissenschaften," 1861, pp. 226-9 and Professor Wilson, "Essays, &c.," ii. p. 136-8. Cf. R. Köhler in "Orient und Occident," ii. pp. 107-14.]

In another story a king is out hunting and becomes thirsty. Seeing a spring near at hand he bends down and is just going to lap up its water, when the Tsar-Medvéd, a King-Bear, seizes him by the beard. The king is unable to free himself from his grasp and is obliged to promise as his ransom "that which he knows not of at home," which turns out to be a couple of children—a boy and a girl—who have been born during his absence. In vain does he attempt to save the twins from their impending fate, by concealing them in a secret abode constructed for that purpose underground. In the course of time the King-Bear arrives to claim them, finds out their hiding-place, digs them up and carries them off on his back to a distant region where no man lives. During his absence they attempt to escape being carried through the air on the back of a friendly falcon but the King-Bear sees them, "strikes his head against the earth and burns the falcon's wings." The twins fall to the ground and are carried by the King-Bear to his home amid inaccessible mountains. There they make a second attempt at escape, trusting this time to an eagle's aid; but it meets with exactly the same fate as their first trial. At last they are rescued by a bull-calf, which succeeds in baffling all the King-Bear's efforts to recover them. At the end of their perilous journey the bull-calf tells the young prince to cut its throat and burn its carcase. He unwillingly consents and from its ashes spring a horse, a dog and an apple-tree, all of which play important parts in the next act of the drama.[138]

In one of the variants of the Water King story,[139] the seizer of the drinking kings' beard is not called the *Morskoi Tsar* but *Chudo Morskoe*, a Water Chudo, whose name recalls to mind

---

138 Afanasief, v. No. 28. In the preceding story, No. 27, the king makes no promise. He hides his children in (or upon) a pillar, hoping to conceal them from a devouring bear, whose fur is of iron. The bear finds them and carries them off. A horse and some geese vainly attempt their rescue; a bull-calf succeeds, as in the former case. In another variant the enemy is an iron wolf. A king had promised his children a wolf. Unable to find a live one, he had one made of iron and gave it to his children. After a time it came to life and began destroying all it found, etc. An interesting explanation of the stories of this class in which they are treated as nature-myths, is given by A. de Gubernatis in his "Zoological Mythology," chap. i. sect. 4.

139 Khudyakof, No. 17.

the Chudo Yudo we have already met with.[140] The Prince who is obliged, in consequence of his father's promise, to surrender himself to the Water Giant, falls in love with a maiden whom he finds in that potentate's palace and who is an enchantress whom the Chudo has stolen. She turns herself into a ring, which he carries about with him and eventually, after his escape from the Chudo, she becomes his bride.

In another story,[141] the being who obtains a child from one of the incautious fathers of the Jephthah type who abound in popular fiction, is of a very singular nature. A merchant is flying across a river on the back of an eagle, when he drops a magic "snuffbox," which had been entrusted to his charge by that bird and it disappears beneath the waters. At the eagle's command the crayfish search for it and bring back word that it is lying "on the knees of an Idol." The eagle summons the Idol and demands the snuff box. Thereupon the Idol says to the merchant—"Give me what you do not know of at home?" The merchant agrees and the Idol gives him back his snuffbox.

In some of the variants of the story, the influence of ideas connected with Christianity makes itself apparent in the names given to the actors. Thus in the "Moujik and Anastasia Adovna,"[142] it is no longer a king of the waters but a devil's imp,[143] who bargains with the thirsting father for his child and the swan-maiden whose shift the devoted youth steals bears the name of Adovna, the daughter of Ad or Hades. In "The Youth,"[144] a moujik, who has lost his way in a forest makes the rash promise to a man who enables him to cross a

140 It has already been observed that the word chudo, which now means a marvel or prodigy, formerly meant a giant.

141 Erlenvein, No. 6, pp. 30-32. The Russian word idol is identical with our own adaptation of *εἴδωλον*

142 Khudyakof, No. 18.

143 Zhidenok, strictly the cub of a zhid, a word which properly means a Jew but is used here for a devil.

144 Khudyakof, No. 118.

great river; "and that man (says the story) was a devil."[145] We shall meet with other instances further on of parents whose "hasty words" condemn their children to captivity among evil spirits. In one of the stories of this class,[146] the father is a hunter who is perishing with cold one night and who makes the usual promise as the condition of his being allowed to warm himself at a fire guarded by a devil. Being in consequence of this deprived of a son, he becomes very sad and drinks himself to death. "The priest will not bury his sinful body, so it is thrust into a hole at a crossway," and he falls into the power of "that very same devil," who turns him into a horse and uses him as a beast of burden. At last he is released by his son, who has forced the devil to free him after several adventures—one of them being a fight with the evil spirit in the shape of a three-headed snake.

In the Hindoo story of "Brave Seventee Bai,"[147] that heroine kills "a very large Cobra" which comes out of a lake. Touching the waters with a magic diamond taken from the snake, she sees them roll back "in a wall on either hand," between which she passes into a splendid garden. In it she finds a lovely girl who proves to be the Cobra's daughter and who is delighted to hear of her serpent-father's death.

Demon haunted waters, which prove fatal to mortals who bathe in or drink of them, often occur in oriental fiction. In one of the Indian stories, for instance,[148] a king is induced to order his escort to bathe in a lake which is the abode of a Rákshasa or demon. They leap into the water simultaneously and are all devoured by the terrible man-eater. From the assaults of such a Rákshasa as this it was that Buddha, who

---

145 Chort, a word which, as has been stated, sometimes means a demon, sometimes the Devil.

146 Afanasief, viii. p. 343.

147 "Old Deccan Days," pp. 34–5. Compare with the conduct of the Cobra's daughter that of Angaraka, the daughter of the Daitya who, under the form of a wild boar, is chased underground by Chandasena. Brockhaus's "Mährchensammlung des Somadeva Bhatta," 1843, vol. i. pp. 110–13.

148 "Panchatantra," v. 10.

was at the time a monkey, preserved himself and 80,000 of his brother monkeys, by suggesting that they should drink from the tank in which the demon lay in wait for them, "through reeds previously made completely hollow by their breath."[149]

* * * * *

From these male personifications of evil—from the Snake, Koshchei and the Water King—we will now turn to their corresponding female forms. By far the most important beings of the latter class are those malevolent enchantresses who form two closely related branches of the same family. Like their sisters all over the world, they are, as a general rule, old, hideous and hateful. They possess all kinds of supernatural powers but their wits are often dull. They wage constant war with mankind but the heroes of storyland find them as easily overcome as the males of their family. In their general character they bear a strong resemblance to the Giantesses, Lamias, female Trolls, Ogresses, Dragonesses, &c., of Europe but in some of their traits they differ from those well-known beings and therefore they are worthy of a detailed notice.

In several of the stories which have already been quoted, a prominent part is played by the Baba Yaga, a female fiend whose name has given rise to much philological discussion of a somewhat unsatisfactory nature.[150] Her appearance is that of a tall, gaunt hag, with dishevelled hair. Sometimes she is seen lying stretched out from one corner to the other of a miserable hut, through the ceiling of which passes her long iron nose; the hut is supported "by fowl's legs," and stands at the edge of a forest towards which its entrance looks. When the proper words are addressed to it, the hut revolves upon its slender supports, so as to turn its back instead of its

---

149 Upham's "Sacred and Historical Books of Ceylon," iii. 287.

150 Afanasief says (P.V.S. iii. 588), "As regards the word yaga (yega, Polish jedza, jadza, jedzi-baba, Slovak, jenzi, jenzi, jezi-baba, Bohemian, jezinka, Galician yazya) it answers to the Sanskrit ahi = snake."

front to the forest. Sometimes, as in the next story, the Baba Yaga appears as the mistress of a mansion, which stands in a courtyard enclosed by a fence made of dead men's bones. When she goes abroad she rides in a mortar, which she urges on with a pestle, while she sweeps away the traces of her flight with a broom. She is closely connected with the Snake in different forms; in many stories, indeed, the leading part has been ascribed by one narrator to a Snake and by another to a Baba Yaga. She possesses the usual magic apparatus by which enchantresses work their wonders; the Day and the Night (according to the following story) are among her servants, the entire animal world lies at her disposal. On the whole she is the most prominent among the strange figures with which the Skazkas make us acquainted. Of the stories which especially relate to her the following may be taken as a fair specimen.

THE BABA YAGA.[151]

To defeat a Baba Yaga, tend her familiars . . .

ONCE UPON A TIME there was an old couple. The husband lost his wife and married again. But he had a daughter by the first marriage, a young girl and she found no favour in the eyes of her evil stepmother, who used to beat her and consider how she could get her killed outright. One day the father went away somewhere or other, so the stepmother said to the girl, "Go to your aunt, my sister and ask her for a needle and thread to make you a shift."

Now that aunt was a Baba Yaga. Well, the girl was no fool, so she went to a real aunt of hers first and says she:

"Good morning, auntie!"

"Good morning, my dear! what have you come for?"

"Mother has sent me to her sister, to ask for a needle and thread to make me a shift."

Then her aunt instructed her what to do. "There is a birch-tree there, niece, which would hit you in the eye—you must tie a ribbon round it; there are doors which would creak and bang—you must pour oil on their hinges; there are dogs which would tear you in pieces—you must throw them these rolls; there is a cat which would scratch your eyes out—you must give it a piece of bacon."

So the girl went away and walked and walked, till she came to the place. There stood a hut and in it sat weaving the Baba Yaga, the Bony-shanks.

"Good morning, auntie," says the girl.

"Good morning, my dear," replies the Baba Yaga.

151 Afanasief, i. No. 3 b. From the Voroneje Government.

"Mother has sent me to ask you for a needle and thread to make me a shift."

"Very well; sit down and weave a little in the meantime."

So the girl sat down behind the loom and the Baba Yaga went outside and said to her servant-maid:

"Go and heat the bath and get my niece washed; and mind you look sharp after her. I want to breakfast off her."

Well, the girl sat there in such a fright that she was as much dead as alive. Presently she spoke imploringly to the servant-maid, saying:

"Kinswoman dear, do please wet the firewood instead of making it burn; and fetch the water for the bath in a sieve." And she made her a present of a handkerchief.

The Baba Yaga waited awhile; then she came to the window and asked:

"Are you weaving, niece? are you weaving, my dear?"

"Oh yes, dear aunt, I'm weaving." So the Baba Yaga went away again and the girl gave the Cat a piece of bacon and asked:

"Is there no way of escaping from here?"

"Here's a comb for you and a towel," said the Cat; "take them and be off. The Baba Yaga will pursue you but you must lay your ear on the ground and when you hear that she is close at hand first of all throw down the towel. It will become a wide, wide river. And if the Baba Yaga gets across the river and tries to catch you, then you must lay your ear on the ground again and when you hear that she is close at hand throw down the comb. It will become a dense, dense forest; through that she won't be able to force her way anyhow."

The girl took the towel and the comb and fled. The dogs would have rent her but she threw them the rolls and they let her go by; the doors would have begun to bang but she poured oil on their hinges and they let her pass through; the birch-tree would have poked her eyes out but she tied the ribbon around it and it let her pass on. And the Cat sat down to the loom and worked away; muddled everything about, if it didn't do much weaving. Up came the Baba Yaga to the window and asked:

"Are you weaving, niece? are you weaving, my dear?"

"I'm weaving, dear aunt, I'm weaving," gruffly replied the Cat.

The Baba Yaga rushed into the hut, saw that the girl was gone and took to beating the Cat and abusing it for not having scratched the girl's eyes out. "Long as I've served you," said the Cat, "you've never given me so much as a bone; but she gave me bacon." Then the Baba Yaga pounced upon the dogs, on the doors, on the birch-tree and on the servant-maid and set to work to abuse them all and to knock them about. Then the dogs said to her, "Long as we've served you, you've never so much as pitched us a burnt crust; but she gave us rolls to eat." And the doors said, "Long as we've served you, you've never poured even a drop of water on our hinges; but she poured oil on us." The birch-tree said, "Long as I've served you, you've never tied a single thread round me; but she fastened a ribbon around me." And the servant-maid said, "Long as I've served you, you've never given me so much as a rag; but she gave me a handkerchief."

The Baba Yaga, bony of limb, quickly jumped into her mortar, sent it flying along with the pestle, sweeping away the while all traces of its flight with a broom and set off in pursuit of the girl. Then the girl put her ear to the ground and when she heard that the Baba Yaga was chasing her and was now close at hand she flung down the towel. And it became a wide, such a wide river! Up came the Baba Yaga to the river and gnashed her teeth with spite; then she went home for her oxen and drove them to the river. The oxen drank up every drop of the river and then the Baba Yaga began the pursuit anew. But the girl put her ear to the ground again and when she heard that the Baba Yaga was near, she flung down the comb and instantly a forest sprang up, such an awfully thick one! The Baba Yaga began gnawing away at it but however hard she worked, she couldn't gnaw her way through it, so she had to go back again.

But by this time the girl's father had returned home and he asked:

"Where's my daughter?"

"She's gone to her aunt's," replied her stepmother.

Soon afterwards the girl herself came running home.

"Where have you been?" asked her father.

"Ah, father!" she said, "mother sent me to aunt's to ask for a needle and thread to make me a shift. But aunt's a Baba Yaga and she wanted to eat me!"

"And how did you get away, daughter?"

"Why like this," said the girl and explained the whole matter. As soon as her father had heard all about it, he became wroth with his wife and shot her. But he and his daughter lived on and flourished and everything went well with them.

~

In one of the numerous variants of this story[152] the heroine is sent by her husband's mother to the Baba Yaga's and the advice which saves her comes from her husband. The Baba Yaga goes into another room "in order to sharpen her teeth," and while she is engaged in that operation the girl escapes, having previously—by the advice of the Cat, to which she had given a lump of butter—spat under the threshold. The spittle answers for her in her absence, behaving as do, in other folktales, drops of blood or rags dipped in blood or apples or eggs or beans or stone images or wooden puppets.[153]

The magic comb and towel, by the aid of which the girl effects her escape, constantly figure in Skazkas of this class and always produce the required effect. A brush, also, is

---

152 Khudyakof, No. 60.
153 See Grimm, KM. iii. 97-8. Cf. R. Köhler in "Orient und Occident," ii. 112.

frequently introduced, from each bristle of which springs up a wood. In one story, however, the brush gives rise to mountains and a *golik* or bathroom whisk, turns into a forest. The towel is used, also, for the purpose of constructing or annihilating a bridge. Similar instruments are found in the folktales of every land whether they appear as the brush, comb and mirror of the German water-sprite;[154] or the rod, stone and pitcher of water of the Norse Troll;[155] or the knife, comb and handful of salt which, in the Modern Greek story, save Asterinos and Pulja from their fiendish mother;[156] or the twig, the stone and the bladder of water, found in the ear of the filly, which saves her master from the Gaelic giant;[157] or the brush, comb and egg, the last of which produces a frozen lake with "mirror-smooth" surface, whereon the pursuing Old Prussian witch slips and breaks her neck;[158] or the wand which causes a river to flow and a mountain to rise between the youth who waves it and the "wicked old Rákshasa" who chases him in the Deccan story;[159] or the handful of earth, cup of water and dry sticks and match, which impede and finally destroy the Rákshasa in the almost identical episode of Somadeva's tale of "The Prince of Varddhamána."[160]

In each instance they appear to typify the influence which the supernatural beings to whom they belonged were supposed to exercise over the elements. It has been thought strange that such stress should be laid on the employment of certain toilet-articles, to the use of which the heroes of folktales do not appear to have been greatly addicted. But it is evident that like produces like in the transformation in question. In

154 Grimm, No. 79. "Die Wassernixe."
155 Asbjörnsen and Moe, No. 14. Dasent, p. 362. "The Widow's Son."
156 Hahn, No. 1.
157 Campbell's "Tales of the West Highlands," No. 2
158 Töppen's "Aberglauben aus Masuren," p. 146.
159 Miss Frere's "Old Deccan Days," p. 63.
160 "Kathásaritságara," vii. ch. xxxix. Translated by Wilson, "Essays," ii. 137. Cf. Brockhaus in the previously quoted "Berichte," 1861, p. 225-9. For other forms, see R. Köhler in "Orient and Occident," vol. ii. p. 112.

the oldest form of the story, the Sanskrit, a handful of earth turns into a mountain, a cup of water into a river. Now, metaphorically speaking, a brush may be taken as a miniature wood; the common use of the term brushwood is a proof of the general acceptance of the metaphor. A comb does not at first sight appear to resemble a mountain but its indented outline may have struck the fancy of many primitive peoples as being a likeness to a serrated mountain range. Thence comes it that in German *Kamm* means not only a comb but also (like the Spanish *Sierra*) a mountain ridge or crest.[161]

In one of the numerous stories[162] about the Baba Yaga, four heroes are wandering about the world together; when they come to a dense forest in which a small izba or hut, is twirling round on "a fowl's leg." Ivan, the youngest of the party, utters the magical formula "Izbushka, Izbushka! stand with back to the forest and front towards us," and "the hut faces towards them, its doors and windows open of their own accord." The heroes enter and find it empty. One of the party then remains indoors, while the rest go out to the chase. The hero who is left alone prepares a meal and then, "after washing his head, sits down by the window to comb his hair." Suddenly a stone is lifted and from under it appears a Baba Yaga, driving in her mortar, with a dog yelping at her heels. She enters the hut and after some short parley, seizes her pestle and begins beating the hero with it until he falls prostrate. Then she cuts a strip out of his back, eats up the whole of the viands he has prepared for his companions and disappears. After a time the beaten hero recovers his senses, "ties up his head with a handkerchief," and sits groaning until his comrades return. Then he makes some excuse for not having got any supper ready for them but says nothing about what has really happened to him.

---

161 See, however, Mr. Campbell's remarks on this subject, in "Tales of the West Highlands," i. pp. lxxvii-lxxxi.

162 Afanasief, viii. No. 6.

On the next day the second hero is treated in the same manner by the Baba Yaga and on the day after that the third undergoes a similar humiliation. But on the fourth day it falls to the lot of the young Ivan to stay in the hut alone. The Baba Yaga appears as usual and begins thumping him with her pestle; but he snatches it from her, beats her almost to death with it, cuts three strips out of her back and then locks her up in a closet. When his comrades return, they are surprised to find him unhurt and a meal prepared for them but they ask no questions. After supper they all take a bath and then Ivan remarks that each of his companions has had a strip cut out of his back. This leads to a full confession, on hearing which Ivan "runs to the closet, takes those strips out of the Baba Yaga and applies them to their backs," which immediately become cured. He then hangs up the Baba Yaga by a cord tied to one foot, at which cord all the party shoot. At length it is severed and she drops. As soon as she touches the ground, she runs to the stone from under which she had appeared, lifts it and disappears.[163]

The rest of the story is very similar to that of "Norka," which has already been given, only instead of the beast of that name we have the Baba Yaga, whom Ivan finds asleep, with a magic sword at her head. Following the advice of her daughters, three fair maidens whom he meets in her palace, Ivan does not attempt to touch the magic sword while she sleeps. But he awakes her gently and offers her two golden apples on a silver dish. She lifts her head and opens her mouth, whereupon he seizes the sword and cuts her head off. As is usual in the stories of this class, his comrades, after hoisting the maidens aloft, cut the cord and let him fall back into the abyss. But he escapes and eventually "he slays all the three heroes and flings their bodies on the plain for wild beasts to devour."

---

163 See the third tale, of the "Siddhi Kür," Jülg's "Kalm. Märchen," pp. 17-19.

This Skazka is one of the many versions of a widespread tale, which tells how the youngest of a party, usually consisting of three persons, overcomes some supernatural foe, generally a dwarf, who had been more than a match for his companions. The most important of these versions is the Lithuanian story of the carpenter who overcomes a Laume—a being in many respects akin to the Baba Yaga—who has proved too strong for his comrades, Perkun and the Devil.[164]

The practice of cutting strips from an enemy's back is frequently referred to in the Skazkas—much more frequently than in the German and Norse stories. It is not often that such strips are turned to good account but in the Skazka with which we have just been dealing, Ivan finding the rope by which he is being lowered into the abyss too short, ties to the end of it the three strips he has cut from the Baba Yaga's back and so makes it sufficiently long. They are often exacted as the penalty of losing a wager, as well in the Skazkas as elsewhere.[165] In a West-Slavonian story about a wager of this kind, the winner cuts off the loser's nose.[166] In the Gaelic stories it is not an uncommon incident for a man to have "a strip of skin cut off him from his crown to his sole."[167]

The Baba Yaga generally kills people in order to eat them. Her house is fenced about with the bones of the men whose flesh she has devoured; in one story she offers a human arm, by way of a meal, to a girl who visits her. But she is also represented in one of the stories[168] as petrifying her victims.

---

164 Schleicher's "Litauische Märchen," No. 39. (I have given an analysis of the story in the "Songs of the Russian People," p. 101.) In the variant of the story in No. 38, the comrades are the hero Martin, a smith and a tailor. Their supernatural foe is a small gnome with a very long beard. He closely resembles the German "Erdmänneken" (Grimm, No. 91) and the "Männchen," in "Der starke Hans" (Grimm, No. 166.)

165 Hahn, No. 11. Schleicher, No. 20, &c., &c.

166 Wenzig, No. 2.

167 "Tales of the West Highlands," ii. p. 15. Mr. Campbell says "I believe such a mode of torture can be traced amongst the Scandinavians, who once owned the Western Islands." But the Gaelic "Binding of the Three Smalls," is unknown to the Skazkas.

168 Erlenvein, No. 3.

This trait connects her with Medusa and the three sister Baba Yagas with the three Gorgones. The Russian Gorgo's method of petrifaction is singular. In the story referred to, Ivan Dévich (Ivan the servant-maid's son) meets a Baba Yaga, who plucks one of her hairs, gives it to him and says, "Tie three knots and then blow." He does so and both he and his horse turn into stone. The Baba Yaga places them in her mortar, pounds them to bits and buries their remains under a stone. A little later comes Ivan Dévich's comrade, Prince Ivan. Him also the Yaga attempts to destroy but he feigns ignorance and persuades her to show him how to tie knots and to blow. The result is that she becomes petrified herself. Prince Ivan puts her in her own mortar and proceeds to pound her therein, until she tells him where the fragments of his comrade are and what he must do to restore them to life.

The Baba Yaga usually lives by herself but sometimes she appears in the character of the house-mother. One of the Skazkas[169] relates how a certain old couple, who had no children, were advised to get a number of eggs from the village—one from each house—and to place them under a sitting hen. From the forty-one eggs thus obtained and treated are born as many boys, all but one of whom develop into strong men but the forty-first long remains a poor weak creature, a kind of "Hop-o'-my-thumb." They all set forth to seek brides and eventually marry the forty-one daughters of a Baba Yaga. On the wedding night she intends to kill her sons-in-law; but they, acting on the advice of him who had been the weakling of their party but who has become a mighty hero, exchange clothes with their brides before "lying down to sleep." Accordingly the Baba Yaga's "trusty servants" cut off the heads of her daughters instead of those of her sons-in-law. Those youths arise, stick the heads of their brides on

169 Afanasief, vii. No. 30.

iron spikes all round the house and gallop away. When the Baba Yaga awakes in the morning, looks out of the window and sees her daughters' heads on their spikes, she flies into a passion, calls for "her burning shield," sets off in pursuit of her sons-in-law and "begins burning up everything on all four sides with her shield." A magic, bridge-creating kerchief, however, enables the fugitives to escape from their irritated mother-in-law.

In one story[170] the heroine is ordered to swing the cradle in which reposes a Baba Yaga's infant son, whom she is ordered to address in terms of respect when she sings him lullabies; in others she is told to wash a Baba Yaga's many children, whose appearance is usually unprepossessing. One girl, for instance, is ordered by a Baba Yaga to heat the bath but the fuel given her for the purpose turns out to be dead men's bones. Having got over this difficulty, thanks to the advice of a sparrow which tells her where to look for wood, she is sent to fetch water in a sieve. Again the sparrow comes to her rescue telling her to line the sieve with clay. Then she is told to wait upon the Baba Yaga's children in the bathroom. She enters it and presently in come "worms, frogs, rats and all sorts of insects." These, which are the Baba Yaga's children, she soaps over and otherwise treats in the approved Russian-bath style and afterwards she does as much for their mother. The Baba Yaga is highly pleased, calls for a "samovar" (or urn) and invites her young bath-woman to drink tea with her. And finally she sends her home with a blue coffer, which turns out to be full of money. This present excites the cupidity of her stepmother, who sends her own daughter to the Baba Yaga's, hoping that she will bring back a similar treasure. The Baba Yaga gives the same orders as before to the new-comer but that conceited young person fails to carry them out. She cannot make the

170 Khudyakof, No. 97.

bones burn, nor the sieve hold water but when the sparrow offers its advice she only boxes its ears. And when the "rats, frogs and all manner of vermin," enter the bathroom, "she crushed half of them to death," says the story; "the rest ran home and complained about her to their mother." And so the Baba Yaga, when she dismisses her, gives her a red coffer instead of a blue one. Out of it, when it is opened, issues fire, which consumes both her and her mother.[171]

Similar to this story in many of its features as well as in its catastrophe is one of the most spirited and dramatic of all the Skazkas, that of—

171 Khudyakof, No. 14. Erlenvein, No. 9.

VASILISSA THE FAIR.[172]

Vasilia, her dolly and the Baba Yaga . . .

IN A CERTAIN KINGDOM there lived a merchant. Twelve years did he live as a married man but he had only one child, Vasilissa the Fair. When her mother died, the girl was eight years old. And on her deathbed the merchant's wife called her little daughter to her, took out from under the bedclothes a doll, gave it to her and said, "Listen, Vasilissa, dear; remember and obey these last words of mine. I am going to die. And now, together with my parental blessing, I bequeath to you this doll. Keep it always by you and never show it to anybody; and whenever any misfortune comes upon you, give the doll food and ask its advice. When it has fed, it will tell you a cure for your troubles." Then the mother kissed her child and died.

After his wife's death, the merchant mourned for her a befitting time and then began to consider about marrying again. He was a man of means. It wasn't a question with him of girls (with dowries); more than all others, a certain widow took his fancy. She was middle-aged and had a couple of daughters of her own just about the same age as Vasilissa. She must needs be both a good housekeeper and an experienced mother.

Well, the merchant married the widow but he had deceived himself, for he did not find in her a kind mother for his Vasilissa. Vasilissa was the prettiest girl[173] in all the village; but her stepmother and stepsisters were jealous of her beauty and tormented her with every possible sort of toil, in order

172 Afanasief, iv. No. 44.
173 The first krasavitsa or beauty.

that she might grow thin from over-work and be tanned by the sun and the wind. Her life was made a burden to her! Vasilissa bore everything with resignation and every day grew plumper and prettier, while the stepmother and her daughters lost flesh and fell off in appearance from the effects of their own spite, notwithstanding that they always sat with folded hands like fine ladies.

But how did that come about? Why, it was her doll that helped Vasilissa. If it hadn't been for it, however could the girl have got through all her work? And therefore it was that Vasilissa would never eat all her share of a meal but always kept the most delicate morsel for her doll; and at night, when all were at rest, she would shut herself up in the narrow chamber[174] in which she slept and feast her doll, saying[175] the while:

"There, dolly, feed; help me in my need! I live in my father's house but never know what pleasure is; my evil stepmother tries to drive me out of the white world; teach me how to keep alive and what I ought to do."

Then the doll would eat and afterwards give her advice and comfort her in her sorrow and next day it would do all Vasilissa's work for her. She had only to take her ease in a shady place and pluck flowers and yet all her work was done in good time; the beds were weeded and the pails were filled and the cabbages were watered and the stove was heated. Moreover, the doll showed Vasilissa herbs which prevented her from getting sunburnt. Happily did she and her doll live together.

Several years went by. Vasilissa grew up and became old enough to be married.[176] All the marriageable young men in

---

174 Chulanchik. The chulan is a kind of closet, generally used as a storeroom for provisions, &c.

175 Prigovarivaya, the word generally used to express the action of a person who utters a charm accompanied by a gesture of the hand or finger.

176 Became a nevyesta, a word meaning "a marriageable maiden," or "a betrothed girl," or "a bride."

the town sent to make an offer to Vasilissa; at her stepmother's daughters not a soul would so much as look. Her stepmother grew even more savage than before and replied to every suitor—

"We won't let the younger marry before her elders."

And after the suitors had been packed off, she used to beat Vasilissa by way of wreaking her spite.

Well, it happened one day that the merchant had to go away from home on business for a long time. Thereupon the stepmother went to live in another house; and near that house was a dense forest and in a clearing in that forest there stood a hut,[177] and in the hut there lived a Baba Yaga. She never let anyone come near her dwelling and she ate up people like so many chickens.

Having moved into the new abode, the merchant's wife kept sending her hated Vasilissa into the forest on one pretence or another. But the girl always got home safe and sound; the doll used to show her the way and never let her go near the Baba Yaga's dwelling.

The autumn season arrived. One evening the stepmother gave out their work to the three girls; one she set to lace-making, another to knitting socks and the third, Vasilissa, to weaving; and each of them had her allotted amount to do. By-and-by she put out the lights in the house, leaving only one candle alight where the girls were working and then she went to bed. The girls worked and worked. Presently the candle wanted snuffing; one of the stepdaughters took the snuffers, as if she were going to clear the wick but instead of doing so, in obedience to her mother's orders, she snuffed the candle out, pretending to do so by accident.

"What shall we do now?" said the girls. "There isn't a spark of fire in the house and our tasks are not yet done. We must go to the Baba Yaga's for a light!"

---

177 Ishbushka, a little izba or cottage.

"My pins give me light enough," said the one who was making lace. "I shan't go."

"And I shan't go, either," said the one who was knitting socks. "My knitting-needles give me light enough."

"Vasilissa, you must go for the light," they both cried out together; "be off to the Baba Yaga's!"

And they pushed Vasilissa out of the room.

Vasilissa went into her little closet, set before the doll a supper which she had provided beforehand and said:

"Now, dolly, feed and listen to my need! I'm sent to the Baba Yaga's for a light. The Baba Yaga will eat me!"

The doll fed and its eyes began to glow just like a couple of candles.

"Never fear, Vasilissa dear!" it said. "Go where you're sent. Only take care to keep me always by you. As long as I'm with you, no harm will come to you at the Baba Yaga's."

So Vasilissa got ready, put her doll in her pocket, crossed herself and went out into the thick forest.

As she walks she trembles. Suddenly a horseman gallops by. He is white and he is dressed in white, under him is a white horse and the trappings of the horse are white—and the day begins to break.

She goes a little further and a second rider gallops by. He is red, dressed in red and sitting on a red horse—and the sun rises.

Vasilissa went on walking all night and all next day. It was only towards the evening that she reached the clearing on which stood the dwelling of the Baba Yaga. The fence around it was made of dead men's bones; on the top of the fence were stuck human skulls with eyes in them; instead of uprights at the gates were men's legs; instead of bolts were arms; instead of a lock was a mouth with sharp teeth.

Vasilissa was frightened out of her wits and stood still as if rooted to the ground.

Suddenly there rode past another horseman. He was black, dressed all in black and on a black horse. He galloped up to the Baba Yaga's gate and disappeared, just as if he had sunk through the ground—and night fell. But the darkness did not last long. The eyes of all the skulls on the fence began to shine and the whole clearing became as bright as if it had been midday. Vasilissa shuddered with fear but stopped where she was, not knowing which way to run.

Soon there was heard in the forest a terrible roar. The trees cracked, the dry leaves rustled; out of the forest came the Baba Yaga, riding in a mortar, urging it on with a pestle, sweeping away her traces with a broom. Up she drove to the gate, stopped short, and snuffing the air around her, cried:—

"Faugh! Faugh! I smell Russian flesh![178] Who's there?"

Vasilissa went up to the hag in a terrible fright, bowed low before her and said:—

"It's me, granny. My stepsisters have sent me to you for a light."

"Very good," said the Baba Yaga; "I know them. If you'll stop awhile with me first and do some work for me, I'll give you a light. But if you won't, I'll eat you!"

Then she turned to the gates and cried:—

"Ho, thou firm fence of mine, be thou divided! And ye, wide gates of mine, do ye fly open!"

The gates opened and the Baba Yaga drove in, whistling as she went and after her followed Vasilissa; and then everything shut to again. When they entered the sitting-room, the Baba Yaga stretched herself out at full length and said to Vasilissa:

"Fetch out what there is in the oven; I'm hungry."

Vasilissa lighted a splinter[179] at one of the skulls which were on the fence and began fetching meat from the oven and

---

178 "Phu, Phu! there is a Russian smell!" the equivalent of our own "Fee, faw, fum, I smell the blood of an Englishman!"

179 Luchina, a deal splinter used instead of a candle.

setting it before the Baba Yaga; and meat enough had been provided for a dozen people. Then she fetched from the cellar kvass, mead, beer and wine. The hag ate up everything, drank up everything. All she left for Vasilissa was a few scraps—a crust of bread and a morsel of sucking-pig. Then the Baba Yaga lay down to sleep, saying:—

"When I go out tomorrow morning, mind you cleanse the courtyard, sweep the room, cook the dinner and get the linen ready. Then go to the corn-bin, take out four quarters of wheat and clear it of other seed.[180] And mind you have it all done—if you don't, I shall eat you!"

After giving these orders the Baba Yaga began to snore. But Vasilissa set the remnants of the hag's supper before her doll, burst into tears and said:—

"Now, dolly, feed, listen to my need! The Baba Yaga has set me a heavy task and threatens to eat me if I don't do it all. Do help me!"

The doll replied:

"Never fear, Vasilissa the Fair! Sup, say your prayers and go to bed. The morning is wiser than the evening!"

Vasilissa awoke very early but the Baba Yaga was already up. She looked out of the window. The light in the skull's eyes was going out. All of a sudden there appeared the white horseman and all was light. The Baba Yaga went out into the courtyard and whistled—before her appeared a mortar with a pestle and a broom. The red horseman appeared—the sun rose. The Baba Yaga seated herself in the mortar and drove out of the courtyard, shooting herself along with the pestle, sweeping away her traces with the broom.

Vasilissa was left alone, so she examined the Baba Yaga's house, wondered at the abundance there was in everything and remained lost in thought as to which work she ought to

---

180 Chernushka, a sort of wild pea.

take to first. She looked up; all her work was done already. The doll had cleared the wheat to the very last grain.

"Ah, my preserver!" cried Vasilissa, "you've saved me from danger!"

"All you've got to do now is to cook the dinner," answered the doll, slipping into Vasilissa's pocket. "Cook away, in God's name and then take some rest for your health's sake!"

Towards evening Vasilissa got the table ready and awaited the Baba Yaga. It began to grow dusky; the black rider appeared for a moment at the gate and all grew dark. Only the eyes of the skulls sent forth their light. The trees began to crack, the leaves began to rustle, up drove the Baba Yaga. Vasilissa went out to meet her.

"Is everything done?" asks the Yaga.

"Please to look for yourself, granny!" says Vasilissa.

The Baba Yaga examined everything, was vexed that there was nothing to be angry about and said:

"Well, well! very good!"

Afterwards she cried:

"My trusty servants, zealous friends, grind this my wheat!"

There appeared three pairs of hands, which gathered up the wheat and carried it out of sight. The Baba Yaga supped, went to bed and again gave her orders to Vasilissa:

"Do just the same tomorrow as to-day; only besides that take out of the bin the poppy seed that is there and clean the earth off it grain by grain. Someone or other, you see, has mixed a lot of earth with it out of spite." Having said this, the hag turned to the wall and began to snore and Vasilissa took to feeding her doll. The doll fed and then said to her what it had said the day before:

"Pray to God and go to sleep. The morning is wiser than the evening. All shall be done, Vasilissa dear!"

The next morning the Baba Yaga again drove out of the courtyard in her mortar and Vasilissa and her doll immediately did all the work. The hag returned, looked at everything and cried, "My trusty servants, zealous friends, press forth oil from the poppy seed!"

Three pairs of hands appeared, gathered up the poppy seed and bore it out of sight. The Baba Yaga sat down to dinner. She ate but Vasilissa stood silently by.

"Why don't you speak to me?" said the Baba Yaga; "there you stand like a dumb creature!"

"I didn't dare," answered Vasilissa; "but if you give me leave, I should like to ask you about something."

"Ask away; only it isn't every question that brings good. 'Get much to know and old soon you'll grow.'"

"I only want to ask you, granny, about something I saw. As I was coming here, I was passed by one riding on a white horse; he was white himself and dressed in white. Who was he?"

"That was my bright Day!" answered the Baba Yaga.

"Afterwards there passed me another rider, on a red horse; red himself and all in red clothes. Who was he?"

"That was my red Sun!"[181] answered the Baba Yaga.

"And who may be the black rider, granny, who passed by me just at your gate?"

"That was my dark Night; they are all trusty servants of mine."

Vasilissa thought of the three pairs of hands but held her peace.

"Why don't you go on asking?" said the Baba Yaga.

"That's enough for me, granny. You said yourself, 'Get too much to know, old you'll grow!'"

"It's just as well," said the Baba Yaga, "that you've only asked about what you saw out of doors, not indoors! In my house I hate having dirt carried out of doors;[182] and as to over-inquisitive people—well, I eat them. Now I'll ask you

181 Krasnoe solnuischko, red (or fair) dear-sun.

182 Equivalent to saying "she liked to wash her dirty linen at home."

something. How is it you manage to do the work I set you to do?"

"My mother's blessing assists me," replied Vasilissa.

"Eh! eh! what's that? Get along out of my house, you bless'd daughter. I don't want bless'd people."

She dragged Vasilissa out of the room, pushed her outside the gates, took one of the skulls with blazing eyes from the fence, stuck it on a stick, gave it to her and said:

"Lay hold of that. It's a light you can take to your stepsisters. That's what they sent you here for, I believe."

Home went Vasilissa at a run, lit by the skull, which went out only at the approach of the dawn; and at last, on the evening of the second day, she reached home. When she came to the gate, she was going to throw away the skull.

"Surely," thinks she, "they can't be still in want of a light at home." But suddenly a hollow voice issued from the skull, saying:

"Throw me not away. Carry me to your stepmother!"

She looked at her stepmother's house and not seeing a light in a single window, she determined to take the skull in there with her. For the first time in her life she was cordially received by her stepmother and stepsisters, who told her that from the moment she went away they hadn't had a spark of fire in the house. They couldn't strike a light themselves anyhow and whenever they brought one in from a neighbour's, it went out as soon as it came into the room.

"Perhaps your light will keep in!" said the stepmother. So they carried the skull into the sitting-room. But the eyes of the skull so glared at the stepmother and her daughters—shot forth such flames! They would fain have hidden themselves but run where they would, everywhere did the eyes follow after them. By the morning they were utterly burnt to cinders. Only Vasilissa was none the worse.[183]

[Next morning Vasilissa "buried the skull," locked up the house and took up her quarters in a neighbouring town. After a time she began to work. Her doll made her a glorious loom and by the end of the winter she had woven a quantity of linen so fine that it might be passed like thread through the eye of a needle. In the spring, after it had been bleached, Vasilissa made a present of it to the old woman with whom she lodged. The crone presented it to the king, who ordered it to be made into shirts. But no seamstress could be found to make them up, until the linen was entrusted to Vasilissa. When a dozen shirts were ready, Vasilissa sent them to the king and as soon as her carrier had started, "she washed herself and combed her hair and dressed herself and sat down at the window." Before long there arrived a messenger demanding her instant appearance at court. And "when she appeared before the royal eyes," the king fell desperately in love with her.

"No; my beauty!" said he, "never will I part with thee; thou shalt be my wife." So he married her; and by-and-by her father returned and took up his abode with her. "And Vasilissa took the old woman into her service and as for the doll—to the end of her life she always carried it in her pocket."]

~

The puppet which plays so important a part in this story is worthy of a special examination. It is called in the original a *Kùkla* (dim. *Kùkolka*), a word designating any sort of puppet or other figure representing either man or beast. In a Little-Russian variant[184] of one of those numerous stories, current in all lands, which commence with the escape of the heroine from an incestuous union, a priest insists on marrying his daughter. She goes to her mother's grave and weeps there. Her dead mother "comes out from her grave," and tells her what to do. The girl obtains from her father a rough dress of pig's skin and two sets of gorgeous apparel; the former she herself

183 I break off the narrative at this point, because what follows is inferior in dramatic interest and I am afraid of diminishing the reader's admiration for one of the best folktales I know. But I give an epitome of the remainder within brackets and in small type.
184 From the Poltava Government. Afanasief, vi. No. 28 b.

assumes, in the latter she dresses up three *Kuklui*, which in this instance were probably mere blocks of wood. Then she takes her place in the midst of the dressed-up forms, which cry, one after the other, "Open, O moist earth, that the fair maiden may enter within thee!" The earth opens and all four sink into it.

This introduction is almost identical with that prefixed to the German story of "Allerleirauh,"[185] except in so far as the puppets are concerned.

Sometimes it is a brother, instead of a father, from whom the heroine is forced to flee. Thus in the story of *Kniaz Danila Govorila*,[186] Prince Daniel the Talker is bent upon marrying his sister, pleading the excuse so often given in stories on this theme, namely, that she is the only maiden whose finger will fit the magic ring which is to indicate to him his destined wife. While she is weeping "like a river," some old women of the mendicant-pilgrim class come to her rescue, telling her to make four *Kukolki* or small puppets and to place one of them in each corner of her room. She does as they tell her. The wedding day arrives, the marriage service is performed in the church and then the bride hastens back to the room. When she is called for—says the story—the puppets in the four corners begin to coo.[187]

"Kuku! Prince Danila!
"Kuku! Govorila.

---

185 Grimm, No. 65. The Wallachian and Lithuanian forms resemble the German (Schott, No. 3. Schleicher, No. 7). In all of them, the heroine is a princess, who runs away from an unnatural father. In one of the Modern Greek versions (Hahn, No. 27), she sinks into the earth. For references to seven other forms of the story, see Grimm, KM., iii. p. 116. In one Russian variant (Khudyakof, No. 54), she hides in a secret drawer, constructed for the purpose in a bedstead; in another (Afanasief, vi. No. 28 a), her father, not recognising her in the pig-skin dress, spits at her and turns her out of the house. In a third, which is of a very repulsive character (ibid. vii. No. 29), the father kills his daughter.

186 Afanasief, vi. No. 18.

187 The Russian word is zakukovali, *i.e.*, "They began to cuckoo." The resemblance between the word kukla, a puppet and the name and cry of the cuckoo (Kukushka) may be merely accidental but that bird has a marked mythological character. See the account of the rite called "the Christening of the Cuckoos," in "Songs of the Russian people," p. 215

"Kuku! He wants to marry,
"Kuku! His own sister.
"Kuku! Split open, O Earth!
"Kuku! Sister, disappear!"

The earth opens and the girl slowly sinks into it. Twice again the puppets sing their song and at the end of its third performance, the earth closes over the head of the rescued bride. Presently in rushes the irritated bridegroom. "No bride is to be seen; only in the corners sit the puppets singing away to themselves." He flies into a passion, seizes a hatchet, chops off their heads and flings them into the fire.[188]

In another version of the same story[189] a son is ordered by his parents to marry his sister after their death. They die and he tells her to get ready to be married. But she has prepared three puppets and when she goes into her room to dress for the wedding, she says to them:

"O Kukolki, (cry) Kuku!"

The first asks, "Why?"

The second replies, "Because the brother his sister takes."

The third says, "Split open, O Earth! disappear, O sister!"

All this is said three times and then the earth opens and the girl sinks "into that world."

In two other Russian versions of the same story, the sister escapes by natural means. In the first[190] she runs away and hides in the hollow of an oak. In the second[191] she persuades a fisherman to convey her across a sea or lake. In a Polish version[192] the sister obtains a magic car, which sinks

---

188 Very like these puppets are the images which reply for the sleeping prince in the opening scene of "De beiden Künigeskinner" (Grimm, No. 113). A doll plays an important part in one of Straparola's stories (Night v. Fable 2). Professor de Gubernatis identifies the Russian puppet with "the moon, the Vedic Râkâ, very small but very intelligent, enclosed in the wooden dress, in the forest of night," "Zoological Mythology," i. 207–8.

189 Afanasief, ii. No. 31.

190 Khudyakof, No. 55.

191 Ibid., No. 83.

192 Wojcicki's "Polnische Volkssagen," &c. Lewestam's translation, iii. No. 8.

underground with her, while the spot on which she has spat replies to every summons which is addressed to her.[193]

Before taking leave of the Baba Yaga, we may glance at a malevolent monster, who seems to be her male counterpart. He appears, however, to be known in South Russia only. Here is an outline of the contents of the solitary story in which he is mentioned. There were two old folks with whom lived two orphan grandchildren, charming little girls. One day the youngest child was sent to drive the sparrows away from her grandfather's peas. While she was thus engaged the forest began to roar and out from it came Verlioka, "of vast stature, one-eyed, crook-nosed, bristly-headed, with tangled beard and moustaches half an ell long and with a wooden boot on his one foot, supporting himself on a crutch and giving vent to a terrible laughter." And Verlioka caught sight of the little girl and immediately killed her with his crutch. And afterwards he killed her sister also and then the old grandmother. The grandfather, however, managed to escape with his life and afterwards, with the help of a drake and other aiders, he wreaked his vengeance on the murderous Verlioka.[194]

We will now turn to another female embodiment of evil, frequently mentioned in the Skazkas—the Witch.[195] She so closely resembles the Baba Yaga both in disposition and in behaviour, that most of the remarks which have been made about that wild being apply to her also. In many cases, indeed, we find that one version of a story will allot to a Baba Yaga

---

193 The germ of all these repulsive stories about incestuous unions, proposed but not carried out, was probably a nature myth akin to that alluded to in the passage of the Rigveda containing the dialogue between Yama and Yami—"where she (the night) implores her brother (the day) to make her his wife and where he declines her offer because, as he says, 'they have called it sin that a brother should marry his sister.'" Max Müller, "Lectures," sixth edition, ii. 557.

194 Afanasief, vii. No. 18.

195 Her name Vyed'ma comes from a Slavonic root véd, answering to the Sanskrit vid—from which springs an immense family of words having reference to knowledge. Vyed'ma and witch are in fact cousins who, though very distantly related, closely resemble each other both in appearance and in character.

the part which in another version is played by a Witch. The name which she bears—that of *Vyed'ma*—is a misnomer; it properly belongs either to the "wise woman," or prophetess, of old times or to her modern representative, the woman to whom Russian superstition attributes the faculties and functions ascribed in olden days by most of our jurisprudents, in more recent times by a few of our rustics, to our own witch. The supernatural being who, in folktales, sways the elements and preys upon mankind, is most inadequately designated by such names as Vyed'ma, *Hexe* or *Witch*, suggestive as those now homely terms are of merely human, though diabolically intensified malevolence. Far more in keeping with the vastness of her powers and the vagueness of her outline, are the titles of Baba Yaga, Lamia, Striga, Troll-Wife, Ogress or Dragoness, under which she figures in various lands. And therefore it is in her capacity of Baba Yaga, rather than in that of Vyed'ma, that we desire to study the behaviour of the Russian equivalent for the terrible female form which figures in the Anglo-Saxon poem as the Mother of Grendel.

From among the numerous stories relating to the *Vyed'ma* we may select the following, which bears her name.

THE WITCH.[196]

The perils of fishing when a witch is close by . . .

THERE ONCE LIVED AN old couple who had one son called Ivashko;[197] no one can tell how fond they were of him!

Well, one day, Ivashko said to his father and mother:

"I'll go out fishing if you'll let me."

"What are you thinking about! you're still very small; suppose you get drowned, what good will there be in that?"

"No, no, I shan't get drowned. I'll catch you some fish; do let me go!"

So his mother put a white shirt on him, tied a red girdle round him and let him go. Out in a boat he sat and said:

Canoe, canoe, float a little farther,
Canoe, canoe, float a little farther!

Then the canoe floated on farther and farther and Ivashko began to fish. When some little time had passed by, the old woman hobbled down to the river side and called to her son:

Ivashechko, Ivashechko, my boy,
Float up, float up, unto the waterside;
I bring thee food and drink.

And Ivashko said:

Canoe, canoe, float to the waterside;
That is my mother calling me.

196 Afanasief, i. No. 4 a. From the Voroneje Government.
197 Ivashko and Ivashechko, are caressing diminutives of Ivan.

The boat floated to the shore: the woman took the fish, gave her boy food and drink, changed his shirt for him and his girdle and sent him back to his fishing. Again he sat in his boat and said:

Canoe, canoe, float a little farther,
Canoe, canoe, float a little farther.

Then the canoe floated on farther and farther and Ivashko began to fish. After a little time had passed by, the old man also hobbled down to the bank and called to his son:

Ivashechko, Ivashechko, my boy,
Float up, float up, unto the waterside;
I bring thee food and drink.

And Ivashko replied:

Canoe, canoe, float to the waterside;
That is my father calling me.

The canoe floated to the shore. The old man took the fish, gave his boy food and drink, changed his shirt for him and his girdle and sent him back to his fishing.

Now a certain witch[198] had heard what Ivashko's parents had cried aloud to him and she longed to get hold of the boy. So she went down to the bank and cried with a hoarse voice:

Ivashechko, Ivashechko, my boy,
Float up, float up, unto the waterside;
I bring thee food and drink.

Ivashko perceived that the voice was not his mother's but was that of a witch and he sang:

198 "Some storytellers," says Afanasief, "substitute the word snake (zmei) in the Skazka for that of witch (vyed'ma)."

Canoe, canoe, float a little farther,
Canoe, canoe, float a little farther;
That is not my mother but a witch
who calls me.

The witch saw that she must call Ivashko with just such a voice as his mother had.

So she hastened to a smith and said to him:

"Smith, smith! make me just such a thin little voice as Ivashko's mother has: if you don't, I'll eat you." So the smith forged her a little voice just like Ivashko's mother's. Then the witch went down by night to the shore and sang:

Ivashechko, Ivashechko, my boy,
Float up, float up, unto the waterside;
I bring thee food and drink.

Ivashko came and she took the fish and seized the boy and carried him home with her. When she arrived she said to her daughter Alenka,[199] "Heat the stove as hot as you can and bake Ivashko well, while I go and collect my friends for the feast." So Alenka heated the stove hot, ever so hot and said to Ivashko,

"Come here and sit on this shovel!"

"I'm still very young and foolish," answered Ivashko: "I haven't yet quite got my wits about me. Please teach me how one ought to sit on a shovel."

"Very good," said Alenka; "it won't take long to teach you."

But the moment she sat down on the shovel, Ivashko instantly pitched her into the oven, slammed to the iron plate in front of it, ran out of the hut, shut the door and hurriedly climbed up ever so high an oak-tree [which stood close by].

Presently the witch arrived with her guests and knocked at the door of the hut. But nobody opened it for her.

---

199 Diminutive of Elena.

"Ah! that cursed Alenka!" she cried. "No doubt she's gone off somewhere to amuse herself." Then she slipped in through the window, opened the door and let in her guests. They all sat down to table and the witch opened the oven, took out Alenka's baked body and served it up. They all ate their fill and drank their fill and then they went out into the courtyard and began rolling about on the grass.

"I turn about, I roll about, having fed on Ivashko's flesh," cried the witch. "I turn about, I roll about, having fed on Ivashko's flesh."

But Ivashko called out to her from the top of the oak:

"Turn about, roll about, having fed on Alenka's flesh!"

"Did I hear something?" said the witch. "No it was only the noise of the leaves." Again the witch began:

"I turn about, I roll about, having fed on Ivashko's flesh!"

And Ivashko repeated:

"Turn about, roll about, having fed on Alenka's flesh!"

Then the witch looked up and saw Ivashko and immediately rushed at the oak on which Ivashko was seated and began to gnaw away at it. And she gnawed and gnawed and gnawed, until at last she smashed two front teeth. Then she ran to a forge and when she reached it she cried, "Smith, smith! make me some iron teeth; if you don't I'll eat you!"

So the smith forged her two iron teeth.

The witch returned and began gnawing the oak again.

She gnawed and gnawed and was just on the point of gnawing it through, when Ivashko jumped out of it into another tree which stood beside it. The oak that the witch had gnawed through fell down to the ground; but then she saw that Ivashko was sitting up in another tree, so she gnashed her teeth with spite and set to work afresh, to gnaw that tree also. She gnawed and gnawed and gnawed—broke two lower teeth and ran off to the forge.

"Smith, smith!" she cried when she got there, "make me some iron teeth; if you don't I'll eat you!"

The smith forged two more iron teeth for her. She went back again and once more began to gnaw the oak.

Ivashko didn't know what he was to do now. He looked out and saw that swans and geese[200] were flying by, so he called to them imploringly:

Oh, my swans and geese,
Take me on your pinions,
Bear me to my father and my mother,
To the cottage of my father and my mother,
There to eat and drink and live in comfort.

"Let those in the centre carry you," said the birds.

Ivashko waited; a second flock flew past and he again cried imploringly:

Oh, my swans and geese!
Take me on your pinions,
Bear me to my father and my mother,
To the cottage of my father and my mother,
There to eat and drink and live in comfort.

"Let those in the rear carry you!" said the birds.

Again Ivashko waited. A third flock came flying up and he cried:

Oh, my swans and geese!
Take me on your pinions,
Bear me to my father and my mother,
To the cottage of my father and my mother,
There to eat and drink and live in comfort.

---

200 Gusi—lebedi, geese—swans.

And those swans and geese took hold of him and carried him back, flew up to the cottage and dropped him in the upper room.

Early the next morning his mother set to work to bake pancakes, baked them and all of a sudden fell to thinking about her boy. "Where is my Ivashko?" she cried; "would that I could see him, were it only in a dream!"

Then his father said, "I dreamed that swans and geese had brought our Ivashko home on their wings."

And when she had finished baking the pancakes, she said, "Now, then, old man, let's divide the cakes: there's for you, father! there's for me! There's for you, father! there's for me."

"And none for me?" called out Ivashko.

"There's for you, father!" went on the old woman, "there's for me."

"And none for me!" [repeated the boy.]

"Why, old man," said the wife, "go and see whatever that is up there."

The father climbed into the upper room and there he found Ivashko. The old people were delighted and asked their boy about everything that had happened. And after that he and they lived on happily together.

~

[That part of this story which relates to the baking and eating of the witch's daughter is well-known in many lands. It is found in the German "Hänsel und Grethel" (Grimm. KM. No. 15 and iii. p. 25, where a number of parallels are mentioned); in the Norse "Askelad" (Asbjörnsen and Moe, No. 1. Dasent, "Boots and the Troll," No. 32), where a Troll's daughter is baked; and "Smörbuk" (Asb. and Moe, No. 52. Dasent, "Buttercup," No. 18), in which the victim is daughter of a "Haugkjoerring," another name for a Troll-wife; in the Servian story of "The Stepmother," &c. (Vuk Karajich, No. 35, pp. 174-5) in which two Chivuti or Jews, are tricked into eating their baked mother; in the Modern Greek stories (Hahn, No. 3 and ii. p. 181), in which the hero bakes (1) a Drakäna, while her husband the

Drakos, is at church, (2) a Lamiopula, during the absence of the Lamia, her mother; and in the Albanian story of "Augenhündin" (Hahn, No. 95), in which the heroine gets rid in a similar manner of Maro, the daughter of that four eyed συκίνεζα. *(See note, ii, 309.) Afanasief also refers (i. p. 121) to Haltrich, No. 37 and Haupt and Schmaler, ii. pp. 172-4. He also mentions a similar tale about a giantess existing among the Baltic Kashoubes. See also the end of the song of Tardanak, showing how he killed "the Seven Headed Jelbegen," Radloff, i. p. 31.]*

A variant of this story (from the Chernigof Government)[201] begins by telling how two old people were childless for a long time. At last the husband went into the forest, felled wood and made a cradle. Into this his wife laid one of the logs he had cut and began swinging it, crooning the while a rune beginning

Swing, blockie dear, swing.

After a little time "behold! the block already had legs. The old woman rejoiced greatly and began singing anew and went on singing until the block became a babe." In this variant the boy rows a silver boat with a golden oar; in another South Russian variant[202] the boat is golden, the oar of silver. In a White-Russian variant quoted by Afanasief (i. p. 118), the place of the witch's daughter is filled by her son, who had been in the habit of alluring to her den by gifts of toys and there devouring, the children from the adjacent villages. Buslaef's "Historical Essays," (i. pp. 313-321) contain a valuable investigation of Kulish's version of this story, which he compares with the romance of "The Knight of the Swan."

In another of the variants of this story[203] Ivanushka is the son of a Baruinya or Lady and he is carried off in a whirlwind by a Baba Yaga. His three sisters go to look for him and each of them in turn finds out where he is and attempts to carry

201 Afanasief, i. No. 4.
202 Kulish, ii. 17.
203 Khudyakof, No. 53.

him off, after sending the Baba Yaga to sleep and smearing her eyelids with pitch. But the two elder sisters are caught on their way home by the Baba Yaga and terribly scratched and torn. The youngest sister, however, succeeds in rescuing her brother, having taken the precaution of propitiating with butter the cat Jeremiah, "who was telling the boy stories and singing him songs." When the Baba Yaga awakes, she tells Jeremiah to scratch her eyes open but he refuses, reminding her that, long as he has lived under her roof, she has never in any way regaled him, whereas the "fair maiden" had no sooner arrived than she treated him to butter. In another variant[204] the bereaved mother sends three servant-maids in search of her boy. Two of them get torn to pieces; the third succeeds in saving Ivanushka from the Baba Yaga, who is so vexed that she pinches her butter-bribed cat to death for not having awakened her when the rescue took place. A comparison of these three stories is sufficient to show how closely connected are the Witch and the Baba Yaga, how readily the name of either of the two may be transferred to the other.

But there is one class of stories in which the *Vyed'ma* is represented as differing from the Baba Yaga, in so far as she is the offspring of parents who are not in any way supernatural or inhuman. Without any apparent cause for her abnormal conduct, the daughter of an ordinary royal house will suddenly begin to destroy and devour all living things which fall in her way—her strength developing as rapidly as her appetite. Of such a nature—to be accounted for only on the supposition that an evil spirit has taken up its abode in a human body[205]—is the witch who appears in the somewhat incomprehensible story that follows.

---

204 Ibid. No. 52.

205 The demonism of Ceylon "represents demons as having human fathers and mothers and as being born in the ordinary course of nature. Though born of human parents, all their qualities are different from those of men. They leave their parents sometime after their birth but before doing so, they generally take care to try their demoniac powers on

THE WITCH AND THE SUN'S SISTER.[206]

Treating strangers with kindness brings reward . . .

IN A CERTAIN FAR-OFF country there once lived a king and queen. And they had an only son, Prince Ivan, who was dumb from his birth. One day, when he was twelve years old, he went into the stable to see a groom who was a great friend of his.

That groom always used to tell him tales [*skazki*] and on this occasion Prince Ivan went to him expecting to hear some stories [*skazochki*] but that wasn't what he heard.

"Prince Ivan!" said the groom, "your mother will soon have a daughter and you a sister. She will be a terrible witch and she will eat up her father and her mother and all their subjects. So go and ask your father for the best horse he has—as if you wanted a gallop—and then, if you want to be out of harm's way, ride away whithersoever your eyes guide you."

Prince Ivan ran off to his father and for the first time in his life, began speaking to him.

At that the king was so delighted that he never thought of asking what he wanted a good steed for but immediately ordered the very best horse he had in his stud to be saddled for the prince.

Prince Ivan mounted and rode off without caring where he went.[207] Long, long did he ride.

At length he came to where two old women were sewing and he begged them to let him live with them. But they said:

---

them." "Demonology and Witchcraft in Ceylon," by Dandris de Silva Gooneratne Modliar. "Journal of Ceylon Branch of Royal Asiatic Society," 1865-6, p. 17.

206 Afanasief, vi. No. 57. From the Ukraine.

207 "Whither [his] eyes look."

"Gladly would we do so, Prince Ivan, only we have now but a short time to live. As soon as we have broken that trunkful of needles and used up that trunkful of thread, that instant will death arrive!"

Prince Ivan burst into tears and rode on. Long, long did he ride. At length he came to where the giant Vertodub was,[208] and he besought him, saying:

"Take me to live with you."

"Gladly would I have taken you, Prince Ivan!" replied the giant, "but now I have very little longer to live. As soon as I have pulled up all these trees by the roots, instantly will come my death!"

More bitterly still did the prince weep as he rode farther and farther on. By-and-by he came to where the giant Vertogor was and made the same request to him but he replied:

"Gladly would I have taken you, Prince Ivan! but I myself have very little longer to live. I am set here, you know, to level mountains. The moment I have settled matters with these you see remaining, then will my death come!"

Prince Ivan burst into a flood of bitter tears and rode on still farther. Long, long did he ride. At last he came to the dwelling of the Sun's Sister. She received him into her house, gave him food and drink and treated him just as if he had been her own son.

The prince now led an easy life. But it was all no use; he couldn't help being miserable. He longed so to know what was going on at home.

He often went to the top of a high mountain and thence gazed at the palace in which he used to live and he could see that it was all eaten away; nothing but the bare walls remained! Then he would sigh and weep. Once when he

---

208 Vertodub, the Tree-extractor (vertyet' = to twirl, dub = tree or oak) is the German Baumdreher or Holzkrummacher; Vertogor the Mountain leveller (gora = mountain) answers to the Steinzerreiber or Felsenkripperer.

returned after he had been thus looking and crying, the Sun's Sister asked him:

"What makes your eyes so red to-day, Prince Ivan?"[209]

"The wind has been blowing in them," said he.

The same thing happened a second time. Then the Sun's Sister ordered the wind to stop blowing. Again a third time did Prince Ivan come back with a blubbered face. This time there was no help for it; he had to confess everything and then he took to entreating the Sun's Sister to let him go, that he might satisfy himself about his old home. She would not let him go but he went on urgently entreating.

So at last he persuaded her and she let him go away to find out about his home. But first she provided him for the journey with a brush, a comb and two youth-giving apples. However old anyone might be, let him eat one of these apples, he would grow young again in an instant.

Well, Prince Ivan came to where Vertogor was. There was only just one mountain left! He took his brush and cast it down on the open plain. Immediately there rose out of the earth, goodness knows whence,[210] high, ever so high mountains, their peaks touching the sky. And the number of them was such that there were more than the eye could see![211] Vertogor rejoiced greatly and blithely recommenced his work.

After a time Prince Ivan came to where Vertodub was and found that there were only three trees remaining there. So he took the comb and flung it on the open plain. Immediately from somewhere or other there came a sound of trees,[212] and forth from the ground arose dense oak forests! each stem more huge than the other! Vertodub was delighted, thanked the Prince and set to work uprooting the ancient oaks.

---

209 Why are you just now so zaplakannoi or blubbered. (Zalplakat' or plakat' = to cry.)
210 Otkuda ni vzyalis.
211 Vidimo—nevidimo, visibly—invisibly.
212 Zashumyeli, they began to produce a shum or noise.

By-and-by Prince Ivan reached the old women and gave each of them an apple. They ate them and straightway became young again. So they gave him a handkerchief; you only had to wave it and behind you lay a whole lake! At last Prince Ivan arrived at home. Out came running his sister to meet him, caressed him fondly.

"Sit thee down, my brother!" she said, "play a tune on the lute while I go and get dinner ready."

The Prince sat down and strummed away on the lute [*gusli*].

Then there crept a mouse out of a hole and said to him in a human voice:

"Save yourself, Prince. Run away quick! your sister has gone to sharpen her teeth."

Prince Ivan fled from the room, jumped on his horse and galloped away back. Meantime the mouse kept running over the strings of the lute. They twanged and the sister never guessed that her brother was off. When she had sharpened her teeth she burst into the room. Lo and behold! not a soul was there, nothing but the mouse bolting into its hole! The witch waxed wroth, ground her teeth like anything and set off in pursuit.

Prince Ivan heard a loud noise and looked back. There was his sister chasing him. So he waved his handkerchief and a deep lake lay behind him. While the witch was swimming across the water, Prince Ivan got a long way ahead. But on she came faster than ever; and now she was close at hand! Vertodub guessed that the Prince was trying to escape from his sister. So he began tearing up oaks and strewing them across the road. A regular mountain did he pile up! there was no passing by for the witch! So she set to work to clear the way. She gnawed and gnawed and at length contrived by hard work to bore her way through; but by this time Prince Ivan was far ahead.

On she dashed in pursuit, chased and chased. Just a little more and it would be impossible for him to escape! But Vertogor spied the witch, laid hold of the very highest of all the mountains, pitched it down all of a heap on the road and flung another mountain right on top of it. While the witch was climbing and clambering, Prince Ivan rode and rode and found himself a long way ahead. At last the witch got across the mountain and once more set off in pursuit of her brother. By-and-by she caught sight of him and exclaimed:

"You shan't get away from me this time!" And now she is close, now she is just going to catch him!

At that very moment Prince Ivan dashed up to the abode of the Sun's Sister and cried:

"Sun, Sun! open the window!"

The Sun's Sister opened the window and the Prince bounded through it, horse and all.

Then the witch began to ask that her brother might be given up to her for punishment. The Sun's Sister would not listen to her, nor would she give him up. Then the witch said:

"Let Prince Ivan be weighed against me, to see which is the heavier. If I am, then I will eat him; but if he is, then let him kill me!"

This was done. Prince Ivan was the first to get into one of the scales; then the witch began to get into the other. But no sooner had she set foot in it than up shot Prince Ivan in the air and that with such force that he flew right up into the sky and into the chamber of the Sun's Sister.

But as for the Witch-Snake, she remained down below on earth.

~

[The word terem (plural terema) which occurs twice in this story (rendered the second time by "chamber") deserves a special notice. It is defined by Dahl, in its antique sense, as "a raised, lofty habitation or part of one—a Boyar's castle—a Seigneur's house—the dwelling-place of a

ruler within a fortress," &c. The "terem of the women," sometimes styled "of the girls," used to comprise the part of a Seigneur's house, on the upper floor, set aside for the female members of his family. Dahl compares it with the Russian tyurma, a prison and the German Thurm. But it seems really to be derived from the Greek τερεμνόν, "anything closely shut fast or closely covered, a room, chamber," &c.

That part of the story which refers to the Cannibal Princess is familiar to the Modern Greeks. In the Syriote tale of "The Strigla" (Hahn, No. 65) a princess devours her father and all his subjects. Her brother, who had escaped while she was still a babe, visits her and is kindly received. But while she is sharpening her teeth with a view towards eating him, a mouse gives him a warning which saves his life. As in the Russian story the mouse jumps about on the strings of a lute in order to deceive the witch, so in the Greek it plays a fiddle. But the Greek hero does not leave his sister's abode. After remaining concealed one night, he again accosts her. She attempts to eat him but he kills her.

In a variant from Epirus (Hahn, ii. p. 283-4) the cannibal princess is called a Chursusissa. Her brother climbs a tree, the stem of which she gnaws almost asunder. But before it falls, a Lamia comes to his aid and kills his sister.

Afanasief (viii. p. 527) identifies the Sun's Sister with the Dawn. The following explanation of the skazka (with the exception of the words within brackets) is given by A. de Gubernatis ("Zool. Myth." i. 183). "Ivan is the Sun, the aurora [or dawn] is his [true] sister; at morning, near the abode of the aurora, that is, in the east, the shades of night [his witch or false sister] go underground and the Sun arises to the heavens; this is the mythical pair of scales. Thus in the Christian belief, St. Michael weighs human souls; those who weigh much sink down into hell and those who are light arise to the heavenly paradise."]

As an illustration of this story, Afanasief (P.V.S. iii. 272) quotes a Little-Russian Skazka in which a man, who is seeking "the Isle in which there is no death," meets with various personages like those with whom the Prince at first wished to stay on his journey and at last takes up his abode with the moon. Death comes in search of him, after a hundred years or so have elapsed and engages in a struggle with the Moon, the result of which is that the man is caught up into the sky and there shines thenceforth "as a star near the moon."

The Sun's Sister is a mythical being who is often mentioned in the popular poetry of the South-Slavonians. A Servian song represents a beautiful maiden, with "arms of silver up to the elbows," sitting on a silver throne which floats on water. A suitor comes to woo her. She waxes wroth and cries,

> Whom wishes he to woo?
> The sister of the Sun,
> The cousin of the Moon,
> The adopted sister of the Dawn.

Then she flings down three golden apples, which the "marriage-proposers" attempt to catch but "three lightnings flash from the sky" and kill the suitor and his friends.

In another Servian song a girl cries to the Sun—

> O brilliant Sun! I am fairer than thou,
> Than thy brother, the bright Moon,
> Than thy sister, the moving star [Venus?].

In South-Slavonian poetry the sun often figures as a radiant youth. But among the Northern Slavonians, as well as the Lithuanians, the sun was regarded as a female being, the bride of the moon. "Thou askest me of what race, of what family I am," says the fair maiden of a song preserved in the Tambof Government—

> My mother is—the beauteous Sun,
> And my father—the bright Moon;

My brothers are—the many Stars,
And my sisters—the white Dawns.[213]

A far more detailed account might be given of the Witch and her near relation the Baba Yaga, as well as of those masculine embodiments of that spirit of evil which is personified in them, the Snake, Koshchei and other similar beings. But the stories which have been quoted will suffice to give at least a general idea of their moral and physical attributes. We will now turn from their forms, so constantly introduced into the skazka-drama, to some of the supernatural figures which are not so often brought upon the stage—to those mythical beings of whom (numerous as may be the traditions about them) the regular "story" does not so often speak, to such personifications of abstract ideas as are less frequently employed to set its conventional machinery in motion.

---

213 Afanasief, P.V.S., i. 80-84. In the Albanian story of "The Serpent Child," (Hahn, No. 100), the heroine, the wife of the man whom forty snake-sloughs encase, is assisted in her troubles by two subterranean beings whom she finds employed in baking. They use their hands instead of shovels and clean out the oven with their breasts. They are called "Sisters of the Sun."

PART III

Mythological

One-eyed Likho, a story of the Polyphemus Cycle—Woe, the Poor Man's Companion—Friday, Wednesday, and Sunday personified as Female Spirits—The Leshy or Wood-Demon—Legends about Rivers—Frost as a Wooer of Maidens—The Whirlwind personified as a species of Snake or Demon—Morfei and Oh, two supernatural beings

SOMEWHAT RESEMBLING THE PICTURE usually drawn of the supernatural Witch in the Skazkas, is that which some of them offer of a personification of evil called Likho. The following story, belonging to the familiar Polyphemus-cycle, will serve to convey an idea of this baleful being, who in it takes a female form.

ONE-EYED LIKHO.[214]

if you go in search of evil . . .

ONCE UPON A TIME there was a smith. "Well now," says he, "I've never set eyes on any harm. They say there's evil (*likho*)[215] in the world. I'll go and seek me out evil." So he went and had a goodish drink and then started in search of evil. On the way he met a tailor.

"Good day," says the Tailor.

"Good day."

"Where are you going?" asks the Tailor.

"Well, brother, everybody says there is evil on earth. But I've never seen any, so I'm going to look for it."

"Let's go together. I'm a thriving man, too and have seen no evil; let's go and have a hunt for some."

Well, they walked and walked till they reached a dark, dense forest. In it they found a small path and along it they went—along the narrow path. They walked and walked along the path and at last they saw a large cottage standing before them. It was night; there was nowhere else to go to. "Look here," they say, "let's go into that cottage." In they went. There was nobody there. All looked bare and squalid. They sat down and remained sitting there some time. Presently in came a tall woman, lank, crooked, with only one eye.

"Ah!" says she, "I've visitors. Good day to you."

---

214 The adjective likhoi has two opposite meanings, sometimes signifying what is evil, hurtful, malicious, &c., sometimes what is bold, vigourous and therefore to be admired. As a substantive, likho conveys the idea of something malevolent or unfortunate. The Polish licho properly signifies uneven. But odd numbers are sometimes considered unlucky. Polish housewives, for instance, think it imprudent to allow their hens to sit on an uneven number of eggs. But the peasantry also describe by Licho an evil spirit, a sort of devil. (Wojcicki in the "Encyklopedyja Powszechna," xvii. p. 17.) "When Likho sleeps, awake it not," says a proverb common to Poland and South Russia.

215 From an article by Borovikovsky in the "Otech. Zap." 1840, No. 2.

"Good day, grandmother. We've come to pass the night under your roof."

"Very good: I shall have something to sup on."

Thereupon they were greatly terrified. As for her, she went and fetched a great heap of firewood. She brought in the heap of firewood, flung it into the stove and set it alight. Then she went up to the two men, took one of them—the Tailor—cut his throat, trussed him and put him in the oven.

Meantime the Smith sat there, thinking, "What's to be done? how's one to save one's life?" When she had finished her supper, the Smith looked at the oven and said:

"Granny, I'm a smith."

"What can you forge?"

"Anything."

"Make me an eye."

"Good," says he; "but have you got any cord? I must tie you up or you won't keep still. I shall have to hammer your eye in."

She went and fetched two cords, one rather thin, the other thicker. Well, he bound her with the one which was thinnest.

"Now then, granny," says he, "just turn over." She turned over and broke the cord.

"That won't do, granny," says he; "that cord doesn't suit."

He took the thick cord and tied her up with it famously.

"Now then, turn away, granny!" says he. She turned and twisted but didn't break the cord. Then he took an awl, heated it red-hot and applied it to her eye—her sound one. At the same moment he caught up a hatchet and hammered away vigourously with the back of it at the awl. She struggled like anything and broke the cord; then she went and sat down at the threshold.

"Ah, villain!" she cried. "You shan't get away from me now!"

He saw that he was in an evil plight again. There he sat, thinking, "What's to be done?"

By-and-by the sheep came home from afield and she drove them into her cottage for the night. Well, the Smith spent the night there, too. In the morning she got up to let the sheep out. He took his sheep-skin pelisse and turned it inside out so that the wool was outside, passed his arms through its sleeves and pulled it well over him and crept up to her as he had been a sheep. She let the flock go out one at a time, catching hold of each by the wool on its back and shoving it out. Well, he came creeping up like the rest. She caught hold of the wool on his back and shoved him out. But as soon as she had shoved him out, he stood up and cried:

"Farewell, Likho! I have suffered much evil (*likha*) at your hands. Now you can do nothing to me."

"Wait a bit!" she replied, "you shall endure still more. You haven't escaped yet!"

The Smith went back through the forest along the narrow path. Presently he saw a golden-handled hatchet sticking in a tree and he felt a strong desire to seize it. Well, he did seize that hatchet and his hand stuck fast to it. What was to be done? There was no freeing it anyhow. He gave a look behind him. There was Likho coming after him and crying:

"There you are, villain! you've not got off yet!"

The Smith pulled out a small knife which he had in his pocket and began hacking away at his hand—cut it clean off and ran away. When he reached his village, he immediately began to show his arm as a proof that he had seen Likho at last.

"Look," says he, "that's the state of things. Here am I," says he, "without my hand. And as for my comrade, she's eaten him up entirely."

~

In a Little-Russian variant of this story, quoted by Afanasief,[216] (III. p. 137) a man, who often hears evil or

216 From an article by Borovikovsky in the "Otech. Zap." 1840, No. 2.

misfortune (*likho*) spoken of, sets out in search of it. One day he sees an iron castle beside a wood, surrounded by a palisade of human bones tipped with skulls. He knocks at the door and a voice cries "What do you want?" "I want evil," he replies. "That's what I'm looking for." "Evil is here," cries the voice. So in he goes and finds a huge, blind giant lying within, stretched on a couch of human bones. "This was Likho (Evil)," says the story, "and around him were seated Zluidni (Woes) and Zhurba (Care)." Finding that Likho intends to eat him, the misfortune-seeker takes to flight. Likho hears the iron doors creak and cries to them to stop the fugitive. "But he had already passed out of doors. Only he lost his right hand on which the door slammed: whereupon he exclaimed 'Here's misfortune, sure enough!'"

The opening of the story of Likho is somewhat similar to that of one of the tales of Indian origin translated by Stanislas Julien from the Chinese. Once upon a time, we are told, a king grew weary of good fortune, so he sent messengers in search of misfortune. A certain god sold it to them, in the shape of a sow which devoured a peck of needles a day. The king's agents took to worrying his subjects for needles and brought such trouble upon the whole kingdom, that his ministers entreated him to have the beast put to death. He consented and it was led forth to die. But neither knife nor axe could penetrate its hide, so they tried to consume it with fire. After a time it became red-hot and then it leaped out from amid the flames and dashed about setting fire to all manner of things. The conflagration spread and was followed by famine, so that the whole land was involved in ruin.[217]

The Polyphemus story has been so thoroughly investigated by Wilhelm Grimm,[218] that there is no occasion to dwell

217 "Les Avadânas," vol. i. No. 9, p. 51.

218 In the "Philogische und historische Abhandlungen," of the Berlin Academy of Sciences for 1857, pp. 1-30. See also Buslaef, "Ist. Och.," i. 327-331.; Campbell's "West Highland Tales," i. p. 132, &c.

upon it here. But the following statement is worthy of notice. The inhabitants of the Ukraine are said still to retain some recollection of the one-eyed nation of Arimaspians of whom Herodotus speaks (Bk. IV. c. 27). According to them the One-Eyes[219] dwell somewhere far off, beyond the seas. The Tartars, during their inroads, used to burn towns and villages, kill old folks and infants and carry off young people. The plumpest of these they used to sell to cannibals who had but one eye apiece, situated in the forehead. And the cannibals would drive away their purchases, like sheep, to their own land and there fatten them up, kill them and eat them. A similar tradition, says Afanasief (VIII. 260) exists also among the Ural Cossacks.

While on the subject of eyes, it may be remarked that the story of "One-Eye, Two-Eyes and Three-Eyes," rendered so familiar to juvenile English readers by translations from the German,[220] appears among the Russian tales in a very archaic and heathenish form. Here is the outline of a version of it found in the Archangel Government.[221] There once was a Princess Marya, whose stepmother had two daughters, one of whom was three-eyed. Now her stepmother hated Marya and used to send her out, with nothing to eat but a dry crust, to tend a cow all day. But "the princess went into the open field, bowed down before the cow's right foot and got plenty to eat and to drink and fine clothes to put on; all day long she followed the cow about dressed like a great lady—when the day came to a close, she again bowed down to the cow's right foot, took off her fine clothes, went home and laid on the table the crust of bread she had brought back with

219 Ednookie (edno or odno = one; oko = eye). A Slavonic equivalent of the name "Arimaspians," from the Scythic arima = one and spû = eye. Mr. Rawlinson associates arima, through farima, with Goth. fruma, Lat. primus, &c. and spû with Lat. root spic or spec—in specio, specto, &c. and with our "spy," &c.

220 Grimm, No. 130, &c.

221 Afanasief, vi. No. 55.

her." Wondering at this, her stepmother sent her two-eyed stepsister to watch her. But Marya uttered the words "Sleep, sleep, one-eye! sleep, sleep, other eye!" till the watcher fell asleep. Then the three-eyed sister was sent and Marya by the same spell sent two of her eyes to sleep but forgot the third. So all was found out and the stepmother had the cow killed. But Marya persuaded her father, who acted as the butcher, to give her a part of the cow's entrails, which she buried near the threshold; and from it there sprang a bush covered with berries and haunted by birds which sang "songs royal and rustic." After a time a Prince Ivan heard of Marya, so he came riding up and offered to marry whichever of the three princesses could fill with berries from the bush a bowl which he brought with him. The stepmother's daughters tried to do so but the birds almost pecked their eyes out and would not let them gather the berries. Then Marya's turn came and when she approached the bush the birds picked the berries for her and filled the bowl in a trice. So she married the prince and lived happily with him for a time.

But after she had borne him a son, she went to pay a visit to her father and her stepmother availed herself of the opportunity to turn her into a goose and to set her own two-eyed daughter in her place. So Prince Ivan returned home with a false bride. But a certain old man took out the infant prince afield and there his mother appeared, flung aside her feather-covering and suckled the babe, exclaiming the while with tears—

"To-day I suckle thee, tomorrow I shall suckle thee but on the third day I shall fly away beyond the dark forests, beyond the high mountains!"

This occurred on two successive days but on the second occasion Prince Ivan was a witness of what took place and he seized her feather-dress and burnt it and then laid hold of her. She first turned into a frog, then assumed various reptile forms and finally became a spindle. This he broke in two and flung one half in front and the other behind him and the spell was broken along with it. So he regained his wife and went home with her. But as for the false wife, he took a gun and shot her.

We will now return to the stories in which Harm or Misery figures as a living agent. To Likho is always attributed a character of unmitigated malevolence and a similar disposition is ascribed by the songs of the people to another being in whom the idea of misfortune is personified. This is *Goré* or Woe, who is frequently represented in popular poetry—sometimes under the name of *Béda* or Misery—as chasing and ultimately destroying the unhappy victims of destiny. In vain do the fugitives attempt to escape. If they enter the dark forest, Woe follows them there; if they rush to the pothouse, there they find Woe sitting; when they seek refuge in the grave, Woe stands over it with a shovel and rejoices.[222] In the following story, however, the gloomy figure of Woe has been painted in a less than usually sombre tone.

---

222 See the "Songs of the Russian People," p. 30.

WOE.[223]

Perhaps, even Woe can be outsmarted . . .

IN A CERTAIN VILLAGE there lived two peasants, two brothers: one of them poor, the other rich. The rich one went away to live in a town, built himself a large house and enrolled himself among the traders. Meanwhile the poor man sometimes had not so much as a morsel of bread and his children—each one smaller than the other—were crying and begging for food. From morning till night the peasant would struggle, like a fish trying to break through ice but nothing came of it all. At last one day he said to his wife:

"Suppose I go to town and ask my brother whether he won't do something to help us."

So he went to the rich man and said:

"Ah, brother mine! do help me a bit in my trouble. My wife and children are without bread. They have to go whole days without eating."

"Work for me this week, then I'll help you," said his brother.

What was there to be done! The poor man betook himself to work, swept out the yard, cleaned the horses, fetched water, chopped firewood.

At the end of the week the rich man gave him a loaf of bread and says:

"There's for your work!"

"Thank you all the same," dolefully said the poor man, making his bow and preparing to go home.

"Stop a bit! come and dine with me tomorrow and bring your wife, too: tomorrow is my name-day, you know."

---

223 Afanasief, v. No. 34. From the Novgorod Government.

"Ah, brother! how can I? you know very well you'll be having merchants coming to you in boots and pelisses but I have to go about in bast shoes and a miserable old grey caftan."

"No matter, come! there will be room even for you."

"Very well, brother! I'll come."

The poor man returned home, gave his wife the loaf and said:

"Listen, wife! we're invited to a party tomorrow."

"What do you mean by a party? who's invited us?"

"My brother! he keeps his name-day tomorrow."

"Well, well! let's go."

Next day they got up and went to the town, came to the rich man's house, offered him their congratulations and sat down on a bench. A number of the name-day guests were already seated at table. All of these the host feasted gloriously but he forgot even so much as to think of his poor brother and his wife; not a thing did he offer them; they had to sit and merely look on at the others eating and drinking.

The dinner came to an end; the guests rose from table and expressed their thanks to their host and hostess; and the poor man did likewise, got up from his bench and bowed down to his girdle before his brother. The guests drove off homewards, full of drink and merriment, shouting, singing songs. But the poor man had to walk back empty.

"Suppose we sing a song, too," he says to his wife.

"What a fool you are!" says she, "people sing because they've made a good meal and had lots to drink; but why ever should you dream of singing?"

"Well, at all events, I've been at my brother's name-day party. I'm ashamed of trudging along without singing. If I sing, everybody will think I've been feasted like the rest."

"Sing away, then, if you like; but I won't!"

The peasant began a song. Presently he heard a voice joining in it. So he stopped and asked his wife:

"Is it you that's helping me to sing with that thin little voice?"

"What are you thinking about! I never even dreamt of such a thing."

"Who is it, then?"

"I don't know," said the woman. "But now, sing away and I'll listen."

He began his song again. There was only one person singing, yet two voices could be heard. So he stopped and asked:

"Woe, is that you that's helping me to sing?"

"Yes, master," answered Woe: "it's I that's helping you."

"Well then, Woe! let's all go on together."

"Very good, master! I'll never depart from you now."

When the peasant got home, Woe bid him to the *kabak* or pothouse.

"I've no money," says the man.

"Out upon you, moujik! What do you want money for? why you've got on a sheep-skin jacket. What's the good of that? It will soon be summer; anyhow you won't be wanting to wear it. Off with the jacket and to the pothouse we'll go."

So the peasant went with Woe into the pothouse and they drank the sheep-skin away.

The next day Woe began groaning—its head ached from yesterday's drinking—and again bade the master of the house have a drink.

"I've no money," said the peasant.

"What do we want money for? Take the cart and the sledge; we've plenty without them."

There was nothing to be done; the peasant could not shake himself free from Woe. So he took the cart and the sledge, dragged them to the pothouse and there he and Woe drank them away. Next morning Woe began groaning more than ever and invited the master of the house to go and drink off the effects of the debauch. This time the peasant drank away his plough and his harrow.

A month hadn't passed before he had got rid of everything he possessed. Even his very cottage he pledged to a neighbour and the money he got that way he took to the pothouse.

Yet another time did Woe come close beside him and say:

"Let us go, let us go to the pothouse!"

"No, no, Woe! it's all very well but there's nothing more to be squeezed out."

"How can you say that? Your wife has got two petticoats: leave her one but the other we must turn into drink."

The peasant took the petticoat, drank it away and said to himself:

"We're cleaned out at last, my wife as well as myself. Not a stick nor a stone is left!"

Next morning Woe saw, on waking, that there was nothing more to be got out of the peasant, so it said:

"Master!"

"Well, Woe?"

"Why, look here. Go to your neighbour and ask him to lend you a cart and a pair of oxen."

The peasant went to the neighbour's.

"Be so good as to lend me a cart and a pair of oxen for a short time," says he. "I'll do a week's work for you in return."

"But what do you want them for?"

"To go to the forest for firewood."

"Well then, take them; only don't overburden them."

"How could you think of such a thing, kind friend!"

So he brought the pair of oxen and Woe got into the cart with him and away he drove into the open plain.

"Master!" asks Woe, "do you know the big stone on this plain?"

"Of course I do."

"Well then if you know it, drive straight up to it."

They came to the place where it was, stopped and got out of the cart. Woe told the peasant to lift the stone; the peasant lifted it, Woe helping him. Well, when they had lifted it there was a pit underneath chock full of gold.

"Now then, what are you staring at!" said Woe to the peasant, "be quick and pitch it into the cart."

The peasant set to work and filled the cart with gold; cleared the pit to the very last ducat. When he saw there was nothing more left:

"Just give a look, Woe," he said; "isn't there some money left in there?"

"Where?" said Woe, bending down; "I can't see a thing."

"Why there; something is shining in yon corner!"

"No, I can't see anything," said Woe.

"Get into the pit; you'll see it then."

Woe jumped in: no sooner had it got there than the peasant closed the mouth of the pit with the stone.

"Things will be much better like that," said the peasant: "if I were to take you home with me, O Woeful Woe, sooner or later you'd be sure to drink away all this money, too!"

The peasant got home, shovelled the money into his cellar, took the oxen back to his neighbour and set about considering how he should manage. It ended in his buying a wood, building a large homestead and becoming twice as rich as his brother.

After a time he went into the town to invite his brother and sister-in-law to spend his name-day with him.

"What an idea!" said his rich brother: "you haven't a thing to eat and yet you ask people to spend your name-day with you!"

"Well, there was a time when I had nothing to eat but now, thank God! I've as much as you. If you come, you'll see for yourself."

"So be it! I'll come," said his brother.

Next day the rich brother and his wife got ready and went to the name-day party. They could see that the former beggar had got a new house, a lofty one, such as few merchants had!

And the moujik treated them hospitably, regaled them with all sorts of dishes, gave them all sorts of meads and spirits to drink. At length the rich man asked his brother:

"Do tell me by what good luck have you grown rich?"

The peasant made a clean breast of everything—how Woe the Woeful had attached itself to him, how he and Woe had drunk away all that he had, to the very last thread, so that the only thing that was left him was the soul in his body. How Woe showed him a treasure in the open field, how he took that treasure and freed himself from Woe into the bargain. The rich man became envious.

"Suppose I go to the open field," thinks he, "and lift up the stone and let Woe out. Of a surety it will utterly destroy my brother and then he will no longer brag of his riches before me!"

So he sent his wife home but he himself hastened into the plain. When he came to the big stone, he pushed it aside and knelt down to see what was under it. Before he had managed to get his head down low enough, Woe had already leapt out and seated itself on his shoulders.

"Ha!" it cried, "you wanted to starve me to death in here! No, no! Now will I never on any account depart from you."

"Only hear me, Woe!" said the merchant: "it wasn't I at all who put you under the stone."

"Who was it then, if it wasn't you?"

"It was my brother put you there but I came on purpose to let you out."

"No, no! that's a lie. You tricked me once; you shan't trick me a second time!"

Woe gripped the rich merchant tight by the neck; the man had to carry it home and there everything began to go wrong with him. From the very first day Woe began again to play its usual part, every day it called on the merchant to renew his drinking.[224] Many were the valuables which went in the pothouse.

"Impossible to go on living like this!" says the merchant to himself. "Surely I've made sport enough for Woe! It's time to get rid of it—but how?"

He thought and thought and hit on an idea. Going into the large yard, he cut two oaken wedges, took a new wheel and drove a wedge firmly into one end of its axle-box. Then he went to where Woe was:

"Hallo, Woe! why are you always idly sprawling there?"

"Why, what is there left for me to do?"

"What is there to do! let's go into the yard and play at hide-and-seek."

Woe liked the idea. Out they went into the yard. First the merchant hid himself; Woe found him immediately. Then it was Woe's turn to hide.

"Now then," says Woe, "you won't find me in a hurry! There isn't a chink I can't get into!"

"Get along with you!" answered the merchant. "Why you couldn't creep into that wheel there and yet you talk about chinks!"

"I can't creep into that wheel? See if I don't go clean out of sight in it!"

Woe slipped into the wheel; the merchant caught up the oaken wedge and drove it into the axle-box from the other side. Then he seized the wheel and flung it, with Woe in it, into the river. Woe was drowned and the merchant began to live again as he had been wont to do of old.

~

In a variant of this story found in the Tula Government we have, in the place of woe, *Nuzhda* or Need. The poor brother and his wife are returning home disconsolately from a party

224 Opokhmyelit'sya: "to drink off the effects of his debauch."

given by the rich brother in honour of his son's marriage. But a draught of water which they take by the way gets into their heads and they set up a song.

"There are two of them singing (says the story) but three voices prolong the strain.

"'Whoever is that?' say they.

"'Thy Need,' answers someone or other.

"'What, my good mother Need!'

"So saying the man laid hold of her and took her down from his shoulders—for she was sitting on them. And he found a horse's head and put her inside it and flung it into a swamp. And afterwards he began to lead a new life—impossible to live more prosperously."

Of course the rich brother becomes envious and takes Need out of the swamp, whereupon she clings to him so tightly that he cannot get rid of her and he becomes utterly ruined.[225]

In another story, from the Viatka Government, the poor man is invited to a house-warming at his rich brother's but he has no present to take with him.

"We might borrow but who would trust us?" says he.

"Why there's Need!" replies his wife with a bitter laugh. "Perhaps she'll make us a present. Surely we've lived on friendly terms with her for an age!"

"Take the feast-day sarafan,"[226] cries Need from behind the stove; "and with the money you get for it buy a ham and take it to your brother's."

"Have you been living here long, Need?" asks the moujik.

"Yes, ever since you and your brother separated."

"And have you been comfortable here?"

"Thanks be to God, I get on tolerably!"

The moujik follows the advice of Need but meets with a cold reception at his brother's. On returning sadly home

225 Erlenvein, No. 21.

226 Our "Sunday gown."

he finds a horse standing by the roadside, with a couple of bags slung across its back. He strikes it with his glove and it disappears, leaving behind it the bags, which turn out to be full of gold. This he gathers up and then goes indoors. After finding out from his wife where she has taken up her quarters for the night, he says:

"And where are you, Need?"

"In the pitcher which stands on the stove."

After a time the moujik asks his wife if she is asleep. "Not yet," she replies. Then he puts the same question to Need, who gives no answer, having gone to sleep. So he takes his wife's last sarafan, wraps up the pitcher in it and flings the bundle into an ice-hole.[227]

In one of the "chapbook" stories (a *lubochnaya skazka*), a poor man "obtained a crust of bread and took it home to provide his wife and boy with a meal but just as he was beginning to cut it, suddenly out from behind the stove jumped Kruchìna,[228] snatched the crust from his hands and fled back again behind the stove. Then the old man began to bow down before Kruchìna and to beseech him[229] to give back the bread, seeing that he and his had nothing to eat. Thereupon Kruchìna replied, "I will not give you back your crust but in return for it I will make you a present of a duck which will lay a golden egg every day," and kept his word.[230]

In Little-Russia the peasantry believe in the existence of small beings, of vaguely defined form, called *Zluidni* who bring *zlo* or evil to every habitation in which they take up their quarters. "May the Zluidni strike him!" is a Little-Russian curse and "The Zluidni have got leave for three days; not in three years will you get rid of them!" is a White-Russian

227 Afanasief, viii. p. 408.

228 Properly speaking "grief," that which morally krushìt or crushes a man.

229 Kruchìna, as an abstract idea, is of the feminine gender. But it is here personified as a male being.

230 Afanasief, v. p. 237.

proverb. In a Little-Russian skazka a poor man catches a fish and takes it as a present to his rich brother, who says, "A splendid fish! thank you, brother, thank you!" but evinces no other sign of gratitude. On his way home the poor man meets an old stranger and tells him his story—how he had taken his brother a fish and had got nothing in return but a "thank ye."

"How!" cries the old man. "A *spasibo*[231] is no small thing. Sell it to me!"

"How can one sell it?" replies the moujik. "Take it pray, as a present!"

"So the *spasibo* is mine!" says the old man and disappears, leaving in the peasant's hands a purse full of gold.

The peasant grows rich and moves into another house. After a time his wife says to him—

"We've been wrong, Ivan, in leaving our millstones in the old house. They nourished us, you see, when we were poor; but now, when they're no longer necessary to us, we've quite forgotten them!"

"Right you are," replies Ivan and sets off to fetch them. When he reaches his old dwelling, he hears a voice saying—

"A bad fellow, that Ivan! now he's rich, he's abandoned us!"

"Who are you?" asks Ivan. "I don't know you a bit."

"Not know us! you've forgotten our faithful service, it seems! Why, we're your Zluidni!"

"God be with you!" says he. "I don't want you!"

"No, no! we will never part from you now!"

"Wait a bit!" thinks Ivan and then continues aloud, "Very good, I'll take you; but only on condition that you bring home my millstones for me."

---

231 Spasibo is the word in popular use as an expression of thanks and it now means nothing more than "thank you!" But it is really a contraction of spasi Bog! "God save (you)!" as our "Good-bye!" is of "God be with you!"

So he laid the millstones on their backs and made them go on in front of him. They all had to pass along a bridge over a deep river; the moujik managed to give the Zluidni a shove and over they went, millstones and all and sank straight to the bottom.[232]

There is a very curious Servian story of two brothers, one of whom is industrious and unlucky and the other idle and prosperous. The poor brother one day sees a flock of sheep and near them a fair maiden spinning a golden thread.

"Whose sheep are these?" he asks.

"The sheep are his whose I myself am," she replies.

"And whose art thou?" he asks.

"I am thy brother's Luck," she answers.

"But where is my Luck?" he continues

"Far away from thee is thy Luck," she replies.

"But can I find her?" he asks.

"Thou canst; go and seek her," she replies.

So the poor man wanders away in search of her. One day he sees a grey-haired old woman asleep under an oak in a great forest, who proves to be his Luck. He asks who it is that has given him such a poor Luck and is told that it is Fate. So he goes in search of Fate. When he finds her, she is living at ease in a large house but day by day her riches wane and her house contracts. She explains to her visitor that her condition at any given hour affects the whole lives of all children born at that time and that he had come into the world at a most unpropitious moment; and she advises him to take his niece Militsa (who had been born at a lucky time) to live in his house and to call all he might acquire her property. This advice he follows and all goes well with him. One day, as he is gazing at a splendid field of corn, a stranger asks him to whom it belongs. In a forgetful moment he replies, "It is

---

232 Maksimovich, "Tri Skazki" (quoted by Afanasief, viii. p. 406).

mine," and immediately the whole crop begins to burn. He runs after the stranger and cries, "Stop, brother! that field isn't mine but my niece Militsa's," whereupon the fire goes out and the crop is saved.[233]

On this idea of a personal Fortune is founded the quaint opening of one of the Russian stories. A certain peasant, known as Ivan the Unlucky, in despair at his constant want of success, goes to the king for advice. The king lays the matter before "his nobles and generals," but they can make nothing of it. At last the king's daughter enters the council chamber and says, "This is my opinion, my father. If he were to be married, the Lord might allot him another sort of Fortune." The king flies into a passion and exclaims:

"Since you've settled the question better than all of us, go and marry him yourself!"

The marriage takes place and brings Ivan good luck along with it.[234]

Similar references to a man's good or bad luck frequently occur in the skazkas. Thus in one of them (from the Grodno Government) a poor man meets "two ladies (*pannui*) and those ladies are—the one Fortune and the other Misfortune."[235] He tells them how poor he is and they agree that it will be well to bestow something on him. "Since he is one of yours," says Luck, "do you make him a present." At length they take out ten roubles and give them to him. He hides the money in a pot and his wife gives it away to a neighbour. Again they assist him, giving him twenty roubles and again his wife gives them away unwittingly. Then the ladies bestow on him two farthings (*groshi*), telling him to give them to fishermen and

233 Vuk Karajich, No. 13.
234 Afanasief, viii. No. 21.
235 Schastie and Neschastie—Luck and Bad-luck—the exact counterparts of the Indian Lakshmí and Alakshmí.

bid them make a cast "for his luck." He obeys and the result is the capture of a fish which brings him in wealth.[236]

In another story[237] a young man, the son of a wealthy merchant, is so unlucky that nothing will prosper with him. Having lost all that his father has left him, he hires himself out, first as a labourer, then as a herdsman. But as, in each capacity, he involves his masters in heavy losses, he soon finds himself without employment. Then he tries another country, in which the king gives him a post as a sort of stoker in the royal distillery, which he soon all but burns down. The king is at first bent upon punishing him but pardons him after hearing his sad tale. "He bestowed on him the name of Luckless,[238] and gave orders that a stamp should be set on his forehead, that no tolls or taxes should be demanded from him and that wherever he appeared he should be given free board and lodging but that he should never be allowed to stop more than twenty-four hours in anyone place." These orders are obeyed and wherever Luckless goes, "nobody ever asks him for his billet or his passport but they give him food to eat and liquor to drink and a place to spend the night in; and next morning they take him by the scruff of the neck and turn him out of doors."[239]

We will now turn from the forms under which popular fiction has embodied some of the ideas connected with Fortune and Misfortune, to another strange group of figures—the

236 Afanasief, iii. No. 9.
237 Afanasief viii. pp. 32-4.
238 Bezdolny (bez = without; dolya = lot, share, etc.).
239 Everyone knows how frequent are the allusions to good and bad fortune in Oriental fiction, so that there is no occasion to do more than allude to the stories in which they occur—one of the most interesting of which is that of Víra-vara in the "Hitopadesa" (chap. iii. Fable 9), who finds one night a young and beautiful woman, richly decked with jewels, weeping outside the city in which dwells his royal master Sudraka and asks her who she is and why she weeps. To which (in Mr. Johnson's translation) she replies "I am the Fortune of this King Sudraka, beneath the shadow of whose arm I have long reposed very happily. Through the fault of the queen the king will die on the third day. I shall be without a protector and shall stay no longer; therefore do I weep." On the variants of this story, see Benfey's "Panchatantra," i. pp. 415-16.

personifications of certain days of the week. Of these, by far the most important is that of Friday.

The Russian name for that day, *Pyatnitsa*,[240] has no such mythological significance as have our own Friday and the French *Vendredi*. But the day was undoubtedly consecrated by the old Slavonians to some goddess akin to Venus or Freyja and her worship in ancient times accounts for the superstitions now connected with the name of Friday. According to Afanasief,[241] the Carinthian name for the day, *Sibne dan*, is a clear proof that it was once holy to Siva, the Lithuanian Seewa, the Slavonic goddess answering to Ceres. In Christian times the personality of the goddess (by whatever name she may have been known) to whom Friday was consecrated became merged in that of St. Prascovia and she is now frequently addressed by the compound name of "Mother Pyatnitsa-Prascovia." As she is supposed to wander about the houses of the peasants on her holy day and to be offended if she finds certain kinds of work going on, they are (or at least they used to be) frequently suspended on Fridays. It is a sin, says a time-honoured tradition, for a woman to sew or spin or weave or buck linen on a Friday and similarly for a man to plait bast shoes, twine cord and the like. Spinning and weaving are especially obnoxious to "Mother Friday," for the dust and refuse thus produced injure her eyes. When this takes place, she revenges herself by plagues of sore-eyes, whitlows and hangnails. In some places the villagers go to bed early on Friday evening, believing that "St. Pyatinka" will punish all whom she finds awake when she roams through the cottage. In others they sweep their floors every Thursday evening, that she may not be annoyed by dust or the like when she comes next day. Sometimes, however, she has been seen, says

240 From pyat = five, Friday being the fifth working day. Similarly Tuesday is called Vtornik, from vtoroi = second; Wednesday is Sereda, "the middle;" Thursday Chetverg, from chetverty = fourth. But Saturday is Subbòta.

241 P.V.S., i. 230. See also Buslaef, "Ist. Och." pp. 323, 503-4.

the popular voice, "all pricked with the needles and pierced by the spindles" of the careless woman who sewed and spun on the day they ought to have kept holy in her honour. As for any work begun on a Friday, it is sure to go wrong.[242]

These remarks will be sufficient to render intelligible the following story of—

242 A tradition of our own relates that the Lords of the Admiralty, wishing to prove the absurdity of the English sailor's horror of Friday, commenced a ship on a Friday, launched her on a Friday, named her "The Friday," procured a Captain Friday to command her and sent her to sea on a Friday, and—she was never heard of again.

FRIDAY.[243]

Do not upset Mother Friday . . .

THERE WAS ONCE A certain woman who did not pay due reverence to Mother Friday but set to work on a distaff-ful of flax, combing and whirling it. She span away till dinnertime, then suddenly sleep fell upon her—such a deep sleep! And when she had gone to sleep, suddenly the door opened and in came Mother Friday, before the eyes of all who were there, clad in a white dress and in such a rage! And she went straight up to the woman who had been spinning, scooped up from the floor a handful of the dust that had fallen out of the flax and began stuffing and stuffing that woman's eyes full of it! And when she had stuffed them full, she went off in a rage—disappeared without saying a word.

When the woman awoke, she began squalling at the top of her voice about her eyes but couldn't tell what was the matter with them. The other women, who had been terribly frightened, began to cry out:

"Oh, you wretch, you! you've brought a terrible punishment on yourself from Mother Friday."

Then they told her all that had taken place. She listened to it all and then began imploringly:

"Mother Friday, forgive me! pardon me, the guilty one! I'll offer thee a taper and I'll never let friend or foe dishonour thee, Mother!"

Well, what do you think? During the night, back came Mother Friday and took the dust out of that woman's eyes, so that she was able to get about again. It's a great sin to

243 fanasief, "Legendui," No. 13. From the Tambof Government.

dishonour Mother Friday—combing and spinning flax, forsooth!

~

Very similar to this story is that about Wednesday which follows. Wednesday, the day consecrated to Odin, the eve of the day sacred to the Thundergod,[244] may also have been held holy by the heathen Slavonians but to some commentators it appears more likely that the traditions now attached to it in Russia became transferred to it from Friday in Christian times—Wednesday and Friday having been associated by the Church as days sacred to the memory of Our Lord's passion and death. The Russian name for the day, *Sereda* or *Sreda*, means "the middle," Wednesday being the middle of the working week.

244 For an account of various similar superstitions connected with Wednesday and Thursday, see Mannhardt's "Germanische Mythen," p. 15, 16 and W. Schmidt's "Das Jahr und seine Tage," p. 19.

WEDNESDAY.[245]

Beat your pails together and make a sign of the cross . . .

A YOUNG HOUSEWIFE WAS spinning late one evening. It was during the night between a Tuesday and a Wednesday. She had been left alone for a long time and after midnight, when the first cock crew, she began to think about going to bed, only she would have liked to finish spinning what she had in hand. "Well," thinks she, "I'll get up a bit earlier in the morning but just now I want to go to sleep." So she laid down her hatchel—but without crossing herself—and said:

"Now then, Mother Wednesday, lend me thy aid, that I may get up early in the morning and finish my spinning." And then she went to sleep.

Well, very early in the morning, long before it was light, she heard someone moving, bustling about the room. She opened her eyes and looked. The room was lighted up. A splinter of fir was burning in the cresset and the fire was lighted in the stove. A woman, no longer young, wearing a white towel by way of head-dress, was moving about the cottage, going to and fro, supplying the stove with firewood, getting everything ready. Presently she came up to the young woman and roused her, saying, "Get up!" The young woman got up, full of wonder, saying:

"But who art thou? What hast thou come here for?"

"I am she on whom thou didst call. I have come to thy aid."

"But who art thou? On whom did I call?"

---

245 Khudyakof, No. 166. From the Orel Government.

"I am Wednesday. On Wednesday surely thou didst call. See, I have spun thy linen and woven thy web: now let us bleach it and set it in the oven. The oven is heated and the irons are ready; do thou go down to the brook and draw water."

The woman was frightened and thought: "What manner of thing is this?" (or, "How can that be?") but Wednesday glared at her angrily; her eyes just did sparkle!

So the woman took a couple of pails and went for water. As soon as she was outside the door she thought: "Mayn't something terrible happen to me? I'd better go to my neighbour's instead of fetching the water." So she set off. The night was dark. In the village all were still asleep. She reached a neighbour's house and rapped away at the window until at last she made herself heard. An aged woman let her in.

"Why, child!" says the old crone; "whatever hast thou got up so early for? What's the matter?"

"Oh, granny, this is how it was. Wednesday has come to me and has sent me for water to buck my linen with."

"That doesn't look well," says the old crone. "On that linen she will either strangle thee or scald[246] thee."

The old woman was evidently well acquainted with Wednesday's ways.

"What am I to do?" says the young woman. "How can I escape from this danger?"

"Well, this is what thou must do. Go and beat thy pails together in front of the house and cry, 'Wednesday's children have been burnt at sea!'[247] She will run out of the house and do thou be sure to seize the opportunity to get into it before she comes back and immediately slam the door to and make the sign of the cross over it. Then don't let her in, however much she may threaten you or implore you but sign a cross

---

246 Doubtful. The Russian word is "Svarit," properly "to cook."

247 Compare the English nursery rhyme addressed to the lady-bird:
"Lady-bird, lady-bird, fly away home, Your house is a-fire, your children at home."

with your hands and draw one with a piece of chalk and utter a prayer. The Unclean Spirit will have to disappear."

Well, the young woman ran home, beat the pails together and cried out beneath the window:

"Wednesday's children have been burnt at sea!"

Wednesday rushed out of the house and ran to look and the woman sprang inside, shut the door and set a cross upon it. Wednesday came running back and began crying: "Let me in, my dear! I have spun thy linen; now will I bleach it." But the woman would not listen to her, so Wednesday went on knocking at the door until cockcrow. As soon as the cocks crew, she uttered a shrill cry and disappeared. But the linen remained where it was.[248]

~

In one of the numerous legends which the Russian peasants hold in reverence, St. Petka or Friday appears among the other saints and together with her is mentioned another canonised day, St. Nedélya or Sunday,[249] answering to the Greek St. Anastasia, to *Der heilige Sonntag* of German peasant-hagiology. In some respects she resembles both Friday and Wednesday, sharing their views about spinning and weaving at unfitting seasons. Thus in Little-Russia she assures untimely spinners that it is not flax they are spinning but her hair and in proof of this she shows them her dishevelled *kosa* or long back plait.

---

248 Wednesday in this and Friday in the preceding story, are the exact counterparts of Lithuanian Laumes. According to Schleicher ("Lituanica," p. 109), Thursday evening is called in Lithuania *Laumiú vákars*, the Laume's Eve. No work ought to be done on a Thursday evening and it is especially imprudent to spin then. For at night, when the Laumes come, as they are accustomed to do between Thursday evening and Friday morning, they seize any spinning which has been begun, work away at it till cockcrow and then carry it off. In modern Greece the women attribute all nightly meddling with their spinning to the *Neraïdes* (the representatives of the Hellenic Nereids. See Bernhard Schmidt's "Volksleben der Neugriechen," p. 111). In some respects the *Neraïda* closely resemble the *Lamia* and both of them have many features in common with the *Laume*. The latter name (which in Lettish is written Lauma) has never been satisfactorily explained. Can it be connected with the Greek *Lamia* which is now written also as Λαμνία, Λαμνα and Λαμνίσσα?

249 The word Nedyelya now means "a week." But it originally meant Sunday, the non-working day (ne = not, dyelat' = to do or work.) After a time, the name for the first day of the week became transferred to the week itself.

In one of the Wallachian tales[250] the hero is assisted in his search after the dragon-stolen heroine by three supernatural females—the holy Mothers Friday, Wednesday and Sunday. They replace the three benignant Baba Yagas of Russian stories. In another,[251] the same three beings assist the Wallachian Psyche when she is wandering in quest of her lost husband. Mother Sunday rules the animal world and can collect her subjects by playing on a magic flute. She is represented as exercising authority over both birds and beasts and in a Slovak story she bestows on the hero a magic horse. He has been sent by an unnatural mother in search of various things hard to be obtained but he is assisted in the quest by St. Nedélka, who provides him with various magical implements and lends him her own steed Tatoschik and so enables him four times to escape from the perils to which he has been exposed by his mother, whose mind has been entirely corrupted by an insidious dragon. But after he has returned home in safety, his mother binds him as if in sport and the dragon chops off his head and cuts his body to pieces. His mother retains his heart but ties up the rest of him in a bundle and sets it on Tatoschik's back. The steed carries its ghastly burden to St. Nedélka, who soon reanimates it and the youth becomes as sound and vigourous as a young man without a heart can be. Then the saint sends him, under the disguise of a begging piper, to the castle in which his mother dwells and instructs him how to get his heart back again. He succeeds and carries it in his hand to St. Nedélka. She gives it to "the bird Pelekan (no mere Pelican but a magic fowl with a very long and slim neck), which puts its head down the youth's throat and restores his heart to its right place."[252]

---

250 That of "Wilisch Witiâsu," Schott, No. 11.

251 That of "Trandafíru," Schott, No. 23.

252 J. Wenzig's "Westslawischer Märchenschatz," pp. 144-155. According to Wenzig Nedélka is "the personified first Sunday after the new moon." The part here attributed to St. Nedélka is played by a Vila in one of the Songs of Montenegro. According to an ancient

St. Friday and St. Wednesday appear to belong to that class of spiritual beings, sometimes of a demoniacal disposition, with which the imagination of the old Slavonians peopled the elements. Of several of these—such as the Domovoy or House-Spirit, the Rusalka or Naiad and the Vodyany or Water-Sprite—I have written at some length elsewhere,[253] and therefore I will not at present quote any of the stories in which they figure. But as a specimen of the class to which such tales as these belong, here is a skazka about one of the wood-sprites or Slavonic Satyrs, who are still believed by the peasants to haunt the forests of Russia. In it we see reduced to a vulgar form and brought into accordance with everyday peasant-life, the myth which appears to have given rise to the endless stories about the theft and recovery of queens and princesses. The leading idea of the story is the same but the Snake or Koshchei has become a paltry wood-demon, the hero is a mere hunter and the princely heroine has sunk to the low estate of a priest's daughter.

Indian tradition, the Aswattha-tree "is to be touched only on a Sunday, for on every other day Poverty or Misfortune abides in it: on Sunday it is the residence of Lakshmí" (Good Fortune). H. H. Wilson "Works," iii. 70.

253 "Songs of the Russian People," pp. 120-153.

THE LÉSHY.[254]

A priest's daughter. a wood-demon and a hunter . . .

A CERTAIN PRIEST'S DAUGHTER went strolling in the forest one day, without having obtained leave from her father or her mother—and she disappeared utterly. Three years went by. Now in the village in which her parents dwelt there lived a bold hunter, who went daily roaming through the thick woods with his dog and his gun. One day he was going through the forest; all of a sudden his dog began to bark and the hair of its back bristled up. The sportsman looked and saw lying in the woodland path before him a log and on the log there sat a moujik plaiting a bast shoe. And as he plaited the shoe, he kept looking up at the moon and saying with a menacing gesture:—

"Shine, shine, O bright moon!"

The sportsman was astounded. "How comes it," thinks he, "that the moujik looks like that?—he is still young; but his hair is grey as a badger's."[255]

He only thought these words but the other replied, as if guessing what he meant:—

"Grey am I, being the devil's grandfather!"[256]

Then the sportsman guessed that he had before him no mere moujik but a Léshy. He levelled his gun and—bang! he let him have it right in the paunch. The Léshy groaned and seemed to be going to fall across the log; but directly afterwards he got up and dragged himself into the thickets. After him ran the dog in pursuit and after the dog followed the sportsman.

---

254 Afanasief, vii. No. 33. The name Léshy or Lyeshy is derived from lyes, a forest.
255 Literally "as a lun," a kind of hawk (falco rusticolus). Lun also means a greyish light.
256 Ottogo ya i cyed chto chortof dyed.

He walked and walked and came to a hill: in that hill was a fissure and in the fissure stood a hut. He entered the hut—there on a bench lay the Léshy stone dead and by his side a damsel, exclaiming, amid bitter tears:—

"Who now will give me to eat and to drink?"

"Hail, fair maiden!" says the hunter. "Tell me whence thou comest and whose daughter thou art?"

"Ah, good youth! I know not that myself, anymore than if I had never seen the free light—never known a father and mother."

"Well, get ready as soon as you can. I will take you back to Holy Russia."

So he took her away with him and brought her out of the forest. And all the way he went along, he cut marks on the trees. Now this damsel had been carried off by the Léshy and had lived in his hut for three years—her clothes were all worn out or had got torn off her back, so that she was stark naked but she wasn't a bit ashamed of that. When they reached the village, the sportsman began asking whether there was anyone there who had lost a girl. Up came the priest and cried, "Why, that's my daughter." Up came running the priest's wife and cried:—

"O thou dear child! where hast thou been so long? I had no hope of ever seeing thee again."

But the girl gazed and just blinked with her eyes, understanding nothing. After a time, however, she began slowly to come back to her senses. Then the priest and his wife gave her in marriage to the hunter and rewarded him with all sorts of good things. And they went in search of the hut in which she had lived while she was with the Léshy. Long did they wander about the forest; but that hut they never found.

~

To another group of personifications belong those of the Rivers. About them many stories are current, generally having reference to their alleged jealousies and disputes. Thus it is said that when God was allotting their shares to the rivers, the Desna did not come in time and so failed to obtain precedence over the Dnieper.

"Try and get before him yourself," said the Lord.

The Desna set off at full speed but in spite of all her attempts, the Dnieper always kept ahead of her until he fell into the sea, where the Desna was obliged to join him.[257]

About the Volga and its affluent, the Vazuza, the following story is told:—

257 Afanasief, P.V.S., ii. 226.

VAZUZA AND VOLGA.[258]

The competitive nature of rivers . . .

VOLGA AND VAZUZA HAD a long dispute as to which was the wiser, the stronger and the more worthy of high respect. They wrangled and wrangled but neither could gain the mastery in the dispute, so they decided upon the following course:—

"Let us lie down together to sleep," they said, "and whichever of us is the first to rise and the quickest to reach the Caspian Sea, she shall be held to be the wiser of us two and the stronger and the worthier of respect."

So Volga lay down to sleep; down lay Vazuza also. But during the night Vazuza rose silently, fled away from Volga, chose the nearest and the straightest line and flowed away. When Volga awoke, she set off neither slowly nor hurriedly but with just befitting speed. At Zubtsof she came up with Vazuza. So threatening was her mien, that Vazuza was frightened, declared herself to be Volga's younger sister and besought Volga to take her in her arms and bear her to the Caspian Sea. And so to this day Vazuza is the first to awake in the Spring and then she arouses Volga from her wintry sleep.

~

In the Government of Tula a similar tradition is current about the Don and the Shat, both of which flow out of Lake Ivan.

Lake Ivan had two sons, Shat and Don. Shat, contrary to his father's wishes, wanted to roam abroad, so he set out on his travels but go whither he would, he could get received nowhere. So, after fruitless wanderings, he returned home.

---

258 Afanasief, iv. No. 40. From the Tver Government.

But Don, in return for his constant quietness (the river is known as "the quiet Don"), obtained his father's blessing and he boldly set out on a long journey. On the way, he met a raven and asked it where it was flying.

"To the blue sea," answered the raven.

"Let's go together!"

Well, they reached the sea. Don thought to himself, "If I dive right through the sea, I shall carry it away with me."

"Raven!" he said, "do me a service. I am going to plunge into the sea but do you fly over to the other side and as soon as you reach the opposite shore, give a croak."

Don plunged into the sea. The raven flew and croaked—but too soon. Don remained just as he appears at the present day.[259]

In White-Russia there is a legend about two rivers, the beginning of which has evidently been taken from the story of Jacob and Esau:—

259 Translated literally from Afanasief, P.V.S. ii. 227.

SOZH AND DNIEPER.

To determine which river will be the strongest . . .

THERE WAS ONCE A blind old man called Dvina. He had two sons—the elder called Sozh and the younger Dnieper. Sozh was of a boisterous turn and went roving about the forests, the hills and the plains; but Dnieper was remarkably sweet-tempered and he spent all his time at home and was his mother's favourite. Once, when Sozh was away from home, the old father was deceived by his wife into giving the elder son's blessing to the younger son. Thus spake Dvina while blessing him:—

"Dissolve, my son, into a wide and deep river. Flow past towns and bathe villages without number as far as the blue sea. Thy brother shall be thy servant. Be rich and prosperous to the end of time!"

Dnieper turned into a river and flowed through fertile meadows and dreamy woods. But after three days, Sozh returned home and began to complain.

"If thou dost desire to become superior to thy brother," said his father, "speed swiftly by hidden ways, through dark untrodden forests and if thou canst outstrip thy brother, he will have to be thy servant!"

Away sped Sozh on the chase, through untrodden places, washing away swamps, cutting out gullies, tearing up oaks by the roots. The Vulture[260] told Dnieper of this and he put on extra speed, tearing his way through high hills rather than turn on one side. Meanwhile Sozh persuaded the Raven to fly straight to Dnieper, and as soon as it had come up with him to

---

260 Yastreb = vulture or goshawk

croak three times; he himself was to burrow under the earth, intending to leap to the surface at the cry of the Raven and by that means to get before his brother. But the Vulture fell on the Raven; the Raven began to croak before it had caught up the river Dnieper. Up burst Sozh from underground and fell straight into the waves of the Dnieper.[261]

~

Here is an account of—

261 Quoted from Borichefsky (pp. 183-5) by Afanasief.

THE METAMORPHOSIS OF THE DNIEPER, THE VOLGA, AND THE DVINA.[262]

To become a river . . .

THE DNIEPER, VOLGA AND Dvina used once to be living people. The Dnieper was a boy and the Volga and Dvina his sisters. While they were still in childhood they were left complete orphans, and as they hadn't a crust to eat, they were obliged to get their living by daily labour beyond their strength. "When was that?" Very long ago, say the old folks; beyond the memory even of our great-grandfathers.

Well, the children grew up but they never had even the slightest bit of good luck. Every day, from morn till eve, it was always toil and toil and all merely for the day's subsistence. As for their clothing, it was just what God sent them! They sometimes found rags on the dust-heaps and with these they managed to cover their bodies. The poor things had to endure cold and hunger. Life became a burden to them.[263]

One day, after toiling hard afield, they sat down under a bush to eat their last morsel of bread. And when they had eaten it, they cried and sorrowed for a while and considered and held counsel together as to how they might manage to live and to have food and clothing, and without toiling, to supply others with meat and drink. Well, this is what they resolved: to set out wandering about the wide world in search of good luck and a kindly welcome and to look for and find out the best places in which they could turn into great rivers—for that was a possible thing then.

---

262 Tereshchenko, v. 43, 44.

263 Literally "Life disgusted them worse than a bitter radish."

Well, they walked and walked; not one year only, nor two years but all but three; and they chose the places they wanted and came to an agreement as to where the flowing of each one should begin. And all three of them stopped to spend the night in a swamp. But the sisters were more cunning than their brother. No sooner was Dnieper asleep than they rose up quietly, chose the best and most sloping places and began to flow away.

When the brother awoke in the morning, not a trace of his sisters was to be seen. Then he became wroth and made haste to pursue them. But on the way he bethought himself and decided that no man can run faster than a river. So he smote the ground and flowed in pursuit as a stream. Through gullies and ravines he rushed and the further he went the fiercer did he become. But when he came within a few versts of the seashore, his anger calmed down and he disappeared in the sea. And his two sisters, who had continued running from him during his pursuit, separated in different directions and fled to the bottom of the sea. But while the Dnieper was rushing along in anger, he drove his way between steep banks. Therefore is it that his flow is swifter than that of the Volga and the Dvina; therefore also is it that he has many rapids and many mouths.

~

There is a small stream which falls into Lake Ilmen on its western side and which is called Chorny Ruchei, the Black Brook. On the banks of this brook, a long time ago, a certain man set up a mill and the fish came and implored the stream to grant them its aid, saying, "We used to have room enough and be at our ease but now an evil man is taking away the water from us." And the result was this. One of the inhabitants of Novgorod was angling in the brook Chorny. Up came a stranger to him, dressed all in black, who greeted him and said:—

"Do me a service and I will show thee a place where the fish swarm."

"What is the service?"

"When thou art in Novgorod, thou wilt meet a tall, big moujik in a plaited blue caftan, wide blue trowsers and a high blue hat. Say to him, 'Uncle Ilmen! the Chorny has sent thee a petition and has told me to say that a mill has been set in his way. As thou may'st think fit to order, so shall it be!'"

The Novgorod man promised to fulfil this request and the black stranger showed him a place where the fish swarmed by thousands. With rich booty did the fisherman return to Novgorod, where he met the moujik with the blue caftan and gave him the petition. The Ilmen answered:—

"Give my compliments to the brook Chorny and say to him about the mill: there used not to be one and so there shall not be one!"

This commission also the Novgorod man fulfilled and behold! during the night the brook Chorny ran riotous, Lake Ilmen waxed boisterous, a tempest arose and the raging waters swept away the mill.[264]

In old times sacrifices were regularly paid to lakes and streams in Russia, just as they were in Germany[265] and in other lands. And even at the present day the common people are in the habit of expressing, by some kind of offering, their thanks to a river on which they have made a prosperous voyage. It is said that Stenka Razin, the insurgent chief of the Don Cossacks in the seventeenth century, once offered a human sacrifice to the Volga. Among his captives was a Persian princess, to whom he was warmly attached. But one day "when he was fevered with wine, as he sat at the ship's side and musingly regarded the waves, he said: 'Oh, Mother Volga, thou great river! much hast thou given me of gold and of silver and of all good things; thou hast nursed me and nourished me and covered me with glory and honour. But

---

264 Translated literally from Afanasief, P.V.S. ii. 230.
265 "Deutsche Mythologie," 462.

I have in no way shown thee my gratitude. Here is somewhat for thee; take it!' And with these words he caught up the princess and flung her into the water."[266]

Just as rivers might be conciliated by honour and sacrifice, so they could be irritated by disrespect. One of the old songs tells how a youth comes riding to the Smorodina and beseeches that stream to show him a ford. His prayer is granted and he crosses to the other side. Then he takes to boasting and says, "People talk about the Smorodina, saying that no one can cross it whether on foot or on horseback—but it is no better than a pool of rain-water!" But when the time comes for him to cross back again, the river takes its revenge and drowns him in its depths, saying the while: "It is not I but thy own boasting that drowns thee."

From these vocal rivers we will now turn to that elementary force by which in winter they are often rendered mute. In the story which is now about to be quoted will be found a striking personification of Frost. As a general rule, Winter plays by no means so important a part as might have been expected in Northern tales. As in other European countries, so in Russia, the romantic stories of the people are full of pictures bathed in warm sunlight but they do not often represent the aspect of the land when the sky is grey and the earth is a sheet of white and outdoor life is sombre and still. Here and there, it is true, glimpses of snowy landscapes are offered by the skazkas. But it is seldom that a wintry effect is so deliberately produced in them as is the case in the following remarkable version of a well-known tale.

266 Afanasief, loc. cit. p. 231.

FROST.[267]

It pays to properly respect the elements . . .

THERE WAS ONCE AN old man who had a wife and three daughters. The wife had no love for the eldest of the three, who was her stepdaughter, but was always scolding her. Moreover, she used to make her get up ever so early in the morning and gave her all the work of the house to do. Before daybreak the girl would feed the cattle and give them to drink, fetch wood and water indoors, light the fire in the stove, give the room a wash, mend the dresses and set everything in order. Even then her stepmother was never satisfied but would grumble away at Marfa, exclaiming:—

"What a lazybones! what a slut! Why here's a brush not in its place and there's something put wrong and she's left the muck inside the house!"

The girl held her peace and wept; she tried in every way to accommodate herself to her stepmother and to be of service to her stepsisters. But they, taking pattern by their mother, were always insulting Marfa, quarrelling with her and making her cry: that was even a pleasure to them! As for them, they lay in bed late, washed themselves in water got ready for them, dried themselves with a clean towel and didn't sit down to work till after dinner.

Well, our girls grew and grew, until they grew up and were old enough to be married. The old man felt sorry for his eldest daughter, whom he loved because she was industrious and obedient, never was obstinate, always did as she was bid and never uttered a word of contradiction. But he didn't

267 Afanasief, iv. No. 42. From the Vologda Government.

know how he was to help her in her trouble. He was feeble, his wife was a scold and her daughters were as obstinate as they were indolent.

Well, the old folks set to work to consider—the husband how he could get his daughters settled, the wife how she could get rid of the eldest one. One day she says to him:—

"I say, old man! let's get Marfa married."

"Gladly," says he, slinking off (to the sleeping-place) above the stove. But his wife called after him:—

"Get up early tomorrow, old man, harness the mare to the sledge and drive away with Marfa. And Marfa, get your things together in a basket and put on a clean shift; you're going away tomorrow on a visit."

Poor Marfa was delighted to hear of such a piece of good luck as being invited on a visit and she slept comfortably all night. Early next morning she got up, washed herself, prayed to God, got all her things together, packed them away in proper order, dressed herself (in her best things) and looked something like a lass!—a bride fit for any place whatsoever!

Now it was wintertime and out of doors was a rattling frost. Early in the morning, between daybreak and sunrise, the old man harnessed the mare to the sledge and led it up to the steps. Then he went indoors, sat down on the window-sill and said:—

"Now then! I've got everything ready."

"Sit down to table and swallow your victuals!" replied the old woman.

The old man sat down to table and made his daughter sit by his side. On the table stood a pannier; he took out a loaf,[268] and cut bread for himself and his daughter. Meantime his wife served up a dish of old cabbage soup and said:—

268 Chelpan, a sort of dough cake or pie without stuffing.

"There, my pigeon, eat and be off; I've looked at you quite enough! Drive Marfa to her bridegroom, old man. And look here, old greybeard! drive straight along the road at first and then turn off from the road to the right, you know, into the forest—right up to the big pine that stands on the hill and there hand Marfa over to Morozko (Frost)."

The old man opened his eyes wide, also his mouth and stopped eating and the girl began lamenting.

"Now then, what are you hanging your chaps and squealing about?" said her stepmother. "Surely your bridegroom is a beauty and he's that rich! Why, just see what a lot of things belong to him, the firs, the pine-tops and the birches, all in their robes of down—ways and means that anyone might envy; and he himself a *bogatir*!"[269]

The old man silently placed the things on the sledge, made his daughter put on a warm pelisse and set off on the journey. After a time, he reached the forest, turned off from the road; and drove across the frozen snow.[270] When he got into the depths of the forest, he stopped, made his daughter get out, laid her basket under the tall pine and said:—

"Sit here and await the bridegroom. And mind you receive him as pleasantly as you can."

Then he turned his horse round and drove off homewards.

The girl sat and shivered. The cold had pierced her through. She would fain have cried aloud but she had not strength enough; only her teeth chattered. Suddenly she heard a sound. Not far off, Frost was cracking away on a fir. From fir to fir was he leaping and snapping his fingers. Presently he appeared on that very pine under which the maiden was sitting and from above her head he cried:—

"Art thou warm, maiden?"

---

269 Bogatir is the regular term for a Russian "hero of romance." Its origin is disputed but it appears to be of Tartar extraction.

270 Nast, snow that has thawed and frozen again.

"Warm, warm am I, dear Father Frost," she replied.

Frost began to descend lower, all the more cracking and snapping his fingers. To the maiden said Frost:—

"Art thou warm, maiden? Art thou warm, fair one?"

The girl could scarcely draw her breath but still she replied:

"Warm am I, Frost dear: warm am I, father dear!"

Frost began cracking more than ever and more loudly did he snap his fingers and to the maiden he said:—

"Art thou warm, maiden? Art thou warm, pretty one? Art thou warm, my darling?"

The girl was by this time numb with cold and she could scarcely make herself heard as she replied:—

"Oh! quite warm, Frost dearest!"

Then Frost took pity on the girl, wrapped her up in furs and warmed her with blankets.

Next morning the old woman said to her husband:—

"Drive out, old greybeard and wake the young couple!"

The old man harnessed his horse and drove off. When he came to where his daughter was, he found she was alive and had got a good pelisse, a costly bridal veil and a pannier with rich gifts. He stowed everything away on the sledge without saying a word, took his seat on it with his daughter and drove back. They reached home and the daughter fell at her stepmother's feet. The old woman was thunderstruck when she saw the girl alive and the new pelisse and the basket of linen.

"Ah, you wretch!" she cries. "But you shan't trick me!"

Well, a little later the old woman says to her husband:—

"Take my daughters, too, to their bridegroom. The presents he's made are nothing to what he'll give them."

Well, early next morning the old woman gave her girls their breakfast, dressed them as befitted brides and sent them off on their journey. In the same way as before the old man left the girls under the pine.

There the girls sat and kept laughing and saying:

"Whatever is mother thinking of! All of a sudden to marry both of us off! As if there were no lads in our village, forsooth! Some rubbishy fellow may come and goodness knows who he may be!"

The girls were wrapped up in pelisses but for all that they felt the cold.

"I say, Prascovia! the frost's skinning me alive. Well, if our bridegroom[271] doesn't come quick, we shall be frozen to death here!"

"Don't go talking nonsense, Mashka; as if suitors[272] generally turned up in the forenoon. Why it's hardly dinnertime yet!"

"But I say, Prascovia! if only one comes, which of us will he take?"

"Not you, you stupid goose!"

"Then it will be you, I suppose!"

"Of course it will be me!"

"You, indeed! there now, have done talking stuff and treating people like fools!"

Meanwhile, Frost had numbed the girl's hands, so our damsels folded them under their dress and then went on quarrelling as before.

"What, you fright! you sleepy-face! you abominable shrew! why, you don't know so much as how to begin weaving: and as to going on with it, you haven't an idea!"

"Aha, boaster! and what is it you know? Why, nothing at all except to go out to merry-makings and lick your lips there. We'll soon see which he'll take first!"

While the girls went on scolding like that, they began to freeze in downright earnest. Suddenly they both cried out at once:

---

271 Suzhenoi-ryazhenoi.
272 Zhenikhi.

"Whyever is he so long coming. Do you know, you've turned quite blue!"

Now, a good way off, Frost had begun cracking, snapping his fingers and leaping from fir to fir. To the girls it sounded as if someone was coming.

"Listen, Prascovia! He's coming at last and with bells, too!"

"Get along with you! I won't listen; my skin is peeling with cold."

"And yet you're still expecting to get married!"

Then they began blowing on their fingers.

Nearer and nearer came Frost. At length he appeared on the pine, above the heads of the girls and said to them:

"Are ye warm, maidens? Are ye warm, pretty ones? Are ye warm, my darlings?"

"Oh, Frost, it's awfully cold! we're utterly perished! We're expecting a bridegroom but the confounded fellow has disappeared."

Frost slid lower down the tree, cracked away more, snapped his fingers oftener than before.

"Are ye warm, maidens? Are ye warm, pretty ones?"

"Get along with you! Are you blind that you can't see our hands and feet are quite dead?"

Still lower descended Frost, still more put forth his might,[273] and said:

"Are ye warm, maidens?"

"Into the bottomless pit with you! Out of sight, accursed one!" cried the girls—and became lifeless forms.[274]

Next morning the old woman said to her husband:

"Old man, go and get the sledge harnessed; put an armful of hay in it and take some sheep-skin wraps. I daresay the girls are half-dead with cold. There's a terrible frost outside! And mind you, old greybeard, do it quickly!"

---

273 Sil'no priudaril, mightily smote harder.
274 Okostenyeli, were petrified.

Before the old man could manage to get a bite he was out of doors and on his way. When he came to where his daughters were, he found them dead. So he lifted the girls on to the sledge, wrapped a blanket round them and covered them up with a bark mat. The old woman saw him from afar, ran out to meet him and called out ever so loud:

"Where are the girls?"

"In the sledge."

The old woman lifted the mat, undid the blanket and found the girls both dead.

Then, like a thunderstorm, she broke out against her husband abusing him saying:

"What have you done, you old wretch? You have destroyed my daughters, the children of my own flesh and blood, my never-enough-to-be-gazed-on seedlings, my beautiful berries! I will thrash you with the tongs; I will give it you with the stove-rake."

"That's enough, you old goose! You flattered yourself you were going to get riches but your daughters were too stiff-necked. How was I to blame? it was you yourself would have it."

The old woman was in a rage at first and used bad language; but afterwards she made it up with her stepdaughter and they all lived together peaceably and thrived and bore no malice. A neighbour made an offer of marriage, the wedding was celebrated and Marfa is now living happily. The old man frightens his grandchildren with (stories about) Frost and doesn't let them have their own way.

~

In a variant from the Kursk Government (Afanasief IV. No. 42. *b*), the stepdaughter is left by her father "in the open plain." There she sits, "trembling and silently offering up a prayer." Frost draws near, intending "to smite her and to freeze her to death." But when he says to her, "Maiden,

maiden, I am Frost the Red-Nosed," she replies "Welcome, Frost; doubtless God has sent you for my sinful soul." Pleased by her "wise words," Frost throws a warm cloak over her and afterwards presents her with "robes embroidered with silver and gold and a chest containing rich dowry." The girl puts on the robes and appears "such a beauty!" Then she sits on the chest and sings songs. Meantime her stepmother is baking cakes and preparing for her funeral. After a time her father sets out in search of her dead body. But the dog beneath the table barks—"Taff! Taff! The master's daughter in silver and gold by the wedding party is borne along but the mistress's daughter is wooed by none!" In vain does its mistress throw it a cake and order it to modify its remarks. It eats the cake but it repeats its offensive observations, until the stepdaughter appears in all her glory. Then the old woman's own daughter is sent afield. Frost comes to have a look at his new guest, expecting "wise words" from her too. But as none are forthcoming, he waxes wroth and kills her. When the old man goes to fetch her, the dog barks—"Taff! Taff! The master's daughter will be borne along by the bridal train but the bones of the mistress's daughter are being carried in a bag," and continues to bark in the same strain until the yard-gates open. The old woman runs out to greet her daughter and "instead of her embraces a cold corpse."

To the Russian peasants, it should be observed, Moroz, our own Jack Frost, is a living personage. On Christmas Eve it is customary for the oldest man in each family to take a spoonful of kissel, a sort of pudding and then, having put his head through the window, to cry:

"Frost, Frost, come and eat kissel! Frost, Frost, do not kill our oats! drive our flax and hemp deep into the ground."

The Tcheremisses have similar ideas and are afraid of knocking the icicles off their houses, thinking that, if they do so, Frost will wax wroth and freeze them to death. In one of the Skazkas, a peasant goes out one day to a field of buckwheat and finds it all broken down. He goes home and tells the bad news to his wife, who says, "It is Frost who has done this. Go and find him and make him pay for the damage!" So the peasant goes into the forest and after wandering about for some time, lights upon a path which leads him to a cottage made of ice, covered with snow and hung with icicles. He knocks at the door and out comes an old man—"all white." This is Frost, who presents him with the magic cudgel and tablecloth which work wonders in so many of the tales.[275] In another story, a peasant meets the Sun, the Wind and the Frost. He bows to all three but adds an extra salutation to the Wind. This enrages the two others and the Sun cries out that he will burn up the peasant. But the Wind says, "I will blow cold and temper the heat." Then the Frost threatens to freeze the peasant to death but the Wind comforts him, saying, "I will blow warm and will not let you be hurt."[276]

Sometimes the Frost is described by the people as a mighty smith who forges strong chains with which to bind the earth and the waters—as in the saying "The Old One has built a bridge without axe and without knife," *i.e.*, the river is frozen over. Sometimes Moroz-Treskun, the Crackling Frost, is spoken of without disguise as the preserver of the hero who is ordered to enter a bath which has been heated red-hot. Frost goes into the bath and breathes with so icy a breath that the heat of the building turns at once to cold.[277]

The story in which Frost so singularly figures is one which is known in many lands and of which many variants are current in Russia. The jealous hatred of a stepmother, who exposes her stepdaughter to some great peril, has been made

275 Afanasief, P.V.S. i. 318–19.

276 Ibid. i. 312.

277 As with Der Frostige in the German story of "Die sechs Diener," KM., No. 134, p. 519 and "The Man with the White Hat," in that of "Sechse kommen durch die ganze Welt," No. 71, p. 295 and their variants in different lands. See Grimm, iii. p. 122.

the theme of countless tales. What gives its special importance, as well as its poetical charm, to the skazka which has been quoted, is the introduction of Frost as the power to which the stepmother has recourse for the furtherance of her murderous plans and by which she, in the persons of her own daughters, is ultimately punished. We have already dealt with one specimen of the skazkas of this class, the story of Vasilissa, who is sent to the Baba Yaga's for a light. Another, still more closely connected with that of "Frost," occurs in Khudyakof's collection.[278]

A certain woman ordered her husband (says the story) to make away with his daughter by a previous marriage. So he took the girl into the forest and left her in a kind of hut, telling her to prepare some soup while he was cutting wood. "At that time there was a gale blowing. The old man tied a log to a tree; when the wind blew, the log rattled. She thought the old man was going on cutting wood but in reality he had gone away home."

When the soup was ready, she called out to her father to come to dinner. No reply came from him, "but there was a human head in the forest and it replied, 'I'm coming immediately!' And when the Head arrived, it cried, 'Maiden, open the door!' She opened it. 'Maiden, Maiden! lift me over the threshold!' She lifted it over. 'Maiden, Maiden! put the dinner on the table!' She did so and she and the Head sat down to dinner. When they had dined, 'Maiden, Maiden!' said the Head, 'take me off the bench!' She took it off the bench and cleared the table. It lay down to sleep on the bare floor; she lay on the bench. She fell asleep but it went into the forest after its servants. The house became bigger; servants, horses, everything one could think of suddenly appeared. The servants came to the maiden and said, 'Get up! it's time to

278 No. 13, "The Stepmother's Daughter and the Stepdaughter," written down in Kazan.

go for a drive!' So she got into a carriage with the Head but she took a cock along with her. She told the cock to crow; it crowed. Again she told it to crow; it crowed again. And a third time she told it to crow. When it had crowed for the third time, the Head fell to pieces and became a heap of golden coins."[279]

Then the stepmother sent her own daughter into the forest. Everything occurred as before, until the Head arrived. Then she was so frightened that she tried to hide herself and she would do nothing for the Head, which had to dish up its own dinner and eat it by itself. And so "when she lay down to sleep, it ate her up."

In a story in Chudinsky's collection, the stepdaughter is sent by night to watch the rye in an *ovin*,[280] or corn-kiln. Presently a stranger appears and asks her to marry him. She replies that she has no wedding-clothes, upon which he brings her everything she asks for. But she is very careful not to ask for more than one thing at a time and so the cock crows before her list of indispensable necessaries is exhausted. The stranger immediately disappears and she carries off her presents in triumph.

The next night her stepsister is sent to the *ovin* and the stranger appears as before and asks her to marry him. She, also, replies that she has no wedding-clothes and he offers to supply her with what she wants. Whereupon, instead of asking for a number of things one after the other, she demands them all at once—"Stockings, garters, a petticoat, a dress, a comb, earrings, a mirror, soap, white paint and rouge and everything which her stepsister had got." Then follows the catastrophe.

---

279 This is a thoroughly Buddhistic idea. According to Buddhist belief, the treasure which has belonged to anyone in a former existence may come to him in the shape of a man who, when killed, turns to gold. The first story of the fifth book of the "Panchatantra," is based upon an idea of this kind. A man is told in a vision to kill a monk. He does so and the monk becomes a heap of gold. A barber, seeing this, kills several monks but to no purpose. See Benfey's Introduction, pp. 477–8.

280 For an account of the ovin and the respect paid to it or to the demons supposed to haunt it see "The Songs of the Russian People," p. 257.

The stranger brought her everything, all at once.

"Now then," says he, "will you marry me now?"

"Wait a bit," said the stepmother's daughter, "I'll wash and dress and whiten myself and rouge myself and then I'll marry you." And straightway she set to work washing and dressing—and she hastened and hurried to get all that done—she wanted so awfully to see herself decked out as a bride. By-and-by she was quite dressed—but the cock had not yet crowed.

"Well, maiden!" says he, "will you marry me now?"

"I'm quite ready," says she.

Thereupon he tore her to pieces.[281]

There is one other of those personifications of natural forces which play an active part in the Russian tales, about which a few words may be said. It often happens that the heroine-stealer whom the hero of the story has to overcome is called, not Koshchei nor the Snake but Vikhor,[282] the whirlwind. Here is a brief analysis of part of one of the tales in which this elementary abducer figures. There was a certain king, whose wife went out one day to walk in the garden. "Suddenly a gale (*vyeter*) sprang up. In the gale was the Vikhor-bird. Vikhor seized the Queen and carried her off." She left three sons and they, when they came to man's estate, said to their father—"Where is our mother? If she be dead, show us her grave; if she be living, tell us where to find her."

"I myself know not where your mother is," replied the King. "Vikhor carried her off."

"Well then," they said, "since Vikhor carried her off and she is alive, give us your blessing. We will go in search of our mother."

All three set out but only the youngest, Prince Vasily, succeeded in climbing the steep hill, whereon stood the

281 Chudinsky, No. 13. "The Daughter and the Stepdaughter." From the Nijegorod Government.

282 Vikhr' or Vikhor' from vit', to whirl or twist.

palace in which his mother and Vikhor lived. Entering it during Vikhor's absence, the Prince made himself known to his mother, "who straightway gave him to eat and concealed him in a distant apartment, hiding him behind a number of cushions, so that Vikhor might not easily discover him." And she gave him these instructions. "If Vikhor comes and begins quarrelling, don't come forth but if he takes to chatting, come forth and say, 'Hail father!' and seize hold of the little finger of his right hand and wherever he flies do you go with him."

Presently Vikhor came flying in and addressed the Queen angrily. Prince Vasily remained concealed until his mother gave him a hint to come forth. This he did and then greeted Vikhor and caught hold of his right little finger. Vikhor tried to shake him off, flying first about the house and then out of it but all in vain. At last Vikhor, after soaring on high, struck the ground and fell to pieces, becoming a fine yellow sand. "But the little finger remained in the possession of Prince Vasily, who scraped together the sand and burnt it in the stove."[283]

* * * * *

With a mention of two other singular beings who occur in the Skazkas, the present chapter may be brought to a close. The first is a certain Morfei (Morpheus?) who figures in the following variant of a well-known tale.

There was a king and he had a daughter with whom a general who lived over the way fell in love. But the king would not let him marry her unless he went where none had been and brought back thence what none had seen. After much consideration the general set out and travelled "over swamps, hill and rivers." At last he reached a wood in which was a hut and inside the hut was an old crone. To her he told

283 Khudyakof, No. 82. The story ends in the same way as that of Norka. See supra, p. 73.

his story, after hearing which, she cried out, "Ho, there! Morfei, dish up the meal!" and immediately a dinner appeared of which the old crone made the general partake. And next day "she presented that cook to the general, ordering him to serve the general honourably, as he had served her. The general took the cook and departed." By-and-by he came to a river and was appealed to for food by a shipwrecked crew. "Morfei, give them to eat!" he cried and immediately excellent viands appeared, with which the mariners were so pleased that they gave the general a magic volume in exchange for his cook—who, however, did not stay with them but secretly followed his master. A little later the general found another shipwrecked crew, who gave him, in exchange for his cook, a sabre and a towel, each of magic power. Then the general returned to his own city and his magic properties enabled him to convince the king that he was an eligible suitor for the hand of the Princess.[284]

The other is a mysterious personage whose name is "Oh!" The story in which he appears is one with which many countries are familiar and of which numerous versions are to be found in Russia. A father sets out with his boy for "the bazaar," hoping to find a teacher there who will instruct the child in such science as enables people "to work little and feed delicately and dress well." After walking a long way the man becomes weary and exclaims, "Oh! I'm so tired!" Immediately there appears "an old magician," who says—

"Why do you call me?"

"I didn't call you," replies the old man. "I don't even know who you are."

---

284 Khudyakof, No. 86. Morfei the Cook is merely a development of the magic cudgel which in so many stories (e.g. the sixth of the Calmuck tales) is often exchanged for other treasures by its master, to whom it soon returns—it being itself a degraded form of the hammer of Thor, the lance of Indra, which always came back to the divine hand that had hurled it.

"My name is Oh," says the magician, "and you cried 'Oh!' Where are you taking that boy?"

The father explains what it is he wants and the magician undertakes to give the boy the requisite education, charging "one assignat rouble" for a year's tuition.[285]

The teacher, in this story, is merely called a magician; but as in other Russian versions of it his counterpart is always described as being demoniacal and is often openly styled a devil, it may be assumed that Oh belongs to the supernatural order of beings. It is often very difficult, however, to distinguish magicians from fiends in storyland the same powers being generally wielded and that for the same purposes, by the one set of beings as by the other. Of those powers and of the end to which the stories represent them as being turned, some mention will be made in the next chapter.

285 Khudyakof, No. 19. The rest of the story is that of "Der Gaudief un sin Meester," Grimm's KM. No. 68. (See also vol. iii. p. 118 of that work, where a long list is given of similar stories in various languages.)

PART IV

Magic and Witchcraft

The Waters of Life and Death, and of Strength and Weakness — Aid given to Children by Dead Parents—Magic Horses, Fish, &c.—Stories about Brides won by a Leap, &c.—Stories about Wizards and Witches—The Headless Piincess—Midnight Watchings over Corpses—The Fire Bird, its connexion with the Golden Bird and the Phoenix

Most of the magical "properties" of the "skazka-drama," closely resemble those which have already been rendered familiar to us by well-known folktales. Of such as these—of "caps of darkness," of "seven-leagued boots," of "magic cudgels," of "Fortunatus's purses," and the like[286]—it is unnecessary, for the present, to say more than that they are of as common occurrence in Slavonic as in other stories. But there are some among them which materially differ from their counterparts in more western lands and are therefore worthy of special notice. To the latter class belong the Dolls of which mention has already been made and the Waters of Life and Death of which I am now about to speak.

A Water of Life plays an important part in the folktales of every land.[287] When the hero of a "fairy story" has been done to death by evil hands, his resuscitation by means of a

286 About which, see Professor Wilson's note on Somadeva's story of the "Origin of Pátaliputra," "Essays," i. p. 168-9, with Dr. Rost's reference to L. Deslongchamps, "Essai sur les Fables Indiennes," Paris, 1838, p. 35 and Grässe, "Sagenkreise des Mittelalters," Leipsig, 1842, p. 191. See also the numerous references given by Grimm, KM. iii. pp. 168-9.

287 As well as in all the mythologies. For the magic draught of the fairy-story appears to be closely connected with the Greek ambrosia, the Vedic soma or amrita, the Zend haoma.

healing and vivifying lotion or ointment[288] follows almost as a matter of course. And by common consent the Raven (or some sort of crow) is supposed to know where this invaluable specific is to be found,[289] a knowledge which it shares with various supernatural beings as well as with some human adepts in magic and sometimes with the Snake. In all these matters the Russian and the Western tales agree but the Skazka differs from most stories of its kind in this respect, that it almost invariably speaks of *two* kinds of magic waters as being employed for the restoration of life. We have already seen in the story of "Marya Morevna," that one of these, sometimes called the mertvaya voda—the "dead water," or "Water of Death"—when sprinkled over a mutilated corpse, heals all its wounds; while the other, which bears the name of the zhivaya voda,—the "living water," or "Water of Life"—endows it once more with vitality.

[In a Norse tale in Asbjörnsen's new series, No. 72, mention is made of a Water of Death, as opposed to a Water of Life. The Death Water (Doasens Vana) throws all whom it touches into a magic sleep, from which only Life Water (Livsens Vand) can rouse them (p. 57). In the Rámáyana, Hanuman fetches four different kinds of herbs in order to resuscitate his dead monkeys: "the first restore the dead to life, the second drive away all pain, the third join broken parts, the fourth cure all wounds, &c." Talboys Wheeler, "History of India," ii. 368. In the Egyptian story already mentioned (at p. 113), Satou's corpse quivers and opens its eyes when his heart has become saturated with a healing liquid. But he does not actually come to life till the remainder of the liquid has been poured down his throat.

288 A water, "Das Wasser des Lebens," in two German stories (Grimm, Nos. 92 and 97 and iii. p. 178) and in many Greek tales (Hahn, Nos. 32, 37, &c.). An oil or ointment in the Norse tale (Asbjörnsen and Moe, No. 35, Dasent, No. 3). A balsam in Gaelic tales, in which a "Vessel of Balsam" often occurs. According to Mr. Campbell ("West Highland Tales," i. p. 218), "Ballan Iocshlaint, teat, of ichor, of health, seems to be the meaning of the words." The juice squeezed from the leaves of a tree in a modern Indian tale ("Old Deccan Days," p. 139).

289 The mythical bird Garuda, the Indian original of the Roc of the Arabian Nights, was similarly connected with the Amrita. See the story of Garuda and the Nágas in Brockhaus's translation of the "Kathásaritságara," ii. pp. 98-105. On the Vedic falcon which brings the Soma down to earth, see Kuhn's "Herabkunft des Feuers," pp. 138-142.

In a Kirghiz story, quoted by Bronevsky,[290] a golden-haired hero finds, after long search, the maiden to whom he had in very early life been betrothed. Her father has him murdered. She persuades the murderer to show her the body of her dead love and weeps over it bitterly. A spirit appears and tells her to sprinkle it with water from a neighbouring well. The well is very deep but she induces the murderer to allow her to lower him into it by means of her remarkably long hair. He descends and hands up to her a cup of water. Having received it, she cuts off her hair and lets the murderer drop and be drowned. Then she sprinkles her lover's corpse with the water and he revives. But he lives only three days. She refuses to survive him and is buried by his side. From the graves of the lovers spring two willows, which mingle their boughs as if in an embrace. And the neighbours set up near the spot three statues, his and hers and her nurse's.

Such is the story, says Bronevsky, which the Kirghiz tell with respect to some statues of unknown origin which stand (or used to stand) near the Ayaguza, a river falling into Lake Balkhash. A somewhat similar Armenian story is quoted by Haxthausen in his Transcaucasia (p. 350 of the English translation).

In the Kalevala, when Lemmenkäinen has been torn to pieces, his mother collects his scattered remains and by a dexterous synthetical operation restores him to physical unity. But the silence of death still possesses him. Then she entreats the Bee to bring vivifying honey. After two fruitless journeys, the Bee succeeds in bringing back honey "from the cellar of the Creator." When this has been applied, the dead man returns to life, sits up and says in the words of the Russian heroes—"How long I have slept!"[291]

Here is another instance of a life-giving operation of a double nature. There is a well-known Indian story about four suitors for the hand of one girl. She dies but is restored to life by one of her lovers, who happens one day to see a dead child resuscitated and learns how to perform similar miracles. In two Sanskrit versions of the "Vetálapanchavinsati,"[292] as well

---

290 In the Russian periodical, "Otechestvennuiya Zapiski," vol. 43 (for 1830) pp. 252-6.

291 Schiefners's translation, 1852, pp. 80, 81.

292 In that attributed to Sivadása, tale 2 (Lassen's "Anthologia Sanscritica," pp. 16-19) and in the "Kathásaritságara," chap. lxxvi. See Brockhaus's summary in the "Berichte der phil. hist. Classe der Kön. Sächs. Gesellschaft der Wissenschaften," December 3, 1853, pp. 194-5.

as in the Hindi version,[293] *the life-giving charm consists in a spell taken from a book of magic. But in the Tamil version, the process is described as being of a different and double nature. According to it, the mother of the murdered child "by the charm called sisupàbam re-created the body, and by the incantation called sanjìvi, restored it to life." The suitor, having learnt the charm and the incantation, "took the bones and the ashes (of the dead girl) and having created out of them the body, by virtue of the charm sisupàbam gave life to that body by the sanjìvi incantation." According to Mr. Babington, "Sanjìvi is defined by the Tamuls to be a medicine which restores to life by dissipating a mortal swoon . . . In the text the word is used for the art of using this medicine."*[294]*]*

As a general rule, the two waters of which mention is made in the Skazkas possess the virtues and are employed in the manner, mentioned above; but there are cases in which their powers are of a different nature. Sometimes we meet with two magic fluids, one of which heals all wounds and restores sight to the blind and vigour to the cripple, while the other destroys all that it touches. Sometimes, also, recourse is had to magic draughts of two kinds, the one of which strengthens him who quaffs it, while the other produces the opposite effect. Such liquors as these are known as the "Waters of Strength and Weakness," and are usually described as being stowed away in the cellar of some many-headed Snake. For the Snake is often mentioned as the possessor or at least the guardian, of magic fluids. Thus one of the Skazkas[295] speaks of a wondrous garden, in which are two springs of healing and vivifying water and around that garden is coiled like a ring a mighty serpent. Another tells how a flying Snake brought two heroes to a lake, into which they flung a green bough and immediately the bough broke into flame and was

---

293 The "Baitál-Pachísí," translated by Ghulam Mohammad Munshi, Bombay 1868, pp. 23-24.

294 B. G. Babington's translation of "The Vedàla Cadai," p. 32. contained in the "Miscellaneous Translations" of the Oriental Translation Fund, 1831, vol. i. pt

295 Afanasief, P.V.S. ii. 551.

consumed. Then it took them to another lake, into which they cast a mouldy log. And the log straightway began to put forth buds and blossoms.[296]

In some cases the magic waters are the property, not of a Snake but of one of the mighty heroines who so often occur in these stories and who bear so great a resemblance to Brynhild, as well in other respects as in that of her enchanted sleep. Thus in one of the Skazkas297 an aged king dreams that "beyond thrice nine lands, in the thirtieth country, there is a fair maiden from whose hands and feet water is flowing, of which water he who drinks will become thirty years younger." His sons go forth in search of this youth-giving liquid, and after many adventures, the youngest is directed to the golden castle in which lives the "fair maiden," whom his father has seen in his vision. He has been told that when she is awake her custom is to divert herself in the green fields with her Amazon host—"for nine days she rambles about and then for nine days she sleeps a heroic slumber." The Prince hides himself among the bushes near the castle and sees a fair maiden come out of it surrounded by an armed band "and all the band consists of maidens, each one more beautiful than the other. And the most beautiful, the most never-enough-to-be-gazed-upon, is the Queen herself." For nine days he watches the fair band of Amazons as they ramble about. On the tenth day all is still and he enters the castle. In the midst of her slumbering guards sleeps the Queen on a couch of down, the healing water flowing from her hands and feet. With it he fills two flasks and then he retires. When the Queen awakes, she becomes conscious of the theft and pursues the Prince. Coming up with him, she slays him with a single blow but then takes compassion on him and restores him to life.

---

296 Afanasief, viii. p. 205.

297 Afanasief, vii. No. 5 b.

In another version of the story, the precious fluid is contained in a flask which is hidden under the pillow of the slumbering "Tsar Maiden." The Prince steals it and flees but he bears on him the weight of sin and so, when he tries to clear the fence which girds the enchanted castle, his horse strikes one of the cords attached to it and the spell is broken which maintains the magic sleep in which the realm is locked. The Tsar Maiden pursues the thief but does not succeed in catching him. He is killed, however, by his elder brothers, who "cut him into small pieces," and then take the flask of magic water to their father. The murdered prince is resuscitated by the mythical bird known by the name of the *Zhar-Ptitsa*, which collects his scattered fragments, puts them together and sprinkles them first with "dead water" and then with "live-water,"—conveyed for that purpose in its beak—after which the prince gets up, thanks his reviver and goes his way.[298]

In one of the numerous variants of the story in which a prince is exposed to various dangers by his sister—who is induced to plot against his life by her demon lover, the Snake—the hero is sent in search of "a healing and a vivifying water," preserved between two lofty mountains which cleave closely together, except during "two or three minutes" of each day. He follows his instructions, rides to a certain spot and there awaits the hour at which the mountains fly apart. "Suddenly a terrible hurricane arose, a mighty thunder smote and the two mountains were torn asunder. Prince Ivan spurred his heroic steed, flew like a dart between the mountains, dipped two flasks in the waters and instantly turned back." He himself escapes safe and sound but the hind legs of his horse are caught between the closing cliffs and smashed to pieces.

298 Afanasief, vii. No. 5 a. For the *Zhar-Ptitsa*, see infra, p. 285.

The magic waters, of course, soon remedy this temporary inconvenience.[299]

In a Slovak version of this story, a murderous mother sends her son to two mountains, each of which is cleft open once in every twenty-four hours—the one opening at midday and the other at midnight; the former disclosing the Water of Life, the latter the Water of Death.[300] In a similar story from the Ukraine, mention is made of two springs of healing and life-giving water, which are guarded by iron-beaked ravens and the way to which lies between grinding hills. The Fox and the Hare are sent in quest of the magic fluid. The Fox goes and returns in safety but the Hare, on her way back, is not in time quite to clear the meeting cliffs and her tail is jammed in between them. Since that time, hares have had no tails.[301]

On the Waters of Strength and Weakness much stress is laid in many of the tales about the many-headed Snakes which carry off men's wives and daughters to their metallic castles. In one of these, for instance, the golden-haired Queen Anastasia has been torn away by a whirlwind from her husband "Tsar Byel Byelyanin" [the White King]. As in the variant of the story already quoted,[302] her sons go in search of her and the youngest of them, after finding three palaces—the first of copper, the second of silver, the third of

---

299 Afanasief, vi. p. 249. For a number of interesting legends, collected from the most distant parts of the world, about grinding mountains and crashing cliffs, &c., see Tylor's "Primitive Culture," pp. 313-16. After quoting three mythic descriptions found among the Karens, the Algonquins and the Aztecs, Mr. Tylor remarks, "On the suggestion of this group of solar conceptions and that of Maui's death, we may perhaps explain as derived from a broken-down fancy of solar-myth, that famous episode of Greek legend, where the good ship Argo passed between the Symplêgades, those two huge cliffs that opened and closed again with swift and violent collision."
Several of the Modern Greek stories are very like the skazka mentioned above. In one of these (Hahn, ii. p. 234), a Lamia guards the water of life (άβανατο νερό) which flows within a rock; in another (ii. p. 280) a mountain opens at midday and several springs are disclosed, each of which cries "Draw from me!" but the only one which is life-giving is that to which a bee flies.

300 Wenzig, p. 148.

301 Afanasief, P.V.S. ii. 353.

302 See above, p. 233.

gold, each containing a princess held captive by Vikhor, the whirlwind—comes to a fourth palace gleaming with diamonds and other precious stones. In it he discovers his long-lost mother, who gladly greets him and at once takes him into Vikhor's cellar. Here is the account of what ensued.

Well, they entered the cellar; there stood two tubs of water, the one on the right hand the other on the left. Says the Queen—

"Take a draught of the water that stands on the right hand." Prince Ivan drank of it.

"Now then, how strong do you feel?" said she.

"So strong that I could upset the whole palace with one hand," he replied.

"Come now, drink again."

The Prince drank once more.

"How strong do you feel now?" she asked.

"Why now, if I wanted, I could give the whole world a jolt."

"Oh that's plenty then! Now make these tubs change places—that which stands on the right, set on the left: and that which is on the left, change to the right."

Prince Ivan took the tubs and made them change places. Says the Queen—

"See now, my dear son; in one of these tubs is the 'Water of Strength,' in the other is the 'Water of Weakness.'[303] He who drinks of the former becomes a mighty hero but he who drinks of the second loses all his vigour. Vikhor always quaffs the Strong Water and places it on the right-hand side; therefore you must deceive him or you will never be able to hold out against him."

The Queen proceeds to tell her son that, when Vikhor comes home, he must hide beneath her purple cloak and watch for

303 Silnaya voda or potent water and bezsilnaya voda or impotent water (sila = strength).

an opportunity of seizing her gaoler's magic mace.[304] Vikhor will fly about till he is tired and will then have recourse to what he supposes is the "Strong Water;" this will render him so feeble that the Prince will be able to kill him. Having received these instructions and having been warned not to strike Vikhor after he is dead, the Prince conceals himself. Suddenly the day becomes darkened, the palace quivers and Vikhor arrives; stamping on the ground, he becomes a noble gallant, who enters the palace, "holding in his hands a battle mace." This Prince Ivan seizes it and a long struggle takes place between him and Vikhor, who flies away with him over seas and into the clouds. At last, Vikhor becomes exhausted and seeks the place where he expects to find the invigourating draught on which he is accustomed to rely. The result is as follows:

Dropping right into his cellar, Vikhor ran to the tub which stood on the right and began drinking the Water of Weakness. But Prince Ivan rushed to the left, quaffed a deep draught of the Water of Strength and became the mightiest hero in the whole world. Then seeing that Vikhor was perfectly enfeebled, he snatched from him his keen faulchion and with a single blow struck off his head. Behind him voices began to cry:

"Strike again! strike again! or he will come to life!"

"No," replied the Prince, "a hero's hand does not strike twice but finishes its work with a single blow." And straightway he lighted a fire, burnt the head and the trunk and scattered the ashes to the winds.[305]

The part played by the Water of Strength in this story may be compared with "the important share which the exhilarating juice of the Soma-plant assumes in bracing Indra for his conflict with the hostile powers in the atmosphere," and

304 Palitsa = a cudgel, etc. In the variant of the story quoted in the preceding section the prince seized Vikhor by the right little finger, mizinets. Palets meant a finger. The similarity of the two words may have led to a confusion of ideas.

305 Afanasief, vii. pp. 97–103.

Vikhor's sudden debility with that of Indra when the Asura Namuchi "drank up Indra's strength along with a draught of wine and soma."[306]

Sometimes, as has already been remarked, one of the two magic waters is even more injurious than the Water of Weakness.[307] The following may be taken as a specimen of the stories in which there is introduced a true Water of Death—one of those deadly springs which bear the same relation to the healing and vivifying founts that the enfeebling bears to the strengthening water. The Baba Yaga who figures in it is, as is so often the case, replaced by a Snake in the variant to which allusion has already been made.

---

306 Muir's "Sanskrit Texts," v. p. 258 and p. 94. See, also Mannhardt's "Germ. Mythen," pp. 96-97.

307 Being as destructive as the poison which was created during the churning of the Amrita.

THE BLIND MAN AND THE CRIPPLE.[308]

The legless and the blind are heroes . . .

IN A CERTAIN KINGDOM there lived a king and queen; they had a son, Prince Ivan and to look after that son was appointed a tutor named Katoma.[309] The king and queen lived to a great age but then they fell ill and despaired of ever recovering. So they sent for Prince Ivan and strictly enjoined him:

"When we are dead, do you in everything respect and obey Katoma. If you obey him, you will prosper; but if you choose to be disobedient, you will perish like a fly."

The next day the king and queen died. Prince Ivan buried his parents and took to living according to their instructions. Whatever he had to do, he always consulted his tutor about it.

Some time passed by. The Prince attained to man's estate and began to think about getting married. So one day he went to his tutor and said:

"Katoma, I'm tired of living alone, I want to marry."

"Well, Prince! what's to prevent you? you're of an age at which it's time to think about a bride. Go into the great hall. There's a collection there of the portraits of all the princesses in the world; look at them and choose for yourself; whichever pleases you, to her send a proposal of marriage."

Prince Ivan went into the great hall and began examining the portraits. And the one that pleased him best was that of the Princess Anna the Fair—such a beauty! the like of her wasn't

---

308 Afanasief, v. No. 35.

309 In the original he is generally designated as Katòma—dyàd'ka, dubovaya shàpka, "Katòma-governor, oaken-hat." Not being able to preserve the assonance, I have dropped the greater part of his title.

to be found in the whole world! Underneath her portrait were written these words:

"If anyone asks her a riddle and she does not guess it, him shall she marry; but he whose riddle she guesses shall have his head chopped off."

Prince Ivan read this inscription, became greatly afflicted and went off to his tutor.

"I've been in the great hall," says he, "and I picked out for my bride Anna the Fair; only I don't know whether it's possible to win her."

"Yes, Prince; she's hard to get. If you go alone, you won't win her anyhow. But if you will take me with you and if you will do what I tell you, perhaps the affair can be managed."

Prince Ivan begged Katoma to go with him and gave his word of honour to obey him whether in joy or grief.

Well, they got ready for the journey and set off to sue for the hand of the Princess Anna the Fair. They travelled for one year, two years, three years and traversed many countries. Says Prince Ivan—

"We've been travelling all this time, uncle and now we're approaching the country of Princess Anna the Fair; and yet we don't know what riddle to propound."

"We shall manage to think of one in good time," replied Katoma. They went a little farther. Katoma was looking down on the road and on it lay a purse full of money. He lifted it up directly, poured all the money out of it into his own purse and said—

"Here's a riddle for you, Prince Ivan! When you come into the presence of the Princess, propound a riddle to her in these words: 'As we were coming along, we saw Good lying on the road and we took up the Good with Good and placed it in our own Good!' That riddle she won't guess in a lifetime; but any other one she would find out directly. She would only have to look into her magic-book and as soon as she had guessed it, she'd order your head to be cut off."

Well, at last Prince Ivan and his tutor arrived at the lofty palace in which lived the fair Princess. At that moment she happened to be out on the balcony and when she saw the newcomers, she sent out to know whence they came and what they wanted. Prince Ivan replied—

"I have come from such-and-such a kingdom and I wish to sue for the hand of the Princess Anna the Fair."

When she was informed of this, the Princess gave orders that the Prince should enter the palace and there in the presence of all the princes and boyars of her council should propound his riddle.

"I've made this compact," she said. "Anyone whose riddle I cannot guess, him I must marry. But anyone whose riddle I can guess, him I may put to death."

"Listen to my riddle, fair princess!" said Prince Ivan. "As we came along, we saw Good lying on the road and we took up the Good with Good and placed it in our own Good."

Princess Anna the Fair took her magic-book and began turning over its leaves and examining the answers of riddles. She went right through the book but she didn't get at the meaning she wanted. Thereupon the princes and boyars of her council decided that the Princess must marry Prince Ivan. She wasn't at all pleased but there was no help for it and so she began to get ready for the wedding. Meanwhile she considered within herself how she could spin out the time and do away with the bridegroom and she thought the best way would be to overwhelm him with tremendous tasks.

So she called Prince Ivan and said to him—

"My dear Prince Ivan, my destined husband! It is meet that we should prepare for the wedding; pray do me this small service. On such and such a spot of my kingdom there stands a lofty iron pillar. Carry it into the palace kitchen and chop it into small chunks by way of fuel for the cook."

"Excuse me, Princess," replied the prince. "Was it to chop fuel that I came here? Is that the proper sort of employment for me? I have a servant for that kind of thing, Katoma *dyadka*, of the oaken *shapka*."

The Prince straightway called for his tutor and ordered him to drag the iron pillar into the kitchen and to chop it into small chunks by way of fuel for the cook. Katoma went to the spot indicated by the Princess, seized the pillar in his arms, brought it into the palace kitchen and broke it into little pieces; but four of the iron chips he put into his pocket, saying—

"They'll prove useful by-and-by!"

Next day the princess says to Prince Ivan—

"My dear Prince, my destined husband! tomorrow we have to go to the wedding. I will drive in a carriage but you should ride on a heroic steed and it is necessary that you should break him in beforehand."

"I break a horse in myself! I keep a servant for that."

Prince Ivan called Katoma and said—

"Go into the stable and tell the grooms to bring forth the heroic steed; sit upon him and break him in; tomorrow I've got to ride him to the wedding."

Katoma fathomed the subtle device of the Princess, but without stopping long to talk, he went into the stable and told the grooms to bring forth the heroic steed. Twelve grooms were mustered, they unlocked twelve locks, opened twelve doors and brought forth a magic horse bound in twelve chains of iron. Katoma went up to him. No sooner had he managed to seat himself than the magic horse leaped up from the ground and soared higher than the forest—higher than the standing forest, lower than the flitting cloud. Firm sat Katoma, with one hand grasping the mane; with the other he took from his pocket an iron chunk and began taming the horse with it between the ears. When he had used up one chunk, he betook himself to another; when two were used up, he took to a third; when three were used up, the fourth came into play. And so grievously did he punish the heroic steed that it could not hold out any longer but cried aloud with a human voice—

"Batyushka Katoma! don't utterly deprive me of life in the white world! Whatever you wish, that do you order: all shall be done according to your will!"

"Listen, O meat for dogs!" answered Katoma; "tomorrow Prince Ivan will ride you to the wedding. Now mind! when the grooms bring you out into the wide courtyard and the Prince goes up to you and lays his hand on you, do you stand quietly, not moving so much as an ear. And when he is seated on your back, do you sink into the earth right up to your fetlocks and then move under him with a heavy step, just as if an immeasurable weight had been laid upon your back."

The heroic steed listened to the order and sank to earth scarcely alive. Katoma seized him by the tail and flung him close to the stable, crying—

"Ho there! coachmen and grooms; carry off this dog's-meat to its stall!"

The next day arrived; the time drew near for going to the wedding. The carriage was brought round for the Princess and the heroic steed for Prince Ivan. The people were gathered together from all sides—a countless number. The bride and bridegroom came out from the white stone halls. The Princess got into the carriage and waited to see what would become of Prince Ivan; whether the magic horse would fling his curls to the wind and scatter his bones across the open plain. Prince Ivan approached the horse, laid his hand upon its back, placed his foot in the stirrup—the horse stood just as if petrified, didn't so much as wag an ear! The Prince got on its back, the magic horse sank into the earth up to its fetlocks. The twelve chains were taken off the horse, it began to move with an even heavy pace, while the sweat poured off it just like hail.

"What a hero! What immeasurable strength!" cried the people as they gazed upon the Prince.

So the bride and bridegroom were married and then they began to move out of the church, holding each other by the hand. The Princess took it into her head to make one more trial of Prince Ivan, so she squeezed his hand so hard that he could not bear the pain. His face became suffused with blood, his eyes disappeared beneath his brows.

"A fine sort of hero you are!" thought the Princess. "Your tutor has tricked me splendidly; but you shan't get off for nothing!"

Princess Anna the Fair lived for some time with Prince Ivan as a wife ought to live with a God-given[310] husband flattered him in every way in words but in reality never thought of anything except by what means she might get rid of Katoma. With the Prince, without the tutor, there'd be no difficulty in settling matters! she said to herself. But whatever slanders she might invent, Prince Ivan never would allow himself to be influenced by what she said but always felt sorry for his tutor. At the end of a year he said to his wife one day—

"Beauteous Princess, my beloved spouse! I should like to go with you to my own kingdom."

"By all means," replied she, "let us go. I myself have long been wishing to see your kingdom."

Well they got ready and went off; Katoma was allotted the post of coachman. They drove and drove and as they drove along Prince Ivan went to sleep. Suddenly the Princess Anna the Fair awoke him, uttering loud complaints—

---

310 Bogodanny (bog = God; dat', davat' = to give). One of the Russian equivalents for our hideous "father-in-law" is "God-given father" (bogodanny otets) and for "mother-in-law," bogodanny mat' or "God-given mother." (Dahl.)

"Listen, Prince, you're always sleeping, you hear nothing! But your tutor doesn't obey me a bit, drives the horses on purpose over hill and dale, just as if he wanted to put an end to us both. I tried speaking him fair but he jeered at me. I won't go on living any longer if you don't punish him!"

Prince Ivan, 'twixt sleeping and waking, waxed very wroth with his tutor and handed him over entirely to the Princess, saying—

"Deal with him as you please!"

The Princess ordered his feet to be cut off. Katoma submitted patiently to the outrage.

"Very good," he thinks; "I shall suffer, it's true; but the Prince also will know what to lead a wretched life is like!"

When both of Katoma's feet had been cut off, the Princess glanced around and saw that a tall tree-stump stood on one side; so she called her servants and ordered them to set him on that stump. But as for Prince Ivan, she tied him to the carriage by a cord, turned the horses round and drove back to her own kingdom. Katoma was left sitting on the stump, weeping bitter tears.

"Farewell, Prince Ivan!" he cries; "you won't forget me!"

Meanwhile Prince Ivan was running and bounding behind the carriage. He knew well enough by this time what a blunder he had made but there was no turning back for him. When the Princess Anna the Fair arrived in her kingdom, she set Prince Ivan to take care of the cows. Every day he went afield with the herd at early morn and in the evening he drove them back to the royal yard. At that hour the Princess was always sitting on the balcony and looking out to see that the number of the cows were all right.[311]

Katoma remained sitting on the stump one day, two days, three days, without anything to eat or drink. To get down was

311 Four lines are omitted here. See A. de Gubernatis, "Zool. Mythology," i. 181, where a solar explanation of the whole story will be found.

utterly impossible, it seemed as if he must die of starvation. But not far away from that place there was a dense forest. In that forest was living a mighty hero who was quite blind. The only way by which he could get himself food was this: whenever he perceived by the sense of smell that any animal was running past him, whether a hare or a fox or a bear, he immediately started in chase of it, caught it—and dinner was ready for him. The hero was exceedingly swift-footed and there was not a single wild beast which could run away from him. Well, one day it fell out thus. A fox slunk past; the hero heard it and was after it directly. It ran up to the tall stump and turned sharp off on one-side; but the blind hero hurried on, took a spring and thumped his forehead against the stump so hard that he knocked the stump out by the roots. Katoma fell to the ground and asked:

"Who are you?"

"I'm a blind hero. I've been living in the forest for thirty years. The only way I can get my food is this: to catch some game or other and cook it at a wood fire. If it had not been for that, I should have been starved to death long ago!"

"You haven't been blind all your life?"

"No, not all my life; but Princess Anna the Fair put my eyes out!"

"There now, brother!" says Katoma; "and it's thanks to her, too, that I'm left here without any feet. She cut them both off, the accursed one!"

The two heroes had a talk and agreed to live together and join in getting their food. The blind man says to the lame:

"Sit on my back and show me the way; I will serve you with my feet and you me with your eyes."

So he took the cripple and carried him home and Katoma sat on his back, kept a look out all round and cried out from time to time: "Right! Left! Straight on!" and so forth.

Well, they lived some time in the forest in that way and caught hares, foxes and bears for their dinner. One day the cripple says—

"Surely we can never go on living all our lives without a soul [to speak to]. I have heard that in such and such a town lives a rich merchant who has a daughter; and that merchant's daughter is exceedingly kind to the poor and crippled. She gives alms to everyone. Suppose we carry her off, brother and let her live here and keep house for us."

The blind man took a cart, seated the cripple in it and rattled it into the town, straight into the rich merchant's courtyard. The merchant's daughter saw them out of window and immediately ran out and came to give them alms. Approaching the cripple, she said:

"Take this, in Christ's name, poor fellow!"

He [seemed to be going] to take the gift but he seized her by the hand pulled her into the cart and called to the blind man, who ran off with it at such a pace that no one could catch him, even on horseback. The merchant sent people in pursuit—but no, they could not come up with him.

The heroes brought the merchant's daughter into their forest hut and said to her:

"Be in the place of a sister to us, live here and keep house for us; otherwise we poor sufferers will have no one to cook our meals or wash our shirts. God won't desert you if you do that!"

The merchant's daughter remained with them. The heroes respected her, loved her, acknowledged her as a sister. They used to be out hunting all day but their adopted sister was always at home. She looked after all the housekeeping, prepared the meals, washed the linen.

But after a time a Baba Yaga took to haunting their hut and sucking the breasts of the merchant's daughter. No sooner have the heroes gone off to the chase, than the Baba Yaga is there in a moment. Before long the fair maiden's face began to fall away and she grew weak and thin. The blind man could see nothing but Katoma remarked that things weren't going well. He spoke about it to the blind man and they went together to their adopted sister and began questioning her. But the Baba Yaga had strictly forbidden her to tell the truth. For a long time she was afraid to acquaint them with her trouble, for a long time she held out but at last her brothers talked her over and she told them everything without reserve.

"Every time you go away to the chase," says she, "there immediately appears in the cottage a very old woman with a most evil face and long grey hair. And she sets me to dress her head and meanwhile she sucks my breasts."

"Ah!" says the blind man, "that's a Baba Yaga. Wait a bit; we must treat her after her own fashion. Tomorrow we won't go to the chase but we'll try to entice her and lay hands upon her!"

So next morning the heroes didn't go out hunting.

"Now then, Uncle Footless!" says the blind man, "you get under the bench and lie there ever so still and I'll go into the yard and stand under the window. And as for you, sister, when the Baba Yaga comes, sit down just here, close by the window; and as you dress her hair, quietly separate the locks and throw them outside through the window. Just let me lay hold of her by those grey hairs of hers!"

What was said was done. The blind man laid hold of the Baba Yaga by her grey hair and cried—

"Ho there, Uncle Katoma! Come out from under the bench and lay hold of this viper of a woman, while I go into the hut!"

The Baba Yaga hears the bad news and tries to jump up to get her head free. (*Where are you off to? That's no go, sure enough!*[312]) She tugs and tugs but cannot do herself any good!

312 These ejaculations belong to the storyteller.

Just then from under the bench crawled Uncle Katoma, fell upon her like a mountain of stone, took to strangling her until the heaven seemed to her to disappear.[313] Then into the cottage bounded the blind man, crying to the cripple—

"Now we must heap up a great pile of wood and consume this accursed one with fire and fling her ashes to the wind!"

The Baba Yaga began imploring them:

"My fathers! my darlings! forgive me. I will do all that is right."

"Very good, old witch! Then show us the fountain of healing and life-giving water!" said the heroes.

"Only don't kill me and I'll show it you directly!"

Well, Katoma sat on the blind man's back. The blind man took the Baba Yaga by her back hair and she led them into the depths of the forest, brought them to a well,[314] and said—

"That is the water that cures and gives life."

"Look out, Uncle Katoma!" cried the blind man; "don't make a blunder. If she tricks us now we shan't get right all our lives!"

Katoma cut a green branch off a tree and flung it into the well. The bough hadn't so much as reached the water before it all burst into a flame!

"Ha! so you're still up to your tricks," said the heroes and began to strangle the Baba Yaga, with the intention of flinging her, the accursed one, into the fiery fount. More than ever did the Baba Yaga implore for mercy, swearing a great oath that she would not deceive them this time.

"On my troth I will bring you to good water," says she.

The heroes consented to give her one more trial and she took them to another fount.

---

313 Literally, "Seemed to her as small as a lamb."

314 Kolòdez, a word connected with kolòda a log, trough, &c.

Uncle Katoma cut a dry spray from a tree and flung it into the fount. The spray had not yet reached the water when it already turned green, budded and put forth blossoms.

"Come now, that's good water!" said Katoma.

The blind man wetted his eyes with it and saw directly. He lowered the cripple into the water and the lame man's feet grew again. Then they both rejoiced greatly and said to one another, "Now the time has come for us to get all right! We'll get everything back again we used to have! Only first we must make an end of the Baba Yaga. If we were to pardon her now, we should always be unlucky; she'd be scheming mischief all her life."

Accordingly they went back to the fiery fount and flung the Baba Yaga into it; didn't it soon make an end of her!

After this Katoma married the merchant's daughter and the three companions went to the kingdom of Anna the Fair in order to rescue Prince Ivan. When they drew near to the capital, what should they see but Prince Ivan driving a herd of cows!

"Stop, herdsman!" says Katoma; "where are you driving these cows?"

"I'm driving them to the Princess's courtyard," replied the Prince. "The Princess always sees for herself whether all the cows are there."

"Here, herdsman; take my clothes and put them on and I will put on yours and drive the cows."

"No, brother! that cannot be done. If the Princess found it out, I should suffer harm!"

"Never fear, nothing will happen! Katoma will guarantee you that."

Prince Ivan sighed and said—

"Ah, good man! If Katoma had been alive, I should not have been feeding these cows afield!"

Then Katoma disclosed to him who he was. Prince Ivan warmly embraced him and burst into tears.

"I never hoped even to see you again," said he.

So they exchanged clothes. The tutor drove the cows to the Princess's courtyard. Anna the Fair went into the balcony, looked to see if all the cows were there and ordered them to be driven into the sheds. All the cows went into the sheds except the last one, which remained at the gate. Katoma sprang at it, exclaiming—

"What are you waiting for, dog's-meat?"

Then he seized it by the tail and pulled it so hard that he pulled the cow's hide right off! The Princess saw this and cried with a loud voice:

"What is that brute of a cowherd doing? Seize him and bring him to me!"

Then the servants seized Katoma and dragged him to the palace. He went with them, making no excuses, relying on himself. They brought him to the Princess. She looked at him and asked—

"Who are you? Where do you come from?"

"I am he whose feet you cut off and whom you set on a stump. My name is Katoma *dyadka*, oaken *shapka*."

"Well," thinks the Princess, "now that he's got his feet back again, I must act straight-forwardly with him for the future."

And she began to beseech him and the Prince to pardon her. She confessed all her sins and swore an oath always to love Prince Ivan and to obey him in all things. Prince Ivan forgave her and began to live with her in peace and concord. The hero who had been blind remained with them but Katoma and his wife went to the house of [her father] the rich merchant and took up their abode under his roof.

~

[There is a story in the "Panchatantra" (v. 12) which, in default of other parallels, may be worth comparing with that part of this Skazka which refers to the blind man and the cripple in the forest. Here is an outline of it:—

To a certain king a daughter is born who has three breasts. Deeming her presence unfortunate, he offers a hundred thousand purses of gold to anyone who will marry her and take her away. For a long time no man takes advantage of the offer but at last a blind man, who goes about led by a hunchback named Mantharaka or Cripple, marries her, receives the gold and is sent far away with his wife and his friend. All three live together in the same house. After a time the wife falls in love with the hunchback and conspires with him to kill her husband. For this purpose she boils a snake, intending to poison her husband with it. But he stirs the snake-broth as it is cooking and the steam which rises from it cures his blindness. Seeing the snake in the pot, he guesses what has occurred, so he pretends to be still blind and watches his wife and his friend. They, not knowing he can see, embrace in his presence, whereupon he catches up the "cripple" by the legs and dashes him against his wife. So violent is the blow that her third breast is driven out of sight and the hunchback is beaten straight. Benfey (whose version of the story differs at the end from that given by Wilson, "Essays," ii. 74) in his remarks on this story (i. p. 510-15), which he connects with Buddhist legends, observes that it occurs also in the "Tuti-Nameh" (Rosen, ii. 228) but there the hunchback is replaced by a comely youth and the similarity with the Russian story disappears. For a solar explanation of the Indian story see A. de Gubernatis, "Zool. Mythology," i. 85.]

Of this story there are many variants. In one of them[315] a king promises to reward with vast wealth anyone who will find him "a bride fairer than the sun, brighter than the moon and whiter than snow." A certain moujik, named Nikita Koltoma, offers to show him where a princess lives who answers to this description and goes forth with him in search of her. On the way, Nikita enters several forges, desiring to have a war mace cast for him and in one of them

315 Afanasief, viii. No. 23 a.

he finds fifty smiths tormenting an old man. Ten of them are holding him by the beard with pincers, the others are thundering away at his ribs with their hammers. Finding that the cause of this punishment is an unpaid debt of fifty roubles, Nikita ransoms the greybeard, who straightway disappears. Nikita obtains the mace he wants, which weighs fifty poods or nearly a ton and leaves the forge. Presently the old man whom he has ransomed comes running up to him, thanks him for having rescued him from a punishment which had already lasted thirty years and bestows on him, as a token of gratitude, a Cap of Invisibility.

Soon after this Nikita, attended by the king and his followers, reaches the palace of the royal heroine, Helena the Fair. She at first sends her warriors to capture or slay the unwelcome visitors but Nikita attacks them with his mace and leaves scarce one alive. Then she invites the king and his suite to the palace, having prepared in the meantime a gigantic bow fitted with a fiery arrow, wherewith to annihilate her guests. Guessing this, Nikita puts on his Cap of Invisibility, bends the bow and shoots the arrow into the queen's *terema* [the women's chambers] and in a moment the whole upper story is in a blaze. After that the queen submits and is married to the king.

But Nikita warns him that for three nights running his bride will make trial of his strength by laying her hand on his breast and pressing it hard—so hard that he will not be able to bear the pressure. When that happens, he must slip out of the room and let Nikita take his place. All this comes to pass; the bride lays her hand on the bridegroom's breast and says—

"Is my hand heavy?"

"As a feather on water!" replies the king, who can scarcely draw his breath beneath the crushing weight of the hand he has won. Then he leaves the room, under the pretext of giving an order and Nikita takes his place. The queen renews the experiment, presses with one hand presses with both and with all her might. Nikita catches her up and then flings her down on the floor. The room shakes beneath the blow, the bride "arises, lies down quietly and goes to sleep," and Nikita is replaced by the king. By the end of the third night the queen gives up all hope of squeezing her husband to death and makes up her mind to conjugal submission.[316]

But before long, she, like Brynhild, finds out that she has been tricked and resolves on revenge. Throwing Nikita into a slumber which lasts for twenty-four hours, she has his feet cut off and sets him adrift in a boat; then she degrades her husband turning him into a swineherd and she puts out the eyes of Nikita's brother Timofei. In the course of time the brothers obtain from a Baba Yaga the healing and vivifying waters and so recover the eyes and feet they had lost. The Witch-Queen is put to death and Nikita lives happily as the King's Prime Minister. The specific actions of the two waters are described with great precision in this story. When the lame man sprinkles his legs with the Healing Water, they become whole at once; "his legs are quite sound, only they don't move." Then he applies the Vivifying Water and the use of his legs returns to him. Similarly when the blind man applies the Healing Water to his empty orbits, he obtains new eyes—"perfectly faultless eyes, only he cannot see with them;" he applies the Vivifying Water, "and begins to see even better than before."

In a Ryazan variant of the story,[317] Ivan Dearly-Bought, after his legs have been cut off at the knees and he has been

316 To this episode a striking parallel is offered by that of Gunther's wedding night in the "Nibelungenlied," in which Brynhild flings her husband Gunther across the room, kneels on his chest and finally binds him hand and foot and suspends him from a nail till daybreak. The next night Siegfried takes his place and wrestles with the mighty maiden. After a long struggle he flings her on the floor and forces her to submit. Then he leaves the room and Gunther returns. A summary of the story will be found in the "Tales of the Teutonic Lands," by G. W. Cox and E. H. Jones, pp. 94-5.
317 Khudyakof, i. No. 19. pp. 73-7.

left in a forest, is found by a giant who has no arms but who is so fleet that "no post could catch him up." The two maimed heroes form an alliance. After a time, they carry off a princess who is suffering from some mysterious disease and take her to their forest home. She tells them that her illness is due to a Snake, which comes to her every night, entering by the chimney and sucks away her strength. The heroes seizes the Snake, which takes them to the healing lake and they are cured. Then they restore the princess, also cured, to her father. Ivan returns to the palace of the Enchantress Queen who had maimed him and beats her with red-hot iron bars until he has driven out of her all her magic strength, "leaving her only one woman's strength and that a very poor one."

In a Tula variant[318] the wicked wife, who has set her confiding husband to tend her pigs, is killed by the hero. She had put out his eyes and had cut off the feet of another companion of her husband; in this variant also the Healing Waters are found by the aid of a snake.

The supernatural steed which Katoma tamed belongs to an equine race which often figures in the Skazkas. A good account of one of these horses is given in the following story of—

318 Erlenvein, No. 19, pp. 95-7. For a Little-Russian version see Kulish, ii. pp. 59-82.

PRINCESS HELENA THE FAIR.[319]

With the assistance of a magical horse . . .

We say that we are wise folks but our old people dispute the fact, saying: "No, no, we were wiser than you are." But skazkas tell that, before our grandfathers had learnt anything, before their grandfathers320 were born—[321]

THERE LIVED IN A certain land an old man of this kind who instructed his three sons in reading and writing[322] and all book learning. Then said he to them: "Now, my children! When I die, mind you come and read prayers over my grave."

"Very good, father, very good," they replied.

The two elder brothers were such fine strapping fellows! so tall and stout! But as for the youngest one, Ivan, he was like a half-grown lad or a half-fledged duckling, terribly inferior to the others. Well, their old father died. At that very time there came tidings from the King, that his daughter, the Princess Helena the Fair, had ordered a shrine to be built for her with twelve columns, with twelve rows of beams. In that shrine she was sitting upon a high throne and awaiting her bridegroom, the bold youth who, with a single bound of his swift steed, should reach high enough to kiss her on the lips. A stir ran through the whole youth of the nation. They took to licking their lips and scratching their heads and wondering to whose share so great an honour would fall.

---

319 Afanasief, vi. No. 26. From the Kursk Government.

320 *Prashchurui.*

321 The sentence in italics is a good specimen of the *priskazka* or preface.

322 *Gramota* = γράμματα whence comes *gràmotey*, able to read and write = γραμματικό

"Brothers!" said Vanyusha,[323] "our father is dead; which of us is to read prayers over his grave?"

"Whoever feels inclined, let him go!" answered the brothers.

So Vanya went. But as for his elder brothers they did nothing but exercise their horses and curl their hair and dye their moustaches.

The second night came.

"Brothers!" said Vanya, "I've done my share of reading. It's your turn now; which of you will go?"

"Whoever likes can go and read. We've business to look after; don't you meddle."

And they cocked their caps and shouted and whooped and flew this way and shot that way and roved about the open country.

So Vanyusha read prayers this time also—and on the third night, too.

Well, his brothers got ready their horses, combed out their moustaches and prepared to go next morning to test their mettle before the eyes of Helena the Fair.

"Shall we take the youngster?" they thought. "No, no. What would be the good of him? He'd make folks laugh and put us to confusion; let's go by ourselves."

So away they went. But Vanyusha wanted very much to have a look at the Princess Helena the Fair. He cried, cried bitterly; and went out to his father's grave. And his father heard him in his coffin and came out to him, shook the damp earth off his body and said:

"Don't grieve, Vanya. I'll help you in your trouble."

And immediately the old man drew himself up and straightened himself and called aloud and whistled with a ringing voice, with a shrill[324] whistle.

---

323 Vanya and Vanyusha are diminutives of Ivan (John), answering to our Johnny; Vanka is another, more like our Jack.

324 Literally "with a Solovei-like whistle." The word *solovei* generally means a nightingale but it was also the name of a mythical hero, a robber whose voice or whistle had the power of killing those who heard it.

From goodness knows whence appeared a horse, the earth quaking beneath it, a flame rushing from its ears and nostrils. To and fro it flew and then stood still before the old man, as if rooted in the ground and cried,

"What are thy commands?"

Vanya crept into one of the horse's ears and out of the other and turned into such a hero as no skazka can tell of, no pen describe! He mounted the horse, set his arms akimbo and flew, just like a falcon, straight to the home of the Princess Helena. With a wave of his hand with a bound aloft, he only failed by the breadth of two rows of beams. Back again he turned, galloped up, leapt aloft and got within one beam-row's breadth. Once more he turned, once more he wheeled, then shot past the eye like a streak of fire, took an accurate aim and kissed[325] the fair Helena right on the lips!

"Who is he? Who is he? Stop him! Stop him!" was the cry. Not a trace of him was to be found!

Away he galloped to his father's grave, let the horse go free, prostrated himself on the earth and besought his father's counsel. And the old man held counsel with him.

When he got home he behaved as if he hadn't been anywhere. His brothers talked away, describing where they had been, what they had seen and he listened to them as of old.

The next day there was a gathering again. In the princely halls there were more boyars and nobles than a single glance could take in. The elder brothers rode there. Their younger brother went there too but on foot, meekly and modestly, just as if he hadn't kissed the Princess and seated himself in a distant corner. The Princess Helena asked for her bridegroom, wanted to show him to the world at large, wanted to give him half her kingdom; but the bridegroom did not put in an appearance! Search was made for him among the boyars,

---

325 Chmoknuel, smacked.

among the generals; everyone was examined in his turn—but with no result! Meanwhile, Vanya looked on, smiling and chuckling and waiting till the bride should come to him herself.

"I pleased her then," says he, "when I appeared as a gay gallant; now let her fall in love with me in my plain caftan."

Then up she rose, looked around with bright eyes that shed a radiance on all who stood there and saw and knew her bridegroom and made him take his seat by her side and speedily was wedded to him. And he—good heavens! how clever he turned out and how brave and what a handsome fellow! Only see him mount his flying steed, give his cap a cock and stick his elbows akimbo! why, you'd say he was a king, a born king! you'd never suspect he once was only Vanyusha.

~

The incident of the midnight watch by a father's grave, kept by a son to whom the dead man appears and gives a magic horse, often occurs in the Skazkas. It is thoroughly in accordance with Slavonic ideas about the residence of the dead in their tombs and their ability to assist their descendants in time of trouble. Appeals for aid to a dead parent are of frequent occurrence in the songs still sung by the Russian peasantry at funerals or over graves; especially in those in which orphans express their grief, calling upon the grave to open and the dead to appear and listen and help.[326] So in the Indian story of Punchkin, the seven hungry stepmother-persecuted princesses go out every day and sit by their dead mother's tomb and cry and say, "Oh, mother, mother, cannot you see your poor children, how unhappy we are," etc., until a tree grows up out of the grave laden with fruits for their relief.[327] So in the German tale,[328] Cinderella is aided by the

326 See Barsof's rich collection of North-Russian funeral poetry, entitled "Prichitaniya Syevernago Kraya," Moscow, 1872. Also the "Songs of the Russian People," pp. 334-345.

327 Miss Frere's "Old Deccan Days," pp. 3, 4.

328 Grimm, KM. No. 21.

white bird, which dwells in the hazel tree growing out of her mother's grave.

In one of the Skazkas[329] a stepdaughter is assisted by her cow. The girl, following its instructions, gets in at one ear and out of the other and finds all her tasks performed, all her difficulties removed. When it is killed, there springs from its bones a tree which befriends the girl and gains her a lordly husband. In a Servian variant of the story, it is distinctly stated that the protecting cow had been the girl's mother—manifestly in a previous state of existence, a purely Buddhistic idea.[330]

In several of the Skazkas we find an account of a princess who is won in a similar manner to that described in the story of Helena the Fair. In one case,[331] a king promises to give his daughter to anyone "who can pluck her portrait from the house, from the other side of ever so many beams." The youngest brother, Ivan the Simpleton, carries away the portrait and its cover at the third trial. In another, a king offers his daughter and half his kingdom to him "who can kiss the princess through twelve sheets of glass."[332] The usual youngest brother is carried towards her so forcibly by his magic steed that, at the first trial, he breaks through six of the sheets of glass; at the second, says the story, "he smashed all twelve of the sheets of glass and he kissed the Princess Priceless-Beauty and she immediately stamped a mark upon his forehead." By this mark, after he has disappeared for some time, he is eventually recognised and the princess is obliged to marry him.[333] In a third story,[334] the conditions of winning the princely bride are easier, for "he who takes a leap on

329 Afanasief, vi. No. 54.
330 Ona krava shto yoy ye bila mati, Vuk Karajich, p. 158. In the German translation (p. 188) Wie dies nun die Kuh sah, die einst seine Mutter gewesen war.
331 Afanasief, ii. p. 254.
332 Cherez dvyenadtsat' stekol. Steklo means a glass or a pane of glass.
333 Afanasief, ii. p. 269.
334 Khudyakof, No. 50.

horseback and kisses the king's daughter on the balcony, to him will they give her to wife." In a fourth, the princess is to marry the man "who, on horseback, bounds up to her on the third floor." At the first trial, the *Durak* or Fool, reaches the first floor, at the next, the second; and the third time, "he bounds right up to the princess and carries off from her a ring."[335]

In the Norse story of "Dapplegrim,"[336] a younger brother saves a princess who had been stolen by a Troll and hidden in a cave above a steep wall of rock as smooth as glass. Twice his magic horse tries in vain to surmount it but the third time it succeeds and the youth carries off the princess, who ultimately becomes his wife. Another Norse story still more closely resembles the Russian tales. In "The Princess on the Glass Hill"[337] the hero gains a Princess as his wife by riding up a hill of glass, on the top of which she sits with three golden apples in her lap and by carrying off these precious fruits. He is enabled to perform this feat by a magic horse, which he obtains by watching his father's crops on three successive St. John's Nights.

In a Celtic story,[338] a king promises his daughter and two-thirds of his kingdom, to anyone who can get her out of a turret which "was aloft, on the top of four carraghan (?fortified) towers." The hero Conall kicks "one of the posts that was keeping the turret aloft," the post breaks and the turret falls but Conall catches it in his hands before it reaches the ground, a door opens and out comes the Princess Sunbeam and throws her arms about Conall's neck.

In most of these stories the wife-gaining leap is so vaguely described that it is allowable to suppose that the original idea has been greatly obscured in the course of travel. In some

---

335 Afanasief, iii. p. 25.
336 Dasent's "Norse Tales," No. 40. Asbjörnsen and Moe, No. 37. "Grimsborken."
337 Dasent, No. 13. Asbjörnsen and Moe, No. 51. "Jomfruen paa Glasberget."
338 Campbell's "West-Highland Tales," iii. pp. 265, 266.

Eastern stories it is set in a much plainer light; in one modern collection for instance,[339] it occurs four times. A princess is so fond of her marble bath, which is "like a little sea," with high spiked walls all around it, that she vows she will marry no one who cannot jump across it on horseback. Another princess determines to marry him only who can leap into the glass palace in which she dwells, surrounded by a wide river; and many kings and princes perish miserably in attempting to perform the feat. A third king's daughter lives in a garden "hedged round with seven hedges made of bayonets," by which her suitors are generally transfixed. A fourth "has vowed to marry no man who cannot jump on foot over the seven hedges made of spears and across the seven great ditches that surround her house;" and "hundreds of thousands of Rajahs have tried to do it and died in the attempt."

The secluded princess of these stories may have been primarily akin to the heroine of the "Sleeping Beauty" tales but no special significance appears now to be attributable to her isolation. The original idea seems to have been best preserved in the two legends of the wooing of Brynhild by Sigurd, in the first of which he awakens her from her magic sleep, while in the second he gains her hand (for Gunnar) by a daring and difficult ride—for "him only would she have who should ride through the flaming fire that was drawn about her hall." Gunnar fails to do so but Sigurd succeeds; his horse leaps into the fire, "and a mighty roar arose as the fire burned ever madder and the earth trembled and the flames went up even unto the heavens, nor had any dared to ride as he rode, even as it were through the deep murk."[340]

We will take next a story which is a great favourite in Russia and which will serve as another illustration of the use made of magical "properties" in the Skazkas.

---

339 Miss Frere's "Old Deccan Days," pp. 31, 73, 95, 135.

340 "Völsunga Saga," translated by E. Magnússon and W. Morris, pp. 95-6.

EMILIAN THE FOOL.[341]

By the Pike's command . . .

THERE WERE ONCE THREE brothers, of whom two were sharp-witted but the third was a fool. The elder brothers set off to sell their goods in the towns down the river,[342] and said to the fool:

"Now mind, fool! obey our wives and pay them respect as if they were your own mothers. We'll buy you red boots and a red caftan and a red shirt."

The fool said to them:

"Very good; I will pay them respect."

They gave the fool their orders and went away to the downstream towns; but the fool stretched himself on top of the stove and remained lying there. His brothers' wives say to him—

"What are you about, fool! your brothers ordered you to pay us respect and in return for that each of them was going to bring you a present but there you lie on the stove and don't do a bit of work. Go and fetch some water, at all events."

The fool took a couple of pails and went to fetch the water. As he scooped it up, a pike happened to get into his pail. Says the fool:

"Glory to God! now I will cook this pike and will eat it all myself; I won't give a bit of it to my sisters-in-law. I'm savage with them!"

The pike says to him with a human voice:

"Don't eat me, fool! if you'll put me back again into the water you shall have good luck!"

---

341 Afanasief, vi. No. 32. From the Novgorod Government. A "chapbook" version of this story will be found in Dietrich's collection (pp. 152–68 of the English translation); also in Keightley's "Tales and Popular Fictions."

342 Nijnie, lower. Thus Nijny Novgorod is the lower (down the Volga) Novgorod. (Dahl.)

Says the fool, "What sort of good luck shall I get from you?"

"Why, this sort of good luck: whatever you say, that shall be done. Say, for instance, 'By the Pike's command at my request, go home, ye pails and be set in your places.'"

As soon as the fool had said this, the pails immediately went home of their own accord and became set in their places. The sisters-in-law looked and wondered.

"What sort of a fool is this!" they say. "Why, he's so knowing, you see, that his pails have come home and gone to their places of their own accord!"

The fool came back and lay down on the stove. Again did his brothers' wives begin saying to him—

"What are you lying on the stove for, fool? there's no wood for the fire; go and fetch some."

The fool took two axes and got into a sledge but without harnessing a horse to it.

"By the Pike's command," he says, "at my request, drive, into the forest, O sledge!"

Away went the sledge at a rattling pace, as if urged on by someone. The fool had to pass by a town and the people he met were jammed into corners by his horseless sledge in a way that was perfectly awful. They all began crying out:

"Stop him! Catch him!"

But they couldn't lay hands on him. The fool drove into the forest, got out of the sledge, sat down on a log and said—

"One of you axes fell the trees, while the other cuts them up into billets."

Well, the firewood was cut up and piled on the sledge. Then says the fool:

"Now then, one of you axes! go and cut me a cudgel,[343] as heavy a one as I can lift."

---

343 Kukova, a stick or cudgel, one end of which is bent and rounded like a ball.

The axe went and cut him a cudgel and the cudgel came and lay on top of the load.

The fool took his seat and drove off. He drove by the town but the townspeople had met together and had been looking out for him for ever so long. So they stopped the fool, laid hands upon him and began pulling him about. Says the fool—

"By the Pike's command at my request, go, O cudgel and bestir thyself."

Out jumped the cudgel and took to thumping and smashing and knocked over ever such a lot of people. There they lay on the ground, strewed about like so many sheaves of corn. The fool got clear of them and drove home, heaped up the wood and then lay down on the stove.

Meanwhile, the townspeople got up a petition against him and denounced him to the King, saying:

"Folks say there's no getting hold of him the way we tried;[344] we must entice him by cunning and the best way of all will be to promise him a red shirt and a red caftan and red boots."

So the King's runners came for the fool.

"Go to the King," they say, "he will give you red boots, a red caftan and a red shirt."

Well, the fool said:

"By the Pike's command at my request, do thou, O stove, go to the King!"

He was seated on the stove at the time. The stove went; the fool arrived at the King's.

The King was going to put him to death but he had a daughter and she took a tremendous liking to the fool. So she began begging her father to give her in marriage to the fool. Her father flew into a passion. He had them married and then ordered them both to be placed in a tub and the tub to be tarred over and thrown into the water; all which was done.

---

344 Tak de ego ne vzat'.

Long did the tub float about on the sea. His wife began to beseech the fool:

"Do something to get us cast on shore!"

"By the Pike's command at my request," said the fool, "cast this tub ashore and tear it open!"

He and his wife stepped out of the tub. Then she again began imploring him to build some sort of a house. The fool said:

"By the Pike's command at my request, let a marble palace be built and let it stand immediately opposite the King's palace!"

This was all done in an instant. In the morning the King saw the new palace and sent to enquire who it was that lived in it. As soon as he learnt that his daughter lived there, that very minute he summoned her and her husband. They came. The King pardoned them and they all began living together and flourishing.[345]

~

"The Pike," observes Afanasief, "is a fish of great repute in northern mythology." One of the old Russian songs still sung at Christmas, tells how a Pike comes from Novgorod, its scales of silver and gold, its back woven with pearls, a costly diamond gleaming in its head instead of eyes. And this song is one which promises wealth, a fact connecting the Russian fish with that Scandinavian pike which was a shape assumed by Andvari—the dwarf-guardian of the famous treasure, from which sprang the woes recounted in the *Völsunga Saga* and the

---

345 There are numerous variants of this story among the Skazkas. In one of these (Afanasief, vii. No. 31) the man on whom the pike has bestowed supernatural power uses it to turn a Maiden princess into a mother. This renders the story wholly in accordance with (1) the Modern Greek tale of "The Half Man," (Hahn, No. 8) in which the magic formula runs, "according to the first word of God and the second of the fish shall such and such a thing be done!" (2) The Neapolitan story of "Pervonto" (Basile's "Pentamerone," No. 3) who obtains his magic power from three youths whom he screens from the sun as they lie asleep one hot day and who turn out to be sons of a fairy. Afanasief compares the story also with the German tale of "The Little Grey Mannikin," in the "Zeitschrift für Deutsche Mythologie," &c., i. pp. 38-40. The incident of wishes being fulfilled by a fish occurs in many stories, as in that of "The Fisherman," in the "Arabian Nights," "The Fisherman and his Wife," in Grimm (KM., No. 19). A number of stories about the Pike are referred to by A. de Gubernatis ("Zoolog. Mythology," ii. 337-9).

Nibelungenlied. According to a Lithuanian tradition,[346] there is a certain lake which is ruled by the monstrous pike Strukis. It sleeps only once a year and then only for a single hour. It used always to sleep on St. John's Night but a fisherman once took advantage of its slumber to catch a quantity of its scaly subjects. Strukis awoke in time to upset the fisherman's boat; but fearing a repetition of the attempt, it now changes each year the hour of its annual sleep. A gigantic pike figures also in the *Kalevala*.

It would be easy to fill with similar stories, not only a section of a chapter but a whole volume; but instead of quoting anymore of them, I will take a few specimens from a different, though a somewhat kindred group of tales—those which relate to the magic powers supposed to be wielded in modern times by dealers in the Black Art. Such narratives as these are to be found in every land but Russia is especially rich in them, the faith of the peasantry in the existence of Witches and Wizards, Turnskins and Vampires, not having been as yet seriously shaken. Some of the stories relating to the supernatural Witch, who evidently belongs to the demon world, have already been given. In those which I am about to quote, the wizard or witch who is mentioned is a human being but one who has made a compact with evil spirits and has thereby become endowed with strange powers. Such monsters as these are, throughout their lives, a terror to the district they inhabit; nor does their evil influence die with them, for after they have been laid in the earth, they assume their direst aspect and as Vampires bent on blood, night after night, they go forth from their graves to destroy. As I have elsewhere given some account of Slavonic beliefs in witchcraft,[347] I will do little more at present than allow the stories to speak for themselves. They will be recognised as being akin to the tales

346 Quoted by Afanasief from Siemienski's "Podania," Posen, 1845, p. 42.
347 "Songs of the Russian People," pp. 387–427.

about sorcery current farther west but they are of a more savage nature. The rustic warlocks and witches of whom we are accustomed to hear have little, if any, of that thirst for blood which so unfavourably characterizes their Slavonic counterparts. Here is a story, by way of example, of a most gloomy nature.

THE WITCH GIRL.[348]

The cossack and the witch . . .

LATE ONE EVENING, A Cossack rode into a village, pulled up at its last cottage and cried—

"Heigh, master! will you let me spend the night here?"

"Come in, if you don't fear death!"

"What sort of a reply is that?" thought the Cossack, as he put his horse up in the stable. After he had given it its food he went into the cottage. There he saw its inmates, men and women and little children, all sobbing and crying and praying to God; and when they had done praying, they began putting on clean shirts.

"What are you crying about?" asked the Cossack.

"Why you see," replied the master of the house, "in our village Death goes about at night. Into whatsoever cottage she looks, there, next morning, one has to put all the people who lived in it into coffins and carry them off to the graveyard. To-night it's our turn."

"Never fear, master! 'Without God's will, no pig gets its fill!'"

The people of the house lay down to sleep; but the Cossack was on the look-out and never closed an eye. Exactly at midnight the window opened. At the window appeared a witch all in white. She took a sprinkler, passed her arm into the cottage and was just on the point of sprinkling—when the Cossack suddenly gave his sabre a sweep and cut her arm off close to the shoulder. The witch howled, squealed, yelped like

348 Afanasief, vii. No. 36 a. This story has no special title in the original.

a dog and fled away. But the Cossack picked up the severed arm, hid it under his cloak, washed away the stains of blood and lay down to sleep.

Next morning the master and mistress awoke and saw that everyone, without a single exception, was alive and well and they were delighted beyond expression.

"If you like," says the Cossack, "I'll show you Death! Call together all the Sotniks and Desyatniks[349] as quickly as possible and let's go through the village and look for her."

Straightway all the Sotniks and Desyatniks came together and went from house to house. In this one there's nothing, in that one there's nothing, until at last they come to the Ponomar's[350] cottage.

"Is all your family present?" asks the Cossack.

"No, my own! one of my daughters is ill. She's lying on the stove there."

The Cossack looked towards the stove—one of the girl's arms had evidently been cut off. Thereupon he told the whole story of what had taken place and he brought out and showed the arm which had been cut off. The commune rewarded the Cossack with a sum of money and ordered that witch to be drowned.

~

Stories of this kind are common in all lands but the witches about whom they are told generally assume the forms of beasts of prey, especially of wolves or of cats. A long string of similar tales will be found in Dr. Wilhelm Hertz's excellent and exhaustive monograph on werewolves.[351] Very important also is the Polish story told by Wojcicki[352] of the village which

349 The rural police. Sotnick = centurion, from sto = 100. Desyatnik is a word of the same kind from desyat = 10.

[360] A Ponomar is a kind of sacristan.

350 A Ponomar is a kind of sacristan.

351 "Der Werewolf, Beitrag zur Sagengeschichte," Stuttgart, 1862. For Russian ideas on the subject see "Songs of the Russian people," pp. 403-9.

352 "Polnische Volkssagen" (translated by Lewestam), p. 61

is attacked by the Plague, embodied in the form of a woman, who roams from house to house in search of victims. One night, as she goes her rounds, all doors and windows have been barred against her except one casement. This has been left open by a nobleman who is ready to sacrifice himself for the sake of others. The Pest Maiden arrives and thrusts her arm in at his window. The nobleman cuts it off and so rids the village of its fatal visitor. In an Indian story,[353] a hero undertakes to watch beside the couch of a haunted princess. When all is still a Rákshasa appears on the threshold, opens the door and thrusts into the room an arm—which the hero cuts off. The fiend disappears howling and leaves his arm behind.

The horror of the next story is somewhat mitigated by a slight infusion of the grotesque—but this may arise from a mere accident and be due to the exceptional cheerfulness of some link in the chain of its narrators.

353 Brockhaus's "Mährchensammlung des Somadeva Bhatta," ii. p. 24.

THE HEADLESS PRINCESS.[354]

A removable head leads to a stake through the heart . . .

IN A CERTAIN COUNTRY there lived a King; and this King had a daughter who was an enchantress. Near the royal palace there dwelt a priest and the priest had a boy of ten years old, who went every day to an old woman to learn reading and writing. Now it happened one day that he came away from his lessons late in the evening and as he passed by the palace he looked in at one of the windows. At that window the Princess happened to be sitting and dressing herself. She took off her head, lathered it with soap, washed it with clean water, combed its hair, plaited its long back braid and then put it back again in its proper place. The boy was lost in wonder.

"What a clever creature!" thinks he. "A downright witch!"

And when he got home he began telling everyone how he had seen the Princess without her head.

All of a sudden the King's daughter fell grievously ill and she sent for her father and strictly enjoined him, saying—

"If I die, make the priest's son read the psalter over me three nights running."

The Princess died; they placed her in a coffin and carried it to church. Then the king summoned the priest and said—

"Have you got a son?"

"I have, your majesty."

"Well then," said the King, "let him read the psalter over my daughter three nights running."

354 Afanasief, vii. No. 36 b. This story, also, is without special title.

The priest returned home and told his son to get ready. In the morning the priest's son went to his lessons and sat over his book looking ever so gloomy.

"What are you unhappy about?" asked the old woman.

"How can I help being unhappy, when I'm utterly done for?"

"Why what's the matter? Speak out plainly."

"Well then, granny, I've got to read psalms over the princess, and do you know, she's a witch!"

"I knew that before you did! But don't be frightened, there's a knife for you. When you go into the church, trace a circle round you; then read away from your psalter and don't look behind you. Whatever happens there, whatever horrors may appear, mind your own business and go on reading, reading. But if you look behind you, it will be all over with you!"

In the evening the boy went to the church, traced a circle round him with the knife and betook himself to the psalter. Twelve o'clock struck. The lid of the coffin flew up; the Princess arose, leapt out and cried—

"Now I'll teach you to go peeping through my windows and telling people what you saw!"

She began rushing at the priest's son but she couldn't anyhow break into the circle. Then she began to conjure up all sorts of horrors. But in spite of all that she did, he went on reading and reading and never gave a look round. And at daybreak the Princess rushed at her coffin and tumbled into it at full length, all of a heap.

The next night everything went on just the same. The priest's son wasn't a bit afraid, went on reading without a stop right up to daybreak and in the morning went to the old woman. She asked him—

"Well! have you seen horrors?"

"Yes, granny!"

"It will be still more horrible this time. Here's a hammer for you and four nails. Knock them into the four corners of the coffin and when you begin reading the psalter, stick up the hammer in front of you."

In the evening the priest's son went to the church and did everything just as the old woman had told him. Twelve o'clock struck, the coffin lid fell to the ground, the Princess jumped up and began tearing from side to side and threatening the youth. Then she conjured up horrors, this time worse than before. It seemed to him as if a fire had broken out in the church; all the walls were wrapped in flames! But he held his ground and went on reading, never once looking behind him. Just before daybreak the Princess rushed to her coffin—then the fire seemed to go out immediately and all the deviltry vanished!

In the morning the King came to the church and saw that the coffin was open and in the coffin lay the princess, face downwards.

"What's the meaning of all this?" says he.

The lad told him everything that had taken place. Then the king gave orders that an aspen stake should be driven into his daughter's breast and that her body should be thrust into a hole in the ground. But he rewarded the priest's son with a heap of money and various lands.

~

Perhaps the most remarkable among the stories of this class is the following, which comes from Little Russia. Those readers who are acquainted with the works of Gogol, the great Russian novelist, who was a native of that part of the country, will observe how closely he has kept to popular traditions in his thrilling story of the *Vy*, which has been translated into English, from the French, under the title of "The King of the Gnomes."[355]

355 In Mr. Hain Friswell's collection of "Ghost Stories," 1858.

THE SOLDIER'S MIDNIGHT WATCH.[356]

God knows who breaks in whom . . .

ONCE UPON A TIME there was a Soldier who served God and the great Gosudar for fifteen years, without ever setting eyes on his parents. At the end of that time there came an order from the Tsar to grant leave to the soldiers—to twenty-five of each company at a time—to go and see their families. Together with the rest our Soldier, too, got leave to go and set off to pay a visit to his home in the government of Kief. After a time he reached Kief, visited the *Lavra*, prayed to God, bowed down before the holy relics and then started again for his birthplace, a provincial town not far off. Well, he walked and walked. Suddenly there happens to meet him a fair maiden who was the daughter of a merchant in that same town; a most remarkable beauty. Now everyone knows that if a soldier catches sight of a pretty girl, nothing will make him pass her by quietly but he hooks on to her somehow or other. And so this Soldier gets alongside of the merchant's daughter and says to her jokingly—

"How now, fair damsel! not broken in to harness yet?"

"God knows, soldier, who breaks in whom," replies the girl. "I may do it to you or you to me."

So saying she laughed and went her way. Well, the Soldier arrived at home, greeted his family and rejoiced greatly at finding they were all in good health.

Now he had an old grandfather, as white as a *lun*, who had lived a hundred years and a bit. The Soldier was gossiping with him and said:

---

356 Afanasief, vii. No. 36 c. Also without special title.

"As I was coming home, grandfather, I happened to meet an uncommonly fine girl, and sinner that I am, I chaffed her and she said to me:

"'God knows, soldier, whether you'll break me in to harness or I'll break you.'"

"Eh, sirs! whatever have you done? Why that's the daughter of our merchant here, an awful witch! She's sent more than one fine young fellow out of the white world."

"Well, well! I'm not one of the timid ones, either! You won't frighten me in a hurry. We'll wait and see what God will send."

"No, no, grandson!" says the grandfather. "If you don't listen to me, you won't be alive tomorrow!"

"Here's a nice fix!" says the Soldier.

"Yes, such a fix that you've never known anything half so awful, even when soldiering."

"What must I do then, grandfather?"

"Why this. Provide yourself with a bridle and take a thick aspen cudgel and sit quietly in the izba—don't stir a step anywhere. During the night she will come running in and if she manages to say before you can 'Stand still, my steed!' you will straightway turn into a horse. Then she will jump upon your back and will make you gallop about until she has ridden you to death. But if you manage to say before she speaks, 'Tprru! stand still, jade!' she will be turned into a mare. Then you must bridle her and jump on her back. She will run away with you over hill and dale but do you hold your own; hit her over the head with the aspen cudgel and go on hitting her until you beat her to death."

The Soldier hadn't expected such a job as this but there was no help for it. So he followed his grandfather's advice, provided himself with a bridle and an aspen cudgel, took his seat in a corner and waited to see what would happen. At the midnight hour the passage door creaked and the sound of steps was heard; the witch was coming! The moment the door of the room opened, the Soldier immediately cried out—

"Tprru! stand still, jade!"

The witch turned into a mare and he bridled her, led her into the yard and jumped on her back. The mare carried him off over hills and dales and ravines and did all she could to try and throw her rider. But no! the Soldier stuck on tight and thumped her over the head like anything with the aspen cudgel and went on treating her with a taste of the cudgel until he knocked her off her feet and then pitched into her as she lay on the ground, gave her another half-dozen blows or so and at last beat her to death.

By daybreak he got home.

"Well, my friend! how have you got on?" asks his grandfather.

"Glory be to God, grandfather! I've beaten her to death!"

"All right! now lie down and go to sleep."

The Soldier lay down and fell into a deep slumber. Towards evening the old man awoke him—

"Get up, grandson."

He got up.

"What's to be done now? As the merchant's daughter is dead, you see, her father will come after you and will bid you to his house to read psalms over the dead body."

"Well, grandfather, am I to go or not?"

"If you go, there'll be an end of you; and if you don't go, there'll be an end of you! Still, it's best to go."

"But if anything happens, how shall I get out of it?"

"Listen, grandson! When you go to the merchant's he will offer you brandy; don't you drink much—drink only a moderate allowance. Afterwards the merchant will take you into the room in which his daughter is lying in her coffin and will lock you in there. You will read out from the psalter all the evening and up to midnight. Exactly at midnight a strong wind will suddenly begin to blow, the coffin will begin to shake, its lid will fall off. Well, as soon as these horrors begin, jump on to the stove as quick as you can, squeeze yourself into a corner and silently offer up prayers. She won't find you there."

Half an hour later came the merchant and besought the Soldier, crying:

"Ah, Soldier! there's a daughter of mine dead; come and read the psalter over her."

The Soldier took a psalter and went off to the merchant's house. The merchant was greatly pleased, seated him at his table and began offering him brandy to drink. The Soldier drank but only moderately and declined to drink anymore. The merchant took him by the hand and led him to the room in which the corpse lay.

"Now then," he says, "read away at your psalter."

Then he went out and locked the door. There was no help for it, so the Soldier took to his psalter and read and read. Exactly at midnight there was a great blast of wind, the coffin began to rock, its lid flew off. The Soldier jumped quickly on to the stove, hid himself in a corner, guarded himself by a sign of the cross and began whispering prayers. Meanwhile the witch had leapt out of the coffin and was rushing about from side to side—now here, now there. Then there came running up to her countless swarms of evil spirits; the room was full of them!

"What are you looking for?" say they.

"A soldier. He was reading here a moment ago and now he's vanished!"

The devils eagerly set to work to hunt him up. They searched and searched; they rummaged in all the corners. At last they cast their eyes on the stove; at that moment, luckily for the Soldier, the cocks began to crow. In the twinkling of an eye all the devils had vanished and the witch lay all of a heap on the floor. The Soldier got down from the stove, laid her body in the coffin, covered it up all right with the lid and betook himself again to his psalter. At daybreak came the master of the house, opened the door and said—

"Hail, Soldier!"

"I wish you good health, master merchant."

"Have you spent the night comfortably?"

"Glory be to God! yes."

"There are fifty roubles for you but come again, friend and read another night."

"Very good, I'll come."

The Soldier returned home, lay down on the bench and slept till evening. Then he awoke and said—

"Grandfather, the merchant bid me go and read the psalter another night. Should I go or not?"

"If you go, you won't remain alive and if you don't go, just the same! But you'd better go. Don't drink much brandy, drink just what is right; and when the wind blows and the coffin begins to rock, slip straight into the stove. There no one will find you."

The Soldier got ready and went to the merchant's, who seated him at table and began plying him with brandy. Afterwards he took him to where the corpse was and locked him into the room.

The Soldier went on reading, reading. Midnight came, the wind blew, the coffin began to rock, the coffin lid fell afar off on the ground. He was into the stove in a moment. Out jumped the witch and began rushing about; round her swarmed devils, the room was full of them!

"What are you looking for?" they cry.

"Why, there he was reading a moment ago and now he's vanished out of sight. I can't find him."

The devils flung themselves on the stove.

"Here's the place," they cried, "where he was last night!"

There was the place but he wasn't there! This way and that they rushed. Suddenly the cocks began to crow, the devils vanished, the witch lay stretched on the floor.

The Soldier stayed awhile to recover his breath, crept out of the stove, put the merchant's daughter back in her coffin and took to reading the psalter again. Presently he looks round, the day has already dawned. His host arrives:

"Hail, Soldier!" says he.

"I wish you good health, master merchant."

"Has the night passed comfortably?"

"Glory be to God! yes."

"Come along here, then."

The merchant led him out of the room, gave him a hundred roubles and said—

"Come, please and read here a third night; I shan't treat you badly."

"Good, I'll come."

The Soldier returned home.

"Well, grandson, what has God sent you?" says his grandfather.

"Nothing much, grandfather! The merchant told me to come again. Should I go or not?"

"If you go, you won't remain alive and if you don't go, you won't remain alive! But you'd better go."

"But if anything happens where must I hide?"

"I'll tell you, grandson. Buy yourself a frying-pan and hide it so that the merchant shan't see it. When you go to his house he'll try to force a lot of brandy on you. You look out, don't drink much, drink just what you can stand. At midnight, as soon as the wind begins to roar and the coffin to rock, do you that very moment climb on to the stovepipe and cover yourself over with the frying-pan. There no one will find you out."

The Soldier had a good sleep, bought himself a frying-pan,[357] hid it under his cloak and towards evening went to the merchant's house. The merchant seated him at table and took to plying him with liquor—tried every possible kind of invitation and cajolery on him.

"No," says the Soldier, "that will do. I've had my whack. I won't have anymore."

"Well, then, if you won't drink, come along and read your psalter."

The merchant took him to his dead daughter, left him alone with her and locked the door.

The Soldier read and read. Midnight came, the wind blew, the coffin began to rock, the cover flew afar off. The Soldier jumped up on the stovepipe, covered himself with the frying-pan, protected himself with a sign of the cross and awaited what was going to happen. Out jumped the witch and began rushing about. Round her came swarming countless devils, the izba was full of them! They rushed about in search of the Soldier; they looked into the stove—

"Here's the place," they cried, "where he was last night."

"There's the place but he's not there."

This way and that they rush,—cannot see him anywhere. Presently there stepped across the threshold a very old devil.

"What are you looking for?"

"The Soldier. He was reading here a moment ago and now he's disappeared."

"Ah! no eyes! And who's that sitting on the stovepipe there?"

The Soldier's heart thumped like anything; he all but tumbled down on the ground!

"There he is, sure enough!" cried the devils, "but how are we to settle him. Surely it's impossible to reach him there?"

---

357 The Russian skovoroda is a sort of stew-pan, of great size, without a handle.

"Impossible, forsooth! Run and lay your hands on a candle-end which has been lighted without a blessing having been uttered over it."

In an instant the devils brought the candle-end, piled up a lot of wood right under the stovepipe and set it alight. The flame leapt high into the air, the Soldier began to roast: first one foot, then the other, he drew up under him.

"Now," thinks he, "my death has come!"

All of a sudden, luckily for him, the cocks began to crow, the devils vanished, the witch fell flat on the floor. The soldier jumped down from the stovepipe and began putting out the fire. When he had put it out he set every thing to rights, placed the merchant's daughter in her coffin, covered it up with the lid and betook himself to reading the psalter. At daybreak came the merchant and listened at the door to find out whether the Soldier was alive or not. When he heard his voice he opened the door and said—

"Hail, Soldier!"

"I wish you good health, master merchant."

"Have you passed the night comfortably?"

"Glory be to God, I've seen nothing bad."

The merchant gave him a hundred and fifty roubles and said—

"You've done a deal of work, Soldier! do a little more. Come here to-night and carry my daughter to the graveyard."

"Good, I'll come."

"Well, grandson, what has God given?" asked his grandfather.

"Glory be to God, grandfather, I've got off safe! The merchant has asked me to be at his house to-night, to carry his daughter to the graveyard. Should I go or not?"

"If you go, you won't be alive and if you don't go, you won't be alive. But you must go; it will be better so."

"But what must I do? tell me."

"Well this. When you get to the merchant's, everything will be ready there. At ten o'clock the relations of the deceased will begin taking leave of her; and afterwards they will fasten three iron hoops round the coffin and place it on the funeral car; and at eleven o'clock they will tell you to take it to the graveyard. Do you drive off with the coffin but keep a sharp look-out. One of the hoops will snap. Never fear, keep your seat bravely; a second will snap, keep your seat all the same; but when the third hoop snaps, instantly jump on to the horse's back and through the *duga* (the wooden arch above its neck) and run away backwards. Do that and no harm will come to you."

The Soldier lay down to sleep, slept till the evening and then went to the merchant's. At ten o'clock the relations began taking leave of the deceased; then they set to work to fasten iron hoops round the coffin. They fastened the hoops, set the coffin on the funeral car and cried—

"Now then, Soldier! drive off and God speed you!"

The Soldier got into the car and set off: at first he drove slowly but as soon as he was out of sight he let the horse go full split. Away he galloped but all the while he kept an eye on the coffin. Snap went one hoop—and then another. The witch began gnashing her teeth.

"Stop!" she cried, "you shan't escape! I shall eat you up in another moment."

"No, dovey! Soldiers are crown property; no one is allowed to eat them."

Here the last hoop snapped: on to the horse jumped the Soldier and through the duga and then set off running backwards. The witch leapt out of the coffin and tore away in pursuit. Lighting on the Soldier's footsteps she followed them back to the horse, ran right round it, saw the soldier wasn't there and set off again in pursuit of him. She ran and ran, lighted again on his footsteps and again came back to the horse. Utterly at her wit's end, she did the same thing some ten times over. Suddenly the cocks began crowing. There lay the witch stretched out flat on the road! The Soldier picked her up, put her in the coffin, slammed the lid down and drove her to the graveyard. When he got there he lowered the coffin into the grave, shovelled the earth on top of it and returned to the merchant's house.

"I've done it all," says he; "catch hold of your horse."

When the merchant saw the Soldier he stared at him with wide-open eyes.

"Well, Soldier!" said he, "I know a good deal! and as to my daughter, we needn't speak of her. She was awfully sharp, she was! But really, you know more than we do!"

"Come now, master merchant! pay me for my work."

So the merchant handed him over two hundred roubles. The soldier took them, thanked him and then went home and gave his family a feast.

~

[The next chapter will contain a number of vampire stories which, in some respects, resemble these tales of homicidal corpses. But most of them belong, I think, to a separate group, due to a different myth or superstition from that which has given rise to such tales as those quoted above. The vampire is actuated by a thirst which can be quenched only by blood and which impels it to go forth from the grave and destroy. But the enchanted corpses which rise at midnight and attempt to rend their watchers, appear to owe their ferocity to demoniacal possession. After the death of a witch her body is liable, says popular tradition, to be tenanted by a devil (as may be seen from No. iii.) and to corpses thus possessed have been attributed by the storytellers the terrible deeds which Indian tales relate of Rákshasas and other evil spirits. Thus in the story of Nischayadatta, in the seventh book of the "Kathásaritságara," the hero and the four pilgrims, his companions, have to pass a night in a deserted temple of Siva. It is haunted by a Yakshini, a female demon, who turns men by spells into brutes and then eats them; so

they sit watching and praying beside a fire round which they have traced a circle of ashes. At midnight the demon-enchantress arrives, dancing and "blowing on a flute made of a dead man's bone." Fixing her eyes on one of the pilgrims, she mutters a spell, accompanied by a wild dance. Out of the head of the doomed man grows a horn; he loses all command over himself, leaps up and dances into the flames. The Yakshini seizes his half-burnt corpse and devours it. Then she treats the second and the third pilgrim in the same way. But just as she is turning to the fourth, she lays her flute on the ground. In an instant the hero seizes it and begins to blow it and to dance wildly around the Yakshini, fixing his eyes upon her and applying to her the words of her own spell. Deprived by it of all power, she submits and from that time forward renders the hero good service.[358]*]*

In one of the skazkas a malignant witch is destroyed by a benignant female power. It had been predicted that a certain baby princess would begin flying about the world as soon as she was fifteen. So her parents shut her up in a building in which she never saw the light of day, nor the face of a man. For it was illuminated by artificial means and none but women had access to it. But one day, when her nurses and *Mamzeli* had gone to a feast at the palace, she found a door unlocked and made her way into the sunlight. After this her attendants were obliged to allow her to go where she wished, when her parents were away. As she went roaming about the palace she came to a cage "in which a *Zhar-Ptitsa*,[359] lay [as if] dead." This bird, her guardians told her, slept soundly all day but at night her papa flew about on it. Farther on she came to a veiled portrait. When the veil was lifted, she cried in astonishment "Can such beauty be?" and determined to fly on the *Zhar-Ptitsa* to the original of the picture. So at night she sought the *Zhar-Ptitsa*, which was sitting up and flapping its wings and asked whether she might fly abroad

358 From Professor Brockhaus's summary in the "Berichte der phil. hist. Classe der Königl. Sächs. Gesellschaft der Wissenschaften," 1861, pp. 215, 16.

359 For an account of this mythological bird, see the note on next page. Ornithologically, the *Zhar-ptitsa* is the Cassowary.

on its back. The bird consented and bore her far away. Three times it carried her to the room of the prince whose portrait she had so much admired. On the first and second occasion he remained asleep during her visit, having been plunged into a magic slumber by the *Zhar-Ptitsa*. But during her third visit he awoke, "and he and she wept and wept and exchanged betrothal rings." So long did they remain talking that, before the *Zhar-Ptitsa* and his rider could get back, "the day began to dawn—the bird sank lower and lower and fell to the ground." Then the princess, thinking it was really dead, buried it in the earth—having first cut off its wings and "attached them to herself so as to walk more lightly."

After various adventures she comes to a land of mourning. "Why are you so mournful?" she asks. "Because our king's son has gone out of his mind," is the reply. "He eats a man every night." Thereupon she goes to the king and obtains leave to watch the prince by night. As the clock strikes twelve the prince, who is laden with chains, makes a rush at her; but the wings of the *Zhar-Ptitsa* rustle around her and he sits down again. This takes place three times, after which the light goes out. She leaves the room in search of the means of rekindling it, sees a glimmer in the distance and sets off with a lantern in search of it. Presently she finds an old witch who is sitting before a fire, above which seethes a cauldron. "What have you got there?" she asks. "When this cauldron seethes," replies the witch, "within it does the heart of Prince Ivan rage madly."

Pretending to be merely getting a light, the Princess contrives to splash the seething liquid over the witch, who immediately falls dead. Then she looks into the cauldron and there, in truth, she sees the Prince's heart. When she returns to his room he has recovered his senses. "Thank you for bringing a light," he says. "Why am I in chains?" "Thus and thus," says she. "You went out of your mind and ate people." Whereat he wonders greatly.[360]

The *Zhar-Ptitsa* or Fire-Bird, which plays so important a part in this story, is worthy of special notice. Its name is sufficient to show its close connection with flame or light,[361] and its appearance corresponds with its designation. Its feathers blaze with silvery or golden sheen, its eyes shine like crystal, it dwells in a golden cage. In the depth of the night it flies into a garden and lights it up as brightly as could a thousand burning fires. A single feather from its tail illuminates a dark room. It feeds upon golden apples which have the power of bestowing youth and beauty or according to a Croatian version, on magic-grasses. Its song, according to Bohemian legends, heals the sick and restores sight to the blind. We have already seen that, as the Phoenix, of which it seems to be a Slavonic counterpart, dies in the flame from which it springs again into life, so the *Zhar-Ptitsa* sinks into a death-like slumber when the day dawns, to awake to fresh life after the sunset.

One of the skazkas[362] about the *Zhar-Ptitsa* closely resembles the well-known German tale of the Golden Bird.[363] But it is a "Chapbook" story and therefore of doubtful origin. King Vuislaf has an apple-tree which bears golden fruits. These are stolen by a *Zhar-Ptitsa* which flies every night into the garden, so he orders his sons to keep watch there by turns. The elder brothers cannot keep awake and see nothing; but the youngest of the three, Prince Ivan, though he fails to capture the bird, secures one of its tail-feathers. After a time he leaves his home and goes forth in search of the bird. Aided

---

360 Khudyakof, No. 110. From the Nijegorod Government.

361 Zhar = glowing heat, as of a furnace; *zhar-ptitsa* = the glow-bird. Its name among the Czekhs and Slovaks is Ptak Ohnivák. The heathens Slavonians are said to have worshipped Ogon or Agon, Fire, the counterpart of the Vedic Agni. Agon is still the ordinary Russian word for fire, the equivalent of the Latin ignis.

362 Afanasief, vii. No. 11. See also the notes in viii. p. 620, etc.

363 Grimm's KM., No. 57. See the notes in Bd. iii. p. 98.

by a wolf, he reaches the garden in which the *Zhar-Ptitsa* lives and succeeds in taking it out of its golden cage. But trying, in spite of the wolf's warning, to carry off the cage itself, an alarm is sounded and he is taken prisoner. After various other adventures he is killed by his envious brothers but of course all comes right in the end. In a version of the story which comes from the Bukovina, one of the incidents is detailed at greater length than in either the German or the Russian tale. When the hero has been killed by his brothers and they have carried off the *Zhar-Ptitsa* and their victim's golden steed and his betrothed princess—as long as he lies dead, the princess remains mute and mournful, the horse refuses to eat, the bird is silent and its cage is lustreless. But as soon as he comes back to life, the princess regains her spirits and the horse its appetite. The *Zhar-Ptitsa* recommences its magic song and its cage flashes anew like fire.

In another skazka[364] a sportsman finds in a forest "a golden feather of the *Zhar-Ptitsa*; like fire does the feather shine!" Against the advice of his "heroic steed," he picks up the feather and takes it to the king, who sends him in search of the bird itself. Then he has wheat scattered on the ground and at dawn he hides behind a tree near it. "Presently the forest begins to roar, the sea rises in waves and the *Zhar-Ptitsa* flies up, lights upon the ground and begins to peck the wheat." Then the "heroic steed" gallops up, sets its hoof upon the bird's wing and presses it to the ground, so that the shooter is able to bind it with cords and take it to the king. In a variant of the story the bird is captured by means of a trap—a cage in which "pearls large and small" have been strewed.

* * * * *

---

364 Afanasief, vii. No. 12.

I had intended to say something about the various golden haired or golden-horned animals which figure in the Skazkas but it will be sufficient for the present to refer to the notices of them which occur in Prof. de Gubernatis's "Zoological Mythology." And now I will bring this chapter to a close with the following weird story of

THE WARLOCK.[365]

The way to the Warlock's fortune . . .

THERE WAS ONCE A Moujik and he had three married sons. He lived a long while and was looked upon by the village as a *Koldun* [or wizard]. When he was about to die, he gave orders that his sons' wives should keep watch over him [after his death] for three nights, taking one night apiece; that his body should be placed in the outer chamber,[366] and that his sons' wives should spin wool to make him a caftan. He ordered, moreover, that no cross should be placed upon him and that none should be worn by his daughters-in-law.

Well, that same night the eldest daughter-in-law took her seat beside him with some grey wool and began spinning. Midnight arrives. Says the father-in-law from his coffin:

"Daughter-in-law, art thou there?"

She was terribly frightened but answered, "I am." "Art thou sitting?" "I sit." "Dost thou spin?" "I spin." "Grey wool?" "Grey." "For a caftan?" "For a caftan."

He made a movement towards her. Then a second time he asked again—

"Daughter-in-law, art thou there?"

"I am." "Art thou sitting?" "I sit." "Dost thou spin?" "I spin." "Grey wool?" "Grey." "For a caftan?" "For a caftan."

She shrank into the corner. He moved again, came a couple of yards nearer her.

A third time he made a movement. She offered up no prayer. He strangled her and then lay down again in his coffin.

---

365 Khudyakof, No. 104. From the Orel Government

366 The kholodnaya izba—the "cold izba," as opposed to the "warm izba" or living room.

His sons removed her body and next evening, in obedience to his paternal behest, they sent another of his daughters-in-law to keep watch. To her just the same thing happened: he strangled her as he had done the first one.

But the third was sharper than the other two. She declared she had taken off her cross but in reality she kept it on. She took her seat and spun but said prayers to herself all the while.

Midnight arrives. Says her father-in-law from his coffin—

"Daughter-in-law, art thou there?"

"I am," she replies. "Art thou sitting?" "I sit." "Dost thou spin?" "I spin." "Grey wool?" "Grey." "For a caftan?" "For a caftan."

Just the same took place a second time. The third time, just as he was going to rush at her, she laid the cross upon him. He fell down and died. She looked into the coffin; there lay ever so much money. The father-in-law wanted to take it away with him, or, at all events, that only someone who could outdo him in cunning should get it.[367]

~

In one of the least intelligible of the West Highland tales, there is a scene which somewhat resembles the "lykewake" in this skazka. It is called "The Girl and the Dead Man," and relates, among other strange things, how a youngest sister took service in a house where a corpse lay. "She sat to watch the dead man and she was sewing; in the middle of night he rose up and screwed up a grin. 'If thou dost not lie down properly, I will give thee the one leathering with a stick.' He lay down. At the end of a while, he rose on one elbow and screwed up a grin; and the third time he rose and screwed up a grin. When he rose the third time, she struck him a lounder of the stick; the stick stuck to the dead man and the hand

367 The etymology of the word koldun is still, I believe, a moot point. The discovery of the money in the warlock's coffin seems an improbable incident. In the original version of the story the wizard may, perhaps, have turned into a heap of gold (see above, p. 231, on "Gold-men").

stuck to the stick and out they were." Eventually "she got a peck of gold and a peck of silver and the vessel of cordial" and returned home.[368]

The obscurity of the Celtic tale forms a striking contrast to the lucidity of the Slavonic. The Russian peasant likes a clear statement of facts; the Highlander seems, like Coleridge's Scotch admirer, to find a pleasure in seeing "an idea looming out of the mist."

---

368 Campbell, No. 13, vol. i. p. 215.

PART V

Ghost Stories

Slavonic Ideas about the Dead—On Heaven and Hell—On the Jack and the Beanstalk Story—Harmless Ghosts—The Rip van Winkle Story—the attachment #f Ghosts to their Shrouds and Coffin-Lids—Murderous Ghosts—Stories about Vampires—on the name Vampire, and the belief in Vampirism

The Russian peasants have very confused ideas about the local habitation of the disembodied spirit, after its former tenement has been laid in the grave. They seem, from the language of their funeral songs, sometimes to regard the departed spirit as residing in the coffin which holds the body from which it has been severed, sometimes to imagine that it hovers around the building which used to be its home or flies abroad on the wings of the winds. In the food and money and other necessaries of existence still placed in the coffin with the corpse, may be seen traces of an old belief in a journey which the soul was forced to undertake after the death of the body; in the *pomniki* or feasts in memory of the dead, celebrated at certain short intervals after a death and also on its anniversary, may be clearly recognised the remains of a faith in the continued residence of the dead in the spot where they had been buried and in their subjection to some physical sufferings, their capacity for certain animal enjoyments.

The two beliefs run side by side with each other, sometimes clashing and producing strange results—all the more strange when they show signs of an attempt having been made to reconcile them with Christian ideas.[369]

Of a heavenly or upper-world home of departed spirits, neither the songs nor the stories of the people, so far as I am aware, make mention. But that there is a country beyond the sky, inhabited by supernatural beings of magic power and unbounded wealth, is stated in a number of tales of the well-known "Jack and the Beanstalk" type. Of these the following may be taken as a specimen.

369 Some account of Russian funeral rites and beliefs and of the dirges which are sung at buryings and memorials of the dead, will be found in the "Songs of the Russian People," pp. 309–344.

THE FOX-PHYSICIAN.[370]

Do not place your faith in a Fox-Physician . . .

THERE ONCE WAS AN old couple. The old man planted a cabbage-head in the cellar under the floor of his cottage; the old woman planted one in the ash-hole. The old woman's cabbage, in the ash-hole, withered away entirely; but the old man's grew and grew, grew up to the floor. The old man took his hatchet and cut a hole in the floor above the cabbage. The cabbage went on growing again; grew, grew right up to the ceiling. Again the old man took his hatchet and cut a hole in the ceiling above the cabbage. The cabbage grew and grew, grew right up to the sky. How was the old man to get a look at the head of the cabbage? He began climbing up the cabbage-stalk, climbed and climbed, climbed and climbed, climbed right up to the sky, cut a hole in the sky and crept through. There he sees a mill[371] standing. The mill gives a turn—out come a pie and a cake with a pot of stewed grain on top.

The old man ate his fill, drank his fill and then lay down to sleep. When he had slept enough he slid down to earth again and cried:

"Old woman! why, old woman! how one does live up in heaven! There's a mill there—every time it turns, out come a pie and a cake, with a pot of *kasha* on top!"

"How can I get there, old man?"

"Slip into this sack, old woman. I'll carry you up."

The old woman thought a bit and then got into the sack. The old man took the sack in his teeth and began climbing up

370 Afanasief, iv. No. 7. From the Archangel Government.

371 Zhornovtsui, *i.e.* millstones or a hand-mill.

to heaven. He climbed and climbed, long did he climb. The old woman got tired of waiting and asked:

"Is it much farther, old man?"

"We've half the way to go still."

Again he climbed and climbed, climbed and climbed. A second time the old woman asked:

"Is it much farther, old man?"

The old man was just beginning to say: "Not much farther—" when the sack slipped from between his teeth and the old woman fell to the ground and was smashed all to pieces. The old man slid down the cabbage-stalk and picked up the sack. But it had nothing in it but bones and those broken very small. The old man went out of his house and wept bitterly.

Presently a fox met him.

"What are you crying about, old man?"

"How can I help crying? My old woman is smashed to pieces."

"Hold your noise! I'll cure her."

The old man fell at the fox's feet.

"Only cure her! I'll pay whatever is wanted."

"Well, then, heat the bathroom, carry the old woman there along with a bag of oatmeal and a pot of butter and then stand outside the door; but don't look inside."

The old man heated the bathroom, carried in what was wanted and stood outside at the door. But the fox went into the bathroom, shut the door and began washing the old woman's remains; washed and washed and kept looking about her all the time.

"How's my old woman getting on?" asked the old man.

"Beginning to stir!" replied the fox, who then ate up the old woman, collected her bones and piled them up in a corner and set to work to knead a hasty pudding.

The old man waited and waited. Presently he asked;

"How's my old woman getting on?"

"Resting a bit!" cried the fox, as she gobbled up the hasty pudding.

When she had finished it she cried:

"Old man! open the door wide."

He opened it and the fox sprang out of the bathroom and ran off home. The old man went into the bathroom and looked about him. Nothing was to be seen but the old woman's bones under the bench—and those picked so clean! As for the oatmeal and the butter, they had all been eaten up. So the old man was left alone and in poverty.

~

This story is evidently a combination of two widely differing tales. The catastrophe we may for the present pass over but about the opening some few words may be said. The Beanstalk myth is one which is found among so many peoples in such widely distant regions and it deals with ideas of such importance, that no contribution to its history can be considered valueless. Most remarkable among its numerous forms are those American and Malayo-Polynesian versions of the "heaven-tree" story which Mr. Tylor has brought together in his "Early History of mankind."[372] In Europe it is usually found in a very crude and fragmentary form, having been preserved, for the most part, as the introduction to some other story which has proved more attractive to the popular fancy. The Russian versions are all, as far as I am aware, of this nature. I have already[373] mentioned one of them, in which, also, the Fox plays a prominent part. Its opening words are, "There once lived an old man and an old woman and they had a little daughter. One day she was eating beans and she let one fall on the ground. The bean grew and grew and grew right up to heaven. The old man climbed up to heaven, slipped in

372 Pp. 341-349 of the first edition. See, also, for some other versions of the story, as well as for an attempt to explain it, A. de Gubernatis, "Zoological Mythology," i. 243, 244.

373 See supra, chap. I. p. 36.

there, walked and walked, admired and admired and said to himself, 'I'll go and fetch the old woman; won't she just be delighted!'" So he tries to carry his wife up the bean stalk but grows faint and lets her fall; she is killed and he calls in the Fox as Wailer.[374]

In a variant of the "Fox Physician" from the Vologda Government, it is a pea which gives birth to the wondrous tree. "There lived an old man and an old woman; the old man was rolling a pea about and it fell on the ground. They searched and searched a whole week but they couldn't find it. The week passed by and the old people saw that the pea had begun to sprout. They watered it regularly and the pea set to work and grew higher than the izba. When the peas ripened, the old man climbed up to where they were, plucked a great bundle of them and began sliding down the stalk again. But the bundle fell out of the old man's hands and killed the old woman."[375]

According to another variant, "There once lived a grandfather and a grandmother and they had a hut. The grandfather sowed a bean under the table and the grandmother a pea. A hen gobbled up the pea but the bean grew up as high as the table. They moved the table and the bean grew still higher. They cut away the ceiling and the roof; it went on growing until it grew right up to the heavens (*nebo*). The grandfather climbed up to heaven, climbed and climbed—there stood a hut (*khatka*), its walls of pancakes, its benches of white bread, the stove of buttered curds. He began to eat, ate his fill and lay down above the stove to sleep. In came twelve sister-goats. The first had one eye, the second two eyes, the third three and so on with the rest, the last having twelve eyes. They saw that someone had been meddling with their hut, so they put it to rights and when they went out they left the one-eyed to keep

374 Afanasief, iv. No. 9.
375 Ibid., iv. No. 7. p. 34.

watch. Next day the grandfather again climbed up there, saw One-Eye and began to mutter[376] 'Sleep, eye, sleep!' The goat went to sleep. The man ate his fill and went away. Next day the two-eyed kept watch and after it the three-eyed and so on. The grandfather always muttered his charm 'Sleep, eye! Sleep, second eye! Sleep, third eye!' and so on. But with the twelfth goat he failed, for he charmed only eleven of her eyes. The goat saw him with the twelfth and caught him,"—and there the story ends.[377]

In another instance the myth has been turned into one of those tales of the Munchausen class, the title of which is the "saw" *Ne lyubo, ne slushai*, *i.e.*, "If you don't like, don't listen"—the final words being understood; "but let me tell you a story." A cock finds a pea in the part of a cottage under the floor and begins calling to the hens; the cottager hears the call, drives away the cock and pours water over the pea. It grows up to the floor, up to the ceiling, up to the roof; each time way is made for it and finally it grows right up to heaven (d*o nebushka*). Says the moujik to his wife:

"Wife! wife, I say! shall I climb up into heaven and see what's going on there? May be there's sugar there and mead—lots of everything!"

"Climb away, if you've a mind to," replies his wife.

So he climbs up and there he finds a large wooden house. He enters in and sees a stove, garnished with sucking pigs and geese and pies "and everything which the soul could desire." But the stove is guarded by a seven-eyed goat; the moujik charms six of the eyes to sleep but overlooks the seventh. With it the goat sees him eat and drink and then go to sleep. The housemaster comes in, is informed by the goat of all that has occurred, flies into a passion, calls his servants and has the intruder turned out of the house. When the moujik comes to

376 Prigovarivat' = to say or sing while using certain (usually menacing) gestures.

377 Afanasief, iv. p. 35.

the place where the pea-stalk had been, "he looks around—no pea-stalk is there." He collects the cobwebs "which float on the summer air," and of them he makes a cord; this he fastens "to the edge of heaven" and begins to descend. Long before he reaches the earth he comes to the end of his cord, so he crosses himself and lets go. Falling into a swamp, he remains there some time. At last a duck builds her nest on his head and lays an egg in it. He catches hold of the duck's tail and the bird pulls him out of the swamp; whereupon he goes home rejoicing, taking with him the duck and her egg and tells his wife all that has happened.[378]

In another variant it is an acorn which is sown under the floor. From it springs an oak which grows to the skies. The old man of the story climbs up it in search of acorns and reaches heaven. There he finds a hand-mill and a cock with a golden comb, both of which he carries off. The mill grinds pies and pancakes and the old man and his wife live in plenty. But after a time a Barin or Seigneur steals the mill. The old people are in despair but the golden-combed cock flies after the mill, perches on the Barin's gates and cries—

"Kukureku! Boyarin, Boyarin! Give us back our golden, sky-blue mill!"

The cock is flung into the well but it drinks all the water, flies up to the Barin's house and there reiterates its demand. Then it is thrown into the fire but it extinguishes the flames, flies right into the Barin's guest-chamber and crows as before. The guests disperse, the Barin runs after them and the golden-combed cock seizes the mill and flies away with it.[379]

In a variant from the Smolensk Government, it is the wife who climbs up the pea-stalk, while the husband remains down below. When she reaches the top, she finds an *izbushka* or cottage there, its walls made of pies, its tables of cheese, its

---

378 Afanasief, vi. No. 2.
379 Afanasief, "Legendui," No. 33.

stove of pancakes and so forth. After she has feasted and gone to sleep in a corner, in come three goats, of which the first has two eyes and two ears, the second has three of each of these organs and the third has four. The old woman sends to sleep the ears and the eyes of the first and the second goat; but when the third watches it retains the use of its fourth eye and fourth ear, in spite of the incantations uttered by the intruder and so finds her out. On being questioned, she explains that she has come "from the earthly realm into the heavenly," and promises not to repeat her visit if she is dismissed in peace. So the goats let her go and give her a bag of nuts, apples and other good things to take with her. She slides down the pea-stalk and tells her husband all that has happened. He persuades her to undertake a second ascent together with him, so off they set in company, their young granddaughter climbing after them. Suddenly the pea-stalk breaks, they fall headlong and are never heard of again. "Since that time," says the story, "no one has ever set foot in that heavenly izbushka—so no one knows anything more about it."[380]

Clearer and fuller than these vague and fragmentary sketches of a "heavenly realm," are the pictures contained in the Russian folktales of the underground world. But it is very doubtful how far the stories in which they figure represent ancient Slavonic ideas. In the name, if not in the nature, of the *Ad* or subterranean abode of evil spirits and sinful souls, we recognize the influence of the Byzantine Hades; but most of the tales in which it occurs are supposed to draw their original inspiration from Indian sources, while they owe to Christian, Brahmanic, Buddhistic and Mohammedan influences the form in which they now appear. To these "legends," as the folktales are styled in which the saints or their ghostly enemies occur, belongs the following narrative of—

380 Chudinsky, No. 9.

THE FIDDLER IN HELL.[381]

A bridge to be rekeased from hell . . .

THERE WAS A CERTAIN moujik who had three sons. His life was a prosperous one and he laid by money enough to fill two pots. The one he buried in his corn-kiln, the other under the gate of his farmyard. Well, the moujik died and never said a word about the money to anyone. One day there was a festival in the village. A fiddler was on his way to the revel when, all of a sudden, he sank into the earth—sank right through and tumbled into hell, lighting exactly there where the rich moujik was being tormented.

"Hail, friend!" says the Fiddler.

"It's an ill wind that's brought you hither!"[382] answers the moujik; "this is hell and in hell here I sit."

"What was it brought you here, uncle?"

"It was money! I had much money: I gave none to the poor, two pots of it did I bury underground. See now, they are going to torment me, to beat me with sticks, to tear me with nails."

"Whatever shall I do?" cried the Fiddler. "Perhaps they'll take to torturing me too!"

"If you go and sit on the stove behind the chimney-pipe and don't eat anything for three years—then you will remain safe."

The Fiddler hid behind the stovepipe. Then came fiends,[383] and they began to beat the rich moujik, reviling him the while and saying:

"There's for thee, O rich man. Pots of money didst thou bury but thou couldst not hide them. There didst thou bury

381 Afanasief, v. No. 47. From the Tver Government.

382 "You have fallen here" neladno. Ladno means "well," "propitiously," &c., also "in tune."

383 Nenashi = not ours.

them that we might not be able to keep watch over them. At the gate people are always riding about, the horses crush our heads with their hoofs and in the corn-kiln we get beaten with flails."

As soon as the fiends had gone away the moujik said to the Fiddler:

"If you get out of here, tell my children to dig up the money—one pot is buried at the gate and the other in the corn-kiln—and to distribute it among the poor."

Afterwards there came a whole roomful of evil ones and they asked the rich moujik:

"What have you got here that smells so Russian?"

"You have been in Russia and brought away a Russian smell with you," replied the moujik.

"How could that be?" they said. Then they began looking, they found the Fiddler and they shouted:

"Ha, ha, ha! Here's a Fiddler."

They pulled him off the stove and set him to work fiddling. He played three years, though it seemed to him only three days. Then he got tired and said:

"Here's a wonder! After playing a whole evening I used always to find all my fiddle-strings snapped. But now, though I've been playing for three whole days, they are all sound. May the Lord grant us his blessing!"[384]

No sooner had he uttered these words than everyone of the strings snapped.

"There now, brothers!" says the Fiddler, "you can see for yourselves. The strings are snapped; I've nothing to play on!"

"Wait a bit!" said one of the fiends. "I've got two hanks of catgut; I'll fetch them for you."

He ran off and fetched them. The Fiddler took the strings, screwed them up and again uttered the words:

---

384 Gospodi blagoslovi! exactly our "God bless us;" with us now merely an expression of surprise.

"May the Lord grant us his blessing!"

In a moment snap went both hanks.

"No, brothers!" said the Fiddler, "your strings don't suit me. I've got some of my own at home; by your leave I'll go for them."

The fiends wouldn't let him go. "You wouldn't come back," they say.

"Well, if you won't trust me, send someone with me as an escort."

The fiends chose one of their number and sent him with the Fiddler. The Fiddler got back to the village. There he could hear that, in the farthest cottage, a wedding was being celebrated.

"Let's go to the wedding!" he cried.

"Come along!" said the fiend.

They entered the cottage. Everyone there recognised the Fiddler and cried:

"Where have you been hiding these three years?"

"I have been in the other world!" he replied.

They sat there and enjoyed themselves for some time. Then the fiend beckoned to the Fiddler, saying, "It's time to be off!" But the Fiddler replied: "Wait a little longer! Let me fiddle away a bit and cheer up the young people." And so they remained sitting there till the cocks began to crow. Then the fiend disappeared.

After that, the Fiddler began to talk to the sons of the rich moujik and said:

"Your father bids you dig up the money—one potful is buried at the gate and the other in the corn-kiln—and distribute the whole of it among the poor."

Well, they dug up both the pots and began to distribute the money among the poor. But the more they gave away the money, the more did it increase. Then they carried out the pots to a crossway. Everyone who passed by took out of them as much money as his hand could grasp and yet the money wouldn't come to an end. Then they presented a petition to the Emperor and he ordained as follows. There was a certain town, the road to which was a very roundabout one. It was some fifty versts long, whereas if it had been made in a straight line it would not have been more than five. And so the Emperor ordained that a bridge should be made the whole way. Well, they built a bridge five versts long and this piece of work cleared out both the pots.

About that time a certain maid bore a son and deserted him in his infancy. The child neither ate nor drank for three years and an angel of God always went about with him. Well, this child came to the bridge and cried:

"Ah! what a glorious bridge! God grant the kingdom of heaven to him at whose cost it was built!"

The Lord heard this prayer and ordered his angels to release the rich moujik from the depths of hell.[385]

~

With the bridge-building episode in this "legend" may be compared the opening of another Russian story. In it a merchant is described as having much money but no children. So he and his wife "began to pray to God, entreating him to give them a child—for solace in their youth, for support in their old age, for soul-remembrance[386] after death. And they took to feeding the poor and distributing alms. Besides all this, they resolved to build, for the use of all the faithful, a long bridge across swamps and where no man could find a footing. Much wealth did the merchant expend but he built the bridge and when the work was completed he sent his manager Fedor, saying—

"'Go and sit under the bridge and listen to what folks say about me—whether they bless me or revile me.'

---

385 Iz adu kromyeshnago = from the last hell. Kromyeshnaya t'ma = utter darkness. Kromyeshny or kromyeshnaya, is sometimes used by itself to signify hell.

386 Ha pomin dushi. Pomin = "remembrance," also "prayers for the dead."

"Fedor set off, sat under the bridge and listened. Presently three Holy Elders went over the bridge and said one to another—

"'How ought the man who built this bridge to be rewarded?' 'Let there be born to him a fortunate son. Whatsoever that son says—it shall be done: whatsoever he desires—that will the Lord bestow!'"[387]

The rest of the story closely resembles the German tale of "The Pink."[388] In the corresponding Bohemian story of "The Treacherous Servant,"[389] it may be observed, the bridge-building incident has been preserved.

But I will not dwell any longer on the story of the Fiddler, as I propose to give some account in the next chapter of several other tales of the same class, in most of which such descriptions of evil spirits are introduced as have manifestly been altered into what their narrators considered to be in accordance with Christian teaching. And so I will revert to those ideas about the dead and about their abiding-place, which the modern Slavonians seem to have inherited from their heathen ancestors and I will attempt to illustrate them by a few Russian ghost-stories. Those stories are, as a general rule, of a most ghastly nature but there are a few into the composition of which the savage element does not enter. The "Dead Mother," which has already been quoted,[390] belongs to the latter class; and so does the following tale—which, as it bears no title in the original, we may name,

---

387 Afanasief, vii. No. 20. In some variants of this story, instead of the three holy elders appear the Saviour, St. Nicholas and St. Mitrofan.

388 "Die Nelke," Grimm, KM., No. 76 and vol. iii. pp. 125-6.

389 Wenzig, No. 17, pp. 82-6.

390 See Chap. I. p. 32.

THE RIDE ON THE GRAVESTONE.[391]

The consequence of too-jovial feasting . . .

LATE ONE EVENING A certain artisan happened to be returning home from a jovial feast in a distant village. There met him on the way an old friend, one who had been dead some ten years.

"Good health to you!" said the dead man.

"I wish you good health!" replied the reveller and straight away forgot that his acquaintance had ever so long ago bidden the world farewell.

"Let's go to my house. We'll quaff a cup or two once more."

"Come along. On such a happy occasion as this meeting of ours, we may as well have a drink."

They arrived at a dwelling and there they drank and revelled.

"Now then, good-bye! It's time for me to go home," said the artisan.

"Stay a bit. Where do you want to go now? Spend the night here with me."

"No, brother! don't ask me; it cannot be. I've business to do tomorrow, so I must get home as early as possible."

"Well, good-bye! but why should you walk? Better get on my horse; it will carry you home quickly."

"Thanks! let's have it."

He got on its back and was carried off—just as a whirlwind flies! All of a sudden a cock crew. It was awful! All around were graves and the rider found he had a gravestone under him!

~

Of a somewhat similar nature is the story of—

---

391 Afanasief, v. p. 144.

THE TWO FRIENDS.[392]

Promises that endure beyond the grave have consequences . . .

IN THE DAYS OF old there lived in a certain village two young men. They were great friends, went to *besyedas*[393] together, in fact, regarded each other as brothers. And they made this mutual agreement. Whichever of the two should marry first was to invite his comrade to his wedding. And it was not to make any difference whether he was alive or dead.

About a year after this one of the young men fell ill and died. A few months later his comrade took it into his head to get married. So he collected all his kinsmen and set off to fetch his bride. Now it happened that they drove past the graveyard and the bridegroom recalled his friend to mind and remembered his old agreement. So he had the horses stopped, saying:

"I'm going to my comrade's grave. I shall ask him to come and enjoy himself at my wedding. A right trusty friend was he to me."

So he went to the grave and began to call aloud:

"Comrade dear! I invite thee to my wedding."

Suddenly the grave yawned, the dead man arose and said:

"Thanks be to thee, brother, that thou hast fulfilled thy promise. And now, that we may profit by this happy chance, enter my abode. Let us quaff a glass apiece of grateful drink."

---

392 Afanasief, vi, p. 322, 323.

393 Evening gatherings of young people.

"I'd have gone, only the marriage procession is stopping outside; all the folks are waiting for me."

"Eh, brother!" replied the dead man, "surely it won't take long to toss off a glass!"

The bridegroom jumped into the grave. The dead man poured him out a cup of liquor. He drank it off—and a hundred years passed away.

"Quaff another cup, dear friend!" said the dead man.

He drank a second cup—two hundred years passed away.

"Now, comrade dear, quaff a third cup!" said the dead man, "and then go, in God's name and celebrate thy marriage!"

He drank the third cup—three hundred years passed away.

The dead man took leave of his comrade. The coffin lid fell; the grave closed.

The bridegroom looked around. Where the graveyard had been, was now a piece of waste ground. No road was to be seen, no kinsmen, no horses. All around grew nettles and tall grass.

He ran to the village—but the village was not what it used to be. The houses were different; the people were all strangers to him. He went to the priest's—but the priest was not the one who used to be there—and told him about everything that had happened. The priest searched through the church-books and found that, three hundred years before, this occurrence had taken place: a bridegroom had gone to the graveyard on his wedding-day and had disappeared. And his bride, after some time had passed by, had married another man.

~

[The "Rip van Winkle" story is too well-known to require more than a passing allusion. It was doubtless founded on one of the numerous folktales which correspond to the Christian legend of "The Seven Sleepers of Ephesus"—itself an echo of an older tale (see Baring Gould, "Curious Myths," 1872, pp. 93-112 and Cox, "Mythology of the Aryan Nations," i. 413)—and to that of the monk who listens to a bird singing in the convent garden and remains entranced for the space of many years: of which latter

legend a Russian version occurs in Chudinsky's collection (No. 17, pp. 92-4). Very close indeed is the resemblance between the Russian story of "The Two Friends," and the Norse "Friends in Life and Death" (Asbjörnsen's New Series, No. 62, pp. 5-7). In the latter the bridegroom knocks hard and long on his dead friend's grave. At length its occupant appears and accounts for his delay by saying he had been far away when the first knocks came and so had not heard them. Then he follows the bridegroom to church and from church and afterwards the bridegroom sees him back to his tomb. On the way the living man expresses a desire to see something of the world beyond the grave and the corpse fulfils his wish, having first placed on his head a sod cut in the graveyard. After witnessing many strange sights, the bridegroom is told to sit down and wait till his guide returns. When he rises to his feet, he is all overgrown with mosses and shrub (var han overvoxen med Mose og Busker) and when he reaches the outer world he finds all things changed.]

But from these dim sketches of a life beyond or rather within the grave, in which memories of old days and old friendships are preserved by ghosts of an almost genial and entirely harmless disposition, we will now turn to those more elaborate pictures in which the dead are represented under an altogether terrific aspect. It is not as an incorporeal being that the visitor from the other world is represented in the Skazkas. He comes not as a mere phantom, intangible, impalpable, incapable of physical exertion, haunting the dwelling which once was his home or the spot to which he is drawn by the memory of some unexpiated crime. It is as a vitalised corpse that he comes to trouble mankind, often subject to human appetites, constantly endowed with more than human strength and malignity. His apparel is generally that of the grave and he cannot endure to part with it, as may be seen from the following story—

THE SHROUD.[394]

The obligations of the shroud . . .

IN A CERTAIN VILLAGE there was a girl who was lazy and slothful, hated working but would gossip and chatter away like anything. Well, she took it into her head to invite the other girls to a spinning party. For in the villages, as everyone knows, it is the lazybones who gives the spinning-feast and the sweet-toothed are those who go to it.

Well, on the appointed night she got her spinners together. They span for her and she fed them and feasted them. Among other things they chatted about was this—which of them all was the boldest?

Says the lazybones (*lezhaka*):

"I'm not afraid of anything!"

"Well then," say the spinners, "if you're not afraid, go past the graveyard to the church, take down the holy picture from the door and bring it here."

"Good, I'll bring it; only each of you must spin me a distaff-ful."

That was just her sort of notion: to do nothing herself but to get others to do it for her. Well, she went, took down the picture and brought it home with her. Her friends all saw that sure enough it was the picture from the church. But the picture had to be taken back again and it was now the midnight hour. Who was to take it? At length the lazybones said:

"You girls go on spinning. I'll take it back myself. I'm not afraid of anything!"

394 Afanasief, v. No. 30 a, pp. 140-2. From the Voroneje Government.

So she went and put the picture back in its place. As she was passing the graveyard on her return, she saw a corpse in a white shroud, seated on a tomb. It was a moonlight night; everything was visible. She went up to the corpse and drew away its shroud from it. The corpse held its peace, not uttering a word; no doubt the time for it to speak had not come yet. Well, she took the shroud and went home.

"There!" says she, "I've taken back the picture and put it in its place; and what's more, here's a shroud I took away from a corpse."

Some of the girls were horrified; others didn't believe what she said and laughed at her.

But after they had supped and lain down to sleep, all of a sudden the corpse tapped at the window and said:

"Give me my shroud! Give me my shroud!"

The girls were so frightened they didn't know whether they were alive or dead. But the lazybones took the shroud, went to the window, opened it and said:

"There, take it."

"No," replied the corpse, "restore it to the place you took it from."

Just then the cocks suddenly began to crow. The corpse disappeared.

Next night, when the spinners had all gone home to their own houses, at the very same hour as before, the corpse came, tapped at the window and cried:

"Give me my shroud!"

Well, the girl's father and mother opened the window and offered him his shroud.

"No," says he, "let her take it back to the place she took it from."

"Really now, how could one go to a graveyard with a corpse? What a horrible idea!" she replied.

Just then the cocks crew. The corpse disappeared.

Next day the girl's father and mother sent for the priest, told him the whole story and entreated him to help them in their trouble.

"Couldn't a service[395] be performed?" they said.

The priest reflected awhile; then he replied:

"Please to tell her to come to church tomorrow."

Next day the lazybones went to church. The service began, numbers of people came to it. But just as they were going to sing the cherubim song,[396] there suddenly arose, goodness knows whence, so terrible a whirlwind that all the congregation fell flat on their faces. And it caught up that girl and then flung her down on the ground. The girl disappeared from sight; nothing was left of her but her back hair.[397]

~

They are generally the corpses of wizards or of other sinners who have led especially unholy lives, which leave their graves by night and wander abroad. Into such bodies, it is held, demons enter and the combination of fiend and corpse goes forth as the terrible Vampire thirsting for blood. Of the proceedings of such a being the next story gives a detailed account, from which, among other things, may be learnt the fact that Slavonic corpses attach great importance to their coffin-lids as well as to their shrouds.

395 Obyednya, the service answering to the Latin mass.

396 At the end of the obyednya.

397 The kosa or single braid in which Russian girls wear their hair. See "Songs of the Russian People," pp. 272-5. On a story of this kind Goethe founded his weird ballad of "Der Todtentanz." Cf. Bertram's "Sagen," No. 18.

THE COFFIN-LID.[398]

The corpse cpntrolled by means of a coffin lid . . .

A MOUJIK WAS DRIVING along one night with a load of pots. His horse grew tired and all of a sudden it came to a standstill alongside of a graveyard. The moujik unharnessed his horse and set it free to graze; meanwhile he laid himself down on one of the graves. But somehow he didn't go to sleep.

He remained lying there some time. Suddenly the grave began to open beneath him: he felt the movement and sprang to his feet. The grave opened and out of it came a corpse—wrapped in a white shroud and holding a coffin lid—came out and ran to the church, laid the coffin-lid at the door and then set off for the village.

The moujik was a daring fellow. He picked up the coffin-lid and remained standing beside his cart, waiting to see what would happen. After a short delay the dead man came back and was going to snatch up his coffin-lid—but it was not to be seen. Then the corpse began to track it out, traced it up to the moujik and said:

"Give me my lid: if you don't, I'll tear you to bits!"

"And my hatchet, how about that?" answers the moujik. "Why, it's I who'll be chopping you into small pieces!"

"Do give it back to me, good man!" begs the corpse.

"I'll give it when you tell me where you've been and what you've done."

"Well, I've been in the village and there I've killed a couple of youngsters."

---

398 Afanasief, v. pp. 142–4. From the Tambof Government.

"Well then, now tell me how they can be brought back to life."

The corpse reluctantly made answer:

"Cut off the left skirt of my shroud and take it with you. When you come into the house where the youngsters were killed, pour some live coals into a pot and put the piece of the shroud in with them and then lock the door. The lads will be revived by the smoke immediately."

The moujik cut off the left skirt of the shroud and gave up the coffin-lid. The corpse went to its grave—the grave opened. But just as the dead man was descending into it, all of a sudden the cocks began to crow and he hadn't time to get properly covered over. One end of the coffin-lid remained sticking out of the ground.

The moujik saw all this and made a note of it. The day began to dawn; he harnessed his horse and drove into the village. In one of the houses he heard cries and wailing. In he went—there lay two dead lads.

"Don't cry," says he, "I can bring them to life!"

"Do bring them to life, kinsman," say their relatives. "We'll give you half of all we possess."

The moujik did everything as the corpse had instructed him and the lads came back to life. Their relatives were delighted but they immediately seized the moujik and bound him with cords, saying:

"No, no, trickster! We'll hand you over to the authorities. Since you knew how to bring them back to life, maybe it was you who killed them!"

"What are you thinking about, true believers! Have the fear of God before your eyes!" cried the moujik.

Then he told them everything that had happened to him during the night. Well, they spread the news through the village; the whole population assembled and swarmed into the graveyard. They found out the grave from which the dead man had come out, they tore it open and they drove an aspen stake right into the heart of the corpse, so that it might no more rise up and slay. But they rewarded the moujik richly and sent him away home with great honour.

~

It is not only during sleep that the Vampire is to be dreaded. At cross-roads or in the neighbourhood of cemeteries, an animated corpse of this description often lurks, watching for some unwary wayfarer whom it may be able to slay and eat. Past such dangerous spots as these the belated villager will speed with timorous steps, remembering, perhaps, some such uncanny tale as that which comes next.

THE TWO CORPSES.[399]

The hunger of corpses . . .

A SOLDIER HAD OBTAINED leave to go home on furlough—to pray to the holy images and to bow down before his parents. And as he was going his way, at a time when the sun had long set and all was dark around, it chanced that he had to pass by a graveyard. Just then he heard that someone was running after him and crying:

"Stop! you can't escape!"

He looked back and there was a corpse running and gnashing its teeth. The Soldier sprang on one side with all his might to get away from it, caught sight of a little chapel,[400] and bolted straight into it.

There wasn't a soul in the chapel but stretched out on a table there lay another corpse, with tapers burning in front of it. The Soldier hid himself in a corner and remained there, hardly knowing whether he was alive or dead but waiting to see what would happen. Presently up ran the first corpse—the one that had chased the Soldier—and dashed into the chapel. Thereupon the one that was lying on the table jumped up and cried to it:

"What hast thou come here for?"

"I've chased a soldier in here, so I'm going to eat him."

"Come now, brother! he's run into my house. I shall eat him myself."

"No, I shall!"

"No, I shall!"

---

399 Afanasief, vi. pp. 324, 325.

400 Chasovenka, a small chapel, shrine or oratory.

And they set to work fighting; the dust flew like anything. They'd have gone on fighting ever so much longer, only the cocks began to crow. Then both the corpses fell lifeless to the ground and the Soldier went on his way homeward in peace, saying:

"Glory be to Thee, O Lord! I am saved from the wizards!"

~

Even the possession of arms and the presence of a dog will not always, it seems, render a man secure from this terrible species of cut-throat.

THE DOG AND THE CORPSE.[401]

Do not abandon those who try to help you . . .

A MOUJIK WENT OUT in pursuit of game one day and took a favourite dog with him. He walked and walked through woods and bogs but got nothing for his pains. At last the darkness of night surprised him. At an uncanny hour he passed by a graveyard and there, at a place where two roads met, he saw standing a corpse in a white shroud. The moujik was horrified and knew not which way to go—whether to keep on or to turn back.

"Well, whatever happens, I'll go on," he thought; and on he went, his dog running at his heels. When the corpse perceived him, it came to meet him; not touching the earth with its feet but keeping about a foot above it—the shroud fluttering after it. When it had come up with the sportsman, it made a rush at him; but the dog seized hold of it by its bare calves and began a tussle with it. When the moujik saw his dog and the corpse grappling with each other, he was delighted that things had turned out so well for himself and he set off running home with all his might. The dog kept up the struggle until cockcrow, when the corpse fell motionless to the ground. Then the dog ran off in pursuit of its master, caught him up just as he reached home and rushed at him, furiously trying to bite and to rend him. So savage was it and so persistent, that it was as much as the people of the house could do to beat it off.

"Whatever has come over the dog?" asked the moujik's old mother. "Why should it hate its master so?"

---

401 Afanasief, vi. pp 321, 322.

The moujik told her all that had happened.

"A bad piece of work, my son!" said the old woman. "The dog was disgusted at your not helping it. There it was fighting with the corpse—and you deserted it and thought only of saving yourself! Now it will owe you a grudge for ever so long."

Next morning, while the family were going about the farmyard, the dog was perfectly quiet. But the moment its master made his appearance, it began to growl like anything.

They fastened it to a chain; for a whole year they kept it chained up. But in spite of that, it never forgot how its master had offended it. One day it got loose, flew straight at him and began trying to throttle him.

So they had to kill it.

~

In the next story a most detailed account is given of the manner in which a Vampire sets to work and also of the best means of ridding the world of it.

THE SOLDIER AND THE VAMPIRE.[402]

The way to deal with a dead Warlock . . .

A CERTAIN SOLDIER WAS allowed to go home on furlough. Well, he walked and walked and after a time he began to draw near to his native village. Not far off from that village lived a miller in his mill. In old times the Soldier had been very intimate with him: why shouldn't he go and see his friend? He went. The Miller received him cordially and at once brought out liquor; and the two began drinking and chattering about their ways and doings. All this took place towards nightfall and the Soldier stopped so long at the Miller's that it grew quite dark.

When he proposed to start for his village, his host exclaimed:

"Spend the night here, trooper! It's very late now and perhaps you might run into mischief."

"How so?"

"God is punishing us! A terrible warlock has died among us and by night he rises from his grave, wanders through the village and does such things as bring fear upon the very boldest! How could even you help being afraid of him?"

"Not a bit of it! A soldier is a man who belongs to the crown and 'crown property cannot be drowned in water nor burnt in fire.' I'll be off: I'm tremendously anxious to see my people as soon as possible."

Off he set. His road lay in front of a graveyard. On one of the graves he saw a great fire blazing. "What's that?" thinks he. "Let's have a look." When he drew near, he saw that the Warlock was sitting by the fire, sewing boots.

402 Afanasief, v. pp. 144–7. From the Tambof Government.

"Hail, brother!" calls out the Soldier.

The Warlock looked up and said:

"What have you come here for?"

"Why, I wanted to see what you're doing."

The Warlock threw his work aside and invited the Soldier to a wedding.

"Come along, brother," says he, "let's enjoy ourselves. There's a wedding going on in the village."

"Come along!" says the Soldier.

They came to where the wedding was; there they were given drink and treated with the utmost hospitality. The Warlock drank and drank, revelled and revelled and then grew angry. He chased all the guests and relatives out of the house, threw the wedded pair into a slumber, took out two phials and an awl, pierced the hands of the bride and bridegroom with the awl and began drawing off their blood. Having done this, he said to the Soldier:

"Now let's be off."

Well, they went off. On the way the Soldier said:

"Tell me; why did you draw off their blood in those phials?"

"Why, in order that the bride and bridegroom might die. Tomorrow morning no one will be able to wake them. I alone know how to bring them back to life."

"How's that managed?"

"The bride and bridegroom must have cuts made in their heels and some of their own blood must then be poured back into those wounds. I've got the bridegroom's blood stowed away in my right-hand pocket and the bride's in my left."

The Soldier listened to this without letting a single word escape him. Then the Warlock began boasting again.

"Whatever I wish," says he, "that I can do!"

"I suppose it's quite impossible to get the better of you?" says the Soldier.

"Why impossible? If anyone were to make a pyre of aspen boughs, a hundred loads of them and were to burn me on that pyre, then he'd be able to get the better of me. Only he'd have to look out sharp in burning me; for snakes and worms and different kinds of reptiles would creep out of my inside and crows and magpies and jackdaws would come flying up. All these must be caught and flung on the pyre. If so much as a single maggot were to escape, then there'd be no help for it; in that maggot I should slip away!"

The Soldier listened to all this and did not forget it. He and the Warlock talked and talked and at last they arrived at the grave.

"Well, brother," said the Warlock, "now I'll tear you to pieces. Otherwise you'd be telling all this."

"What are you talking about? Don't you deceive yourself; I serve God and the Emperor."

The Warlock gnashed his teeth, howled aloud and sprang at the Soldier—who drew his sword and began laying about him with sweeping blows. They struggled and struggled; the Soldier was all but at the end of his strength. "Ah!" thinks he, "I'm a lost man—and all for nothing!" Suddenly the cocks began to crow. The Warlock fell lifeless to the ground.

The Soldier took the phials of blood out of the Warlock's pockets and went on to the house of his own people. When he had got there and had exchanged greetings with his relatives, they said:

"Did you see any disturbance, Soldier?"

"No, I saw none."

"There now! Why we've a terrible piece of work going on in the village. A Warlock has taken to haunting it!"

After talking awhile, they lay down to sleep. Next morning the Soldier awoke and began asking:

"I'm told you've got a wedding going on somewhere here?"

"There was a wedding in the house of a rich moujik," replied his relatives, "but the bride and bridegroom have died this very night—what from, nobody knows."

"Where does this moujik live?"

They showed him the house. Thither he went without speaking a word. When he got there, he found the whole family in tears.

"What are you mourning about?" says he.

"Such and such is the state of things, Soldier," say they.

"I can bring your young people to life again. What will you give me if I do?"

"Take what you like, even were it half of what we've got!"

The Soldier did as the Warlock had instructed him and brought the young people back to life. Instead of weeping there began to be happiness and rejoicing; the Soldier was hospitably treated and well rewarded. Then—left about, face! off he marched to the Starosta and told him to call the peasants together and to get ready a hundred loads of aspen wood. Well, they took the wood into the graveyard, dragged the Warlock out of his grave, placed him on the pyre and set it alight—the people all standing round in a circle with brooms, shovels and fireirons. The pyre became wrapped in flames, the Warlock began to burn. His corpse burst and out of it crept snakes, worms and all sorts of reptiles and up came flying crows, magpies and jackdaws. The peasants knocked them down and flung them into the fire, not allowing so much as a single maggot to creep away! And so the Warlock was thoroughly consumed and the Soldier collected his ashes and strewed them to the winds. From that time forth there was peace in the village.

The Soldier received the thanks of the whole community. He stayed at home some time, enjoying himself thoroughly. Then he went back to the Tsar's service with money in his pocket. When he had served his time, he retired from the army and began to live at his ease.

~

The stories of this class are very numerous, all of them based on the same belief—that in certain cases the dead, in a material shape, leave their graves in order to destroy and prey upon the living. This belief is not peculiar to the Slavonians but it is one of the characteristic features of their spiritual creed. Among races which burn their dead, remarks Hertz in his exhaustive treatise on the Werewolf (p. 126), little is known of regular "corpse-spectres." Only vague apparitions, dream-like phantoms, are supposed, as a general rule, to issue from graves in which nothing more substantial than ashes has been laid.[403] But where it is customary to lay the dead body in the ground, "a peculiar half-life" becomes attributed to it by popular fancy and by some races it is supposed to be actuated at intervals by murderous impulses. In the East these are generally attributed to the fact of its being possessed by an evil spirit but in some parts of Europe no such explanation of its conduct is given, though it may often be implied. "The belief in vampires is the specific Slavonian form of the universal belief in spectres (*Gespenster*)," says Hertz and certainly vampirism has always made those lands peculiarly its own which are or have been tenanted or greatly influenced by Slavonians.

But animated corpses often play an important part in the traditions of other countries. Among the Scandinavians and especially in Iceland were they the cause of many fears, though they were not supposed to be impelled by a thirst for blood so much as by other carnal appetites,[404] or by a kind of local malignity.[405] In Germany tales of horror

403 On this account Hanush believes that the Old Slavonians, as burners of their dead, must have borrowed the vampire belief from some other race. See the "Zeitschrift für deutsche Mythologie," &c., vol. iv. p. 199. But it is not certain that burial by cremation was universally practised by the heathen Slavonians. Kotlyarevsky, in his excellent work on their funeral customs, arrives at the conclusion that there never was any general rule on the subject but that some Slavonians buried without burning, while others first burned their dead and then inhumed their ashes. See "Songs of the Russian People," p. 325.

404 See the strange stories in Maurer's "Isländische Volkssagen," pp. 112 and 300, 301.

405 As in the case of Glam, the terrible spectre which Grettir had so much difficulty in overcoming. To all who appreciate a shudder may be recommended chap. xxxv. of "The Story

similar to the Icelandic are by no means unknown but the majority of them are to be found in districts which were once wholly Lettic or Slavonic, though they are now reckoned as Teutonic, such as East Prussia or Pomerania or Lusatia. But it is among the races which are Slavonic by tongue as well as by descent, that the genuine vampire tales flourish most luxuriantly: in Russia, in Poland and in Servia—among the Czekhs of Bohemia and the Slovaks of Hungary and the numerous other subdivisions of the Slavonic family which are included within the heterogeneous empire of Austria. Among the Albanians and Modern Greeks they have taken firm root but on those peoples a strong Slavonic influence has been brought to bear. Even Prof. Bernhard Schmidt, although an uncompromising opponent of Fallmerayer's doctrines with regard to the Slavonic origin of the present inhabitants of Greece, allows that the Greeks, as they borrowed from the Slavonians a name for the Vampire, may have received from them also certain views and customs with respect to it.[406] Beyond this he will not go and he quotes a number of passages from Hellenic writers to prove that in ancient Greece spectres were frequently represented as delighting in blood and sometimes as exercising a power to destroy. Nor will he admit that any very great stress ought to be laid upon the fact that the Vampire is generally called in Greece by a name of Slavonic extraction; for in the islands, which were, he says, little if at all affected by Slavonic influences, the Vampire bears a thoroughly Hellenic designation.[407] But the

---

of Grettir the Strong," translated from the Icelandic by E. Magnússon and W. Morris, 1869.

406 The ordinary Modern-Greek word for a vampire, *βουρκόλακας*, he says, "is undoubtedly of Slavonic origin, being identical with the Slavonic name of the werewolf, which is called in Bohemian *vlkodlak*, in Bulgarian and Slovak, *vrkolak*, &c.," the vampire and the werewolf having many points in common. Moreover, the Regular name for a vampire in Servian, he remarks, is *vukodlak*. This proves the Slavonian nature (*die Slavicität*) of the name beyond all doubt.—"Volksleben der Neugriechen," 1871, p. 159.

407 In Crete and Rhodes, *καταχανάς*; in Cyprus, *σαρκωμενος*; in Tenos, *αυαικαθούευος*. The Turks, according to Mr. Tozer, give the name of *vurkolak* and some of the Albanians, says Hahn, give that of *βουρβολάχ-ου* to the restless dead. Ibid, p. 160.

thirst for blood attributed by Homer to his shadowy ghosts seems to have been of a different nature from that evinced by the material Vampire of modern days, nor does that ghastly *revenant* seem by any means fully to correspond to such ghostly destroyers as the spirit of Gello or the spectres of Medea's slaughtered children. It is not only in the Vampire, however, that we find a point of close contact between the popular beliefs of the New-Greeks and the Slavonians. Prof. Bernhard Schmidt's excellent work is full of examples which prove how intimately they are connected.

The districts of the Russian Empire in which a belief in vampires mostly prevails are White Russia and the Ukraine. But the ghastly bloodsucker, the *Upir*,[408] whose name has become naturalised in so many alien lands under forms resembling our "Vampire," disturbs the peasant-mind in many other parts of Russia, though not perhaps with the same intense fear which it spreads among the inhabitants of the above-named districts or of some other Slavonic lands. The numerous traditions which have gathered around the original idea vary to some extent according to their locality but they are never radically inconsistent.

Some of the details are curious. The Little-Russians hold that if a vampire's hands have grown numb from remaining long crossed in the grave, he makes use of his teeth, which are like steel. When he has gnawed his way with these through all obstacles, he first destroys the babes he finds in a house and then the older inmates. If fine salt be scattered on the floor of a room, the vampire's footsteps may be traced to his grave, in which he will be found resting with rosy cheek and gory mouth.

The Kashoubes say that when a *Vieszcy*, as they call the Vampire, wakes from his sleep within the grave, he begins to

---

408 Russian vampir, South-Russian upuir, anciently *upir*; Polish *upior*, Polish and Bohemian *upir*. Supposed by some philologists to be from pit' = drink, whence the Croatian name for a vampire *pijawica*. See "Songs of the Russian People," p. 410.

gnaw his hands and feet; and as he gnaws, one after another, first his relations, then his other neighbours, sicken and die. When he has finished his own store of flesh, he rises at midnight and destroys cattle or climbs a belfry and sounds the bell. All who hear the ill-omened tones will soon die. But generally he sucks the blood of sleepers. Those on whom he has operated will be found next morning dead, with a very small wound on the left side of the breast, exactly over the heart. The Lusatian Wends hold that when a corpse chews its shroud or sucks its own breast, all its kin will soon follow it to the grave. The Wallachians say that a *murony*—a sort of cross between a werewolf and a vampire, connected by name with our nightmare—can take the form of a dog, a cat or a toad and also of any blood-sucking insect. When he is exhumed, he is found to have long nails of recent growth on his hands and feet and blood is streaming from his eyes, ears, nose and mouth.

The Russian stories give a very clear account of the operation performed by the vampire on his victims. Thus, one night, a peasant is conducted by a stranger into a house where lie two sleepers, an old man and a youth. "The stranger takes a pail, places it near the youth and strikes him on the back; immediately the back opens and forth flows rosy blood. The stranger fills the pail full and drinks it dry. Then he fills another pail with blood from the old man, slakes his brutal thirst and says to the peasant, 'It begins to grow light! let us go back to my dwelling.'"[409]

Many skazkas also contain, as we have already seen, very clear directions how to deprive a vampire of his baleful power. According to them, as well as to their parallels elsewhere, a stake must be driven through the murderous corpse. In Russia an aspen stake is selected for that purpose but in some places

---

409 Afanasief, P.V.S. iii. 558. The story is translated in full in "Songs of the Russian People," pp. 411, 412

one made of thorn is preferred. But a Bohemian vampire, when staked in this manner in the year 1337, says Mannhardt,[410] merely exclaimed that the stick would be very useful for keeping off dogs; and a *strigon* (or Istrian vampire) who was transfixed with a sharp thorn cudgel near Laibach, in 1672, pulled it out of his body and flung it back contemptuously. The only certain methods of destroying a vampire appear to be either to consume him by fire or to chop off his head with a grave-digger's shovel. The Wends say that if a vampire is hit over the back of the head with an implement of that kind, he will squeal like a pig.

The origin of the Vampire is hidden in obscurity. In modern times it has generally been a wizard or a witch or a suicide,[411] or a person who has come to a violent end or who has been cursed by the Church or by his parents, who takes such an unpleasant means of recalling himself to the memory of his surviving relatives and acquaintances. But even the most honourable dead may become vampires by accident. He whom a vampire has slain is supposed, in some countries, himself to become a vampire. The leaping of a cat or some other animal across a corpse, even the flight of a bird above it, may turn the innocent defunct into a ravenous demon.[412] Sometimes, moreover, a man is destined from his birth to be a vampire, being the offspring of some unholy union. In some instances the Evil One himself is the father of such a doomed victim,

---

410 In a most valuable article on "Vampirism" in the "Zeitschrift für deutsche Mythologie und Sittenkunde," Bd. iv. 1859, pp. 259–82.

411 How superior our intelligence is to that of Slavonian peasants is proved by the fact that they still drive stakes through supposed vampires, whereas our law no longer demands that a suicide shall have a stake driven through his corpse. That rite was abolished by 4 Geo. iv. c. 52.

412 Compare with this belief the Scotch superstition mentioned by Pennant, that if a dog or cat pass over a corpse the animal must be killed at once. As illustrative of this idea, Mr. Henderson states, on the authority of "an old Northumbrian hind," that "in one case, just as a funeral was about to leave the house, the cat jumped over the coffin and no one would move till the cat was destroyed." In another, a colly dog jumped over a coffin which a funeral party had set on the ground while they rested. "It was felt by all that the dog must be killed, without hesitation, before they proceeded farther and killed it was." With us the custom survives; its explanation has been forgotten. See Henderson's "Notes on the Folk Lore of the Northern Counties of England," 1866, p. 43.

in others a temporarily animated corpse. But whatever may be the cause of a corpse's "vampirism," it is generally agreed that it will give its neighbours no rest until they have at least transfixed it. What is very remarkable about the operation is, that the stake must be driven through the vampire's body by a single blow. A second would restore it to life. This idea accounts for the otherwise unexplained fact that the heroes of folktales are frequently warned that they must on no account be tempted into striking their magic foes more than one stroke. Whatever voices may cry aloud "Strike again!" they must remain contented with a single blow.[413]

---

413 A great deal of information about vampires and also about turnskins, wizards and witches, will be found in Afanasief, P.V.S. iii. chap. xxvi., on which I have freely drawn. The subject has been treated with his usual judgment and learning by Mr. Tylor in his "Primitive Culture," ii. 175, 176. For several ghastly stories about the longing of Rákshasas and Vetálas for human flesh, some of which bear a strong resemblance to Slavonic vampire tales, see Brockhaus's translation of the first five books of the "Kathásaritságara," vol. i. p. 94; vol. ii. pp. 13, 142, 147.

PART VI

Legends

1. Saints, &

Legends connected with the Dog, the Izba, the Creation of Man, the Rye, the Snake, Ox, Sole, &c.; with Birds, the Peewit, Sparrow, Swallow, &c.—Legends about SS. Nicholas, Andrew, George, Kasian, &c

As besides the songs or *pyesni* there are current among the people a number of *stikhi* or poems on sacred subjects, so together with the *skazki* there have been retained in the popular memory a multitude of *legendui* or legends relating to persons or incidents mentioned in the Bible or in ecclesiastical history. Many of them have been extracted from the various apocryphal books which in olden times had so wide a circulation and many also from the lives of the Saints; some of them may be traced to such adaptations of Indian legends as the "Varlaam and Josaphat" attributed to St. John of Damascus; and others appear to be ancient heathen traditions, which, with altered names and slightly modified incidents, have been made to do service as Christian narratives. But whatever may be their origin, they all bear witness to the fact of their having been exposed to various influences and many of them may fairly be considered as relics of hoar antiquity, memorials of that misty period when the pious Slavonian chronicler struck by the confusion of Christian with heathen ideas and ceremonies then prevalent, styled his countrymen a two-faithed people.[414]

---

414 Afanasief, Legendui, p. 6.

On the popular tales of a religious character current among the Russian peasantry, the duality of their creed or of that of their ancestors, has produced a twofold effect. On the one hand into narratives drawn from purely Christian sources there has entered a pagan element, most clearly perceptible in stories which deal with demons and departed spirits; on the other hand an attempt has been made to give a Christian nature to what are manifestly heathen legends, by lending saintly names to their characters and clothing their ideas in an imitation of biblical language. Of such stories as these, it will be as well to give a few specimens.

Among the legends borrowed from the apocryphal books and similar writings, many of which are said to be still carefully preserved among the "Schismatics," concealed in hiding-places of which the secret is handed down from father to son—as was once the case with the Hussite books among the Bohemians—there are many which relate to the creation of the world and the early history of man. One of these states that when the Lord had created Adam and Eve, he stationed at the gates of Paradise the dog, then a clean beast, giving it strict orders not to give admittance to the Evil One. But "the Evil One came to the gates of Paradise and threw the dog a piece of bread and the dog went and let the Evil One into Paradise. Then the Evil One set to work and spat over Adam and Eve—covered them all over with spittle, from the head to the little toe of the left foot." Thence is it that spittle is impure (*pogana*). So Adam and Eve were turned out of Paradise and the Lord said to the dog:

"Listen, O Dog! thou wert a Dog (*Sobaka*), a clean beast; through all Paradise the most holy didst thou roam. Henceforward shalt thou be a Hound (*Pes* or *Pyos*), an unclean beast. Into a dwelling it shall be a sin to admit thee; into a church if thou dost run, the church must be consecrated anew."

And so—the story concludes—"ever since that time it has been called not a dog but a hound—skin-deep it is unclean (*pogana*) but clean within."

According to another story, when men first inhabited the earth, they did not know how to build houses, so as to keep themselves warm in winter. But instead of asking aid from the Lord, they applied to the Devil, who taught them how to make an *izba* or ordinary Russian cottage. Following his instructions, they made wooden houses, each of which had a door but no window. Inside these huts it was warm; but there was no living in them, on account of the darkness. "So the people went back to the Evil One. The Evil one strove and strove but nothing came of it, the izba still remained pitch dark. Then the people prayed unto the Lord. And the Lord said: 'Hew out a window!' So they hewed out windows and it became light."[415]

Some of the Russian traditions about the creation of man are closely connected with Teutonic myths. The Schismatics called *Dukhobortsui* or Spirit-Wrestlers, for instance, hold that man was composed of earthly materials but that God breathed into his body the breath of life. "His flesh was made of earth, his bones of stone, his veins of roots, his blood of water, his hair of grass, his thought of the wind, his spirit of the cloud."[416] Many of the Russian stories about the early ages of the world, also, are current in Western Europe, such as that about the rye—which in olden days was a mass of ears from top to bottom. But some lazy harvest-women having cursed "God's corn," the Lord waxed wroth and began to strip the ears from the stem. But when the last ear was about to fall, the Lord had pity upon the penitent culprits and allowed the single ear to remain as we now see it.[417]

415

416 Buslaef, "Ist. Och," i. 147, where the Teutonic equivalents are given

417 Tereshchenko, v. 48. For a German version of the story, see the KM., No. 124, "Die Kornähre."

A Little-Russian variant of this story says that Ilya (Elijah), was so angry at seeing the base uses to which a woman turned "God's corn," that he began to destroy all the corn in the world. But a dog begged for and received a few ears. From these, after Ilya's wrath was spent, mankind obtained seed and corn began to grow again on the face of the earth but not in its pristine bulk and beauty. It is on account of the good service thus rendered to our race that we ought to cherish and feed the dog.[418]

Another story, from the Archangel Government, tells how a certain King, as he roamed afield with his princes and boyars, found a grain of corn as large as a sparrow's egg. Marvelling greatly at its size, he tried in vain to obtain from his followers some explanation thereof. Then they bethought them of "a certain man from among the old people, who might be able to tell them something about it." But when the old man came, "scarcely able to crawl along on a pair of crutches," he said he knew nothing about it but perhaps his father might remember something. So they sent for his father, who came limping along with the help of one crutch and who said:

"I have a father living, in whose granary I have seen just such a seed."

So they sent for his father, a man a hundred and seventy years old. And the patriarch came, walking nimbly needing neither guide nor crutch. Then the King began to question him, saying:

"Who sowed this sort of corn?"

"I sowed it and reaped it," answered the old man, "and now I have some of it in my granary. I keep it as a memorial. When I was young, the grain was large and plentiful but after a time it began to grow smaller and smaller."

---

418 Afanasief, P.V.S. i. 482.

"Now tell me," asked the King, "how comes it, old man, that thou goest more nimbly than thy son and thy grandson?"

"Because I lived according to the law of the Lord," answered the old man. "I held mine own, I grasped not at what was another's."[419]

The existence of hills is accounted for by legendary lore in this wise. When the Lord was about to fashion the face of the earth, he ordered the Devil to dive into the watery depths and bring thence a handful of the soil he found at the bottom. The Devil obeyed but when he filled his hand he filled his mouth also. The Lord took the soil, sprinkled it around and the Earth appeared, all perfectly flat. The Devil, whose mouth was quite full, looked on for some time in silence. At last he tried to speak but choked and fled in terror. After him followed the thunder and the lightning and so he rushed over the whole face of the earth, hills springing up where he coughed and sky-cleaving mountains where he leaped.[420]

As in other countries, a number of legends are current respecting various animals. Thus the Old Ritualists will not eat the crayfish (*rak*), holding that it was created by the Devil. On the other hand the snake (*uzh*, the harmless or common snake) is highly esteemed, for tradition says that when the Devil, in the form of a mouse, had gnawed a hole in the Ark and thereby endangered the safety of Noah and his family, the snake stopped up the leak with its head.[421] The flesh of the horse is considered unclean, because when the infant Saviour was hidden in the manger the horse kept eating the hay under which the babe was concealed, whereas the ox not only would not touch it but brought back hay on its horns to replace what the horse had eaten. According to

---

419 Afanasief, Legendui, p. 19.

420 Tereshchenko, v. p. 45. Some of these legends have been translated by O. von. Reinsberg-Düringsfeld in the "Ausland," Dec. 9, 1872.

421 According to a Bohemian legend the Devil created the mouse, that it might destroy "God's corn," whereupon the Lord created the cat.

an old Lithuanian tradition, the shape of the sole is due to the fact that the Queen of the Baltic Sea once ate one half of it and threw the other half into the sea again. A legend from the Kherson Government accounts for it as follows. At the time of the Angelical Salutation, the Blessed Virgin told the Archangel Gabriel that she would give credit to his words "if a fish, one side of which had already been eaten, were to come to life again. That very moment the fish came to life and was put back in the water."

With the birds many graceful legends are connected. There is a bird, probably the peewit, which during dry weather may be seen always on the wing and piteously crying *Peet, Peet*,[422] as if begging for water. Of it the following tale is told. When God created the earth and determined to supply it with seas, lakes and rivers, he ordered the birds to convey the waters to their appointed places. They all obeyed except this bird, which refused to fulfil its duty, saying that it had no need of seas, lakes or rivers, to slake its thirst. Then the Lord waxed wroth and forbade it and its posterity ever to approach a sea or stream, allowing it to quench its thirst with that water only which remains in hollows and among stones after rain. From that time it has never ceased its wailing cry of "Drink, Drink," Peet, Peet.[423]

When the Jews were seeking for Christ in the garden, says a Kharkof legend, all the birds, except the sparrow, tried to draw them away from his hiding-place. Only the sparrow attracted them thither by its shrill chirruping. Then the Lord cursed the sparrow and forbade that men should eat of its flesh. In other parts of Russia, tradition tells that before the crucifixion the swallows carried off the nails provided for the use of the executioners but the sparrows brought them back. And while our Lord was hanging on the cross the sparrows

422 Pit', = to drink.
423 Tereshchenko, v. 47.

were maliciously exclaiming *Jif! Jif*! or "He is living! He is living!" in order to urge on the tormentors to fresh cruelties. But the swallows cried, with opposite intent, *Umer! Umer*! "He is dead! He is dead." Therefore it is that to kill a swallow is a sin and that its nest brings good luck to a house. But the sparrow is an unwelcome guest, whose entry into a cottage is a presage of woe. As a punishment for its sins, its legs have been fastened together by invisible bonds and therefore it always hops, not being able to run.[424]

A great number of the Russian legends refer to the visits which Christ and his Apostles are supposed to pay to men's houses at various times but especially during the period between Easter Sunday and Ascension Day. In the guise of indigent wayfarers, the sacred visitors enter into farmhouses and cottages and ask for food and lodging; therefore to this day the Russian peasant is ever unwilling to refuse hospitality to any man, fearing lest he might repulse angels unawares. Tales of this kind are common in all Christian lands, especially in those in which their folklore has preserved some traces of the old faith in the heathen gods who once walked the earth and in patriarchal fashion dispensed justice among men. Many of the Russian stories closely resemble those of a similar nature which occur in German and Scandinavian collections; all of them, for instance, agreeing in the unfavourable light in which they place St. Peter. The following abridgment of the legend of "The Poor Widow,"[425] may be taken as a specimen of the Russian tales of this class.

Long, long ago, Christ and his twelve Apostles were wandering about the world and they entered into a village one evening and asked a rich moujik to allow them to spend the night in his house. But he would not admit them, crying:

"Yonder lives a widow who takes in beggars; go to her."

424 Afanasief, Legendui, p. 13.
425 Afanasief, Legendui, No. 3. From the Voroneje Government.

So they went to the widow and asked her. Now she was so poor that she had nothing in the house but a crust of bread and a handful of flour. She had a cow but it had not calved yet and gave no milk. But she did all she could for the wayfarers, setting before them all the food she had and letting them sleep beneath her roof. And her store of bread and flour was wonderfully increased, so that her guests fed and were satisfied. And the next morning they set out anew on their journey.

As they went along the road there met them a wolf. And it fell down before the Lord and begged for food. Then said the Lord, "Go to the poor widow's; slay her cow and eat."

The Apostles remonstrated in vain. The wolf set off, entered the widow's cowhouse and killed her cow. And when she heard what had taken place, she only said:

"The Lord gave, the Lord has taken away. Holy is His will!"

As the sacred wayfarers pursued their journey, there came rolling towards them a barrel full of money. Then the Lord addressed it, saying:

"Roll, O barrel, into the farmyard of the rich moujik!"

Again the Apostles vainly remonstrated. The barrel went its way and the rich moujik found it and stowed it away, grumbling the while:

"The Lord might as well have sent twice as much!"

The sun rose higher and the Apostles began to thirst. Then said the Lord:

"Follow that road and ye will find a well; there drink your fill."

They went along that road and found the well. But they could not drink thereat, for its water was foul and impure and swarming with snakes and frogs and toads. So they returned to where the Lord awaited them, described what they had seen and resumed their journey. After a time they were sent in search of another well. And this time they found a place wherein was water pure and cool and around grew wondrous trees, whereon heavenly birds sat singing. And when they had slaked their thirst, they returned unto the Lord, who said:

"Wherefore did ye tarry so long?"

"We only stayed while we were drinking," replied the Apostles. "We did not spend above three minutes there in all."

"Not three minutes did ye spend there but three whole years," replied the Lord. "As it was in the first well, so will it be in the other world with the rich moujik! But as it was in the second well, so will it be in that world with the poor widow!"

Sometimes our Lord is supposed to wander by himself, under the guise of a beggar. In the story of "Christ's Brother"[426] a young man—whose father, on his deathbed, had charged him not to forget the poor—goes to church on Easter Day, having provided himself with red eggs to give to the beggars with whom he should exchange the Pascal greeting. After exhausting his stock of presents, he finds that there remains one beggar of miserable appearance to whom he has nothing to offer, so he takes him home to dinner. After the meal the beggar exchanges crosses with his host,[427] giving him "a cross which blazes like fire," and invites him to pay him a visit on the following Tuesday. To an enquiry about the way, he replies, "You have only to go along yonder path and say, 'Grant thy blessing, O Lord!' and you will come to where I am."

The young man does as he is told and commences his journey on the Tuesday. On his way he hears voices, as though of children, crying, "O Christ's brother, ask Christ for us—have we to suffer long?" A little later he sees a group of girls who are ladling water from one well into another, who make the same request. At last he arrives at

426 Afanasief, Legendui, No. 8.

427 Who thus becomes his "brother of the cross." This cross-brothership is considered a close spiritual affinity.

the end of his journey, finds the aged mendicant who had adopted him as his brother and recognizes him as "the Lord Jesus Christ Himself." The youth relates what he has seen and asks:

"Wherefore, O Lord, are the children suffering?"

"Their mothers cursed them while still unborn," is the reply. "Therefore is it impossible for them to enter into Paradise."

"And the girls?"

"They used to sell milk and they put water into the milk. Now they are doomed to pour water from well to well eternally."

After this the youth is taken into Paradise and brought to the place there provided for him.[428]

Sometimes the sacred visitor rewards with temporal goods the kindly host who has hospitably received him. Thus the story of "Beer and Corn"[429] tells how a certain man was so poor that when the rest of the peasants were brewing beer and making other preparations to celebrate an approaching feast of the Church, he found his cupboard perfectly bare. In vain did he apply to a rich neighbour, who was in the habit of lending goods and money at usurious rates; having no security to offer, he could borrow nothing. But on the eve of the festival, when he was sitting at home in sadness, he suddenly rose and drew near to the sacred painting which hung in the corner and sighed heavily and said,

"O Lord! forgive me, sinner that I am! I have not even wherewith to buy oil, so as to light the lamp before the image[430] for the festival!"

---

428 Afanasief, in his notes to this story, gives several of its variants. The rewards and punishments awarded in a future life form the theme of a great number of moral parables, apparently of Oriental extraction. For an interesting parallel from the Neilgherry Hills, see Gover's "Folksongs of Southern India," pp. 81-7.

429 Afanasief, Legendui, No. 7.

430 The icona, *εικών* or holy picture.

Soon afterwards an old man entered the cottage and obtained leave to spend the night there. After a time the guest enquired why his host was so sad and on learning the reason, told him to go again to his rich neighbour and borrow a quarter of malt. The moujik obeyed and soon returned with the malt, which the old man ordered him to throw into his well. When this was done the villager and his guest went to bed.

Next morning the old man told the moujik to borrow a number of tubs and fill them with liquor drawn from the well and then to make his neighbours assemble and drink it. He did so and the buckets were filled with "such beer as neither fancy nor imagination can conceive but only a skazka can describe." The villagers, excited by the news, collected in crowds and drank the beer and rejoiced. Last of all came the rich neighbour, begging to know how such wonderful beer was brewed. The moujik told him the whole story, whereupon he straightway commanded his servants to pour all his best malt into his well. And next day he hastened to the well to taste the liquor it contained; but he found nothing but malt and water; not a drop of beer was there.

We may take next the legends current among the peasantry about various saints. Of these, the story of "The Prophet Elijah and St. Nicholas," will serve as a good specimen. But in order to render it intelligible, a few words about "Ilya the Prophet," as Elijah is styled in Russia, may as well be prefixed.

It is well-known that in the days of heathenism the Slavonians worshipped a thunder-god, Perun,[431] who occupied in their mythological system the place which in the Teutonic was assigned to a Donar or a Thor. He was believed, if traditions may be relied upon, to sway the elements, often

---

431 For some account of Perun — the Lithuanian Perkunas — whose name and attributes appear to be closely connected with those of the Indian Parjanya, see the "Songs of the Russian Nation," pp. 86-102.

driving across the sky in a flaming car and launching the shafts of the lightning at his demon foes. His name is still preserved by the western and southern Slavonians in many local phrases, especially in imprecations; but with the introduction of Christianity into Slavonic lands, all this worship of his divinity came to an end. Then took place, as had occurred before in other countries, the merging of numerous portions of the old faith in the new, the transferring of many of the attributes of the old gods to the sacred personages of the new religion.[432] During this period of transition the ideas which were formerly associated with the person of Perun, the thunder-god, became attached to that of the Prophet Ilya or Elijah.

One of the causes which conduced to this result may have been—if Perun really was considered in old times, as he is said to have been, the Lord of the Harvest—that the day consecrated by the Church to Elijah, July 20, occurs in the beginning of the harvest season and therefore the peasants naturally connected their new saint with their old deity. But with more certainty may it be accepted that, the leading cause was the similarity which appeared to the recent converts to prevail between their dethroned thunder-god and the prophet who was connected with drought and with rain, whose enemies were consumed by fire from on high and on whom waited "a chariot of fire and horses of fire," when he was caught up by a whirlwind into heaven. And so at the present day, according to Russian tradition, the Prophet Ilya thunders across the sky in a flaming car and smites the clouds with the darts of the lightning. In the Vladimir Government he is said "to destroy devils with stone arrows,"—weapons corresponding to the hammer of Thor and

432 A Servian song, for instance, quoted by Buslaef ("Ist. Och." i. 361) states that "The Thunder" (*i.e.*, the Thunder-God or Perun) "began to divide gifts. To God (Bogu) it gave the heavenly heights; to St. Peter the summer" (Petrovskie so called after the Saint) "heats; to St. John, the ice and snow; to Nicholas, power over the waters, and to Ilya the lightning and the thunderbolt."

the lance of Indra. On his day the peasants everywhere expect thunder and rain and in some places they set out rye and oats on their gates and ask their clergy to laud the name of Ilya, that he may bless their cornfields with plenteousness. There are districts, also, in which the people go to church in a body on Ilya's day and after the service is over they kill and roast a beast which has been purchased at the expense of the community. Its flesh is cut up into small pieces and sold, the money paid for it going to the church. To stay away from this ceremony or not to purchase a piece of the meat, would be considered a great sin; to mow or make hay on that day would be to incur a terrible risk, for Ilya might smite the field with the thunder or burn up the crop with the lightning. In the old Novgorod there used to be two churches, the one dedicated to "Ilya the Wet," the other to "Ilya the Dry." To these a cross-bearing procession was made when a change in the weather was desired: to the former in times of drought, to the latter when injury was being done to the crops by rain. Diseases being considered to be evil spirits, invalids used to pray to the thunder-god for relief.

And so, at the present day, a *zagovor* or spell against the Siberian cattle-plague entreats the "Holy Prophet of God Ilya," to send "thirty angels in golden array, with bows and with arrows" to destroy it. The Servians say that at the division of the world Ilya received the thunder and lightning as his share and that the crash and blaze of the storm are signs of his contest with the devil. Wherefore the faithful ought not to cross themselves when the thunder peals, lest the evil one should take refuge from the heavenly weapons behind the protecting cross. The Bulgarians say that forked lightning is the lance of Ilya who is chasing the Lamia fiend: summer lightning is due to the sheen of that lance or to the fire issuing from the nostrils of his celestial steeds. The white clouds of summer are named by them his heavenly sheep and they say that he compels the spirits of dead Gypsies to form pellets of snow—by men styled hail—with which he scourges in summer the fields of sinners.[433]

Such are a few of the ideas connected by Slavonian tradition with the person of the Prophet Elijah or Ilya. To St. Nicholas, who has succeeded to the place occupied by an ancient ruler of the waters, a milder character is attributed than to Ilya, the thunder-god's successor. As Ilya is the counterpart of Thor, so does Nicholas in some respects resemble Odin. The special characteristics of the Saint and the Prophet are fairly contrasted in the following story.

433 Afanasief, Legendui, pp. 137-40, P.V.S., i. 469-83. Cf. Grimm's "Deutsche Mythologie," pp. 157-59.

ELIJAH THE PROPHET AND NICHOLAS.[434]

The saints competing amongst themselves . . .

A long while ago there lived a Moujik. Nicholas's day he always kept holy but Elijah's not a bit; he would even work upon it. In honour of St. Nicholas he would have a taper lighted and a service performed but about Elijah the Prophet he forgot so much as to think.

Well, it happened one day that Elijah and Nicholas were walking over the land belonging to this Moujik; and as they walked they looked—in the cornfields the green blades were growing up so splendidly that it did one's heart good to look at them.

"Here'll be a good harvest, a right good harvest!" says Nicholas, "and the Moujik, too, is a good fellow sure enough, both honest and pious: one who remembers God and thinks about the Saints! It will fall into good hands—"

"We'll see by-and-by whether much will fall to his share!" answered Elijah; "when I've burnt up all his land with lightning and beaten it all flat with hail, then this Moujik of yours will know what's right and will learn to keep Elijah's day holy."

Well, they wrangled and wrangled; then they parted asunder. St. Nicholas went off straight to the Moujik and said:

"Sell all your corn at once, just as it stands, to the Priest of Elijah.[435] If you don't, nothing will be left of it: it will all be beaten flat by hail."

Off rushed the Moujik to the Priest.

---

434 Afanasief, Legendui, No. 10. From the Yaroslaf Government.

435 Il'inskomu bat'kye — to the Elijah father.

"Won't your Reverence buy some standing corn? I'll sell my whole crop. I'm in such pressing need of money just now. It's a case of pay up with me! Buy it, Father! I'll sell it cheap."

They bargained and bargained and came to an agreement. The Moujik got his money and went home.

Some little time passed by. There gathered together, there came rolling up, a storm cloud; with a terrible raining and hailing did it empty itself over the Moujik's cornfields, cutting down all the crop as if with a knife—not even a single blade did it leave standing.

Next day Elijah and Nicholas walked past. Says Elijah:

"Only see how I've devastated the Moujik's cornfield!"

"The Moujik's! No, brother! Devastated it you have splendidly, only that field belongs to the Elijah Priest, not to the Moujik."

"To the Priest! How's that?"

"Why, this way. The Moujik sold it last week to the Elijah Priest and got all the money for it. And so, methinks, the Priest may whistle for his money!"

"Stop a bit!" said Elijah. "I'll set the field all right again. It shall be twice as good as it was before."

They finished talking and went each his own way. St. Nicholas returned to the Moujik and said:

"Go to the Priest and buy back your crop—you won't lose anything by it."

The Moujik went to the Priest, made his bow and said:

"I see, your Reverence, God has sent you a misfortune—the hail has beaten the whole field so flat you might roll a ball over it. Since things are so, let's go halves in the loss. I'll take my field back and here's half of your money for you to relieve your distress."

The Priest was rejoiced and they immediately struck hands on the bargain.

Meanwhile—goodness knows how—the Moujik's ground began to get all right. From the old roots shot forth new tender stems. Rainclouds came sailing exactly over the cornfield and gave the soil to drink. There sprang up a marvellous crop—tall and thick. As to weeds, there positively was not one to be seen. And the ears grew fuller and fuller, till they were fairly bent right down to the ground.

Then the dear sun glowed and the rye grew ripe—like so much gold did it stand in the fields. Many a sheaf did the Moujik gather, many a heap of sheaves did he set up; and now he was beginning to carry the crop and to gather it together into ricks.

At that very time Elijah and Nicholas came walking by again. Joyfully did the Prophet gaze on all the land and say:

"Only look, Nicholas! what a blessing! Why, I have rewarded the Priest in such wise, that he will never forget it all his life."

"The Priest? No, brother! the blessing indeed is great but this land you see, belongs to the Moujik. The Priest hasn't got anything whatsoever to do with it."

"What are you talking about?"

"It's perfectly true. When the hail beat all the cornfield flat, the Moujik went to the Priest and bought it back again at half price."

"Stop a bit!" says Elijah. "I'll take the profit out of the corn. However many sheaves the Moujik may lay on the threshing-floor, he shall never thresh out of them more than a peck[436] at a time."

"A bad piece of work!" thinks St. Nicholas. Off he went at once to the Moujik.

"Mind," says he, "when you begin threshing your corn, never put more than one sheaf at a time on the threshing-floor."

The Moujik began to thresh: from every sheaf he got a peck of grain. All his bins, all his storehouses, he crammed with

436 Strictly speaking, a chetverìk = 5.775 gallons.

rye; but still much remained over. So he built himself new barns and filled them as full as they could hold.

Well, one day Elijah and Nicholas came walking past his homestead and the Prophet began looking here and there and said:

"Do you see what barns he's built? has he got anything to put into them?"

"They're quite full already," answers Nicholas.

"Why, wherever did the Moujik get such a lot of grain?"

"Bless me! Why, everyone of his sheaves gave him a peck of grain. When he began to thresh he never put more than one sheaf at a time on the threshing-floor."

"Ah, brother Nicholas!" said Elijah, guessing the truth, "it's you who go and tell the Moujik everything!"

"What an idea! that I should go and tell—"

"As you please; that's your doing! But that Moujik shan't forget me in a hurry!"

"Why, what are you going to do to him?"

"What I shall do, that I won't tell you," replies Elijah.

"There's a great danger coming," thinks St. Nicholas and he goes to the Moujik again and says:

"Buy two tapers, a big one and a little one and do thus and thus with them."

Well, next day the Prophet Elijah and St. Nicholas were walking along together in the guise of wayfarers and they met the Moujik, who was carrying two wax tapers—one, a big rouble one and the other, a tiny copeck one.

"Where are you going, Moujik?" asked St. Nicholas.

"Well, I'm going to offer a rouble taper to Prophet Elijah; he's been ever so good to me! When my crops were ruined by the hail, he bestirred himself like anything and gave me a plentiful harvest, twice as good as the other would have been."

"And the copeck taper, what's that for?"

"Why, that's for Nicholas!" said the peasant and passed on.

"There now, Elijah!" says Nicholas, "you say I go and tell everything to the Moujik—surely you can see for yourself how much truth there is in that!"

Thereupon the matter ended. Elijah was appeased and didn't threaten to hurt the Moujik anymore. And the Moujik led a prosperous life and from that time forward he held in equal honour Elijah's Day and Nicholas's Day.

~

It is not always to the Prophet Ilya that the power once attributed to Perun is now ascribed. The pagan wielder of the thunderbolt is represented in modern traditions by more than one Christian saint. Sometimes, as St. George, he transfixes monsters with his lance; sometimes, as St. Andrew, he smites with his mace a spot given over to witchcraft. There was a village (says one of the legends of the Chernigof Government) in which lived more than a thousand witches and they used to steal the holy stars, until at last "there was not one left to light our sinful world." Then God sent the holy Andrew, who struck with his mace—and all that village was swallowed up by the earth and the place thereof became a swamp.[437]

About St. George many stories are told and still more ballads (if we may be allowed to call them so) are sung. Under the names of Georgy, Yury and Yegory the Brave, he is celebrated as a patron as well of wolves as of flocks and herds, as a Christian Confessor struggling and suffering for the faith amid pagan foes and as a chivalrous destroyer of snakes and dragons. The discrepancies which exist between the various representations given of his character and his functions are very glaring but they may be explained by the fact that a number of legendary ideas sprung from separate sources have become associated with his name; so that in one story his

437 Afanasief, P.V.S., iii. 455.

actions are in keeping with the character of an old Slavonian deity, in another, with that of a Christian or a Buddhist saint.

In some parts of Russia, when the cattle go out for the first time to the spring pastures, a pie, made in the form of a sheep, is cut up by the chief herdsman and the fragments are preserved as a remedy against the diseases to which sheep are liable. On St. George's Day in spring, April 23, the fields are sanctified by a church service, at the end of which they are sprinkled with holy water. In the Tula Government a similar service is held over the wells. On the same day, in some parts of Russia, a youth (who is called by the Slovenes the Green Yegory) is dressed like our own "Jack in the Green," with foliage and flowers. Holding a lighted torch in one hand and a pie in the other, he goes out to the cornfields, followed by girls singing appropriate songs. A circle of brushwood is then lighted, in the centre of which is set the pie. All who take part in the ceremony then sit down around the fire and eventually the pie is divided among them.

Numerous legends speak of the strange connection which exists between St. George and the Wolf. In Little Russia that animal is called "St. George's Dog," and the carcases of sheep which wolves have killed are not used for human food, it being held that they have been assigned by divine command to the beasts of the field. The human victim whom St. George has doomed to be thus destroyed nothing can save. A man, to whom such a fate had been allotted, tried to escape from his assailants by hiding behind a stove; but a wolf transformed itself into a cat and at midnight, when all was still, it stole into the house and seized the appointed prey. A hunter, who had been similarly doomed, went on killing wolves for some time and hanging up their skins; but when the fatal hour arrived, one of the skins became a wolf and slew him by whom it had before been slain. In Little Russia the wolves have their own herdsman[438]—a being like unto a man, who is often seen in company with St. George. There were two brothers (says a popular tale), the one rich, the other poor. The poor brother had climbed up a tree one night and suddenly he saw beneath him what seemed to be two men—the one driving a pack of wolves, the other attending to the conveyance of a quantity of bread. These two beings were St. George and the Lisun. And St. George distributed the bread among the wolves and one loaf which remained over he gave to the poor brother, who afterwards found that it was of a miraculous nature, always renewing itself and so supplying its owner with an inexhaustible store of bread. The rich brother, hearing the story, climbed up the tree one night in hopes of obtaining a similar present. But that night St. George found that he had no bread to give to one of his wolves, so he gave it the rich brother instead.[439]

One of the legends attributes strange forgetfulness on one occasion to St. George. A certain Gypsy who had a wife and seven children and nothing to feed them with, was standing by a roadside lost in reflection, when Yegory the Brave came riding by. Hearing that the saint was on his way to heaven, the Gypsy besought him to ask of God how he was to support his family. St. George promised to do so but forgot. Again the Gypsy saw him riding past and again the saint promised and forgot. In a third interview the Gypsy asked him to leave behind his golden stirrup as a pledge.

A third time St. George leaves the presence of the Lord without remembering the commission with which he has been entrusted. But when he is about to mount his charger the sight of the solitary stirrup recalls it to his mind. So he returns and states the Gypsy's request and obtains the reply that "the

---

438 Called Lisun, Lisovik, Polisun, &c. He answers to the Lyeshy or wood-demon (lyes = a forest) mentioned above, p. 212.

439 Afanasief, P.V.S. i. 711.

Gypsy's business is to cheat and to swear falsely." As soon as the Gypsy is told this, he thanks the Saint and goes off home.

"Where are you going?" cries Yegory. "Give me back my golden stirrup."

"What stirrup?" asks the Gypsy.

"Why, the one you took from me."

"When did I take one from you? I see you now for the first time in my life and never a stirrup did I ever take, so help me Heaven!"

So Yegory had to go away without getting his stirrup back.[440]

There is an interesting Bulgarian legend in which St. George appears in his Christian capacity of dragonslayer but surrounded by personages belonging to heathen mythology. The inhabitants of the pagan city of Troyan, it states, "did not believe in Christ but in gold and silver." Now there were seventy conduits in that city which supplied it with spring-water; and the Lord made these conduits run with liquid gold and silver instead of water, so that all the people had as much as they pleased of the metals they worshipped but they had nothing to drink.

After a time the Lord took pity upon them and there appeared at a little distance from the city a deep lake. To this they used to go for water. Only the lake was guarded by a terrible monster, which daily devoured a maiden, whom the inhabitants of Troyan were obliged to give to it in return for leave to make use of the lake. This went on for three years, at the end of which time it fell to the lot of the king's daughter to be sacrificed by the monster. But when the Troyan Andromeda was exposed on the shore of the lake, a Perseus arrived to save her in the form of St. George. While waiting for the monster to appear, the saint laid his head on her knees and she dressed his locks. Then he fell into so deep a slumber that the monster drew nigh

440 Afanasief, Legendui, No. 12.

without awaking him. But the Princess began to weep bitterly and her scalding tears fell on the face of St. George and awoke him and he slew the monster and afterwards converted all the inhabitants of Troyan to Christianity.[441]

St. Nicholas generally maintains in the legends the kindly character attributed to him in the story in which he and the Prophet Ilya are introduced together. It is to him that at the present day the anxious peasant turns most readily for help and it is he whom the legends represent as being the most prompt of all the heavenly host to assist the unfortunate among mankind. Thus in one of the stories a peasant is driving along a heavy road one autumn day, when his cart sticks fast in the mire. Just then St. Kasian comes by.

"Help me, brother, to get my cart out of the mud!" says the peasant.

"Get along with you!" replies St. Kasian. "Do you suppose I've got leisure to be dawdling here with you!"

Presently St. Nicholas comes that way. The peasant addresses the same request to him and he stops and gives the required assistance.

When the two saints arrive in heaven, the Lord asks them where they have been.

"I have been on the earth," replies St. Kasian. "And I happened to pass by a moujik whose cart had stuck in the mud. He cried out to me, saying, 'Help me to get my cart out!' But I was not going to spoil my heavenly apparel."

"I have been on the earth," says St. Nicholas, whose clothes were all covered with mud. "I went along that same road and I helped the moujik to get his cart free."

Then the Lord says, "Listen, Kasian! Because thou didst not assist the moujik, therefore shall men honour thee by

441 Quoted by Buslaef, "Ist. Och." i. 389. Troyan is also the name of a mythical king who often figures in Slavonic legends.

thanksgiving once only every four years. But to thee, Nicholas, because thou didst assist the moujik to set free his cart, shall men twice every year offer up thanksgiving."

"Ever since that time," says the story, "it has been customary to offer prayers and thanksgiving (*molebnui*) to Nicholas twice a year but to Kasian only once every leap-year."[442]

In another story St. Nicholas comes to the aid of an adventurer who watches beside the coffin of a bewitched princess. There were two moujiks in a certain village, we are told, one of whom was very rich and the other very poor. One day the poor man, who was in great distress, went to the house of the rich man and begged for a loan.

"I will repay it, on my word. Here is Nicholas as a surety," he cried, pointing to a picture of St. Nicholas.

Thereupon the rich man lent him twenty roubles. The day for repayment came but the poor man had not a single copeck. Furious at his loss, the rich man rushed to the picture of St. Nicholas, crying—

"Why don't you pay up for that pauper? You stood surety for him, didn't you?"

And as the picture made no reply, he tore it down from the wall, set it on a cart and drove it away, flogging it as he went and crying—

"Pay me my money! Pay me my money!"

As he drove past the inn a young merchant saw him and cried—

"What are you doing, you infidel!"

The moujik explained that as he could not get his money back from a man who was in his debt, he was proceeding against a surety; whereupon the merchant paid the debt and thereby ransomed the picture, which he hung up in a place of honour and kept a lamp burning before it. Soon afterwards an

---

442 Afanasief, Legendui, No. 11. From the Orel district.

old man offered his services to the merchant, who appointed him his manager; and from that time all things went well with the merchant.

But after a while a misfortune befell the land in which he lived, for "an evil witch enchanted the king's daughter, who lay dead all day long but at night got up and ate people." So she was shut up in a coffin and placed in a church and her hand with half the kingdom as her dowry, was offered to anyone who could disenchant her. The merchant, in accordance with his old manager's instructions, undertook the task and after a series of adventures succeeded in accomplishing it. The last words of one of the narrators of the story are, "Now this old one was no mere man. He was Nicholas himself, the saint of God."[443]

With one more legend about this favourite saint, I will conclude this section of the present chapter. In some of its incidents it closely resembles the story of "The Smith and the Demon," which was quoted in the first chapter.

---

443 Afanasief, Legendui, pp. 141-5. With this story may be compared that of "The Cross-Surety." See above, p. 40.

THE PRIEST WITH THE GREEDY EYES.[444]

So greedy he ate the loaves . . .

IN THE PARISH OF St. Nicholas there lived a Pope. This Pope's eyes were thoroughly pope-like.[445] He served Nicholas several years and went on serving until such time as there remained to him nothing either for board or lodging. Then our Pope collected all the church keys, looked at the picture of Nicholas, thumped him, out of spite, over the shoulders with the keys and went forth from his parish as his eyes led him. And as he walked along the road he suddenly lighted upon an unknown man.

"Hail, good man!" said the stranger to the Pope. "Whence do you come and whither are you going? Take me with you as a companion."

Well, they went on together. They walked and walked for several versts, then they grew tired. It was time to seek repose. Now the Pope had a few biscuits in his cassock and the companion he had picked up had a couple of small loaves.[446]

"Let's eat your loaves first," says the Pope, "and afterwards we'll take to the biscuits, too."

"Agreed!" replies the stranger. "We'll eat my loaves and keep your biscuits for afterwards."

Well, they ate away at the loaves; each of them ate his fill but the loaves got no smaller. The Pope grew envious: "Come," thinks he, "I'll steal them from him!" After the meal the old man lay down to take a nap but the Pope kept scheming how to steal the loaves from him. The old man went to sleep. The

444 Afanasief, Legendui, No. 5. From the Archangel Government.

445 Popovskie, from pop, the vulgar name for a priest, the Greek παππάς.

446 The prosvirka or prosfora, is a small loaf, made of fine wheat flour. It is used for the communion service but before consecration it is freely sold and purchased.

Pope drew the loaves out of his pocket and began quietly nibbling them at his seat. The old man awoke and felt for his loaves; they were gone!

"Where are my loaves?" he exclaimed; "who has eaten them? was it you, Pope?"

"No, not I, on my word!" replied the Pope.

"Well, so be it," said the old man.

They gave themselves a shake and set out again on their journey. They walked and walked; suddenly the road branched off in two different directions. Well, they both went the same way and soon reached a certain country. In that country the King's daughter lay at the point of death and the King had given notice that to him who should cure his daughter he would give half of his kingdom and half of his goods and possessions; but if anyone undertook to cure her and failed, he should have his head chopped off and hung up on a stake. Well, they arrived, elbowed their way among the people in front of the King's palace and gave out that they were doctors. The servant came out from the King's palace and began questioning them:

"Who are you? from what cities, of what families? what do you want?"

"We are doctors," they replied, "we can cure the Princess!"

"Oh! if you are doctors, come into the palace."

So they went into the palace, saw the Princess and asked the King to supply them with a private apartment, a tub of water, a sharp sword and a big table. The King supplied them with all these things. Then they shut themselves up in the private apartment, laid the Princess on the big table, cut her into small pieces with the sharp sword, flung them into the tub of water, washed them and rinsed them. Afterwards they began putting the pieces together; when the old man breathed on them the different pieces stuck together. When he had put all the pieces together properly, he gave them a final puff of breath: the Princess began to quiver and then arose alive and well! The King came in person to the door of their room and cried:

"In the name of the Father and the Son and the Holy Ghost!"

"Amen!" they replied.

"Have you cured the Princess?" asked the King.

"We've cured her," say the doctors. "Here she is!"

Out went the Princess to the King, alive and well.

Says the King to the doctors: "What sort of valuables will you have? would you like gold or silver? Take whatever you please."

Well, they began taking gold and silver. The old man used only a thumb and two fingers but the Pope seized whole handfuls and kept on stowing them away in his wallet—shovelling them into it and then lifting it a bit to see if he was strong enough to carry it.

At last they took their leave of the King and went their way. The old man said to the Pope, "We'll bury this money in the ground and go and make another cure." Well, they walked and walked and at length they reached another country. In that country, also, the King had a daughter at the point of death and he had given notice that whoever cured his daughter should have half of his kingdom and of his goods and possessions; but if he failed to cure her he should have his head chopped off and hung up on a stake.[447] Then the Evil One afflicted the envious Pope, suggesting to him "Why shouldn't he go and perform the cure by himself, without saying a word to the old man and so lay hold of all the gold and silver for himself?" So the Pope walked about in front of the royal gates, forced himself on the notice of the people there and gave out that he was a doctor. In the same way as before he asked the

447 A few lines are here omitted as being superfluous. In the original the second princess is cured exactly as the first had been. The doctors then proceed to a third country, where they find precisely the same position of affairs.

King for a private room, a tub of water, a large table and a sharp sword. Shutting himself up in the private room, he laid the Princess on the table and began chopping her up with the sharp sword; and however much the Princess might scream or squeal, the Pope, without paying any attention to either screaming or squealing, went on chopping and chopping just as if she had been so much beef. And when he had chopped her up into little pieces, he threw them into the tub, washed them, rinsed them and then put them together bit by bit, exactly as the old man had done, expecting to see all the pieces unite with each other. He breathes on them—but nothing happens! He gives another puff—worse than ever! See, the Pope flings the pieces back again into the water, washes and washes, rinses and rinses and again puts them together bit by bit. Again he breathes on them—but still nothing comes of it.

"Woe is me," thinks the Pope; "here's a mess!"

Next morning the King arrives and looks—the doctor has had no success at all—he's only messed the dead body all over with muck!

The King ordered the doctor off to the gallows. Then our Pope besought him, crying—

"O King! O free to do thy will! Spare me for a little time! I will run for the old man, he will cure the Princess."

The Pope ran off in search of the old man. He found the old man and cried:

"Old man! I am guilty, wretch that I am! The Devil got hold of me. I wanted to cure the King's daughter all by myself but I couldn't. Now they're going to hang me. Do help me!"

The old man returned with the Pope.

The Pope was taken to the gallows. Says the old man to the Pope:

"Pope! who ate my loaves?"

"Not I, on my word! So help me Heaven, not I!"

The Pope was hoisted on to the second step. Says the old man to the Pope:

"Pope! who ate my loaves?"

"Not I, on my word! So help me Heaven, not I!"

He mounted the third step—and again it was "Not I!" And now his head was actually in the noose—but it's "Not I!" all the same. Well, there was nothing to be done! Says the old man to the King:

"O King! O free to do thy will! Permit me to cure the Princess. And if I do not cure her, order another noose to be got ready. A noose for me and a noose for the Pope!"

Well, the old man put the pieces of the Princess's body together, bit by bit and breathed on them—and the Princess stood up alive and well. The King recompensed them both with silver and gold.

"Let's go and divide the money, Pope," said the old man.

So they went. They divided the money into three heaps. The Pope looked at them and said:

"How's this? There's only two of us. For whom is this third share?"

"That," says the old man, "is for him who ate my loaves."

"I ate them, old man," cries the Pope; "I did really, so help me Heaven!"

"Then the money is yours," says the old man. "Take my share too. And now go and serve in your parish faithfully; don't be greedy and don't go hitting Nicholas over the shoulders with the keys."

Thus spake the old man and straightway disappeared.

~

[The principal motive of this story is, of course, the same as that of "The Smith and the Demon," in No. 13 (see above, p. 70). A miraculous cure is effected by a supernatural being. A man attempts to do likewise but fails. When about to undergo the penalty of his failure, he is saved by that being, who reads him a moral lesson. In the original form of the tale

the supernatural agent was probably a demigod, whom a vague Christian influence has in one instance degraded into the Devil, in another, canonised as St. Nicholas.

The Medea's cauldron episode occurs in very many folktales, such as the German "Bruder Lustig" (Grimm, No. 81) and "Das junge geglühte Männlein" (Grimm, No. 147), in the latter of which our Lord, accompanied by St. Peter, spends a night in a Smith's house and makes an old beggar-man young by first placing him in the fire and then plunging him into water. After the departure of his visitors, the Smith tries a similar experiment on his mother-in-law but quite unsuccessfully. In the corresponding Norse tale of "The Master-Smith," (Asbjörnsen and Moe, No. 21, Dasent, No. 16) an old beggar-woman is the victim of the Smith's unsuccessful experiment. In another Norse tale, that of "Peik" (Asbjörnsen's New Series, No. 101, p. 219) a king is induced to kill his wife and his daughter in the mistaken belief that he will be able to restore them to life. In one of the stories of the "Dasakumáracharita," a king is persuaded to jump into a certain lake in the hope of obtaining a new and improved body. He is then killed by his insidious adviser, who usurps his throne, pretending to be the renovated monarch. In another story in the same collection a king believes that his wife will be able to confer on him by her magic skill "a most celestial figure," and under that impression confides to her all his secrets, after which she brings about his death. See Wilson's "Essays," ii. 217, &c. and 262, &c. Jacob's "Hindoo Tales," pp. 180, 315.]

2. *Demons, &*

Part played by Demons in the Skazkas—On " Hasty Words, "and Parental Curses; their power to subject persons to demoniacal possession—The dulness of Demons ; Stories about Tricks played upon them—Their Gratitude to those who treat them with Kindness and their General Behavior—Various Legends about Devils—Moral Tale of the Gossip's Bedstead.

From the stories which have already been quoted some idea may be gained of the part which evil spirits play in Russian popular fiction. In one of them (No. 1) figures the ghoul which feeds on the dead, in several (Nos. 37, 38, 45-48) we see the fiend-haunted corpse hungering after human flesh and blood; the history of *The Bad Wife* (No. 7) proves how a demon may suffer at a woman's hands, that of *The Dead Witch* (No. 3) shows to what indignities the remains of a wicked woman may be subjected by the fiends with whom she has chosen to associate. In the *Awful Drunkard* (No. 6) and the *Fiddler in Hell* (No. 41), the abode of evil spirits is portrayed and some light is thrown on their manners and customs; and in the *Smith and the Demon* (No. 13), the portrait of one of their number is drawn in no unkindly spirit. The difference which exists between the sketches of fiends contained in these stories is clearly marked, so much so that it would of itself be sufficient to prove that there is no slight confusion of ideas in the minds of the Russian peasants with regard to the demoniacal beings whom they generally call *chorti* or devils. Still more clearly is the contrast between those ideas brought out by the other stories, many in number, into which those powers of darkness enter. It is evident that the traditions from which the popular conception of the ghostly enemy has been evolved must have been of a complex and even conflicting character.

Of very heterogeneous elements must have been composed the form under which the popular fancy, in Russia as well as in other lands, has embodied the abstract idea of evil. The diabolical characters in the Russian tales and legends are constantly changing the proportions of their figures, the nature of their attributes. In one story they seem to belong to the great and widely subdivided family of Indian demons; in another they appear to be akin to certain fiends of Turanian extraction; in a third they display features which may have been inherited from the forgotten deities of old Slavonic mythology; in all the stories which belong to the "legendary class" they bear manifest signs of having been subjected to Christian influences, the effect of which has been insufficient to do more than slightly to disguise their heathenism.

The old gods of the Slavonians have passed away and left behind but scanty traces of their existence; but still, in the traditions and proverbial expressions of the peasants in various Slavonic lands, there may be recognised some relics of the older faith. Among these are a few referring to a White and to a Black God. Thus, among the peasants of White Russia some vague memory still exists of a white or bright being, now called Byelun,[448] who leads belated travellers out of forests and bestows gold on men who do him good service. "Dark is it in the forest without Byelun" is one phrase; and another, spoken of a man on whom fortune has smiled, is, "He must have made friends with Byelun." On the other hand the memory of the black or evil god is preserved in such imprecations as the Ukraine "May the black god smite thee!"[449] To ancient pagan traditions, also, into which a Christian element has entered, may be assigned the popular belief that infants which have been cursed by their mothers before their birth or which are suffocated during their sleep or which die from any causes unchristened or christened by a drunken priest, become the prey of demons. This idea has given rise

448 Byely = white. See the "Songs of the Russian People," p. 103, the "Deutsche Mythologie," p. 203.

449 Shchob tebe chorny bog ubif! Afanasief, P.V.S., i. 93, 94.

in Russia, as well as elsewhere, to a large group of stories. The Russian peasants believe, it is said, that in order to rescue from the fiends the soul of a babe which has been suffocated in its sleep, its mother must spend three nights in a church, standing within a circle traced by the hand of a priest. When the cocks crow on the third morning, the demons will give her back her dead child.[450]

Great stress is laid in the skazkas and legends upon the terrible power of a parent's curse. The "hasty word" of a father or a mother will condemn even an innocent child to slavery among devils and when it has once been uttered, it is irrevocable. It might have been supposed that the fearful efficacy of such an imprecation would have silenced bad language, as that of the *Vril* rendered war impossible among the Vril-ya of "The Coming Race;" but that such was not the case is proved by the number of narratives which turn on uncalled-for parental cursing. Here is an abridgment of one of these stories.

There was an old man who lived near Lake Onega and who supported himself and his wife by hunting. One day when he was engaged in the pursuit of game, a well-dressed man met him and said,

"Sell me that dog of yours and come for your money to the Mian mountain tomorrow evening."

The old man sold him the dog and went next day to the top of the mountain, where he found a great city inhabited by devils.[451] There he soon found the house of his debtor, who provided him with a banquet and a bath. And in the bathroom he was served by a young man who, when the bath was over, fell at his feet, saying,

"Don't accept money for your dog, grandfather but ask for me!"

450 Afanasief, P.V.S. iii. 314, 315.
451 Lemboï, perhaps a Samoyed word.

The old man consented. "Give me that good youth," said he. "He shall serve instead of a son to me."

There was no help for it; they had to give him the youth. And when the old man had returned home, the youth told him to go to Novgorod, there to enquire for a merchant and ask him whether he had any children.

He did so and the merchant replied,

"I had an only son but his mother cursed him in a passion, crying, 'The devil take thee!'[452] And so the devil carried him off."

It turned out that the youth whom the old man had saved from the devils was that merchant's son. Thereupon the merchant rejoiced greatly and took the old man and his wife to live with him in his house.[453]

And here is another tale of the same kind, from the Vladimir Government.

Once upon a time there was an old couple and they had an only son. His mother had cursed him before he was born but he grew up and married. Soon afterwards he suddenly disappeared. His parents did all they could to trace him but their attempts were in vain.

Now there was a hut in the forest not far off and thither it chanced that an old beggar came one night and lay down to rest on the stove. Before he had been there long, someone rode up to the door of the hut, got off his horse, entered the hut and remained there all night, muttering incessantly:

"May the Lord judge my mother, in that she cursed me while a babe unborn!"

Next morning the beggar went to the house of the old couple and told them all that had occurred. So towards evening the old man went to the hut in the forest and hid himself behind the stove. Presently the horseman arrived,

452 Lemboi te (tebya) voz'mi!

453 Afanasief, P.V.S. iii. pp. 314, 315.

entered the hut and began to repeat the words which the beggar had overheard. The old man recognised his son and came forth to greet him, crying:

"O my dear son! at last I have found thee! never again will I let thee go!"

"Follow me!" replied his son, who mounted his horse and rode away, his father following him on foot. Presently they came to a river which was frozen over and in the ice was a hole.[454] And the youth rode straight into that hole and in it both he and his horse disappeared. The old man lingered long beside the ice-hole, then he returned home and said to his wife:

"I have found our son but it will be hard to get him back. Why, he lives in the water!"

Next night the youth's mother went to the hut but she succeeded no better than her husband had done.

So on the third night his young wife went to the hut and hid behind the stove. And when she heard the horseman enter she sprang forth, exclaiming:

"My darling dear, my life-long spouse! now will I never part from thee!"

"Follow me!" replied her husband.

And when they came to the edge of the ice-hole—

"If thou goest into the water, then will I follow after thee!" cried she.

"If so, take off thy cross," he replied.

She took off her cross, leaped into the ice-hole—and found herself in a vast hall. In it Satan[455] was seated. And when he saw her arrive, he asked her husband whom he had brought with him.

"This is my wife," replied the youth.

---

454 Prolub' (for prorub'), a hole cut in the ice, and kept open, for the purpose of getting at the water.

455 Satana.

"Well then, if she is thy wife, get thee gone hence with her! married folks must not be sundered."[456]

So the wife rescued her husband and brought him back from the devils into the free light.[457]

Sometimes it is a victim's own imprudence and not a parent's "hasty word," which has placed him in the power of the Evil One. There is a well-known story, which has spread far and wide over Europe, of a soldier who abstains for a term of years from washing, shaving and hair-combing and who serves or at least obeys, the devil during that time, at the end of which he is rewarded by the fiend with great wealth. His appearance being against him, he has some difficulty in finding a wife, rich as he is. But after the elder sisters of a family have refused him, the youngest accepts him; whereupon he allows himself to be cleansed, combed and dressed in bright apparel and leads a cleanly and a happy life ever afterwards.[458]

In one of the German versions of this story, a king's elder daughter, when asked to marry her rich but slovenly suitor, replies, "I would sooner go into the deepest water than do that." In a Russian version,[459] the unwashed soldier lends a large sum of money to an impoverished monarch, who cannot pay his troops and asks his royal creditor to give him one of his daughters in marriage by way of recompense. The king reflects. He is sorry for his daughters but at the same time he cannot do without the money. At last, he tells the soldier to get his portrait painted and promises to show it to the princesses and see if one of them will accept him. The soldier has his likeness taken, "touch for touch, just exactly as he is," and

456 The word by which the husband here designates his wife is zakon, which properly signifies (1) law, (2) marriage. Here it stands for "spouse." Satan replies, "If this be thy zakon, go hence therewith! to sever a zakon is impossible."

457 Abridged from Afanasief, P.V.S. iii. 315, 316.

458 See the notes in Grimm's KM. Bd. iii. to stories 100 and 101.

459 Afanasief, v. No. 26.

the king shows it to his daughters. The eldest princess sees that "the picture is that of a monster, with dishevelled hair and uncut nails and unwiped nose," and cries:

"I won't have him! I'd sooner have the devil!"

Now the devil "was standing behind her, pen and paper in hand. He heard what she said and booked her soul."

When the second princess is asked whether she will marry the soldier, she exclaims:

"No indeed! I'd rather die an old maid, I'd sooner be linked with the devil, than marry that man!"

When the devil heard that, "he booked her soul too."

But the youngest princess, the Cordelia of the family, when she is asked whether she will marry the man who has helped her father in his need, replies:

"It's fated I must, it seems! I'll marry him and then—God's will be done!"

While the preparations are being made for the marriage, the soldier arrives at the end of his term of service to "the little devil" who had hired him and from whom he had received his wealth in return for his abstinence and cleanliness. So he calls the "little devil," and says, "Now turn me into a nice young man."

Accordingly "the little devil cut him up into small pieces, threw them into a cauldron and set them on to boil. When they were done enough, he took them out and put them together again properly—bone to bone, joint to joint, vein to vein. Then he sprinkled them with the Waters of Life and Death—and up jumped the soldier, a finer lad than stories can describe or pens portray!"

The story does not end here. When the "little devil" returns to the lake from which he came, "the grandfather" of the demons asks him—

"How about the soldier?"

"He has served his time honestly and honourably," is the reply. "Never once did he shave, have his hair cut, wipe his nose or change his clothes." The "grandfather" flies into a passion.

"What! in fifteen whole years you couldn't entrap a soldier! What, all that money wasted for nothing! What sort of a devil do you call yourself after that?"—and ordered him to be flung "into boiling pitch."

"Stop, grandfather!" replies his grandchild. "I've booked two souls instead of the soldier's one."

"How's that?"

"Why, this way. The soldier wanted to marry one of three princesses but the elder one and the second one told their father that they'd sooner marry the devil than the soldier. So you see both of them are ours."

After he had heard this explanation, "the grandfather acknowledged that the little devil was in the right and ordered him to be set free. The imp, you see, understood his business."

[For two German versions of this story, see the tales of "Des Teufels russiger Bruder," and "Der Bärenhäuter" (Grimm, Nos. 100, 101 and Bd. iii. pp. 181, 182). More than twelve centuries ago, Hiouen-Thsang transferred the following story from India to China. A certain Rishi passed many times ten thousand years in a religious ecstasy. His body became like a withered tree. At last he emerged from his ecstasy and felt inclined to marry, so he went to a neighbouring palace and asked the king to bestow upon him one of his daughters. The king, exceedingly embarrassed, called the princesses together and asked which of them would consent to accept the dreaded suitor (who, of course, had not paid the slightest attention to his toilette for hundreds of centuries). Ninety-nine of those ladies flatly refused to have anything to do with him but the hundredth, the last and youngest of the party, agreed to sacrifice herself for her father's sake. But when the Rishi saw his bride he was discontented and when he heard that her elder and fairer

sisters had all refused him, he pronounced a curse which made all ninety-nine of them humpbacks and so destroyed their chance of marrying at all. Stanislas Julien's "Mémoires sur les contrées occidentales," 1857, i. pp. 244-7.]

As the idea that "a hasty word" can place its utterer or its victim in the power of the Evil One (not only after death but also during this life) has given rise to numerous Russian legends and as it still exists, to some extent, as a living faith in the minds of the Russian peasantry, it may be as well to quote at length one of the stories in which it is embodied. It will be recognised as a variant of the stories about the youth who visits the "Water King" and elopes with one of that monarch's daughters. The main difference between the "legend" we are about to quote and the skazkas which have already been quoted, is that a devil of the Satanic type is substituted in it for the mythical personage—whether Slavonic Neptune or Indian Rákshasa—who played a similar part in them.

THE HASTY WORD.[460]

Taking a bride from the devil . . .

IN A CERTAIN VILLAGE there lived an old couple in great poverty and they had one son. The son grew up,[461] and the old woman began to say to the old man:

"It's time for us to get our son married."

"Well then, go and ask for a wife for him," said he.

So she went to a neighbour to ask for his daughter for her son: the neighbour refused. She went to a second peasant's but the second refused too—to a third but he showed her the door. She went round the whole village; not a soul would grant her request. So she returned home and cried—

"Well, old man! our lad's an unlucky fellow!"

"How so?"

"I've trudged round to every house but no one will give him his daughter."

"That's a bad business!" says the old man; "the summer will soon be coming but we have no one to work for us here. Go to another village, old woman, perhaps you will get a bride for him there."

The old woman went to another village, visited every house from one end to the other but there wasn't an atom of good to be got out of it. Wherever she thrusts herself, they always refuse. With what she left home, with that she returned home.

"No," she says, "no one wants to become related to us poor beggars."

460 Afanasief, v. No. 48.

461 "Entered upon his matured years," from 17 to 21.

"If that's the case," answers the old man, "there's no use in wearing out your legs. Jump up on to the *polati*."[462]

The son was sorely afflicted and began to entreat his parents, saying:

"My born father and my born mother! give me your blessing. I will go and seek my fate myself."

"But where will you go?"

"Where my eyes lead me."

So they gave him their blessing and let him go whithersoever it pleased him.[463]

Well, the youth went out upon the highway, began to weep very bitterly and said to himself as he walked:

"Was I born into the world worse than all other men, that not a single girl is willing to marry me? Methinks if the devil himself would give me a bride, I'd take even her!"

Suddenly, as if rising from the earth, there appeared before him a very old man.

"Good-day, good youth!"

"Good-day, old man!"

"What was that you were saying just now?"

The youth was frightened and did not know what reply to make.

"Don't be afraid of me! I shan't do you any harm and moreover, perhaps I may get you out of your trouble. Speak boldly!"

The youth told him everything precisely.

"Poor creature that I am! There isn't a single girl who will marry me. Well, as I went along I became exceedingly wretched and in my misery I said: 'If the devil offered me a bride, I'd take even her!'"

The old man laughed and said:

"Follow me, I'll let you choose a lovely bride for yourself."

---

462 The sleeping-place.

463 Literally, "to all the four sides."

By-and-by they reached a lake.

"Turn your back to the lake and walk backwards," said the old man. Scarcely had the youth had time to turn round and take a couple of steps, when he found himself under the water and in a white-stone palace—all its rooms splendidly furnished, cunningly decorated. The old man gave him to eat and to drink. Afterwards he introduced twelve maidens, each one more beautiful than the other.

"Choose whichever you like! whichever you choose, her will I bestow upon you."

"That's a puzzling job!" said the youth; "give me till tomorrow morning to think about it, grandfather!"

"Well, think away!" said the old man and led his guest to a private chamber. The youth lay down to sleep and thought:

"Which one shall I choose?"

Suddenly the door opened; a beautiful maiden entered.

"Are you asleep or not, good youth?" says she.

"No, fair maiden! I can't get to sleep, for I'm always thinking which bride to choose."

"That's the very reason I have come to give you counsel. You see, good youth, you've managed to become the devil's guest. Now listen. If you want to go on living in the white world, then do what I tell you. But if you don't follow my instructions, you'll never get out of here alive!"

"Tell me what to do, fair maiden. I won't forget it all my life."

"Tomorrow the fiend will bring you twelve maidens, each one exactly like the others. But you take a good look and choose me. A fly will be sitting above my right eye—that will be a certain guide for you." And then the fair maiden proceeded to tell him about herself, who she was.

"Do you know the priest of such and such a village?" she says. "I'm his daughter, the one who disappeared from home when nine years old. One day my father was angry with me and in his wrath he said, 'May devils fly away with you!'

I went out on the steps and began to cry. All of a sudden the fiends seized me and brought me here; and here I am living with them!"

Next morning the old man brought in the twelve fair maidens—one just like another—and ordered the youth to choose his bride. He looked at them and took her above whose right eye sat a fly. The old man was loth to give her up, so he shifted the maidens about and told him to make a fresh choice. The youth pointed out the same one as before. The fiend obliged him to choose yet a third time. He again guessed his bride aright.

"Well, you're in luck! take her home with you," said the fiend.

Immediately the youth and the fair maiden found themselves on the shore of the lake and until they reached the high road they kept on walking backwards. Presently the devils came rushing after them in hot pursuit:

"Let us recover our maiden!" they cry.

They looked: there were no footsteps going away from the lake; all the footsteps lead into the water! They ran to and fro, they searched everywhere but they had to go back empty handed.

Well, the good youth brought his bride to her village and stopped opposite the priest's house. The priest saw him and sent out his labourer, saying:

"Go and ask who those people are."

"We? we're travellers; please let us spend the night in your house," they replied.

"I have merchants paying me a visit," says the priest, "and even without them there's but little room in the house."

"What are you thinking of, father?" says one of the merchants. "It's always one's duty to accommodate a traveller, they won't interfere with us."

"Very well, let them come in."

So they came in, exchanged greetings and sat down on a bench in the back corner.

"Don't you know me, father?" presently asks the fair maiden. "Of a surety I am your own daughter."

Then she told him everything that had happened. They began to kiss and embrace each other, to pour forth tears of joy.

"And who is this man?" says the priest.

"That is my betrothed. He brought me back into the white world; if it hadn't been for him I should have remained down there for ever!"

After this the fair maiden untied her bundle and in it were gold and silver dishes: she had carried them off from the devils. The merchant looked at them and said:

"Ah! those are my dishes. One day I was feasting with my guests and when I got drunk I became angry with my wife. 'To the devil with you!' I exclaimed and began flinging from the table and beyond the threshold, whatever I could lay my hands upon. At that moment my dishes disappeared!"

And in reality so had it happened. When the merchant mentioned the devil's name, the fiend immediately appeared at the threshold, began seizing the gold and silver wares and flinging in their place bits of pottery.

Well, by this accident the youth got himself a capital bride. And after he had married her he went back to his parents. They had long ago counted him as lost to them for ever. And indeed it was no subject for jesting; he had been away from home three whole years and yet it seemed to him that he had not in all spent more than twenty-four hours with the devils.

~

[A quaint version of the legend on which this story is founded is given by Gervase of Tilbury in his "Otia Imperialia," whence the story passed into the "Gesta Romanorum" (cap. clxii.) and spread widely over mediæval Europe. A certain Catalonian was so much annoyed one day "by the continued and

inappeasable crying of his little daughter, that he commended her to the demons." Whereupon she was immediately carried off. Seven years after this, he learnt (from a man placed by a similar imprecation in the power of the demons, who used him as a vehicle) that his daughter was in the interior of a neighbouring mountain and might be recovered if he would demand her. So he ascended to the summit of the mountain and there claimed his child. She straightway appeared in miserable plight, "arida, tetra, oculis vagis, ossibus et nervis et pellibus vix hærentibus," etc. By the judicious care, however, of her now cautious parent she was restored to physical and moral respectability. For some valuable observations on this story see Liebrecht's edition of the "Otia Imperialia," pp. 137-9. In the German story of "Die sieben Raben" (Grimm, No. 25) a father's "hasty word" turns his six sons into ravens.]

When devils are introduced into a story of this class, it always assumes a grotesque, if not an absolutely comic air. The evil spirits are almost always duped and defeated and that result is generally due to their remarkable want of intelligence. For they display in their dealings with their human antagonists a deficiency of intellectual power which almost amounts to imbecility. The explanation of this appears to be that the devils of European folklore have nothing in common with the rebellious angels of Miltonic theology beyond their vague denomination; nor can any but a nominal resemblance be traced between their chiefs or "grandfathers" and the thunder-smitten but still majestic "Lucifer, Son of the Morning." The demon rabble of "Popular Tales" are merely the lubber fiends of heathen mythology, beings endowed with supernatural might but scantily provided with mental power; all of terrific manual clutch but of weak intellectual grasp. And so the hardy mortal who measures his powers against theirs, even in those cases in which his strength has not been intensified by miraculous agencies, easily overcomes or deludes the slow-witted monsters with whom he strives—whether his antagonist be a Celtic or Teutonic Giant or a French Ogre or a Norse Troll or a Greek Drakos or Lamia or a Lithuanian Laume or a Russian Snake or Koshchei or Baba Yaga or an Indian Rákshasa or Pisácha or any other member of the many species of fiends for which, in Christian parlance, the generic name is that of "devils."

There is no great richness of invention manifested in the stories which deal with the outwitting of evil spirits. The same devices are in almost all cases resorted to and their effect is invariable. The leading characters undergo certain transmutations as the scene of the story is shifted but their mutual relations remain constant. Thus, in a German story[464] we find a schoolmaster deceiving the devil; in one of its Slavonic counterparts[465] a gypsy deludes a snake; in another, current among the Baltic Kashoubes, in place of the snake figures a giant so huge that the thumb of his glove serves as a shelter for the hero of the tale—one which is closely connected with that which tells of Thor and the giant Skrymir.

The Russian stories in which devils are tricked by mortals closely resemble, for the most part, those which are current in so many parts of Europe. The hero of the tale squeezes whey out of a piece of cheese or curd which he passes off as a stone; he induces the fleet demon to compete with his "Hop o' my Thumb" the hare; he sets the strong demon to wrestle with his "greybeard" the bear; he frightens the "grandfather" of the fiends by proposing to fling that potentate's magic staff so high in the air that it will never come down; and he persuades his diabolical opponents to keep pouring gold into a perforated hat or sack. Sometimes, however, a less familiar incident occurs. Thus in a story from the Tambof Government, Zachary the Unlucky is sent by the tailor, his master, to fetch a fiddle from a wolf-fiend. The demon agrees to let him have it on condition that he spends three years in continually weaving nets without ever going to sleep.

464 Haltrich, No. 27.
465 Afanasief, v. No. 25.

Zachary sets to work but at the end of a month he grows drowsy. The wolf asks if he is asleep. "No, I'm not asleep," he replies, "but I'm thinking which fish there are most of in the river—big ones or little ones." The wolf offers to go and enquire and spends three or four months in solving the problem. Meanwhile Zachary sleeps, taking care, however, to be up and at work when the wolf returns to say that the big fishes are in the majority.

Time passes and again Zachary begins to nod. The wolf enquires if he has gone to sleep but is told that he is awake but engrossed by the question as to "which folks are there most of in the world—the living or the dead." The wolf goes out to count them and Zachary sleeps in comfort, till just before it comes back to say that the living are more numerous than the dead. By the time the wolf-fiend has made a third journey in order to settle a doubt which Zachary describes as weighing on his mind—as to the numerical relation of the large beasts to the small—the three years have passed away. So the wolf-fiend is obliged to part with his fiddle and Zachary carries it back to the tailor in triumph.[466]

The demons not unfrequently show themselves capable of being actuated by gratitude. Thus, as we have already seen, the story of the Awful Drunkard[467] represents the devil himself as being grateful to a man who has rebuked an irascible old woman for unjustly blaming the Prince of Darkness. In a skazka from the Orenburg Government, a lad named Vanka [Jack] is set to watch his father's turnip-field by night. Presently comes a boy who fills two huge sacks with turnips and vainly tries to carry them off. While he is tugging away at them he catches sight of Vanka and immediately asks him to help him home with his load. Vanka consents and carries the turnips to a cottage, wherein is seated "an old greybeard with

---

466 Khudyakof, No. 114.
467 Chap. i. p. 46.

horns on his head," who receives him kindly and offers him a quantity of gold as a recompense for his trouble. But acting on the instructions he has received from the boy, Vanka will take nothing but the greybeard's lute, the sounds of which exercise a magic power over all living creatures.[468]

One of the most interesting of the stories of this class is that of the man who unwittingly blesses the devil. As a specimen of its numerous variants we may take the opening of a skazka respecting the origin of brandy.

"There was a moujik who had a wife and seven children and one day he got ready to go afield, to plough. When his horse was harnessed and everything ready, he ran indoors to get some bread; but when he got there and looked in the cupboard, there was nothing there but a single crust. This he carried off bodily and drove away.

"He reached his field and began ploughing. When he had ploughed up half of it, he unharnessed his horse and turned it out to graze. After that he was just going to eat the bread, when he said to himself,

"'Why didn't I leave this crust for my children?'

"So after thinking about it for awhile, he set it aside.

"Presently a little demon came sidling up and carried off the bread. The moujik returned and looked about everywhere but no bread was to be seen. However, all he said was, 'God be with him who took it!'

"The little demon[469] ran off to the devil,[470] and cried:

"'Grandfather! I've stolen Uncle Sidor's[471] bread!'

"'Well, what did he say?'

"'He said, "God be with him!"'

"'Be off with you!' says the devil. 'Hire yourself to him for three years.'

---

468 Afanasief, vii., No. 14.
469 *Byesenok, diminutive of Byes.*
470 Chort.
471 Isidore.

"So the little demon ran back to the moujik."

The rest of the story tells how the imp taught Isidore to make corn-brandy and worked for him a long time faithfully. But at last one day Isidore drank so much brandy that he fell into a drunken sleep. From this he was roused by the imp, whereupon he exclaimed in a rage, "Go to the Devil!" and straightway the "little demon" disappeared.[472]

In another version of the story,[473] when the peasant finds that his crust has disappeared, he exclaims—

"Here's a wonder! I've seen nobody and yet somebody has carried off my crust! Well, here's good luck to him![474] I daresay I shall starve to death."

When Satan heard what had taken place, he ordered that the peasant's crust should be restored. So the demon who had stolen it "turned himself into a good youth," and became the peasant's hireling. When a drought was impending, he scattered the peasant's seed-corn over a swamp; when a wet season was at hand he sowed the slopes of the hills. In each instance his forethought enabled his master to fill his barns while the other peasants lost their crops.

[A Moravian version of this tale will be found in "Der schwarze Knirps" (Wenzig, No. 15, p. 67). In another Moravian story in the same collection (No. 8) entitled "Der böse Geist im Dienste," an evil spirit steals the food which a man had left outside his house for poor passersby. When the demon returns to hell he finds its gates closed and he is informed by "the oldest of the devils," that he must expiate his crime by a three years' service on earth.

A striking parallel to the Russian and the former of the Moravian stories is offered by "a legend of serpent worship," from Bhaunagar in Káthiáwád. A certain king had seven wives, one of whom was badly treated. Feeling hungry one day, she scraped out of the pots which had been given her to wash some remains of rice boiled in milk, set the food on one side and then

472 Erlenvein, No. 33. From the Tula Government.

473 Quoted from Borichefsky, by Afanasief, *Legendui*, p. 182.

474 Emy na zdorovie! "Good health to him!"

went to bathe. During her absence a female Nága (or supernatural snake-being) ate up the rice and then "entering her hole, sat there, resolved to bite the woman if she should curse her but not otherwise." When the woman returned and found her meal had been stolen, she did not lose her temper but only said, "May the stomach of the eater be cooled!" When the Nága heard this, she emerged from her hole and said, "Well done! I now regard you as my daughter," etc. (From the "Indian Antiquary," Bombay, No. 1, 1872, pp. 6, 7.)]

Sometimes the demon of the *legenda* bears a close resemblance to the snake of the *skazka*. Thus, an evil spirit is described as coming every night at twelve o'clock to the chamber of a certain princess and giving her no rest till the dawn of day. A soldier—the fairy prince in a lower form—comes to her rescue and awaits the arrival of the fiend in her room, which he has had brilliantly lighted. Exactly at midnight up flies the evil spirit, assumes the form of a man and tries to enter the room. But he is stopped by the soldier, who persuades him to play cards with him for fillips, tricks him in various ways and fillips him to such effect with a species of "three-man beetle," that the demon beats a hasty retreat.

The next night Satan sends another devil to the palace. The result is the same as before and the process is repeated every night for a whole month. At the end of that time "Grandfather Satan" himself confronts the soldier but he receives so tremendous a beating that he flies back howling "to his swamp." After a time, the soldier induces the whole of the fiendish party to enter his knapsack, prevents them from getting out again by signing it with a cross and then has it thumped on an anvil to his heart's content. Afterwards he carries it about on his back, the fiends remaining under it all the while. But at last some women open it, during his absence from a cottage in which he has left it and out rush the fiends with a crash and a roar. Meeting the soldier on his way back to the cottage, they are so frightened that they fling themselves into the pool below a millwheel; and there, the story declares, they still remain.[475]

This "legend" is evidently nothing more than an adaptation of one of the tales about the dull demons of olden times, whom the Christian storyteller has transformed into Satan and his subject fiends.

By way of a conclusion to this chapter—which might be expanded indefinitely, so numerous are the stories of the class of which it treats—we will take the moral tale of

475 Afanasief, v. No. 43.

"THE GOSSIP'S BEDSTEAD."[476]

It is all on fire and runs on wheels . . .

A certain peasant, was so poor that, in order to save himself from starvation, he took to sorcery. After a time he became an adept in the black art and contracted an intimate acquaintance with the fiendish races. When his son had reached man's estate, the peasant saw it was necessary to find him a bride, so he set out to seek one among "his friends the devils." On arriving in their realm he soon found what he wanted, in the person of a girl who had drunk herself to death and who, in common with other women who had died of drink, was employed by the devils as a water carrier. Her employers at once agreed to give her in marriage to the son of their friend and a wedding feast was instantly prepared. While the consequent revelry was in progress, Satan offered to present to the bridegroom a receipt which a father had given to the devils when he sold them his son. But when the receipt was sought for—the production of which would have enabled the bridegroom to claim the youth in question as his slave—it could not be found; a certain devil had carried it off and refused to say where he had hidden it. In vain did his master cause him to be beaten with iron clubs, he remained obstinately mute. At length Satan exclaimed—

"Stretch him on the Gossip's Bedstead!"

As soon as the refractory devil heard these words, he was so frightened that he surrendered the receipt, which was handed over to the visitor. Astonished at the result, the

476 Afanasief, Legendui, No. 27. From the Saratof Government. This story is merely one of the numerous Slavonic variants of a tale familiar to many lands.

peasant enquired what sort of bedstead that was which had been mentioned with so much effect.

"Well, I'll tell you but don't you tell anyone else," replied Satan, after hesitating for a time. "That bedstead is made for us devils and for our relations, connexions and gossips. It is all on fire and it runs on wheels and turns round and round."

When the peasant heard this, fear came upon him and he jumped up from his seat and fled away as fast as he could.

* * * * *

At this point, though much still remains to be said, I will for the present bring my remarks to a close. Incomplete as is the account I have given of the Skazkas, it may yet, I trust, be of use to students who wish to compare as many types as possible of the Popular Tale. I shall be glad if it proves of service to them. I shall be still more glad if I succeed in interesting the general reader in the tales of the Russian People and through them, in the lives of those Russian men and women of low degree who are wont to tell them, those Russian children who love to hear them.

~END~

More Wild Arancini Classics

Wild Arancini CLassics is preparing a number of publications sourced from the Public Domain. Watch out for these coming releases:

Treasure Island - Robert Louis Stevenson
Alice's Adventures in Wonderland - Lewis Carroll
On Our Selection - Steele Rudd
Joe Wilson's and His Mates - Henry Lawson
The Man From Snowy River and Other Verses -A. B. (The Banjo) Paterson
Heidi - Johanna Spyri
Japanese Fairy Tales - Yei Theodora Ozaki
Russian Fairy Tales - W. R. S. Ralston